11/72

£1-70

A.

A SURVEY OF SOUTHAMPTON
AND ITS REGION

BRITISH ASSOCIATION
FOR THE ADVANCEMENT OF SCIENCE

Southampton Meeting, 1964

LOCAL GENERAL COMMITTEE

Chairman
THE WORSHIPFUL THE MAYOR OF SOUTHAMPTON

Vice-Chairman
THE VICE-CHANCELLOR OF THE UNIVERSITY OF
SOUTHAMPTON
(D. G. James, M.A., LL.D., D.Litt.)

Honorary Local Secretaries
THE TOWN CLERK OF SOUTHAMPTON
(A. Norman Schofield, LL.M.)

THE SECRETARY AND REGISTRAR OF THE
UNIVERSITY OF SOUTHAMPTON
(R. N. M. Robertson, M.A., LL.B.)

Honorary Treasurer
THE BOROUGH TREASURER OF SOUTHAMPTON
(D. W. Pearse, F.I.M.T.A.)

A Survey of Southampton and Its Region

Edited by

F. J. MONKHOUSE, M.A., D.Sc.,

Professor of Geography in the University of Southampton

*Prepared for the meeting of the British Association
held from 26 August to 2 September 1964*

SOUTHAMPTON

Printed in Monotype Bembo 11 on 12 point by
The Camelot Press Limited Southampton
and published by Southampton University Press

CONTENTS

CONTENTS

Part II
The Historical Background

Part III
The Character of the Town of Southampton

vii

CONTENTS

LIST OF MAPS AND DIAGRAMS

LIST OF PLATES

Acknowledgements are gratefully expressed to the following for the provision of photographs:

Aerofilms (Plates VI, VIII, X, XXXIV, XXXVII, LI–LIII, LV)

H. G. Armitage (Plate LIV)

J. A. Bailey (Plates XVIII–XXIV, XXVI)

M. Bradshaw-Bond (Plate XXV)

British Transport Docks Board (Plates XLII–XLV)

Esso Petroleum Company Limited (Plate XXVIII)

Gas Council (Plate XIV)

Eric Kay (Plates I–V, VII, XI–XIII, XV, XXIX–XXXIII, XXXV, XXXVI)

Ordnance Survey (Plates XXXVIII–XL)

E. G. Patience (Plates IX, XVII, XLVI, XLVII, LVI)

Henk Snoek (Plates XLI)

Southampton County Borough Waterworks Department (Plate XVI)

Southern Evening Echo (Plates XLVIII–L)

Allen White (Plate XXVII)

LIST OF TABLES

ACKNOWLEDGEMENTS

THE task of an Editor, frequently laborious though ultimately rewarding, can be immensely lightened, as in the case of the present volume, through the collaboration of his contributors. No fewer than fifty-three have been involved; all have given generously of their specialist knowledge, and have responded willingly to the sometimes peremptory demands of the Editor, an attitude forced on him only through the exigencies of a somewhat rigid time-table.

Much of the organisation of the work devolved upon Mrs. G. A. Trevett, B.A., Secretary to the Department of Geography, University of Southampton, who kept firm control at all stages of the masses of correspondence, manuscript and proofs, as well as carrying out much typing and checking of material. The maps and diagrams were the responsibility of Mr. A. Carson Clark, Senior Cartographer in the Department of Geography, to which task he brought infinite care, patience and skill. Mr. H. Silverwood and Mr. P. Hurn contributed to the drawing of some of the maps. The half-tone illustrations were obtained from a variety of sources, of which due acknowledgement is made on p. xv; special appreciation should be expressed of the assistance in the selection of plates afforded by Mr. Eric Kay, B.A., including the substantial contribution of his own photographs, many of them taken for the specific purpose. The colour map of Southampton Docks (opposite p. 286) was generously supplied by the British Transport Docks Board.

Grateful thanks are due to the Gas Council for providing the original photograph of the Chilcomb structure (Plate XIV); to Dr. D. A. Osmond, head of the Soil Survey of England and Wales, who read and commented upon Chapter V; to the Director and staff of the Computer Laboratory of the University of Southampton, Mr. H. H. Lamb of the Meteorological Office, Mr. T. E. Oliver of the Meteorological Office Archives, and the staff of the Southampton Weather Centre, in connection with Chapter VI; to Mr. P. M. T. Jones, County Agricultural Advisory Officer for Hampshire, and Mr. H. S. Dyer, Divisional Land Commissioner, in connection with Chapter X; to Mr. T. F. Thomson, formerly Hampshire County Planning Officer, under whose direction Chapter XI was initially written; to Thomas Nelson and Sons, for permission to use in Chapter XII material from the forthcoming volume on *Wessex* in their series 'Regions of the British Isles'; to Mr. E. B. Gover, in connection with Chapter XIII; to Professor C. F. C. Hawkes, Miss Jean M. Cook, Mr. F. Cottrill, Mr. Anthony Norton, Mr. John Pallister, Mr. H. de S. Shortt, Dr. Isobel F. Smith, Miss E. M. Samuel and Mr. Barry Cunliffe, in connection with Chapter XIV; to Mr. A. Anderson in connection with Chapter XV; to Dr. P. A. Samet and Dr. G. B. Cook for assistance in computation in connection with Chapter XVI; to Mr. M. J. Clark and Mr. J. Lewin for carrying out the field-work in connection with Figs. 65-67 in Chapter XVII

(Mr. Clark also drew these maps); to Mr. J. P. M. Pannell in connection with Chapter XIX; to individuals too numerous to mention who have assisted in the writing of Chapter XX; and to the Director-General of the Ordnance Survey for making available the copper-plate of Plate XXXVIII. Figures 3 and 4 are based on maps produced by the Geological Survey, by permission. Several Figures are based on various Ordnance Survey and other official maps, reproduced by permission of the Controller of H.M. Stationery Office. The sources of all other Figures are carefully acknowledged in the respective captions.

Finally, the Editor owes an immense debt of gratitude to Mr. H. Oxborough, of the Camelot Press Limited, Southampton, whose skilled assistance and advice went far beyond the normal routine of book production, and with whom it has been a pleasure to work.

Southampton   F. J. M.
December 1963

The City of Southampton

Her Majesty the Queen, on the recommendation of the Home Secretary, was graciously pleased to raise by letters patent the Town and County of Southampton to the title and dignity of a City on 11 February 1964.

As it was not possible to amend accordingly the text of this volume before going to press, the reader will appreciate that references to the Town of Southampton should now imply the City of Southampton.

I

INTRODUCTION

THE pattern of this *Survey*, which falls into three parts, cannot be determined by a rigorous, sharply defined interpretation of the area to be covered. The first part is concerned with the region as a whole, and includes portions of Hampshire, Wiltshire and Dorset and the whole of the Isle of Wight. Even so, certain chapters must logically deal with this wider setting, notably those devoted to the Geomorphology and the Climatology, while others are concerned with the administrative County of Hampshire alone, such as the chapters on the Hydrology and the County Development Plan. Other chapters still, such as that dealing with the Botany, are interested in an 'inner region' in rather greater detail, shown on Fig. 1.

The second part of the *Survey* is concerned with the historical background to both the wider region and the town of Southampton, partly for the inherent interest of such a narrative, partly because '. . . nothing in the past is dead to those who would know how the present has come to be what it is'. A chapter discusses the concept of Wessex, one of those several areas of Britain '. . . which defy definition but which nevertheless have a strong regional characterisation'. Then follows a survey of the place-names of Hampshire, which afford a fascinating mirror of the growth of settlement within the county. A subsequent chapter examines the patterns of settlement in prehistoric and Roman times. Finally, the story is traced of the growth of the town of Southampton, from pre-Conquest days to the end of the nineteenth century.

The third part of the *Survey* is concerned with the County Borough of Southampton itself, focusing interest on the town from the economic, social and administrative points of view. Substantial attention must be paid to the port, for how indeed can we separate our view of the town from that of the port? To this day the Mayor of Southampton bears the title of Admiral of the Port, and the Civic Regalia include a silver oar. So, starting with the Cretaceous geological period within the wider structural region, and ending with a judicious appraisal of the future of the County Borough of Southampton, this *Survey* seeks to portray systematically the diverse, yet intimately associated, facets of the character of the region and the town.

THE FACE OF THE REGION

The outer chalk rim of the Hampshire Basin is for the most part well defined. In the east it forms a marked edge overlooking the wooded ridges of the western Weald, while in the north-east it plunges steeply beneath the Tertiary rocks of the London Basin. In the north-west its escarpments bound the Vales of Pewsey, Warminster and Wardour, and in the west its much indented face contrasts with the claylands of the Vale of Blackmore. In the south the chalk frame is incomplete; the ridge of Ballard Down, ending in the Foreland and the stacks of Old Harry and his family, is interrupted by the broad expanse of Poole Bay. The Chalk appears again in the Needles, and continues as the 'back-bone' of the Isle of Wight.

It is, of course, easy to speak in general terms of a chalk landscape: of wide vistas and smoothly sweeping curves; of downland turf and creamy flint-strewn soils which when newly ploughed reveal almost a sheen; of deeply cut coombes and dry valleys; of sombre yew-groves and thick beech-copses on the sides of the hangers. All these contribute to a most pleasing countryside (Plates I, II).

Structurally, the area under consideration was diversified by the earth movements of mid-Tertiary times, which reached their climax about 35 million years ago, the same 'Alpine Storm' which uplifted the Alps far to the south, for England to experience the 'outer ripples'. Broadly, the Chalk was bent downwards in a downfold or syncline, dipping gently to the south but rising sharply along the edge of what is now the 'backbone' of the Isle of Wight. This great downfold forms the Hampshire Basin. Many other minor wrinkles can be distinguished, the basis of some prominent relief features (Fig. 5). The striking remnants of the contorted limb of one of the upfolds, with its sharply folded rocks, can be seen along the Dorset coast, notably at Stair Hole near Lulworth Cove.

Within this downfold of the Hampshire Basin lie the deposits of the several marine and fluviatile episodes of the Eocene and Oligocene. Over most of Hampshire and eastern Dorset, the Eocene deposits are primarily sandy, notably the Bagshot and Bracklesham Beds, though there are also some areas of clay, such as the London Clay of the Southampton Plateau, a low triangular area lying between the valleys of the rivers Test and Itchen. In the Hampshire Basin the Eocene strata, like the Chalk, dip gently to the south. But in the Isle of Wight, in the steep southern limb of the asymmetrical syncline, they rise again so sharply that their outcrop is narrow, in places only a few hundred yards. At Alum Bay, for example, where the coast bends sharply north–south, the entire range of the Eocene, from the Reading Beds (resting unconformably against the Chalk) to the Barton Beds, is revealed as a series of near-vertical bands of variegated sands and clays.

The Oligocene rocks, covering the southern part of the Basin and the northern third of the Isle of Wight, consist of varied clays and limestones. The latter form some interesting coastal features along the southern shores of the Solent; at the eastern end of the Isle a quite compact and resistant rock, known as the Bembridge Limestone, outcrops along the cliffs. In places this has long been quarried, and in fact the old town walls of Southampton are built of it, as are Winchester Cathedral and Romsey Abbey.

The soils developed on the areas of sand are markedly deficient in basic mineral nutrients: thin, poor and acid. Here therefore occur the extensive heathlands, sombre for much of the year, although in autumn they have a glory all their own. The subdued relief and the well-developed underlying hard-pan result in the presence of many small sheets of stagnant water, surprisingly permanent even during a dry summer. The Dorset heaths are perhaps the most desolate, and much remains of the 'heathy, furzy, briary wilderness' of Thomas Hardy. Sand- and gravel-workings, tank-training grounds, artillery ranges and more recently the Winfrith atomic plant add a man-made desolation to many parts.

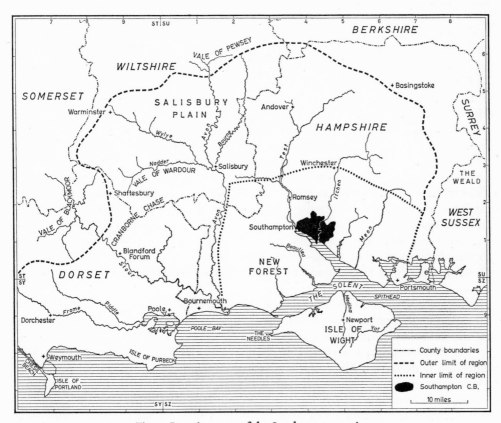

Fig. 1. Location map of the Southampton region

Between Southampton Water and the Avon valley, covering almost 150 square miles, lies the New Forest, which has been described as 'a miraculous survival of pre-Norman England'. A large part of the Forest still consists of open heath, though areas of unenclosed oak and beech flourish in sheltered depressions. A large proportion is Crown land, administered by the Forestry Commission and planted in large blocks of conifers. Apart from forestry, the most important aspects of Forest life today are the grazing of animals and the accommodation of campers and caravanners.

The poverty of the Tertiary sands is accentuated by wide spreads of plateau-gravel, in places as much as 10 feet thick, which cover parts of the New Forest and the Southampton Plateau above about 150 feet. They consist of 'a coarse yet compact deposit of sub-angular flints in a sandy matrix', and they afford an inhospitable habitat for many plants. Yet heaths and heathers, rhododendrons, camellias and azaleas, all acid-tolerant and lime-hating, grow superbly. The show-place for these magnificent shrubs is the famous Rothschild estate at Exbury, on the shores of the Solent.

However, parts of the Tertiary country are of some agricultural value, notably the out-crops of the London Clay and the Bracklesham Beds, which yield medium loams of fair quality. In places even the sands, affording warm and light soils, carry an intensive market-gardening, usually in smallholdings. One striking example of this horticulture is in the area between Swanwick and Fareham, which specialises in soft fruit, particularly straw-berries. Though the acreage is now little more than a quarter of that in pre-1939 days, the fruit is still sent far afield.

The broadly centripetal character of the drainage pattern helps to give a unity to the region; across it rivers such as the Avon, Test, Itchen and Meon drain towards the Channel. The delightful reaches of these chalk-streams offer some of the finest trout-fishing in England, though possibly also the most expensive. Their lower courses are across broad alluvium-floored flood-plains, in which the present rivers are clearly misfits, for they are much too small for their present valleys. It seems evident that these rivers were superimposed from a former cover of Plio-Pleistocene marine deposits, for they cut across the mid-Tertiary fold-lines in a strikingly discordant manner. They were once tributaries to the former drainage-artery of the so-called 'Solent river' (Fig. 7). The west–east line of the Dorset Frome, Poole Harbour and the Solent itself are the product of the disruption by marine denudation of the former southern chalk rim, coupled with the sea-level rise of the Neolithic transgression. This combination of marine erosion and rise of sea-level created the Solent itself, Southampton Water, the Hamble and Beaulieu estuaries and also Ports-mouth, Poole and Christchurch Harbours.

The coastline, from Bridport in the west to Selsey Bill in the east, is in many ways unrivalled in its variety. The rocks have suffered striking differential marine denudation; for example, the outer wall of Portland Limestone along the coast has been breached in many places, forming some striking coastal features, such as Durdle Door and Stair Hole near Lulworth Cove, with a more continuous mass of limestone comprising the Isle of Portland. Further east still, in the Isle of Purbeck, the Portland Stone, nearly horizontal and capped with Purbeck Beds, forms the massive headlands of St. Albans and Durlston. Chalk, too, despite its apparent softness, rises boldly as near-vertical cliffs between Osmington and Lulworth (Plate VI). Elsewhere, as around the curve of Bournemouth Bay, the Tertiary rocks form low earthy cliffs. In places these are of great instability; beach-huts occasionally slump with the clay, and much protective work is required, particularly behind the promenade at Bournemouth itself, and between Highcliffe and Milford (Plate XI).

While erosion is actively attacking parts of the coast, at the same time deposition builds up shingle-beaches and spits, notably Chesil Beach, 16 miles long, and Calshot and Hurst Castle Spits. Elsewhere, in favoured places, are sandy beaches, the profit of such resorts as Weymouth, Swanage and Poole. Within the sheltered estuaries and creeks, salt-marshes have developed from the tidal mud-flats, as behind Hurst Castle Spit. In the formation of these marshes the well-known *Spartina Townsendii*, or perennial rice-grass, with its powers of mud accretion, has played a great part; in this neighbourhood the plant first appeared in Britain as recently as 1870 (Plates X, XXII, XXIII).

This then is the diverse physical setting of the broad Southampton Region. Equally varied are the patterns of settlement. On the chalklands the nucleated villages are sited close to the scarp-foot springs, for within this chalk country the problem of water supply is paramount. Then there are the larger market-towns and service-centres—Dorchester, Andover and the cathedral cities of Salisbury, dominated by its superb spire, and Winchester, which was once indeed capital of England, commanding the gap cut through a prominent chalk ridge by the river Itchen. On the Tertiary outcrops, by contrast, the agricultural villages are straggling and rather shapeless. A few larger settlements include Romsey, the pleasant New Forest centres of Lyndhurst and Brockenhurst, and Eastleigh, just north of Southampton, with its railway workshops and its 'grid-iron' street-pattern dating from the last decade of the nineteenth century.

Most of the coastal resorts, with their thronged beaches and sunshine records, lie to the west of the Solent and on the Isle of Wight. Among them Bournemouth stands supreme; in a century its remarkable growth has spread inland over the heathland, to become a genteelly residential town and resort of over 150,000 people. Indeed, with its contiguous neighbours Christchurch and Poole, it now forms a coastal conurbation of about 270,000 people, representing an increase of 40 per cent over the figures of the 1931 Census. Portsmouth, a city of about 215,000 people, has for so long functioned essentially as a naval port that its future in an age of diminishing sea-power must give cause for concern, and it is now in fact achieving some diversification of industry.

THE FACE OF THE TOWN

Southampton, like most other large towns, reveals itself differently to visitors who approach it from different directions. The traveller by sea enters the port as he starts to move up Southampton Water, and the journey of seven miles or so to the docks is full of interest. The eastern shore is little industrialised. There are some small oil-storage depôts and, in Southampton's south-eastern suburb of Woolston, shipyards, but the fields and trees, the yachts on the Hamble river, and the impressive, though now empty, original building of the Royal Victoria Hospital at Netley, are much more typical of this bank. The western shore is different. Just inside the Water, at Calshot, a site is being prepared for an electricity generating station; then northward appear the Fawley oil refinery with other associated industries nearby, the rapidly expanding town of Hythe, and the power-station at Marchwood. By contrast, this busy waterfront has for its backcloth the attractive New Forest woodlands. On the water, traffic is very mixed as passenger liners, cargo-boats (especially oil tankers), ferries to France, the Isle of Wight and Hythe, and pleasure-craft of many kinds, come and go. The borough, as distinct from the port, begins about a mile south of the nearest part of the docks, at the confluence of the rivers Test and Itchen. From there the boundary runs north-westward along the middle of the Test estuary to its head, whence it sweeps east to enclose the town in a rough semicircle with a radius of approximately four miles. Seen from seaward Southampton is not impressive, for although the town has a few very new tall blocks, the visible central area and eastern suburbs look rather like a toy town from this direction, and the Old Docks on the Itchen seem small and rather dingy. Only the cranes, lining the New Docks along the Test with an almost military precision, seem to provide a setting comparable with the scale and dignity of the large liners which call here. Once in the docks, many travellers see little more of Southampton; they are whisked away to London by boat-train and look out mainly on backyards and gardens.

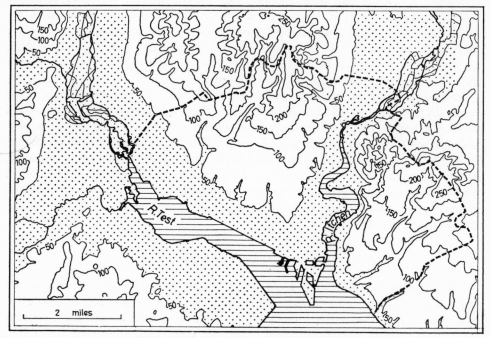

Fig. 2. Relief map of the Southampton district

The boundary of the County Borough is shown as a pecked line. Land under 50 feet O.D. is stippled.

The most attractive approach to the town by road is from the north, from Winchester. Though the ribbon development through Chandler's Ford is dull and monotonous, the journey within the borough itself from Bassett to the docks is pleasant. This route, tree-lined for half its length, runs nearly due north and south and roughly bisects the town. Bassett, with its variety of detached villas, is an obviously expensive district in which to live. On the right a signpost points to the fine municipal Sports Centre. At Bassett cross-roads the houses suddenly cease and for the next mile the road cuts across the Common, a large area of grass and woodland. Away on the left and skirting its eastern fringe rise the predominantly post-1945 University buildings. When the built-up area begins again, there appear successively just off London Road some fine early nineteenth-century domestic architecture in and around Rockstone, Carlton, Brunswick and Cumberland Places, and some late nineteenth-century residences in Winn and Westwood Roads. The last mile of this route forms the main road of the central part of the town, Above Bar Street and then the High Street. Immediately west of Above Bar Street stands the Civic Centre, a low building of Portland Stone, while to the east extensive and attractive parks separate it from a parallel thoroughfare, St. Mary Street. Above Bar Street, with its multiple stores, is a busy shopping area where most of the buildings have obviously been erected since the end of the War of 1939–45. The High Street, guarded by the Bargate (Plate XXIX), is quiet by comparison, and there are some derelict spaces and the beginnings of a park lay-out near the water-front. Here and there are some unmistakably medieval stone buildings.

The dullest way into Southampton is from the west, the immediate approach to and journey through the town being aggravated by memories of the pleasant route through the New Forest as far as Totton. At Redbridge, at the head of the Test estuary, the Bourne-mouth and Ringwood roads converge to form one of the worst bottlenecks in Hampshire. Here, and in the neighbouring suburb of Millbrook, stretch vast post-1945 Corporation housing estates, in which the most striking individual building is the twenty-storey block, Redbridge Towers (Plate LV). From the Millbrook roundabout a road goes north-east to Bassett through the old village and modern residential district of Shirley. The road into the heart of the town runs alongside the estuary, with the land between occupied by the New Docks, light industries and the Southampton to Bournemouth railway line. Millbrook Road and the suburb of Freemantle contain a variety of nineteenth-century dwellings. At Four Posts Hill, just west of the Civic Centre, a road to the right leads past the Central Station and round to the southern end of the High Street, with a fine medieval town wall on its left (Plate XXXI), and the electricity station, the Pirelli cable factory, the new swimming baths and the Royal Pier on the right.

The visitor coming from the east may follow either the main coast road through Bursledon or the more rural inland road through Botley. Both routes bring him into the suburb of Bitterne through large areas of modern Corporation housing at Harefield and Thornhill. Bitterne Road gives the impression of having been built up in the twentieth century, but after a mile or so there are signs of antiquity, for a notice-board on a wall proclaims that here, on the east bank of the Itchen, was the Romano-British port of *Clausentum*. From the new Northam Bridge there are views north-west across a sea of roof-tops towards the Common, and downstream to the wooded heights of Peartree and Woolston beyond. The Southern Television Studios stand on the town side of the bridge and mark the beginning of Northam, the most conspicuous feature of which is a still unfinished redevelopment scheme entailing the replacement of the town's nearest approach to a slum quarter. Despite the changes, plenty of indications from here along to the Six Dials road junction suggest that this district developed as a working-class quarter in the mid-nineteenth century. Straight on at Six Dials the road leads across the parks to the Civic Centre, but the turning to the left, St. Mary Street, runs between the river Itchen and the High Street, past St. Mary's Church and the Terminus Station, and along to the Old Docks with their nearby port services, shipping offices and consulates. A large stone tower, God's House Tower (Plate XXX), now a museum of archaeology, indicates that the traveller has again returned to the medieval quarter, and soon he is once more at the southern end of the High Street.

The routes which the visitors have followed and the main features which they have seen can be traced on Fig. 78, which indicates the situation, site and shape of modern Southampton. If the visitors had time to examine the landscape in detail, they could learn more about the history and present condition of the town. They would see that the buildings as a whole date from three main periods: the Middle Ages (about 1150–1500), the late eighteenth and the early nineteenth centuries, and above all the later nineteenth and twentieth centuries. Nearly all the medieval buildings lie, as has already been noticed, south of the main modern shopping centre in Above Bar Street, and they include impressive defensive walls, towers and gates, stone houses and vaults, and commercial and ecclesiastical structures. Most of the buildings dating from the second period are domestic, with bow windows, stucco fronts and graceful ironwork. They were built after 1800 rather than before, and occur in four groups. One of these is within the medieval walls, while the others lie north-west of the Bargate in Portland Street and Portland Terrace, just off London Road in and near Rockstone Place, and towards the Old Docks. By far the greatest number of the town's buildings have been constructed in the third period, from the mid-nineteenth century onwards: houses, churches and chapels, and administrative, commercial and industrial buildings, most of them very much like their counterparts elsewhere. Although medieval, Georgian and Regency, and nineteenth- and twentieth-century architecture is thus well represented, there is little, apart from Tudor House (Plate XXXII), now a museum, from the early sixteenth to the late eighteenth century.

From this evidence it might be concluded that since the Norman Conquest the town has enjoyed three periods of prosperity and one of decline. It could be dangerous to argue in this way, but it is, in fact, broadly true; the architecture of Southampton reflects its general history since 1066. The Conquest, linking England more closely with the Continent, heralded the first period of prosperity, and the town's political, military and commercial importance increased. Kings, courtiers and pilgrims passed through, as did soldiers, especially during the Hundred Years' War. So too did merchants, exporting amongst other things wool, cloth and tin, and importing, particularly in the eleventh and twelfth centuries, French wine, and later rich Levantine goods carried in Italian galleys and carracks. A small and unimportant borough when Domesday Book was compiled, Southampton had become by the end of the fifteenth century a separate county and the third port of the kingdom.

This medieval heyday was followed by a decline in the town's fortunes, which did not come to an end until the middle of the eighteenth century, when Southampton became a fashionable bathing- and watering-place. With the attraction of the spa gradually ceasing to be its main foundation, this second period of prosperity lasted until about 1830. It then merged into the third, which still continues, the era of docks and railway; the London and Southampton Railway was completed in 1840, and the first modern dock was opened in 1842. Since then Southampton has become the premier passenger port in the country, as well as an important cargo centre. While the town's post-Conquest history is thus reflected in its buildings, there are few indications in the landscape of prehistoric, Roman, and Saxon developments. It is archaeology, not architecture, which provides the clues to these, and the evidence is to be found in the town's museums.

The details of the physical growth of Southampton over the centuries, the outlines of which are suggested by these visual remains, can be filled in from maps and written authorities. The pre-Conquest settlements of Roman *Clausentum* (in modern Bitterne Manor) and Saxon *Hamtun* and *Hamwic* (the former probably in the neighbourhood of the Bargate and the latter near St. Mary's Church) looked towards the Itchen for their port facilities, and it was only with the development of the medieval walled town on the Test side of the narrow projection of land between the rivers that the core was established from which the modern town has grown. This walled area, with a perimeter of about a mile and a quarter, has left substantial remains, as has already been seen. Immediately beyond the walls to the east and north lay the marsh and the common fields of Houndwell, Hoglands and Marlands, now forming the Parks. Beyond these again, though still inside the borough, were the moated manor of Banisters, the common pasture (now the Common), the priory of St. Denys, and the glebe land of St. Mary's at Northam. Outside the boundary on all sides were the heathy wastes of neighbouring small communities. Most of the town's inhabitants lived within the walls, but suburbs and isolated hamlets did develop outside the north and east gates, near St. Mary's Church, and at Hill and Portswood. Even so, in 1596 fewer than a thousand, out of a total population of some 4200, lived outside the walls.

This medieval town, the early development of which is still obscure but whose structure in the fifteenth and sixteenth centuries is well known, underwent few fundamental changes until the late eighteenth century. Since then, however, the growth of the town has been remarkable. Not only most of the available land within the medieval boundary of the town (which followed approximately the line of modern Hill Lane, Burgess Road, Langhorn Road and the river Itchen), but also the areas added by boundary extensions are now covered with buildings. An acreage of 1970 in 1801 had become 13,394 by 1963, and a population of 7913 had risen to about 206,000. The general pattern of this great expansion is clear. By the early nineteenth century rows of small high-density houses had appeared on the low ground towards the Itchen, and dwellings for the wealthier sections of the community were being built beyond the north wall in terraces, and further afield as isolated houses in their own grounds. Long before the end of the century many of these estates were broken up and built over, and the town was already contemplating an extension of its boundary. This first took place in 1895, when Freemantle, Shirley and part of Millbrook were added. The subsequent extensions of 1920 and 1954 in turn brought in Bassett, Swaythling, Bitterne, Bitterne Park, Sholing and Woolston, and the rest of Millbrook, Redbridge, Harefield and part of Thornhill. Much building had of course already taken place in these localities before they were added to the borough, but the amount has greatly increased since. Alongside this landward growth a seaward extension has taken place as the docks have spread southward, leaving the medieval town high and dry. Near the heart of the modern town there has been considerable replacement of older buildings, a natural process quickened by the bomb damage suffered, particularly in the main shopping centre, during the War of 1939-45.

A detailed study of the face of Southampton in the 'sixties illuminates not only the town's history, but also its current developments and problems. Many of these, although having their place in the general story of the town's evolution, have particular relevance to the years since 1945. During this period the town has been recovering from the interruption of its growth and trade and the demolition of many of its buildings during the War of 1939-45; at the same time, it has also been extending its functions, services and amenities. The population is rising, and where people are to live is a major problem. In the late 'forties and early 'fifties large municipal housing estates were built at Millbrook and Harefield; now others are being erected in the adjacent suburbs of Redbridge and Thornhill respectively, but it is easy to see that little building land is left. The last big private estate in the borough, Townhill Park, is being built over, and the next major building scheme will take place in a neighbouring part of the county, at Lordshill, Rownhams.

In this context, two recent modifications of post-war planning ideas are interesting. There has been a movement back to building domestic dwellings in the heart of the old town, on Lansdowne Hill and in Bugle Street, for example. Much more obviously, the construction of the sixteen-storey Millbank House at Northam in 1960 marked the beginning of the surge upwards. Since then several other tall blocks have been completed and others are planned. It seems strange that this method of conserving land should not have been used before; in the last decade, for instance, much of the blitzed Above Bar Street and High Street was rebuilt at low level, and it was rare until a year or two ago to find flats more than three, or at most five, storeys high.

The number of churches and chapels built to serve the new twentieth-century houses is small compared with the number erected in the nineteenth century. Furthermore, the most interesting modern ecclesiastical architecture, of which there is in fact very little, does not appear on the new estates, but in already well-established residential areas. Probably the most noteworthy examples are the Roman Catholic Church of Christ the King at Bitterne, the Congregational Isaac Watts' Memorial Church in Winchester Road, and the rebuilt Anglican Church of St. James in Bernard Street. The most noticeable public buildings on the new estates are the schools; since 1945 twenty-seven new primary and nine new secondary schools have been built. Architecturally, the most important new educational buildings are those connected with the University, to whom Sir Basil Spence was appointed consultant architect in 1956; since then several modern buildings have risen at Highfield. Amongst the halls of residence, Chamberlain Hall at Glen Eyre and the tower at South Stoneham House are the best examples of modern building.

The construction of the Nuffield Theatre at the University is a reminder that Southampton has no permanent theatre; the Grand, south of the Civic Centre, was closed in 1959 and later demolished to make room for shops. The number of cinemas is also declining, largely as a result of the spread of television. Both the B.B.C. and I.T.V. have studios in the town, those of the latter at Northam being much more noticeable than those of the former in South Western House.

The rebuilt main streets, especially Above Bar Street which has taken the place of High

Street as the commercial heart of the town, now constitute a busy regional shopping centre, a very different state of affairs from the immediate post-war years, when even the local inhabitants frequently shopped in Bournemouth or Winchester. The old-established family business has almost entirely disappeared before the advance of the multiple store and its recent successor, the supermarket. Judged by the names on the shops, Southampton's main street could be in almost any large English town. The architecture of these shops is for the most part undistinguished, though it must be recognised that the opportunities for adventurous rebuilding were limited by the fact that reconstruction had to take place along a narrow north–south line. As a result of different planning proposals, the shortage of materials, especially steel, and the great need for houses, the rebuilding of the shopping centre did not really begin before the early 'fifties, and even now there are blitzed areas, at the southern end of the High Street and near the Central Station, for example, which still await redevelopment. Similarly, the long-projected Guildhall Square to the east of the Civic Centre, designed to bring this building more into the heart of the town, has not yet been laid out.

A marked addition to the Southampton scene since 1945 has been the appearance of many new light industries. Before the war the town depended heavily on the docks and service trades for employment. An attempt has been made to remedy this situation and the resulting factories are most evident in two places: the Millbrook Industrial Estate includes several light-engineering businesses, and on the land reclaimed during the construction of the New Docks in the 'twenties and 'thirties firms like A.C.-Delco and Standard Telephones and Cables have established themselves. In the docks themselves new buildings have appeared, such as the passenger and cargo terminals at the Ocean Dock and 102 Berth, the cold store and Dock House. Southampton remains the country's leading passenger port, though in 1958 for the first time the number of passengers crossing the Atlantic by air exceeded the number travelling by sea. In that year, too, the port's marine air base terminal closed and in 1961 the Channel Islands' steamer service was transferred to Weymouth. With the Army's decision in 1962 to conduct troop movements by air, Southampton ceased to be Britain's peace-time port for military personnel. Cargo traffic, however, has increased and may well become more important, especially if the recommendations of the recent Rochdale Committee are implemented. The chief commodity entering the port—oil—does not greatly influence the townscape, but the fruit trade has resulted in the growth of a busy wholesale fruit market in the High Street. The airport for the town lies outside the borough, at Eastleigh.

In Southampton, as elsewhere, motor traffic has produced considerable changes in the scene. Old roads have been altered; Above Bar Street, for example, has been widened, and the High Street, so attractive to travellers for centuries, has been straightened and indeed severed by a cross road (Plate XXXIV). New roads have been cut which often ignore old boundaries and produce a new pattern on the ground. Thus in the heart of the old town the inner ring road (Castle Way on the west and Queensway on the east) has fundamentally changed the locality and its atmosphere. Inevitably, a few buildings of historical interest, some houses in Portland Terrace, for example, have been demolished. Fortunately, nothing of outstanding importance has been completely swept away, and what has gone has been more than compensated for by the development of a new interest on the part of the Corporation in the town's ancient monuments and archaeology and by the expansion of its museums. A formerly familiar sight which has disappeared from the streets is the tram, replaced as the means of public transport by buses in 1950. Road improvements have added many new items to the scene, of which roundabouts (some of which are alleged to impede rather than assist traffic flow), street lights and traffic signs are the most obvious. To find parking-space is increasingly difficult; no non-traditional car-parks have yet been attempted, though it has frequently been suggested that Houndwell and Hoglands, or parts of them, should be used for this purpose. The fundamental reason for many of the traffic problems is that the ways in and out of the town are restricted. There is no land-route southward and in the west the Test estuary is bridged only at its head at Redbridge. Eastward the Itchen is even more of a barrier. Northam Bridge is a fine post-war structure, but the Portsmouth road, to which it gives access, cannot disperse traffic quickly. Moreover, this bridge lies well upstream and a new one is needed to link the southern part of the town with Woolston. There, while the building of a fixed bridge has been planned, the Floating Bridge still operates (Plate XLVI).

The construction of a new bridge at Woolston is just one aspect of the work of planning modern Southampton. It is only since 1945 that the planners have come into their own, but they have certainly left their mark upon the landscape, and the character of the town of the future is likely to owe even more to their efforts. Within the borough itself a future visitor may well see, for example, cars excluded from the central shopping area and a host of sky-scraper blocks, and he may also find access to the waterfront easier. Even more important, the face of Southampton will surely have enlarged through the extension of the borough boundaries. In this respect the problems are already those of keeping the town and port clean and attractive, of regulating the spread of the built-up area into the pleasant surrounding Hampshire countryside, and of reconciling the conflicting interests of different local authorities. These problems are especially obvious at present on the west, where the industrial developments on the New Forest shore of Southampton Water directly involve the Hampshire County Council, the New Forest Rural District Council, the Forestry Commission and the Southampton Harbour Board, though only indirectly the Southampton County Borough Council. On the north, too, the Southampton borough and Hampshire county authorities do not always view the town's expansion in the same light, a difference of opinion which is likely to be repeated on the east when the fixed bridge is built at Woolston. Will difficulties of this sort, which are bound to be aggravated if Southampton continues to prosper, lead to the creation of larger units of local administration? If they do, will one of these new units be the City of Southampton, the town thus being accorded the status which, some claim, it already deserves?

BIBLIOGRAPHICAL NOTE

For a more detailed study of the town's buildings and open spaces, see R. Douch, 'The face of the town', in J. B. Morgan and P. S. Peberdy, eds., *Collected essays on Southampton* (Southampton County Borough Council, 1958).

PART I

THE CHARACTER OF THE REGION

II

GEOLOGY

In the Southampton district and the Isle of Wight, the geologist is fortunate in having a wide range of Mesozoic and Tertiary formations accessible for detailed study along extensive coastlines which vary considerably in detail from year to year. In spite of piecemeal efforts to ward away the inevitable, coastal erosion remains a serious problem (see p. 49), with the result that coastal exposures are changing almost annually, and sections of beds ranging from the Lower Cretaceous Wealden Marls up to the highest British Oligocene strata (the Hamstead Beds) are revealed for study with varying degrees of completeness.

Considerable literature has accumulated on the geology of this area. One might signalise for particular mention the pioneer works of Fitton and the recent authoritative paper by Casey on the Lower Greensand, the work of Rowe and Brydone on Chalk faunal zones, and the meticulous papers of Fisher, Wrigley, St. John-Burton and Curry on various parts of the Tertiary beds, whose work, together with Miss M. E. Chandler's detailed palaeobotanical studies, has greatly supplemented the genius of Forbes in bringing to light the stratigraphical secrets and palaeontological treasures of the 'fluvio-marine' formations.

The limits of the area considered in this account are shown on the accompanying geological sketch map (Fig. 3). The district is represented on the Geological Survey maps listed under the *Bibliographical Note* (see p. 35).

THE STRUCTURE OF THE AREA

Apart from the southern half of the Isle of Wight, the district lies within the confines of the Hampshire Basin, a broad, east–west trending asymmetrical downfold of presumed Miocene age (Fig. 4). The steeply dipping southern limb of the syncline was breached by the sea during the Flandrian post-glacial transgression (see p. 48). Within the major structure is a number of smaller folds of varying importance. Of these, the Winchester and Portsdown anticlines are the most notable. The former, extending from Chilcomb in the east and running westward to the south of Winchester, is responsible for bringing the Lower Chalk (*H. subglobosus* zone) to the surface in the centre of a pericline. The Portsdown anticline results in an outcrop of Chalk (down to the *Marsupites* zone) rimmed by Tertiaries, stretching from east of Fareham to the vicinity of Chichester. To the north-west, this anticline may connect with the gentle anticlinal axis which brings up the London Clay at Swaythling, to the north of Southampton. This fold extends westward as far as the Test to the south of Romsey. It is almost in line with the Dean Hill anticline, responsible for a tongue-like projection of Chalk which almost isolates a Tertiary basin south of Salisbury. It is probable,

Cs

however, that these anticlinal crests are not continuous but arranged *en echelon*, with a trend which is mainly west-north-west by east-south-east. Other minor folds are the Lyndhurst and Thorness Bay synclines. In the Isle of Wight the Sandown–Arreton anticline brings up the Wealden in Sandown Bay. It is an asymmetrical structure, with dips approaching the vertical on the north and gentle dips to the south. Lying out to sea, south-west of the Isle of Wight, is the Brighstone anticline, responsible for the Lower Cretaceous outcrops on the south-western coast.

It is now known from the work of King (1949 and 1954) and Curry (1962) that the structural pattern seen in the Isle of Wight continues southward into the English Channel. The southerly dip of the beds on the south coast of the Isle of Wight becomes reversed so that Kimmeridge Clay outcrops on the floor of the Channel about 20 miles to the south. This formation apparently forms the northern rim of a mid-Channel Tertiary basin, in which beds as high as the Brackleshams are preserved. The Tertiary beds are surrounded by Chalk which ranges as high as the Upper Maestrichtian—that is to say, into Cretaceous beds younger than any yet recorded on the mainland of Great Britain.

Faulting is unimportant within the area. Small step-faults with a combined throw of 10 feet or less are seen to affect some Cretaceous beds. These displacements, however, are merely faults of accommodation. A normal fault with a throw of less than 10 feet occurs to the east of Sandown, affecting the Sandrock, Carstone and Gault. The Chalk shows evidence of shearing; slickensiding, displacement of flint nodule bands between curved shear planes, and the stringing-out of brecciated flint along such planes are all common phenomena. Within certain marl bands in the Lower Chalk, incipient axial plane cleavage has been noted, and worm burrows and ammonites are deformed and orientated along these lines.

THE CONCEALED STRATA

Nine deep exploratory boreholes have been made within the limits of the district here considered (Fig. 3). These are Portsdown No. 1 (6556 feet), Portsdown No. 2 (2871 feet), Arreton, Isle of Wight (5161 feet), Fordingbridge (4487 feet) and Chilcomb Nos. 1-5 (up to 2280 feet) (Table I). The Kingsclere boring to the north and the Henfield boring to the east are also valuable aids to the interpretation of the deeper structure of the Hampshire Basin. A deep boring for water made on Southampton Common penetrated 454 feet of Tertiary beds and a further 859 feet of Chalk.

The thicknesses of the formations encountered are listed in Table I, which has been compiled from the papers of Lees and Taitt (1946), Taitt and Kent (1958), Falcon and Kent (1960), and from information supplied by the Gas Council amplifying the data given by Johnson (1961) concerning the Chilcomb bores. The oldest strata encountered in these boreholes were the Keuper Marls at the base of the Fordingbridge bore. Kent (1949) estimated the depth of the pre-Permian floor of the Hampshire Basin at 12,000 feet. Gravity data, which were often useful in detecting deeply buried structures, were plotted by White (1949) for this region. The main gravity 'low' lies some 8 miles south-east of Salisbury, that is to say, about 20 miles north of the centre of the basin as deduced from stratigraphical

Table I. Succession and Thicknesses of Strata in Deep Boreholes

	A	P_1	P_2	F	C	K	H
Tertiaries	—	—	—	678	—	—	—
Upper Chalk	—	520+	820+			—	—
Middle Chalk	—	210	210	1,319	895+	—	—
Lower Chalk	—	340	350			—	—
Upper Greensand	—	125	110	254	128	111+	—
Gault	—	163	200		237	284	
Lower Greensand	210+	92	78	abs.	90	45	—
Wealden	2,010	825	767	abs.	965	587	1,080+
Purbeck	343	210	248	abs.	75+	539	360
Portland	87	81	28+	abs.	—	143	98
Kimmeridge	1,107	1,102	—	210	—	933	1,082
Corallian	216	111	—	170	—	176	299
Oxford Clay	450	444	—	430	—	312	524
Kellaways	99	29	—		—	60	36
Cornbrash	19	18	—	35	—		13
Great Oolite	196	341	—	404	—	249	207
Fuller's Earth	252	106	—		—		118
Inferior Oolite	172+	388	—	118	—	359	274
Upper Lias	—	281	—	250	—	147	296
Middle Lias	—	286	—	450	—	285	112
Lower Lias	—	802	—		—	752	390
Rhaetic	—	66	—	60	—	78	abs.
Keuper	—	16+	—	106+	—	60+	abs.
Carboniferous	—	—	—	—	—	—	215+

The boreholes are as follows: A. Arreton; P_1. Portsdown No. 1; P_2. Portsdown No. 2; F. Fording-bridge; C. Chilcomb; K. Kingsclere; H. Henfield.

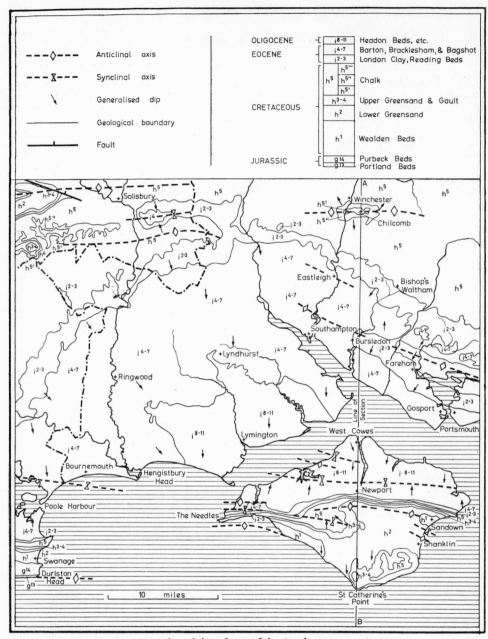

Fig. 3. The solid geology of the Southampton region

Based on the Geological Survey, Quarter Inch Series, sheets 19, 32 (by permission of the Geological Survey).

The line A—B indicates the line of section given in Fig. 4.

and structural considerations. White ascribes this discrepancy 'to the gravitational effect of the high relief uplifted block of the Purbeck anticline'.

The most notable stratigraphical result to emerge from these exploratory boreholes is the evidence for considerable pre-Albian uplift at Fordingbridge. The occurrence of a radio-active 'marker band' near the junction of the Upper Greensand and the Lower Chalk in the Chilcomb bores is an interesting feature which may indicate contamination by volcanic ash.

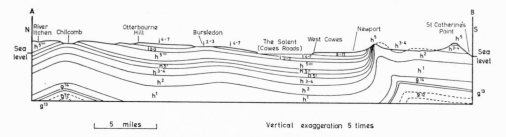

Fig. 4. Geological cross-section

The cross-section, the line of which is shown on Fig. 3, extends from the Itchen valley north of Winchester to St. Catherine's Point, Isle of Wight.

THE CRETACEOUS SYSTEM

The Wealden Series

The Wealden Series of this district is very unequally apportioned between the Wealden Shales (up to 210 feet thick) and the Wealden Marls which attain a thickness of about 1800 feet below the Isle of Wight, although no more than 550 feet are visible at the surface. The sediments of this area have greater affinity with the Wealden type of development seen in Dorset (where the Series attains 2300 feet) than with the Weald itself. The Henfield borehole, to the east of this area, shows the incoming of Wealden facies typical of the Weald. At the surface, the Wealden sediments occur in the cores of the Sandown and Brighstone anticlines on the coast of the Isle of Wight. The Wealden Series probably spans the Valanginian, Hauterivian and Barremian Stages, but it is not possible at the moment to equate levels in the Wealden more precisely with these Stages of the Neocomian.

Wealden Marls. The Wealden Marls consist of a variable series of coloured, variegated clays and marls with impersistent beds of sand, sandstone and sandy limestone laid down in a freshwater environment. The beds are not very fossiliferous, but *Pseudunio*, *Viviparus*, pieces of driftwood and other plant material, together with fish remains and rolled reptilian bones, are to be found. At Hanover Point, scattered trunks of coniferous trees characterise a bed about 450 feet below the top of the Wealden Marls, which has long been known as the 'Pine Raft'.

Wealden Shales. The Wealden Shales are thickest in Compton Bay Chine where they attain 211 feet, although they thin rapidly northward to 100 feet in Compton Bay itself.

The characteristic lithology of the Wealden Shales exhibits dark paper-shales (with bedding-planes abundantly strewn with ostracod carapaces) associated with thin shelly limestones. Where they are thickest some arenaceous beds appear in their lowest levels. On the east coast, where the Wealden Shales are 170 feet thick, one of the limestones, full of the small lamellibrach *Filosina*, has been called the '*Cyrena*' Limestone. Towards the top of the Wealden Shales, oyster *lumachelles* indicates an approach to marine conditions, and concretions in the shales above the '*Cyrena*' Limestone have yielded the undoubted marine echinoid recorded as '*Cidaris*', in addition to bones, teeth and spines of fish. Unfortunately, no ammonites have been found. The upper parts of the Wealden Shales thus foreshadow the widespread marine invasion of the area represented by the *Perna* Bed at the base of the overlying Lower Greensand. Detailed sections of the Wealden Series are available in White (1921).

The Lower Greensand

The Lower Greensand deposits of Aptian and Lower Albian age occupy an extensive tract of the surface of the Isle of Wight. They outcrop on the coast to the north of the Brighstone and Sandown anticlines where, because of their appreciable dip, the width of outcrop is small, and also to the south of these anticlines where gentle southerly dips provide long coastal sections. The highest beds also form the base of the cliffs on the south coast around St. Catherine's Point and Dunnose. The beds have been described in detail by Casey (1961), who has provided a new zonal scheme of classification of the Lower Greensand. The following table is a synopsis of that author's work in so far as it concerns the Hampshire Basin, providing a tabulation of the lithological units corresponding to the palaeontological subdivisions of the Lower Greensand.

Stage	Zone	Formation
LOWER ALBIAN	*Douvilleiceras mammillatum* *Leymeriella tardefurcata*	Carstone Sandrock
UPPER APTIAN	*Hypacanthoplites jacobi* *Parahoplites nutfieldensis* *Cheloniceras martinioides*	 Ferruginous Sands
LOWER APTIAN	*Tropaeum bowerbanki* *Deshayesites deshayesi* *Deshayesites forbesi* *Prodeshayesites fissicostatus*	 Atherfield Clay Series

Casey (1962) raised the top of the Lower Greensand to include the *mammillatum* zone, making the junction of the Lower Greensand and Gault correspond with the divide between the Lower and Middle Albian Stages. It seems that the lowest subzone of the Lower Aptian is not represented in the Isle of Wight, so that the Lower Greensand rests with slight non-sequence on the Wealden.

The formation is thickest (800 feet) in Chale Bay, but decreases to 400 feet in Compton Bay about 8½ miles to the north-east. On the mainland the Lower Greensand, which is only met with in boreholes, is much reduced in thickness. This is due to the thinning of some members, particularly by pre-Gault erosion.

The Atherfield Clay Series. The base of the Lower Greensand is a five-foot bed of sandy clay and calcareous sandstone, known as the *Perna* Bed because of the occurrence of *Mulletia mulleti* formerly assigned to the lamellibranch genus *Perna*. It yields the richest fossil fauna of the Lower Greensand and is the only horizon in that formation with fossil corals (*Holocystis elegans*). The ammonites of the upper part yield the subzonal index *Prodeshayesites obsoletus*, indicative of the upper part of the basal Aptian zone of *P. fissicostatus*.

The Atherfield Clay itself is between 60 and 70 feet thick. It consists of unbedded clay with red and white clay-ironstone nodules. Lamellibranchs are the commonest fossils, ammonites being less frequent, although the zonal index fossil ranges throughout. *Deshayesites fittoni* indicates the basal subzone of the *forbesi* zone.

Casey has extended the top of the Atherfield Clay Series to take in all the strata to the top of the Upper Lobster Bed. The Lower Lobster Bed constitutes a clay division, between 25 and 30 feet thick, named after a fossil prawn *Meyeria magna*, usually recorded as *M. vectense*. True lobsters have also been found, though much more rarely. Lamellibranchs, gastropods and ammonites are well preserved, the last indicating the middle subzone of the *forbesi* zone. The Upper Lobster Bed consists of 40 feet of silty and sandy clays with *Meyeria magna* and ammonites, which occur either crushed or as internal moulds in clay-ironstone or pyritic nodules. The Upper and Lower Lobster Beds are separated by the Crackers, 20 feet of clayey sand with two lines of sandy, calcareous concretions. These have yielded many fossil species of ammonites and lamellibranchs, as well as a fish, a crab and a cirripede. Echinoids and gastropods also occur, but brachiopods are uncommon. The ammonite fauna shows that these beds belong to the uppermost subzone of the *forbesi* zone.

The Ferruginous Sands. The Ferruginous Sands comprise a thick varied series of strata, best exposed on the west coast of the Isle of Wight to the south-east of Atherfield Point. The basal beds are known as the Lower *Gryphaea* Beds. These comprise 28 feet of green clayey sands in the lower half, with brown sands and ironstone fragments in the upper half. The top 2 or 3 feet contain abundant *Exogyra latissima* (formerly assigned to *Gryphaea*), together with phosphatised examples of the subzonal ammonite *Cheloniceras parinodum*. The basal 16 feet contain nodules of indurated sand with a fine ammonite fauna which includes *Deshayesites deshayesi* s.s. In the middle of the Lower *Gryphaea* Beds a 2-foot seam is crowded with *Sellithyris sella* and other brachiopods.

There follows a series of glauconitic clayey sands called the *Scaphites* Group. At the base occur 18 feet of sands with calcareous nodules which have yielded a fine ammonite fauna, including *Deshayesites grandis*, the subzonal index of the upper half of the *deshayesi* zone. In the beds above there are two main levels with nodules and concretions. The lower nodule bed is phosphatic and full of fossils, while the large red-stained, calcareous concretions of the upper layer are aggregated around large ammonite nuclei. The uncoiled ammonite *Australiceras*, formerly called *Scaphites* or *Macroscaphites*, serves to name the division. The upper beds yield large specimens of *Exogyra*.

Above the *Scaphites* Group occur the Lower *Crioceras* Beds, 16 feet thick. The lithology of this division shows grey-green clayey sands, with concretions enclosing giant uncoiling ammonites, formerly assigned to *Crioceras*. Species of the ammonite genus *Dufrenoyia* indicate the basal subzone of the *bowerbanki* zone. Then follows the Walpen Clay and Sand, 57 feet thick in Whale Chine. This division is made up of clayey sands and sandy clays with phosphatic concretions containing numerous ammonites, especially in the lower half. The ammonites indicate the upper half of the *bowerbanki* zone.

Above the Walpen Clay and Sand comes the division known as the Upper *Crioceras* Beds, 46 feet thick, composed of clayey sands with lines of large concretions. These have yielded ammonites indicative of the basal subzone of the *martinioides* zone. The occurrence of the ammonite genus *Tropaeum* (which was formerly identified as *Crioceras*) is reflected in the name of this division of the Lower Greensand, which forms the base of the Upper Aptian Stage. These beds are succeeded by the Walpen and Ladder Sands, composed of 42 feet of sandy beds with calcareous concretions at the base. These enclose multitudes of fossils, mainly small ammonites and brachiopods belonging to the genus *Sellithyris*. Lamellibranchs and the echinoid genera *Phyllobrissus* and *Toxaster* also occur. Serpulid tubes are also common, found in intertwined masses in a sandstone 6 feet above the concretions. The ammonites indicate the middle subzone of the *martinioides* zone.

The next beds make up the Cliff End Sands, 28 feet of glauconitic sands and clays which yield poorly preserved ammonites at the base. In the upper portion, branching cylindrical concretions provide a feature of some interest. The Cliff End Sands are succeeded by 45 feet of unfossiliferous clays and sands, known as the Foliated Clay and Sand. These in turn are followed by 90 feet of glauconitic sands with a conspicuous basal pebble-bed. Fossiliferous nodules about the middle of the division have yielded small *Parahoplites*. The equivalent beds near Shanklin, on the east coast, have provided an ammonoid fauna indicating the lower part of the *nutfieldensis* zone.

The uppermost beds of the Ferruginous Sands are the Ferruginous Bands of Blackgang Chine and the overlying Upper Clays. The Ferruginous Bands, 20 feet thick, consist of iron-stained sands with three layers of ironstone concretions. These concretions are replete with internal moulds and external impressions of gastropods and lamellibranchs, of which *Thetironia* and *Pterotrigonia* are perhaps the commonest. No ammonites have been found in this division. The Ferruginous Bands are succeeded by the Upper Clays, 40 feet of unfossiliferous sandy clays upon which the Sandrock rests.

The Sandrock.   The Sandrock is about 190 feet thick, consisting of pale sand and sandstone. It is usually very unfossiliferous but in Luccombe Chine, south of Shanklin, nodules occur 20 feet above the base which have yielded fossil plants, including the specimens upon which the extinct Cycad order (the Bennettitales) was founded (Carruthers, 1870). Rare ammonites indicating the lower part of the *jacobi* zone have been found in these nodules. A nodule, presumed to have come from the top of the Sandrock, which enclosed a mould of an ammonite, indicates that the upper limit of the Sandrock belongs to the middle subzone of the *tardefurcata* zone. It seems that the uppermost subzone of the *tardefurcata* zone is absent in the Isle of Wight and that the Carstone rests with non-sequence on the Sandrock.

The Carstone.   The Carstone reaches a maximum thickness of 72 feet. It consists of reddish-brown sand containing pebbles and phosphatic nodules. Some of the latter have provided a large fauna which includes the zonal ammonite *Douvilleiceras mammillatum*. These beds were at one time assigned to the Gault.

Intra-Cretaceous Earth-movements

Before and during Albian times, earth-movements occurred which caused folding and erosion in many places. This episode was followed by widespread marine transgression, which extended the Upper Cretaceous marine régime already initiated in Aptian times. Gault sediments thus accumulated in this area on a sea floor formed of strata ranging from Lower Albian (where erosion had been slight) to Kimmeridgian where it had been severe. In eastern Devonshire the Gault rests on beds as old as the Keuper. In our area, the most striking testimony to this orogenic 'spasm' is provided by the Fordingbridge borehole, where strata from Middle Kimmeridge Clay to Lower Greensand inclusive are missing. This is equivalent to an uplift cutting out beds which are 4000 feet thick in Dorset.

The Gault

The Gault and the succeeding Upper Greensand constitute the Middle and Upper Albian Stages. Typically, the Gault is a clay facies and the Upper Greensand is arenaceous, but in different parts of Britain the transition between the two types of sediment takes place at different stratigraphical levels. Generally, the clays predominate in the east and become increasingly replaced by sand as they are traced westward. The palaeontological time-scale of the Middle and Upper Albian is given below, together with the lithological nomenclature applicable to the area under discussion:

Stage	Zone	Subzone	Formation
UPPER ALBIAN	Stoliczkaia dispar	dispar & perinflatum / substudieri	Chert Beds
		aequatorialis	Upper Greensand
	Mortoniceras inflatum	auritus / varicosum	Malm Rock
		orbignyi	Passage Beds
MIDDLE ALBIAN	Euphoplites lautus	cristatum / daviesi / lautus-nitidus / subdelaruei	Possibly absent
	Hoplites dentatus	niobe / intermedius / dentatus-bonarelli	Gault Clay
		benettianus	Beds of Carstone lithology

The Gault of the Isle of Wight is between 90 and 100 feet thick, stretching as a narrow continuous band across the island from the south side of Culver Cliff on the east to Compton Bay on the west. On the south coast of the Isle of Wight the Gault underlies an extensive stretch of foreshore, though it is largely concealed by landslipped masses of Upper Green-sand and Chalk which have slid seawards on the upper lubricated surface of the Gault.

The Carstone type of lithology of the uppermost Lower Greensand persists into the lower portion of the *dentatus* zone Gault, and is succeeded by the typical clay facies. It is possible that the overlying *lautus* zone of the Gault is not represented in the Isle of Wight. The lower half of the succeeding *inflatum* zone (*orbignyi* and *varicosum* subzones) would appear to be represented by the Passage Beds, which are sandy clays and marls 15 to 44 feet thick, forming a transition series passing into the Upper Greensand.

The Gault has been encountered in all the deep boreholes put down on the mainland. In the Fordingbridge bore it rests with great non-sequence on Kimmeridge Clay. Elsewhere it rests on comparatively thin Lower Greensand. It forms an impervious dome in the Winchester pericline, the summit of which reaches to within 300 feet of the surface (Plate XIV). Extensive investigation by the Gas Council has shown that the sandy Lower Greensand would make an excellent gas storage reservoir sealed by the Gault of this structure (Johnson, 1961).

The Upper Greensand (Plate V)

The Upper Greensand at Ventnor in the Isle of Wight has been divided into a lower Malm Rock (70 feet thick) and upper Chert Beds (26 feet thick) (Parkinson, 1881). The lowest 56 feet of the Malm Rock consists mainly of reddish sands and sandstones from which ammonites, recorded by Parkinson, have been re-interpreted by Spath (1943) as indicating the *auritus* subzone of the Upper Albian. The remainder consists of 'building stones' with some chert ascribed on the basis of its ammonite fauna to the *aequatorialis* subzone. The succeeding Chert Beds consist of 26 feet of green sandstone and abundant chert surmounted by a bed of phosphatic nodules lying immediately below the Cenomanian Chloritic Marl. At Ventnor these beds have not yielded ammonites, but in Compton Bay a bed, equivalent to the highest Upper Greensand at Ventnor, contains the subzonal index *S. dispar*. It seems then that the main part of the Chert Beds can be assigned to the *substudieri* subzone.

The Upper Greensand can be studied at Culver Cliff, where it is 80 feet thick. *Exogyra conica*, *Chlamys aspera*, *Neithea quinquecostata* and the worm-tube *Rotularia concava* are common fossils. On the mainland the Upper Greensand has been penetrated in deep boreholes and varies from 110 to 128 feet thick.

The Chalk

The Chalk zones of the Isle of Wight were described by Rowe (1908) and their distribution was mapped by Sherborn (in Rowe, 1908), while those of the Hampshire main-land were worked out and mapped by Brydone (1912). The following scheme, elaborated from Rowe's original proposals, is now adopted for the palaeontological subdivision of the Chalk formations (Wright and Wright, 1951). The thicknesses of the zones in the Isle of Wight and in the Portsdown No. 1 borehole are given in the fourth and fifth columns respectively of the Table opposite.

Formation	Stage	Zone	(Feet)	
UPPER CHALK	UPPER SENONIAN	Belemnella lanceolata	not present	
		Belemnitella mucronata	475	—
		Gonioteuthis quadrata	216	—
		Offaster pilula	130	70+
	LOWER SENONIAN	Marsupites testudinarius	89 ⎫	100
		Uintacrinus westfalicus	40 ⎬	
		Micraster coranguinum	278	230
		Micraster cortestudinarium	52 ⎫	
			⎬ 120	
MIDDLE CHALK	TURONIAN	Holaster planus	60 ⎭	
		Terebratulina lata	⎫	120
		Inoceramus labiatus with basal beds with Actinocamax plenus	⎬ 199	110
LOWER CHALK	CENOMANIAN	Holaster subglobosus	90	170
		Schloenbachia varians	120	170

The total thickness of the Chalk varies from about 1800 feet in the Isle of Wight to 1319 feet in the Fordingbridge borehole. This reduction is due to removal of higher beds by early Tertiary peneplanation, which caused greater erosion in the north as compared with the south (see p. 38).

The *S. varians* zone includes the Chloritic Marl and the Chalk Marl. The zone of *H. subglobosus* is called the Grey Chalk. The *plenus* Marls were formerly placed at the top of the Cenomanian but are now assigned to the base of the Turonian. Above these marls comes the Melbourn Rock, followed by nodular chalk and chalk with marl seams, followed by a bed of nodular chalk which is probably the equivalent of the Chalk Rock of some British localities. The Upper Chalk is by far the thickest of the Chalk formations, and is sometimes called the Chalk-with-Flints.

The Chalk of the Isle of Wight is best examined, tides permitting, at Culver Cliff. Here, above the cherts of the Upper Greensand, may be seen 8 or 9 feet of the so-called Chloritic Marl composed of grey and green glauconitic marly sand which, by increasing clay content, passes transitionally into the Chalk Marl. It contains the sponge *Stauronema carteri*, which has been suggested as an index fossil to this stratigraphical level. *S. varians* occurs, showing that these deposits belong to the Cenomanian Stage. The overlying Chalk Marl is a bluish-grey marly chalk, with abundant siliceous sponges including 'reefs' of *Exanthesis labrosa*. Species belonging to the ammonite genera *Calycoceras* and *Mantelliceras*, together with the lamellibranchs *Chlamys beaveri* and *Inoceramus crippsi*, also occur.

The Grey Chalk of the *H. subglobosus* zone follows, presenting a striped appearance due to alternations of grey marly chalk with more massive whiter chalk. In this bed, about 90 feet thick, the ammonite genera *Turrilites*, *Scaphites* and *Acanthoceras* may be found associated with *Ostrea vesicularis* and *Inoceramus tenuis*. Above the Grey Chalk, the *plenus* Marls may be seen. On the mainland this bed occupies a large part of the denuded core of the pericline at Chilcomb.

The next bed in the sequence is composed of 8 feet of nodular chalk, representing the period of shallowing of the Chalk sea which elsewhere gave rise to the Melbourn Rock. Above this comes almost 200 feet of thick-bedded white chalk with marly partings. On the mainland this bed contributes greatly to the scarp which rims the outcrop of the Lower Chalk around the pericline at Chilcomb. In some areas of Britain, an easily recognised bed of 'Chalk Rock', formerly regarded as the base of the Senonian but now referred to uppermost Turonian, occurs at the top of the Middle Chalk. At Culver Cliff it is represented by about a foot of indurated grey chalk, with a line of green-coated chalk nodules at the top.

The Upper Chalk follows with a distinctive bed containing the bryozoan, *Bicavea rotaformis*, in its lower levels, a band traceable all over the island. The Upper Chalk is a very pure white chalk, massively bedded, and seemed to reach its acme of purity in the *Marsupites* zone. The evolution of the echinoid genus *Micraster* is responsible for a succession of distinctive forms, which enable the stratigraphic level of the beds containing them to be assessed. In addition to the named zonal index fossils, characteristic forms of *Echinocorys* and of the crinoid *Bourgeticrinus* have also been used for the same purpose. Various species of rhynchonellid brachiopods, fish-teeth belonging to such genera as *Lamna* and *Ptychodus*, together with species of the ubiquitous *Inoceramus*, are common Upper Chalk fossils. The Downend Quarries in the Isle of Wight are amongst the best British localities for collecting *Marsupites*, since some specimens still remain as articulated 'cups'. The highest Chalk of the Isle of Wight commonly yields specimens of *Belemnitella mucronata*. Fossiliferous localities on the Hampshire mainland are located on the map accompanying Brydone's (1912) important paper.

THE CRETACEOUS–TERTIARY UNCONFORMITY

The period represented by the Maestrichtian, Danian, Montian and Thanetian Stages comprise a time-interval of which no stratal record exists in this area, and it is probable that for most of the time epeirogenic uplift and slight flexuring of the existing sediments brought them out of the region of deposition into that of erosion. The base of the local Tertiary sequence rests with non-sequence, although without visible angular unconformity, upon various levels in the Senonian Chalk. Generally speaking, the magnitude of the non-sequence increases towards the north. In the Isle of Wight the sub-Tertiary surface is 475 feet above the base of the *mucronata* Chalk. Around the Portsdown anticline, the highest Chalk also belongs to the *mucronata* zone. Along the northern rim of the Hampshire topographic basin from Bledworth to Otterbourne and westward towards Dean Hill, the Tertiaries usually rest on the *quadrata* Chalk. North of the area at Kingsclere, the highest Chalk belongs to the *Marsupites* zone and still further north, at the western end of the London Basin under Crookham Common, the *Uintacrinus* zone is cut into (Hawkins, 1955). Thus, in the 50 miles between Crookham Common and the centre of the Isle of Wight, the equivalent of some 920 feet of Chalk, present in the island, have been eroded. This corresponds to an overstep of 1 foot in 290 feet, corresponding to an angular discrepancy of only one-fifth of a degree.

This overstepping, however, is not uniform. In the Isle of Wight, for instance, between

Alum Bay and Freshwater, only three-quarters of a mile apart, the Tertiaries overstep the *mucronata* zone on to the *quadrata* Chalk. Around the Dean Hill anticline also, Williams-Mitchell (1957) has demonstrated that the Tertiary base channels through the *mucronata* Chalk into the *quadrata* Chalk in a number of places within short distances. Even at Otterbourne, despite Brydone's map, there appears to be *pilula* Chalk locally below the Reading Beds.

THE EOCENE SYSTEM

The formational names applicable to the Eocene Stages of this district are as follows:

Stage	Formation
BARTONIAN	Lower Headon Beds Barton Sands Barton Clays
AUVERSIAN	Upper Bracklesham Beds
LUTETIAN	Lower Bracklesham Beds (part)
CUISIAN	Bagshot Beds and Lower Bracklesham Beds (part)
YPRESIAN	London Clay
SPARNACIAN	Reading Beds
THANETIAN	Not represented

The Reading Beds

On the mainland the Reading Beds occur as a southern fringe bordering the Chalk. Between Romsey and Salisbury they outcrop to form a ring around the synclinal structure north of the Dean Hill anticline and they also loop around the Portsdown anticline. In the Isle of Wight they form a narrow strip of steeply dipping beds, extending from Whitecliff Bay in the east to Alum Bay in the west. The Reading Beds have an average thickness of about 100 feet.

The basement beds are clearly seen in the cliff at Alum Bay. Three or four feet of green silty and sandy clays, weathering brown, contain towards the base impersistent flint pebble-beds, of which patches may occasionally be seen adhering to the chalk surface. The latter shows 'pipes', some of which enclose green-coated flints in a glauconitic sandy matrix. It is probable that this glauconitic basal bed represents the marine oyster-bearing basement bed of the Reading Beds in the type locality. Reid (1902) recorded basal Reading Beds at Fordingbridge and at Sherfield English containing 'masses' of unidentified oysters. In the bore on Southampton Common, 4 to 5 feet of beds with similar lithology occurred above the Chalk at a depth of 450 feet.

Above these glauconitic basal beds, the Reading Beds are composed mainly of red mottled plastic clays, although locally other lithologies predominate. The variegated plastic clays probably represent a lagoonal and/or salt-marsh environment of deposition. Between Otterbourne and Hursley the sediments of the Reading Beds comprise silts, current-bedded sands and pipe-clays with plant remains in the lower levels. The sands are seen with excellent current-bedding in a disused sand-pit west of Otterbourne, where the bases of certain beds channel into the underlying sediments. Reading Beds of sandy facies are also seen in the south-east of the area near Portsmouth. The Reading Beds represent the Sparnacian Stage of the Eocene.

The London Clay

The London Clay varies in thickness from about 300 feet to 400 feet in the south of the area, but it thins and becomes sandier in northern Hampshire. Prestwich's interpretation of the Southampton Common bore assigned 307 feet of beds to this formation. The London Clay outcrops across the centre of the Isle of Wight, where good sections are to be seen in Alum Bay and in Whitecliff Bay. On the mainland it succeeds the Reading Beds down-dip, and is brought again to the surface from under a cover of Bagshot Beds at Bursledon and Swaythling and north-westward to the Test valley. It also outcrops around the Portsdown anticline.

The basal beds can be seen in Whitecliff Bay where 'pellets' of Reading Beds are noted set in a glauconitic sandy or loamy matrix. Seams of the worm-tube *Ditrupa plana* are common at this level. Low horizons, of similar lithology, are seen on the mainland in a clay-pit at Allbrook, near Eastleigh. The more typical clay lithology of the London Clay occurs in the upper half of the formation, well seen at Bursledon where 40 feet of clay is exposed in a clay-pit. Pebble-beds occur in the London Clay, especially in the lower half and sometimes at the junction with the overlying Bagshot Beds. Along the line of the Swaythling anticline, pebble-beds are associated with channelled surfaces, which may indicate shallowing along this line of uplift initiated prior to the Miocene warping of the beds.

Crystals of selenite are common in the London Clay. Typical fossils include *Pinna affinis*, *Arctica planata*, *Pholadomya margaritacea* and various species of turritellid gastropods. The London Clay represents the Ypresian Stage of the Eocene.

The Bagshot Beds

The marine London Clay is succeeded by the Bagshot Beds of continental facies, extremely variable both in thickness and lithology. In the south-west of this region they attain a thickness of 200 feet, though towards the north and east they become much thinner. Around Otterbourne and Chandler's Ford, the Bagshot Beds are represented by an impressive pebble-bed, up to 20 feet thick and composed almost exclusively of flint, with very rare quartz pebbles set in a sparse matrix of sandy clay. This unit is mappable in this area and is still recognisable further south, although the pebbles are more thinly scattered in the matrix. At the site of the University it is between 6 and 10 feet in thickness, and provides a good guide to geological horizon in a variable series of otherwise undistinguished sediments. Below the pebble-bed at the University site, sandy clays of the Bagshot Beds were formerly dug for brick-making.

A more typical lithology of the Bagshot Beds displays grey and yellow sands, with pipe-clays containing impressions of the leaves of tropical plants. In Alum Bay the Bagshot

Beds form the lower part of the well-known succession of brightly coloured sands. In the Bournemouth area the Bagshot Beds are divided into a lower division characterised by important pipe-clays, and an upper division known as the Bournemouth Freshwater Beds, the latter being deltaic deposits of a river draining from the west or south-west. The Bagshots outcrop extensively in the country north of Cadnam and Bramshaw. The Bagshot Beds are usually referred to the base of the Cuisian Stage.

The Bracklesham Beds

The Bracklesham Beds represent part of the Cuisian (characterised by *Nummulites planulatus*), the Lutetian (characterised by *Nummulites laevigatus*) and the Auversian (character-ised by *Nummulites variolarius*). The succession can be seen in Whitecliff Bay, which displays what is perhaps the finest continuous single section in the Lower Tertiaries in Europe. In a succession nearly 600 feet thick, Fisher (1862) recognised 19 beds, with a well-defined pebble-bed at the base. Beds 1 to 5 of Fisher's classification represent the Cuisian. Bed 4, about 140 feet from the base, contains rather rare nummulites (*N. planulatus* below and *N. lucasianus* above), associated with abundant specimens of a form of the lamellibranch *Venericor planicosta*. The highest Cuisian is probably continental, since plant fossils and lignite bands are common and a 4-foot seam of brown coal occurs. The Lutetian is repre-sented by Beds 6 to 8, sandier than the beds below, and the guide fossil, *Nummulites laevigatus*, is common. The remaining Beds 9 to 19 belong to the Auversian. Beds 14 to 17, about 400 feet above the base of the Brackleshams, yield the index species *Nummulites variolarius*, in addition to many marine lamellibranchs and gastropods.

In Alum Bay the Bracklesham Beds are completely different. They consist of 526 feet of brightly and variously coloured continental sands on top of the somewhat similar Bagshot sands. These together make up the spectacular, steeply inclined succession of tinted sands, which afford a well-known tourist attraction.

On the mainland the Bracklesham Beds, of Lutetian age, were exposed during the construction of the dock extensions at the port of Southampton (Wrigley, 1934). No less than 216 species of fossil organisms were found, of which 141 occur in the 'Calcaire Grossier' of France. This correspondence, together with abundant *Nummulites laevigatus*, serves to date the deposits with confidence.

The Brackleshams of the mainland are thinner than their equivalents in the Isle of Wight, the maximum recorded thickness being 320 feet at Netley. In general, the distinction between the dominantly marine eastern facies and the dominantly continental western facies is maintained between Southampton and Bournemouth.

The Barton Beds

The Barton Beds at the type locality of Barton-on-Sea have been carefully described by St. John Burton (1929, 1933) and Curry (1960). The succession is 203 feet thick and has been subdivided into many groups. A convenient lithological base for this formation would be the flint pebble-bed lying about 10 feet below the first occurrence of *N. prestwichianus*, though this latter horizon is commonly taken as the base of the Barton Bed succession. Between the pebble-bed and the *N. prestwichianus* level occur some 10 feet of grey clays, and above *N. prestwichianus* come 33 feet of sandy and glauconitic clays with *Nummulites rectus* in the upper half. These beds are succeeded by 10 feet of sands, followed by the *Pholadomya* Bed which is 4 feet thick. This marks the top of the Lower Barton Beds.

The Middle Barton Beds are 51 feet thick, the basal 6 feet being characterised by the gastropod *Athleta suspensa*. Some 20 feet higher occurs the 'Earthy Bed', from which hundreds of *species* of Bartonian mollusca have been collected. The upper part of the Middle Barton succession consists of 20 feet of brownish-grey clays, with a band of concretionary argillaceous limestone near the top.

The Upper Barton Beds (95 feet thick) commence with the Stone Band, 1 foot thick. Then follows the *Chama* Bed, 18 feet thick, characterised by an abundance of the well-known lamellibranch *Chama squamosa*. Above this level an arenaceous lithology predominates, broken by the Becton Bunny Clays with estuarine, in addition to truly marine, elements in its molluscan fauna. The Upper Barton Beds terminate in 4 feet of lignitic beds. It is evident that these higher beds show a transition from the marine Middle Barton Beds into the continental Lower Headon Beds which form the summit of the local Eocene.

In the Isle of Wight the beds are thicker than at Barton itself. They vary from 338 feet at Alum Bay to 368 feet in Whitecliff Bay, although at the latter locality they are greatly obscured by slipping. In Alum Bay the base of the Barton Beds, characterised by *Nummulites prestwichianus* succeeded by *N. rectus*, is followed by 248 feet of fossiliferous clays reaching to the level of the *Chama* Bed of the mainland. Above these lie 90 feet of the Headon Hill Sands.

The Lower Headon Beds

The Lower Headon Beds have been referred to the Oligocene, but it seems better to consider them as brackish or freshwater sediments at the top of the Bartonian, and to commence the Oligocene with the marine episode represented by the marine Middle Headon clays.

At Headon Hill the Lower Headon Beds are 62 feet thick and comprise clays and pale sands with five thin bands of freshwater limestone, of which the uppermost, which terminates the Eocene, is known as the How Edge Limestone. Freshwater gastropods such as *Planorbis* (*Planorbina*) and *Limnaea* (*Galba*) are common. The Lower Headon Beds are exposed at Hordle Cliff on the mainland, where they are 82 feet thick. These beds have been divided into no less than 33 minor units, authoritatively dealt with by Chandler (1925-6), who has described the fossil flora. This finds its nearest living counterpart in the flora of South-east Asia, although no single species of the Lower Headon flora has survived to the present day. The Mammalia Bed near the base and the Crocodile Bed some 10 feet higher have yielded interesting vertebrate fossils.

I Rake Bottom: a dry valley on the scarp-face of the Chalk to the north of Butser Hill (*N.G. ref.* SU 7120)

II *Micraster* Chalk surface near Broughton, Stockbridge (*N.G. ref.* SU 2935)

III   The undissected surface of the plateau-gravels, Beaulieu Heath (*N.G. ref.* SU 4104)

IV   Seepage-steps in a valley near Picket Post, New Forest (*N.G. ref.* SU 1905)

THE OLIGOCENE SYSTEM

The following beds correspond to the Oligocene Stages:

Stage	Formation
RUPELIAN	⎰ Upper Hamstead Beds ⎱ Lower Hamstead Beds (part)
LATTORFIAN	⎧ Lower Hamstead Beds (part) ⎪ Bembridge Marls ⎨ Bembridge Limestone ⎪ Osborne Beds ⎩ Upper and Middle Headon Beds

The Middle Headon Beds

At Headon Hill, in the Isle of Wight, the Middle Headon Beds are 33 feet thick, consisting of sands and clays, of which the upper part constitutes the *Venus* Bed characterised by the lamellibranch *Sinodia suborbicularis* formerly assigned to the genus *Venus*. On the mainland the Middle Headon Beds are represented by the Brockenhurst Beds of the New Forest, from which a rich molluscan fauna has been collected, testifying to a marine environment of deposition of Lattorfian age.

The Upper Headon Beds

At the type locality these beds are 47 feet thick, the basal 25 feet consisting of limestones interbedded with clays and lignites. The limestones yield well-preserved freshwater mollusca, and less commonly they contain vertebrate bones and teeth. The upper 22 feet consist of clays enclosing freshwater shells. From the Upper Headon Beds of Colwell Bay, where the limestones are not developed, Chandler (1963) records 38 species of fossil plants, constituting a flora which agrees with those Eocene floras from 'horizons where conditions of growth have been affected by the proximity of the sea'. The Upper Headon Beds outcrop on the mainland chiefly under Beaulieu Heath.

The Osborne Beds

With the exception of a small outlier near Lyndhurst on the mainland, these beds are confined to the Isle of Wight, where they are from 70 to 80 feet thick. They consist of coloured clays, sands and shales, with a basal bed of limestone. The poorly preserved fossils indicate a freshwater environment of deposition.

The Bembridge Limestone

This is best seen in Whitecliff Bay, where it consists of 22 feet of hard white limestone, with moulds of freshwater and, more rarely, land shells together with fruits of *Chara*. The

Ds

beds extend seaward where, because of their greater resistance to erosion, they form 'ledges', dangerous to shipping.

The Bembridge Marls

In Whitecliff Bay the base of these beds is marked by the Bembridge Oyster Bed of estuarine facies, succeeded by almost 90 feet of clays which contain freshwater mollusca. Fossil plants also occur, and, exclusive of species of *Chara*, 97 forms have been listed by Chandler, the bulk of which come from the Insect Limestone, a lenticular bed a few feet above the Oyster Bed.

The Lower Hamstead Beds

Davies and Wrigley (1937) place the junction of the Lattorfian and Rupelian Stages within the Lower Hamstead Beds. These beds are only seen on the west coast of the Isle of Wight between Hamstead and Bouldnor. They are 236 feet thick, with the 'Black Band', full of *Viviparus*, at the base. They are mainly freshwater sediments, with some estuarine beds containing a brackish water fauna. About 66 feet from the base is the 'White Band', a discontinuous layer of shells, from which the bulk of the fossil plants listed by Chandler (1963) were extracted. The Lower Hamstead Beds have also yielded vertebrate remains.

The Upper Hamstead Beds

These beds comprise 20 feet of marine clays, sometimes known as the *Corbula* Beds. They are the youngest 'solid' strata of the area. It may be that still younger beds were deposited and have been subsequently eroded, but by this time the régime of deposition was ending, to be succeeded by a period of folding and erosion responsible for the present-day attitude of the strata.

THE QUATERNARY SYSTEM

Pre-glacial

Wooldridge and Linton (1955) consider that a 'Pliocene' sea once occupied the site of the present-day Hampshire *topographical* basin, and that the summit plain at about 550 feet O.D. represents the elevated sea-floor. Everard (1956) believes that the withdrawal of this sea was a consequence of intermittent falling in sea-level and that platforms, notching the dip slope of the Chalk and forming a 'stairway' with steps at 480, 430, 390 and 325 feet, remain as testimony to this halting retreat. The 325-foot platform, which is the best developed, might represent the period of stable sea-level which is known as the Sicilian (or 100 metres) stage of the immediate pre-glacial epoch.

Glacial

Everard (1954) has recognised gravel-covered terraces graded to sea-levels of 230, 185, 165, 150, 100, 70, 35, 15, −30 and −60 feet O.D. He considers that by the time the 185-foot terrace was formed, the sea had completely retreated from this area, although it made temporary short-lived re-incursions into the southern fringe of the district.

The pattern of distribution of the gravel terraces shows the course of the left-bank tributaries of the former 'Solent river' (see p. 46). In the north these gravel terraces are ordinary downstream-sloping fluviatile deposits. A striking feature of their lower reaches, where they border Southampton Water and the Solent, is a horizontal segment characterised by the absence of a longitudinal gradient, although a transverse slope is sometimes seen. Everard considers that such segments represent wave-cut platforms formed during a period of still-stand. On this hypothesis he has constructed a series of migrating strand-lines, successively moving the shore-line to the south-east. The gravels which cover these benches were, he thinks, derived from the marine erosion of cliffs capped with early terrace-gravels, augmented by fluviatile gravels brought to the head of the estuary and redistributed by longshore drift.

Also remaining as evidence to these complex adjustments of the varying position of land and sea are raised beaches, recognised near Portsmouth at 100, 50 and 15 feet O.D. (Palmer and Cooke, 1923) and at Bembridge where a platform covered by shingle and backed by a cliff-line occurs just above sea-level.

Post-glacial

Submerged gravels occur at 60 and 30 feet below sea-level at Fawley and at 34 and 18 feet below sea-level at Southampton Docks. These are tentatively correlated and interpreted as two river terraces drowned by the post-glacial rise in sea-level. This Neolithic or 'Flandrian' transgression also buried the peat-beds, soils and tufaceous marls which overlie the gravels (Godwin and Godwin, 1940). These in turn were covered by alluvium or modern sediments of Southampton Water. The submerged gravels contain remains of mammoth and reindeer and the peats above them have yielded Neolithic implements.

The post-glacial rise in sea-level caused the final breaching of the chalk ridge which connected the Isle of Purbeck with the Isle of Wight and which formed the right bank of the 'Solent river' (see p. 48). This permitted the invasion by the waters of the Channel, which severed the Isle of Wight from the mainland and initiated the outlines of the present-day coastline.

Miscellaneous

Other superficial deposits formed during the relatively recent geological evolution of this region include: (i) the Angular Gravels of the chalk downs of the Isle of Wight, consisting of flints from the Upper Chalk as a consequence of its dissolution; (ii) the Clay-with-Flints composed partly from the insoluble residue of the solution of the Chalk and partly of *remanié* clay derived from the original continuous cover of Tertiary beds; (iii) the Coombe Deposits formed of cemented solifluction debris derived from the Chalk; (iv) the somewhat similar 'Head'; and (v) the Brickearths composed of brown loamy structureless deposits, in which remains of Pleistocene animals and Palaeolithic implements have been found.

BIBLIOGRAPHICAL NOTE

It will be seen from the account presented that the authors have relied on an immense amount of published research rather than on their own investigations in its compilation. They are greatly indebted to the Gas Council for providing information about the Chilcomb boreholes and the original photograph of their model of the Chilcomb structure (Plate XIV).

(1) K. C. Boswell, 'A detailed profile of the river Test', *Proceedings of the Geologists' Association, London* (1946), vol. 57, pp. 102-16.

(2) R. M. Brydone, *The stratigraphy of the Chalk of Hampshire* (London, 1912).

(3) R. M. Brydone, *The Chalk zone of Offaster pilula* (London, 1938).

(4) S. St. J. Burton, 'Faunal horizons of the Barton Beds in Hampshire', *Proceedings of the Geologists' Association, London* (1933), vol. 44, pp. 131-67.

(5) W. Carruthers, 'On fossil Cycadian stems from the Secondary rocks of Britain', *Transactions of the Linnaean Society of London* (1870), vol. 26, pp. 675-708.

(6) R. Casey, 'The stratigraphical palaeontology of the Lower Greensand', *Palaeontology* (1961), vol. 3, pp. 487-621.

(7) M. E. Chandler, 'The Upper Eocene flora of Hordle, Hants.', *Monographs of the Palaeontographical Society of London* (1925-6).

(8) M. E. Chandler, 'Flora of the Lower Headon Beds of Hampshire and the Isle of Wight', *Bulletin of the British Museum (Natural History)* (1961), vol. 5, pp. 93-157.

(9) M. E. Chandler, 'Revision of the Oligocene floras of the Isle of Wight', *Bulletin of the British Museum (Natural History)* (1963), vol. 6, pp. 323-83.

(10) C. P. Chatwin, *British Regional Geology: the Hampshire Basin and adjoining areas* (Geological Survey and Museum, London, 3rd ed., 1960).

(11) D. Curry, 'The English Bartonian Nummulites', *Proceedings of the Geologists' Association, London* (1957), vol. 48, pp. 229-46.

(12) D. Curry, 'A Lower Tertiary outlier in the central English Channel, with notes on the beds surrounding it', *Quarterly Journal of the Geological Society of London* (1962), vol. 118, pp. 177-206.

(13) D. Curry and D. E. Wisden, 'Geology of some British coastal areas: the Southampton district including Barton (Hampshire) and Bracklesham (Sussex) coastal sections', *Geologists' Association, London* (1958): *Excursion Guide No. 14*.

(14) A. G. Davies, 'The Brockenhurst Beds at Victoria Tilery, Brockenhurst, Hampshire', *Proceedings of the Geologists' Association, London* (1952), vol. 63, pp. 215-19.

(15) C. E. Everard, 'The Solent river: a geomorphological study', *Transactions of the Institute of British Geographers* (1954), no. 20, pp. 41-58.

(16) C. E. Everard, 'Erosion platforms on the borders of the Hampshire Basin', *Transactions of the Institute of British Geographers* (1956), no. 22, pp. 33-46.

(17) N. L. Falcon and P. E. Kent, 'Geological results of petroleum exploration in Britain, 1954-7', *Memoirs of the Geological Society of London* (1960), no. 2.

(18) O. Fisher, 'The Bracklesham Beds of the Isle of Wight Basin', *Quarterly Journal of the Geological Society of London* (1862), vol. 18, pp. 65-94.

(19) J. S. Gardner, H. Keeping and H. W. Monckton, 'The Upper Eocene comprising the Barton and Upper Bagshot formations', *Quarterly Journal of the Geological Society of London* (1888), vol. 44, pp. 578-635.

(20) Geological Survey of Great Britain and Northern Ireland, New Series, colour-printed, Geological Survey sheets (one inch to the mile), nos. 298 (*Salisbury*) and memoir, Reid, 1903; 299 (*Winchester*) and memoir, White, 1912; 300 (*Alresford*) and memoir, White, 1910; 314 (*Ringwood*) and memoir, Reid, 1902; 315 (*Southampton*) and memoir, Reid, 1902; 316 (*Fareham*) and memoir, White, 1913; 329 (*Bournemouth*) and memoir, Reid, 1898, and White, 1917; 330 (*Lymington*) and 331 (*Portsmouth*) with joint memoir, White, 1915; 344 and 345 (*Isle of Wight*) with memoirs; Forbes, 1856 (on Tertiary fluvio-marine formations); Bristow, 1862; Reid and Strahan, 1889; White, 1921, on geology.

(21) H. Godwin and M. E. Godwin, 'The submerged peats of Southampton Water', *New Phytologist* (1940), vol. 39, pp. 303-7.

(22) J. F. N. Green, 'The terraces of southernmost England', *Quarterly Journal of the Geological Society of London* (1936), vol. 92, pp. 58-88.

(23) J. F. N. Green, 'The terraces of Bournemouth, Hants', *Proceedings of the Geologists' Association of London* (1946), vol. 57, pp. 82-101.

(24) J. F. N. Green, 'Some gravels and gravel pits in Hampshire and Dorset', *Proceedings of the Geologists' Association, London* (1947), vol. 58, pp. 128-43.

(25) H. L. Hawkins, 'The Eocene succession in the eastern part of the Enborne valley, on the borders of Berkshire and Hampshire', *Quarterly Journal of the Geological Society of London* (1955), vol. 110, pp. 409-30.

(26) R. W. Hooley, 'The history of the drainage of the Hampshire Basin', *Proceedings of the Hampshire Field Club* (1922), vol. 9, pp. 151-72.

(27) C. Johnson, 'Gas reservoirs in British porous rock structures', *Institute of Gas Engineers* (1961), Publication no. 605.

(28) P. E. Kent, 'A structural contour map of the surface of the buried pre-Permian rocks of England and Wales', *Proceedings of the Geologists' Association, London* (1949), vol. 60, pp. 87-104.

(29) W. B. R. King, 'The geology of the eastern part of the English Channel', *Quarterly Journal of the Geological Society of London* (1949), vol. 105, pp. 327-38.

(30) W. B. R. King, 'The geological history of the English Channel', *Quarterly Journal of the Geological Society of London* (1954), vol. 110, pp. 77-101.

(31) G. M. Lees and A. H. Taitt, 'The geological results of the search for oilfields in Great Britain', *Quarterly Journal of the Geological Society of London* (1946), vol. 101, pp. 255-317.

(32) L. S. Palmer and J. H. Cooke, 'The Pleistocene deposits of the Portsmouth district and their relation to man', *Proceedings of the Geologists' Association, London* (1923), vol. 34, pp. 253-82.

(33) C. Parkinson, 'The Upper Greensand and Chloritic Marl, Isle of Wight', *Quarterly Journal of the Geological Society of London* (1881), vol. 37, pp. 370-5.

(34) A. W. Rowe, 'The Zones of the White Chalk of the English coast', Part 5, The Isle of Wight, *Proceedings of the Geologists' Association, London* (1908), vol. 20, pp. 209-352.

(35) T. W. Shore, 'Hampshire mudlands and other alluvium', *Proceedings of the Hampshire Field Club* (1893), vol. 3, pp. 181-200.

(36) T. W. Shore, 'The origin of Southampton Water', *Proceedings of the Hampshire Field Club* (1905), vol. 5, pp. 1-25.

(37) T. W. Shore and J. W. Elwes, 'The new dock excavations at Southampton', *Proceedings of the Hampshire Field Club* (1890), vol. 1, pp. 43-56.

(38) L. F. Spath, 'Ammonoidea of the Gault', *Monograph of the Palaeontographical Society of London* (1943), part 16.

(39) A. H. Taitt and P. E. Kent, 'Deep boreholes at Portsdown (Hants) and Henfield (Sussex)', *British Petroleum Co., Technical Publication, London* (1958).

(40) P. H. N. White, 'Gravity data obtained in Great Britain by the Anglo-American Oil Company Ltd.', *Quarterly Journal of the Geological Society of London* (1949), vol. 104, pp. 339-64.

(41) E. Williams-Mitchell, 'The stratigraphy and structure of the Chalk of the Dean Hill anticline, Wiltshire', *Proceedings of the Geologists' Association, London* (1957), vol. 67, pp. 221-7.

(42) S. W. Wooldridge and D. L. Linton, 'Structure, surface and drainage in south-east England', *Transactions of the Institute of British Geographers* (1939, 1955), no. 10.

(43) C. W. Wright and E. V. Wright, 'A survey of the fossil Cephalopoda of the Chalk of Great Britain', *Monograph of the Palaeontographical Society of London* (1951).

(44) A. Wrigley, 'A Lutetian fauna at Southampton Docks', *Proceedings of the Geologists' Association, London* (1934), vol. 45, pp. 1-16.

(45) A. Wrigley and A. G. Davies, 'The occurrence of *Nummulites planulatus* in the Cuisian of England', *Proceedings of the Geologists' Association, London* (1937), vol. 48, pp. 203-28.

III

GEOMORPHOLOGY

THE Southampton region includes some of the most attractive and unspoiled countryside in lowland England. Particularly delightful to the layman, and perpetually fascinating to the geomorphologist, is the Chalk hill-country of north-central Hampshire, southern Wiltshire and north-eastern Dorset. Smoothly curving slopes, clad in part by beech, juniper and yew, lead down to winding dry valleys, and to occasional broad and deep trenches through which flow with surprising rapidity the clear waters of the few perennial streams; often the landscape has an air of great spaciousness, never more so than on the almost deserted western parts of Salisbury Plain. In sharp contrast, the Tertiary rocks around Southampton itself give rise to much dull and featureless lowland, though even here is found the New Forest, a small region of outstanding beauty.

THE GEOMORPHOLOGY OF THE CHALK COUNTRY

The Chalk of the north-central part of the Southampton region forms a broad belt of mainly upland country, anticlinal in structure, and separating the Tertiary lowlands of the London and Hampshire Basins. To the east the more pronounced Wealden anticlinorium, structurally a continuation of the Hampshire flexuring, has been denuded to reveal older Cretaceous rocks. The Chalk is now confined to the flanks of the Weald, where it gives rise to the north-facing escarpment of the western South Downs (an extension of the hilly country between Winchester and Butser Hill), the east-facing escarpment between Petersfield and Alton, and the narrow east–west Farnham–Guildford 'hog's back' (an extension of the Chalk uplands near Basingstoke). To the north-west the Chalk is bounded by the anticlinal Vale of Pewsey, beyond which rise the Marlborough Downs and their continuations into Berkshire. To the west in Wiltshire the Chalk is terminated by a fine escarpment, deeply indented by the Vales of Warminster and Wardour, but traceable south-westward into the Dorset Downs. In the exteme south of the Southampton region, the Chalk rises steeply from beneath the rocks of the Tertiary basin, and forms the low ridges of Purbeck and the Isle of Wight, together with some broader uplands in the central and south-eastern parts of the latter.

The Chalk country varies considerably in elevation from place to place, and by no means all is hilly or upstanding. Along the margins of the Tertiary rocks, at the foot of the Chalk dip-slope, the average height of the land may be less than 200 feet, though away from here the Chalk rises, sometimes gradually and sometimes steeply, to between 400 and 900 feet. Even so, there are still broad undulating vales and near-horizontal lowlands in parts of central Hampshire and south-eastern Wiltshire lying to the north of the ridges of the Dean Hill and Winchester areas. Within this category fall the valleys of the upper Itchen and the Dever, whose flanks are seamed by numerous shallow dry valleys and whose floors generally do not exceed a height of 300 to 350 feet. These are not simple river valleys, produced by long-continued denudation of the Chalk, but are essentially miniature structural basins, once containing infillings of weak Tertiary sands and clays. The removal of these younger rocks by fluvial action has revealed a Chalk surface which, though slightly dissected, may be equated genetically with the so-called 'sub-Eocene surface', well preserved on the lower dip-slope of the Chalk close to the present Tertiary margins of the Hampshire Basin (Fig. 5). A far more striking lowland area, with barely perceptible relief, occurs on either side of the valley of the Wallop brook, near Broughton. The structure is, however, gently anticlinal, and a different explanation of the origin of the plain must therefore be sought. Again, much of Salisbury Plain, particularly on the Till-Avon interfluve and around Stonehenge, lies well below 500 feet. It is true that the Chalk here forms a shallow syncline, but the simple removal of formerly existing Tertiary formations cannot be adequate to explain the present-day form of the Plain, for it can be conclusively shown that much of the resistant Upper Chalk has also been worn away, as indeed it has in the Broughton area.

In contrast to these Chalk 'lowlands' are the hillier and more deeply dissected areas, which are for the most part confined to the margins of the region, though scarp-like hill-masses diversify much of the triangle between Salisbury, North Tidworth and Stockbridge. In the extreme east an extensive plateau area, 'drained' by a great dry valley running north-eastward through East Tisted to Alton and by the complex valley of the upper Meon, extends between New Alresford and the escarpment overlooking the western Weald. The flat-topped interfluves, which are capped extensively by Clay-with-Flints, form in effect the remains of a broad bench-feature at 600 to 700 feet, above which the scarp crests rise quite sharply to a maximum of 813 feet near Liss. Along the northern margins of the Hampshire Chalk a high ridge trends westward and north-westward past Basingstoke (which commands a marked synclinal gap between the headwaters of the Test and Loddon), and reaches a height of 974 feet at Walbury Hill, near Inkpen. On the northern side of this Chalk upland is a very steep and imposing scarp face, formed in part as a result of the breaching of the arcuate Kingsclere and Shalbourne periclines; to the south, the dip-slope valleys are of exceptional depth, especially above Vernham Dean and near Linkenholt. Farther to the west, along the southern edge of the Vale of Pewsey, the continuity of the Chalk ridge is broken by the large water-gaps at Collingbourne Kingston and Upavon, and by the shallow wind-gap above West Lavington.

The hill-country to the west of Salisbury is the most extensive, impressive and complicated area of Chalk upland within the Southampton region. In essence, it comprises a series of west–east ridges, separating the valleys of the Wylye, Nadder and Ebble. In the north rises the Great Ridge, an elongated upland extending from Maiden Bradley in the west to the confluence of the Wylye and Nadder at Wilton in the east. Like the other Chalk hill-masses of this area, the Great Ridge declines in height eastward, from the isolated mass of Brimsdown Hill (933 feet) to Grovely Wood (approximately 550 feet). In the centre is the majestic Chalk escarpment which forms the southern margin of the Vale of Wardour. This is of special geomorphological interest, in that the scarp-face is marked by huge 'scallops', as at Swallowcliffe, Sutton and Compton Downs. It seems likely that these unusual forms have arisen through the mass-wasting, under periglacial conditions, of narrow interfluves once separating north-trending obsequent valleys, the much modified heads of which in fact form the 'scallops' themselves. To the south of the river Ebble lies the third great upland mass of Chalk, extending from Melbury Hill (862 feet) in the west, past Win Green (911 feet) to Coombe Bissett Down (493 feet) in the east. Between Berwick St. John and Bower Chalke this ridge is bounded on the north by a steep scarp slope, resulting from the partial breaching of the Bower Chalke pericline (see p. 42). Farther to the east the fold remains largely intact, though dissected by many angular dry valleys which run down to the synclinal Ebble between Broad Chalke and Odstock.

To the south of Shaftesbury the Chalk escarpment loses some of its impressiveness owing to its deep penetration by fine escarpment dry valleys (as at Fontmell Magna), and declines in height towards the double water-gap of the Iwerne and Stour, isolating Hambledon and Hod Hills. Beyond the Stour, however, the Chalk crests climb steadily again towards Bulbarrow Hill (901 feet) and beyond.

Before a more detailed analysis of the landforms of the Chalk country can be attempted, some account of the varying lithology and structure of the Chalk itself must be given.

The primary division of the Chalk into Upper, Middle and Lower is of fundamental geomorphological importance. The Upper Chalk, owing to its overall great purity and high degree of permeability, is very resistant to denudation, whereas the Middle and Lower Chalk (particularly the latter, with its high content of marl and relative lack of permeability) are much weaker. As a result, the Upper Chalk tends to form a protective carapace over extensive dip-slope areas and on the crests of anticlinal ridges and escarpments. However, once this resistant overlay has been breached by fluvial erosion and the weaker Middle and Lower Chalk thus exposed to sub-aerial attack, the effects are often striking. The Chalk Rock and the Melbourn Rock, the hard bands separating the three major divisions of the Chalk, do not on the other hand seem to possess much morphological significance, for scarp-profiles and valley-side slopes are in most cases smoothly graded across their outcrops.

Within the Upper Chalk—by far the thickest of the divisions except where thinned by prolonged denudation—further variations of note can be seen. The lowermost part, coinciding with the *Micraster* fossil-zones and sometimes referred to as the *Echinoid* Chalk, forms the most resistant layer in the whole of the Chalk, and not only tops the finest and highest of the Chalk escarpments but in dip-slope and synclinal areas gives rise to 'structural surfaces', from which the overlying weaker Chalk has been removed by denudation. The near-level lowland of the Broughton area, together with the rather more dissected Salisbury Plain, have both been formed in this way (see p. 38). Above the *Echinoid* Chalk is the *Belemnite* Chalk, itself comprising several fossil-zones. Towards the base the Chalk coinciding with the *Marsupites testudinarius* zone is significantly weak, perhaps owing to a comparatively high marl content, and is easily stripped from the surface of the underlying

Micraster Chalk. In areas of dipping strata the *Marsupites* Chalk gives rise to a distinct strike-vale at the foot of the usually well-preserved *Micraster* dip-slope. In the upper part of the *Belemnite* Chalk, the fossil-zone of *Gonioteuthis quadrata* coincides with a resistant band, which under suitable structural conditions—as on the northern fringe of the Hampshire Basin—forms a low and discontinuous cuesta, sometimes referred to as the 'secondary escarpment' to distinguish it from the 'main', and usually higher, feature capped by the *Micraster* Chalk (Fig. 5). To the north and east of Southampton, the secondary escarpment takes the form of a line of prow-shaped hills, at about 350 to 500 feet in height, which can be traced from Farley Mount, west of Winchester, into the South Downs. In Dorset, however, the escarpment is feebly developed, except at Pentridge Hill where a large residual mass of *Belemnite* Chalk rises to 600 feet. In the central part of the Chalk country, between the Avon and Test valleys, the secondary escarpment takes on a rather more complex form. Near Broughton it forms a true scarp feature, commanding a fine view over the *Micraster* structural plain (Plate II), but to the west and north it becomes indented and discontinuous, and eventually forms a number of island-like hills, including those on either side of the Bourne valley near North Tidworth (for example, Sidbury, Clarendon and Pickpit Hills). Over Salisbury Plain itself the *Belemnite* Chalk has, as stated above, been destroyed, but immediately to the east of the Avon it forms a line of hills traceable from Salisbury north-eastward past Bulford to Beacon Hill.

As implied already, the detailed morphology of the Chalk country owes much to the existence of numerous subsidiary fold-axes, formed over a prolonged period in the early and middle Tertiary era. These so-called 'Alpine' structures, which are superimposed in the main on to the broad upswelling of the Hampshire-Wiltshire Chalk, are aligned from west to east, and increase in amplitude both westward and eastward from a comparatively undisturbed 'structural saddle' near Salisbury and Andover. Most striking of the individual folds are the Warminster and Wardour anticlines of the west, the Pewsey anticline of the north-west and the Peasemarsh and Petersfield-Fernhurst anticlines of the east (Fig. 5). In the south are some additional and very important folds, including the Weymouth-Purbeck monocline and the Brighstone and Sandown anticlines of the Isle of Wight. The Alpine folds, in a subdued form, can sometimes be traced across the Tertiary country, but their morphological influences are rarely evident, probably because there is here little marked differentiation in terms of resistance between adjacent strata. In cross-section the Alpine folds are normally asymmetrical, with northern dips of up to 30° to 90° and southern dips not exceeding 5°. The steeper northern limbs are in some instances disrupted by strike-faulting, as in the western Vale of Wardour, where the Mere fault downthrows Chalk against the Kimmeridge Clay and a fine obsequent fault-line scarp has resulted. The individual fold-axes often show a tendency towards periclinal development; thus the Winchester anticline, prior to its erosion, rose to at least two culminating points, at Chilcomb and immediately to the east of the Meon valley near Old Winchester Hill.

It is well known that folded rocks are subjected to a denudational process terminating in 'inverted' relief, comprising anticlinal ridges which have been worn into scarp-rimmed vales, and former synclinal valleys which have been left upstanding as lines of hills. Most of the sequential forms produced by the process can be admirably seen in the Southampton region, though some stages are absent and certain problems of interpretation are thereby posed.

The simplest relationship between geological structure and relief can be observed in a transect north-westward from Portsmouth through New Alresford to Basingstoke. All the main Chalk ridges encountered are anticlinal in structure, and the lowlands are either synclines containing some Tertiary infilling (such as the Forest of Bere) or downfolds from which sands and clays have been worn away (see p. 38). None the less it must be pointed out that the anticlinal ridges have been affected by some erosion; for instance, the *Belemnite* Chalk has been completely removed from the crest of the Winchester anticline, and in that sense its breaching has commenced. However, the first really noteworthy stages of the inversion process are not seen until streams are able to penetrate the *Micraster* Chalk to attack the weak fold-core of Middle and Lower Chalk. At first such breaches are very localised, and occur only at periclinal culminations, where the lower divisions of the Chalk stand highest above base-level. Away from such points, the pitch of the folds carries the weak rocks below the level of possible stream penetration, and only narrow and shallow valleys are cut into the strong Upper Chalk.

The folds appear to have been breached in two distinct ways. In the first—and by far the rarer—the anticlines are crossed discordantly by main streams which, as they cut downwards, eventually expose Middle and Lower Chalk. Valley widening then proceeds rapidly, and infacing scarps overlooking a circular or elliptical 'vale' are formed. The process is best seen today in the Vale of Chilcomb, to the east of Winchester, where the breaching has been extended some two miles to the east of the Itchen by former miniature subsequent streams. The second, more usual, method involves small secondary consequent streams draining the limbs of the fold. In their upper courses these streams in time penetrate the Upper Chalk and hollow out large amphitheatres on or close to the fold-axis. Gradually the hollows are broadened by spring-sapping, solution and mass-wasting, and the interfluves between neighbouring valleys are eventually destroyed; with this growing measure of integration a true anticlinal vale begins to emerge, and the development of a subsequent stream unifying the drainage of the vale quickly follows. The complex nature of the whole process is shown in Fig. 6, which depicts the breaching of the Winchester, Meon valley and Bower Chalke anticlines.

The final outcome of breaching may be best seen in the Isle of Wight, where the anticlinal Vale of Arreton (Sandown) is floored by rocks considerably older than the Chalk and drained by the subsequent eastern Yar, and in the Vale of Wardour, with its Upper Greensand and Portlandian-Purbeckian cuestas framed within the Chalk rim (Fig. 5). To the north of Wardour lies, of course, the desiccated Chalk upland of the Great Ridge, undoubtedly the finest example of a synclinal ridge in lowland England.

It should be stated, however, that the attainment of these final stages in the inversion of relief is somewhat problematical. The most difficult question posed is that of the eventual disappearance of a synclinal stream as a nearby anticlinal subsequent comes into being. Except where the breaching is directly initiated by tributaries of a transfluent stream, as in

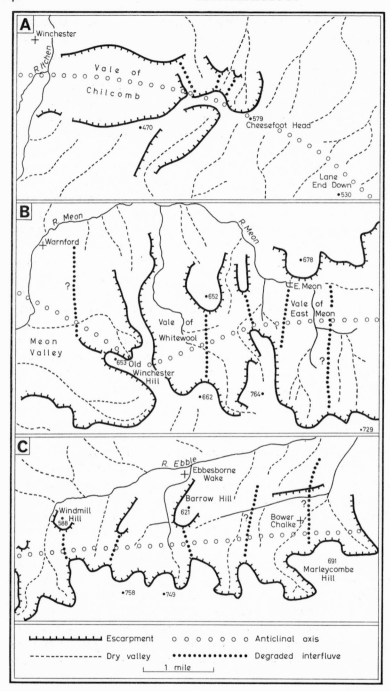

Fig. 6. Anticlines at an early stage of their breaching process

A. The Winchester anticline east of the river Itchen; B. the Meon valley anticline east of the river Meon; and C. the Bower Chalke anticline east of Shaftesbury.

the case of the Itchen at Winchester and the Meon south of Warnford, the drainage of the newly formed vale is effected by a stream or streams tributary to an adjacent synclinal consequent; the latter therefore provides the base-level of breaching, and its disappearance owing to deepening of the anticlinal vale alone cannot be envisaged. The problem is well illustrated by the upper course of the river Ebble, whose southern tributaries have eroded deeply into the Bower Chalke anticline (Fig. 6). The vale developing in the latter naturally stands higher than the valley bottom of the Ebble, which is itself engaged in cutting through the resistant Upper Chalk flooring the syncline, with the eventual result that the Ebble syncline will never be able to form an upland comparable with the Great Ridge, whose capping of Upper Chalk is virtually intact.

The possibility must exist that features such as the anticlinal Vales of Wardour and Warminster and the synclinal Great Ridge do not represent the ultimate stage of a breaching process whose earliest stages are exemplified by the Winchester, Meon and Bower Chalke folds. Instead, it may be necessary to postulate the existence, to the west of Salisbury, of a former high-level marine surface, cut in late Tertiary times across the fold-structures; certainly the general accordance of summit-heights here indicates such an episode of planation, though whether it was marine or sub-aerial is open to controversy. If the geology of the suggested hill-top surface is reconstructed, outcrops of weak rock (Middle and Lower Chalk and even older rocks along the anticlinal axes, and Tertiary sands and clays in the Ebble syncline) occur just where the three main streams, the Wylye, Nadder and Ebble, now flow. All these could therefore be regarded as simple subsequents which have extended their courses headwards from the consequent Avon; the latter, owing to the pitch of the folds here, has itself been subject to prolonged uniclinal shifting towards the east. The Great Ridge, on the other hand, significantly coincides with a major line of strength—the outcrop of the Upper Chalk—at the level of planation.

Dry Valleys

It would be inappropriate to conclude this brief discussion of the landforms of the Chalk country without some reference to the perplexing problem of the origin of the dry valleys. At present the Chalklands are divided into separate blocks by deep valleys of rivers such as the Stour, Avon, Test and Itchen. Away from these drainage arteries, within the interfluvial blocks, are numerous systems of ramifying valleys, which are clearly the product of surface run-off, but now contain no permanent—and in most instances even no temporary —streams. There can be no doubt that the desiccation of most of these Chalk valleys is due in part to a secular fall of the water-table which has been brought about in two ways. First, the formation in the current erosion cycle of the escarpments bordering the Chalk country has been accompanied by a steady decline in elevation of the scarp-foot springs and hence a lowering of the water-table within the Chalk. Secondly, the deep incision of the main Chalk valleys, on whose floors are often found copious springs, has led to a significant lowering of the saturation level within the interfluves. An interesting outcome of this latter process may be observed in the Bourne valley above Salisbury. Deprived of part of its surface catchment in the Vale of Pewsey by the extension of the East Avon, the river Bourne has lost the power to incise its valley at a rate comparable with those of the Avon and Test to west and east. During each summer season, the water-table falls well below the floor of the Bourne valley, and at such times underground abstraction of water from beneath the Bourne by both neighbouring rivers must be proceeding. In fact, the Bourne valley is manifestly being converted at this very moment into a major dry valley, and in the not too distant future its episodic wet-season flows will cease altogether.

However, to demonstrate that the dry valleys have been profoundly affected by this fall of the water-table is not to disprove that other factors and processes have played a part in their formation. Periods of more humid climate and more abundant surface run-off in interglacial and post-glacial times may have been instrumental in accelerating the erosion of the valleys. Some evidence to this end is afforded by the numerous spring-sapped 'coombes', often of spectacular form, cut into Chalk escarpments where today the springs are few and feeble. It has also been argued by many writers that under the periglacial conditions obtaining at times in the Quaternary, when the normally permeable Chalk was rendered impermeable by deep permafrost, active surface erosion may have been promoted by rapid summer snow-melt or even brief spring rains. Certainly many dry valleys now contain infillings of gravel and 'coombe rock', clearly the product of a frost climate. Even so, there are some reasons to believe that periglacial processes were responsible more for the moulding of the valley-side slopes than the actual incision of the valleys. The Chalk is perhaps the most susceptible of all the sedimentary rocks of southern England to frost attack, owing to its close pattern of minor joints (favouring a miniature kind of 'block weathering') and high porosity (resulting in a form of 'granular disintegration' whereby small lumps of chalk are broken by tiny expanding ice-crystals into a pasty sludge, itself forming a lubricant which aids the movement of more angular detritus). On the Chalk slopes, such frost weathering must have been extremely active under periglacial conditions and the resultant rapid solifluxion, even on low gradients, was an effective transporter of the shattered debris. The characteristically mature, smoothly graded landscape of the Chalk country has been ascribed by recent workers to this mass-wasting. The 'linear erosion' involved in the deepening of the dry valleys, on the other hand, may have been impeded by the large loads being fed into contemporary streams. In the bottoms of some valleys the infilling at present approaches 20 feet in depth, and its character often suggests the occupation of the valley by 'solifluxion tongues', with limited powers of corrasion, rather than normal streams.

THE GEOMORPHOLOGY OF THE TERTIARY BASIN

The Tertiary deposits that occupy the major asymmetrical downfold in the Chalk of southern Hampshire and eastern Dorset give rise to a landscape which is largely lacking in striking geomorphological features. Over most of the area the surface is dissected by shallow, gentle-sided valleys running down to the main river trenches (such as those of the lower Avon and Test) or to the coast itself; the interfluves and hills, which are either smoothly rounded or conspicuously flat-topped, rarely exceed 250 feet, except towards the northern margins of the New Forest. The natural monotony of the landscape is emphasised by the extent to which it has been built over, particularly between Southampton and Portsmouth and between Lymington and the Bournemouth conurbation.

It is not therefore surprising to find that, with some notable exceptions, the Tertiary country has not attracted as much geomorphological attention as the Chalklands, and many aspects of its landscape evolution are not well understood. For example, the fundamental relationship between lithology and relief has yet to be investigated in detail, though a cursory examination of topographical and geological maps reveals certain obvious correlations. Thus along the northern margins of the Tertiary basin the Reading Beds form everywhere low-lying ground at the foot of the 'sub-Eocene' Chalk surface. The London Clay, however, sometimes is associated with low undulating country—a southward extension of the Reading Beds vale—and sometimes forms a minor discontinuous cuesta, as at Durley Street and near Shirrell Heath. Between the Test and Itchen valleys, however, this 'outer' Tertiary escarpment is capped by pebbly Bagshot Beds (notably at Otterbourne Hill), and in Dorset there are actually two scarps, topped respectively by the lower London Clay (reaching over 300 feet at Chalbury and Edmondsham) and Bagshot Beds (as at Holt Heath, Horton Common and Cranborne Common) (Fig. 5).

This occasional double form of the outer escarpment, and its association with contrasting rock types, poses something of a problem. It may be that the feature owes its origin to a protective layer of superficial gravels, resting on a bevelled surface of the London Clay and Bagshot Beds and since largely removed by denudation. Some colour is lent to this suggestion by the fact that in Dorset the cuestas are still most evident where capped by small outliers of plateau-gravel, and even more by the fact that there is, in the Tertiary basin, an 'inner' escarpment still extensively topped by gravels. Immediately to the north and east of Southampton, this feature takes the form of a prominent ridge, extending from Toot Hill (276 feet) through Chilworth (298 feet) to West End (269 feet) and beyond. On the north side the ground drops steeply away to the lower country around Eastleigh and Botley, while to the south there is a gentle step-like descent to the shores of Southampton Water and the Solent. The 'escarpment' is developed largely in Bracklesham Beds up-arched along the Swaythling-Bursledon fold-axis, but almost certainly owes its continued existence and its asymmetrical form to a protective overlay of plateau-gravels, made up of hard sub-angular flints set in a sandy matrix and nourishing little effective surface run-off. In the New Forest, a similar and more imposing feature, no longer anticlinal in structure and topped in places (beneath the gravel) by Barton Clay, may be traced north-westward from Minstead, past Bramshaw and Nomansland (where the summits exceed 400 feet) as far as North Charford, on the margins of the Avon valley above Fordingbridge.

Within the New Forest—morphologically as well as scenically the most interesting part of the Tertiary basin—the land descends very gently southward from the crests of the inner scarp to the shores of Christchurch Bay and the western Solent. The dip of the rocks here is in fact noticeably greater than the gradient of the land-surface, so that whereas the northern part of the Forest is underlain by Bracklesham Beds and Barton Clay, towards the centre Barton Sand becomes more extensive, and in the south-east, near the Solent coast, Headon

Beds (of Oligocene age) outcrop. These variegated rocks, which in essence comprise alternating sands and clays, have as yet had little opportunity of influencing the surface morphology of wide tracts of the Forest, for they have been—and often still are—very effectively masked by huge spreads of plateau-gravel. Early stages in the removal of the latter can, however, be distinguished. In the southern part of the Forest, where the gravels are low-lying and probably of late Quaternary age, valley development is as yet in its infancy, so that the gravels are virtually untouched; hence the landscape consists of a series of broad, usually heathy plateaus, declining very gently from 130 to 140 feet (as on Beaulieu Heath) to between 30 feet and sea-level on the Solent shores (Plate III). In the west-central and north-western Forest, where the gravels are higher and of early and mid-Quaternary age, dissection is far more advanced; very wide, almost U-shaped valleys (for example, those of the Ditchend and Latchmore brooks) run down towards the Avon, and are separated by narrow flat-topped ridges on which only tongues of gravel remain.

Many of the valleys around Picket Post show features of special interest. Marked breaks of slope appear on the valley sides, and result from seepages which perhaps mark junctions between permeable and impermeable strata; below these 'seepage-steps' occur masses of slumped material, often convex in profile, leading down to the very boggy valley bottoms (Plate IV). Spring sapping at the base of the permeable plateau-gravels has also been instrumental in the widening of many central and northern Forest valleys, but this is manifestly less important now, if only because the area of the gravels, and hence their catchment, has been in the process gradually diminished.

As stated above (p. 40), the effects of Alpine folding in the Tertiary country are not striking. However, the pattern of the Tertiary outcrops is sometimes clearly affected, as in the Forest of Bere area and in the Alderbury syncline, east of Salisbury. In the vicinity of Southampton some interesting small-scale morphological features have been produced. The Swaythling anticlinal axis passes just to the north of the town, and a few tiny south-flowing streams have been superimposed on to the fold from overlying plateau-gravels. The streams have locally cut through the Bracklesham Beds forming the 'shell' of the anticline to reveal its core of London Clay; the latter has been hollowed out into unusually broad, poorly drained valleys, notably that of the Tanner's Brook to the east of Rownhams and the Southampton Sports Centre 'basin', which contrast sharply with the much narrower valleys found in the town, where the streams are contained by the more resistant Bracklesham Beds on the southern limbs of the anticline.

THE COASTLINE

The 'Solent River'

The main outline of the coastline owes much, both directly and indirectly, to the structures produced by the Alpine folding. In the south the Purbeck, Brighstone and Sandown anticlines, bringing resistant Chalk and older rocks well above base-level, once formed an effective and continuous barrier to wave attack from a southerly direction. To the north, the protected Tertiary basin itself nourished, in late Tertiary times, a major west–east drainage

V   Cliffs formed of Upper Greensand, with slumping on the Gault, Niton, Isle of Wight (*N.G. ref.* SZ 5176)

VI   Lulworth Cove, Dorset, with Portland and Purbeck Limestone along the coast in the foreground, and Chalk backing the Cove (*N.G. ref.* SY 8380)

VII Chalk cliffs in Scratchell's Bay, Isle of Wight (*N.G. ref.* SU 3085). Note the well-defined flint-bands dipping steeply inland

VIII Chalk cliffs and the Old Harry Rocks (*N.G. ref.* SZ 0682) at the Foreland, Swanage, Dorset

artery, the so-called 'Solent river' (Fig. 7), whose upper and lower courses are today represented by the Dorset Frome and the narrow strait between the Isle of Wight and the mainland. This great river, a southern counterpart of the Thames, has suffered many vicissitudes. In the early Quaternary (*Calabrian*) it was overwhelmed by a marine inundation which affected much of southern England up to a height of 690 feet, but after the regression of the sea it re-established its course on the newly emerged sea-floor at about 300 feet. At this stage it was joined by several secondary consequents, including the ancestors of such important streams as the Stour, Avon, Test and Itchen on the present mainland, and lesser streams, including the Medina, on the south side.

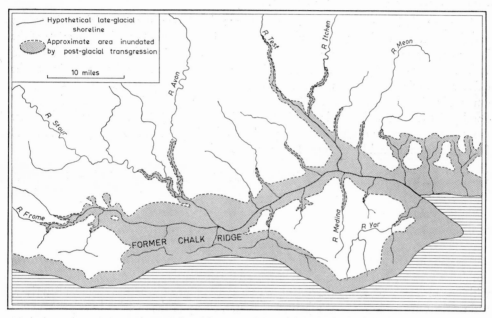

Fig. 7. Hypothetical reconstruction of the 'Solent river'

The greater part of the Quaternary era saw the spasmodic incision of this whole river-system, and the widespread development of terraces, with gravel spreads, below the 300-foot level. Certain of these erosion levels are demonstrably of marine origin, and it seems that partial inundation of the Solent river must have recurred, probably during interglacial periods. However, when the sea-level fell during glacial periods, downcutting was renewed, and during the ultimate glaciation the Solent river may have become graded to a level some 80 to 100 feet below the present, if one may judge from the evidence of 'submerged' terraces preserved beneath alluvium and peat in the Southampton Water-Solent area.

One of the results of this downcutting was the formation of deep water-gaps through the southern Chalk barrier. Such breaches must once have been more numerous than at present,

Es

and those in the area between the Foreland of Swanage and the Needles assumed a very special significance. During periods of high sea-level the gaps were very probably flooded by the sea, and wave action contributed to their widening. As a result, the Chalk ridge, which had also been somewhat weakened by prolonged marine attack from the south, must have been converted into a string of islets, some of which were in turn reduced to lines of stacks comparable with the Needles. In post-glacial times occurred the final and rapid rise of sea-level (the so-called *Flandrian* transgression), and the destruction of the Chalk barrier was completed. At the same time, the valley of the middle and lower Solent river was flooded, and there began a period of very rapid wave attack on the unresistant Tertiary sands and clays of Poole and Christchurch Bays.

The post-glacial transgression led not merely to the dismemberment of the Solent river and the separation of the Isle of Wight from the mainland, but also to the drowning of the lower courses of the affluents of the Solent. Where these rivers had cut deep, confined valleys narrow estuaries were formed, which are sometimes still in existence owing to the effectiveness of natural tidal scour, as in Southampton Water (Plate IX) and the Medina estuary, but in other instances have been converted by rapid alluviation into bluff-bounded flood plains (for example, the lower Avon and Meon valleys). On the other hand, where the valleys were more open in character and complex in pattern, ramifying inlets, such as Poole, Portsmouth and Newtown Harbours, resulted.

Coastal Accretion

In the sheltered localities formed by these inlets, and in the Solent too, marine erosion of the Tertiary rocks and overlying gravels has been inhibited. Cliff features are therefore non-existent or very unimpressive, except at isolated points along the northern shore of the Isle of Wight (for example, Bouldnor Cliff). Instead, coastal accretion has become the dominant process, and widespread mud-flats and salt-marshes have accumulated, notably within Poole Harbour, along the Solent coast between Hurst Castle and the Beaulieu river, and on the western shores of Southampton Water. Many of the marshes have grown even since the latter half of the last century, and have owed much to the activity of the hybrid *Spartina Townsendii* (perennial rice-grass), first reported in Southampton Water in 1870 (see p. 109). This marsh grass thrives in deep mud, and gives a forest of stems which effect-ively retain additional sediment brought in by the tide, so that the marsh grows steadily upwards and drainage is increasingly confined to a close network of meandering creeks (Plates X, XXII, XXIII).

Coastal accretion has not, of course, only taken the form of marsh accumulation. In addition to the usual temporary shingle- and sand-beaches occupying the bays, several well-known sand- and shingle-spits can be seen. The sand-spits are largely confined to the west, and include those at Studland and Sandbanks, which obstruct the entrance to Poole Harbour, and the very unstable bar which has grown northward across the mouth of Christchurch Harbour. The shingle-spits are better developed farther east, perhaps because of the larger supplies of shingle released by erosion of the plateau-gravel there. This shingle is moved predominantly eastwards to the Solent, where it is fashioned by both westerly and easterly waves into complex accumulations, with main ridges, laterals and recurved ends. Hurst Castle and Calshot Spits in particular have attracted much geomorphological attention, but both are now essentially stable features and in fact possess less individuality than a small spit which has grown near Warren Farm, west of the Beaulieu river. The western part of this spit consists of main ridges, trending approximately parallel to each other and enclosing small marsh 'basins', together with upwards of twenty laterals apparently formed by small waves moving episodically westwards through the Solent. The eastern part of the spit, about half a mile in length, consists of a solitary ridge of pebbles formed entirely since 1946. The rapid growth of this eastern beach has undoubtedly been facilitated by the existence of a marsh-mud basement (whose presence has also prevented the formation of laterals), and the shingle supply has itself been derived from erosion of the western part of Warren Farm spit, which incidentally has been driven some 300 feet inland since the beginning of the century.

Coastal Erosion

In contrast to these features of aggradation are the lengthy stretches of cliff-line in the Southampton region. Along the margins of Poole and Christchurch Bays, and at some localities in the Isle of Wight, the Tertiary rocks have been fashioned into low cliffs, often with very complicated profiles. Although waves attack strongly at the base of these cliffs, rendering the slope continually unstable, sub-aerial agencies are more active in causing the recession of the cliff as a whole. Gullying is in places very severe, as at Alum and Whitecliff Bays, where the strata are tilted vertically and lines of weakness can be readily selected by rivulets. Mass slumping is characteristic of many areas, but is nowhere more severe than at Barton-on-Sea. Here permeable plateau-gravels and Barton Sands overlie Barton Clay, and the resultant springs and seepages undermine the gravels and sands, which slip *en masse* over the well-lubricated clay, leaving a steep cliff some way inland (Plate XI). Beneath this is an 'undercliff', essentially a 'bench' of Barton Clay but veneered by a chaotic mass of sand, gravel and clay, often actively flowing in great soggy tongues down to the beach. Measures to prevent such serious cliff recession, including the construction of groynes to hold up beach shingle and thus gain some protection for the cliff base, have met with little success here. It is important to re-emphasise that even if wave action were successfully countered, further sub-aerial wasting of the cliff would proceed for a time, until, in fact, the cliff was replaced by a stable vegetated slope of comparatively low angle.

One interesting by-product of the severe erosion of the cliffs has been the rejuvenation of short streams running down to the coast. These have eroded deeply into the weak sands and clays to form ravine-like valleys, which in the Bournemouth area are known as 'chines' and in Christchurch Bay as 'bunnies' (for example, Chewton and Becton Bunnies). Most spectacular of all, with their sheer walls and many small waterfalls, are the chines cut into the Lower Greensand cliffs of the southern Isle of Wight (for example, Whale and Shepherd's Chines).

The most impressive sea-cliffs are those formed by the Chalk at Culver Cliff, at Scratchell's Bay (both I.W.) (Plate VII), and near Swanage. These rise to a height of nearly 400 feet, and at their bases sometimes occur broad wave-cut platforms, which are revealed at low tide. In detail, the Chalk cliff-forms are much influenced by local conditions of jointing and stratification. Where the Chalk dips steeply seawards, as on the north side of the Culver headland and at Alum Bay, the cliff often approximates in angle to the bedding-planes and takes on a 'slabby' appearance; but where the dip is inland, the bedding planes are very sharply truncated, and near-vertical cliffs may result. Lines of weakness are commonly etched into caves, arches and eventually stacks. Those developed in the steeply tilted and compressed Upper Chalk at the Needles are widely famous, but other interesting examples, similar in origin but on a smaller scale, are found at Freshwater Bay in the Isle of Wight. The splendid stacks of the Foreland near Swanage, including Old Harry, Old Harry's Wife and The Pinnacle, together with the imposing vertical cliffs from which they have been separated, are by contrast formed in near-horizontal *Belemnite* Chalk (Plate VIII).

In the south-eastern quadrant of the Isle of Wight, the Lower Chalk combines with the Upper Greensand to form a line of vertical cliffs rising above the outcrop of the Gault Clay. The rocks here dip very gently towards the south, and in the past huge masses of Greensand and Chalk have broken away to move over the 'blue slipper', as the clay is locally known. The resultant undercliff, most extensive to the west of Ventnor, is altogether grander in scale and, with its woods and secluded glens, more picturesque than that at Barton-on-Sea. At present some small cliff falls and slips are taking place, but it is hard to believe that these movements compare in scale or frequency with those of the recent past (Plate V).

BIBLIOGRAPHICAL NOTE

(1) C. E. Everard, 'Submerged gravel and peat in Southampton Water', *Proceedings of the Hampshire Field Club* (1954), vol. 18, pp. 263-85; 'The Solent River: a geomorphological study', *Transactions of the Institute of British Geographers* (1954), no. 20, pp. 41-58; 'Erosion platforms on the borders of the Hampshire Basin', *Transactions of the Institute of British Geographers* (1956), no. 22, pp. 33-46; and 'The streams in the New Forest: a study in drainage evolution', *Proceedings of the Hampshire Field Club* (1957), vol. 19, pp. 240-52.

(2) P. Pinchemel, *Les plaines de craie* (Paris, 1954).

(3) K. R. Sealy, 'The terraces of the Salisbury Avon', *Geographical Journal* (1955), vol. 121, pp. 50-6.

(4) R. J. Small, 'The morphology of Chalk escarpments: a critical discussion', *Transactions of the Institute of British Geographers* (1961), no. 29, pp. 71-90.

(5) A. J. Stevens, 'Surfaces, soils and land use in north-east Hampshire', *Transactions of the Institute of British Geographers* (1959), no. 26, pp. 51-66.

(6) S. W. Wooldridge and D. L. Linton, *Structure, surface and drainage in south-east England* (London, 1955).

IV

THE HYDROGRAPHY OF THE SOLENT
AND SOUTHAMPTON WATER

INTRODUCTION

FROM ancient times, the remarkable tidal régime observed in the waters behind the Isle of Wight has intrigued the sailors who found profit in braving the English Channel. Often driven up the Channel by the south-westerly gales that raise ocean waves against the south coast of England, they anxiously sought an entrance into the smoother waters of the Solent as a haven of refuge from such a deadly lee shore.

The various contributions to the formation of the present coastline—the Alpine folding, the creation of the English Channel and of the 'Solent river', its dismemberment by the early Quaternary transgression, the separation of the Isle of Wight, the breaching of the

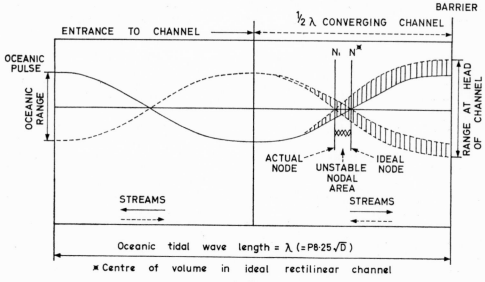

Fig. 8. The stationary tidal oscillation and nodal area in the English Channel

Figs. 8-15 and 18 are based on D. H. Macmillan, 'Tidal features of Southampton Water: Investigation into cause of remarkable phenomena', *Dock & Harbour Authority* (1949), with some revisions.

southern Chalk ridge, wave erosion and shingle accretion—have been described in Chapter III. These events in the geological history of the English Channel, and their results, have had profound effects on the unusually providential tidal phenomena which have made Southampton an obvious and unique terminal for the liners of today.

THE TIDAL PHENOMENA

The creation of the English Channel had two main hydrological consequences. These were (i) the progressive introduction of the semi-diurnal tidal pulse of the North Atlantic Ocean right into the Straits of Dover; and (ii) the opening of this converging gulf to the wave action of the ocean, with an immense 'fetch', along which the prevailing westerly gales can raise wave amplitudes of 30 to 40 feet, with pressures of up to 5 tons per square foot.

If one regards the restricted area lying between Land's End and Dover as a 'stationary wave compartment', with its own natural period of oscillation, one may roughly assume an average depth of 36 fathoms and a length of 300 miles. The resulting natural period of oscillation may be calculated from the following approximate formula★:

$$T = \frac{L}{4\sqrt{D}}$$

Where T = Period of natural oscillation in hours
L = Length of compartment in nautical miles
D = Depth (average) in fathoms

Thus in this case: $T = \dfrac{300}{4\sqrt{36}}$

$$= \frac{300}{24}$$

$$= 12\tfrac{1}{2} \text{ hours}$$

As this closely approximates to the diurnal tidal period of the Atlantic Ocean, it is clear that the English Channel is kept in continuous oscillation by the kinetic energy of the oceanic tidal pulse applied in perfect synchronism at the western entrance (Fig. 8).

A modern cotidal map of the English Channel (Fig. 9) indicates the tidal régime which has prevailed since about 4500 B.C., when the outline of the English Channel had begun to

★ This formula is derived from the standard formula for a standing oscillation—namely:

$$T = \frac{2l}{\sqrt{gh}}$$

Where T = period in seconds
l = length in feet
h = depth in feet
g = acceleration due to gravity

assume its present shape. It has been shown that if one assumes a tidal compartment equal in length to the English Channel and with its average depth, the period of oscillation will coincide with the diurnal oceanic tidal oscillation at its western entrance off Land's End. This in itself is a phenomenal synchronism of natural forces, but it must, of course, be realised that this assumption is based on a uniform rectangular shape, and discrepancies from theory when the natural boundaries deviate from the rectilinear are inevitable. If the English Channel were of uniform depth and truly rectangular in plan, one would expect no

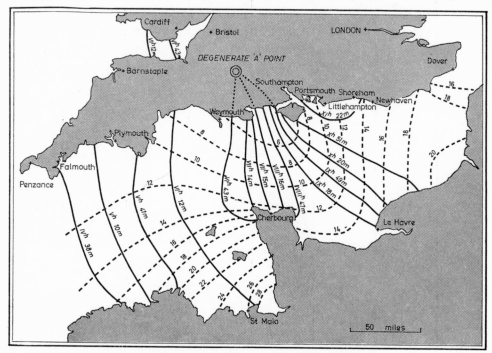

Fig. 9. Cotidal map of the English Channel

The degenerate amphidromic point is indicated by A. Lunitidal intervals and ranges (in feet) are given.

variation in vertical tidal level at the centre of its major axis or 'node', but only an alternation of tidal stream movement during each period of oscillation ($12\frac{1}{2}$ hours). The transverse nodal line would run from somewhere near the western end of the Isle of Wight to the eastern side of the Cherbourg peninsula.

On the other hand, a glance at the map reveals a roughly converging Channel section, and the intrusion of the Cherbourg peninsula drastically reduces the cross-sectional area at that point. One must, therefore, expect the 'node' to be unstable, due to the resistance to normal flow, which will, of course, be highest at the time of its greatest rate. Thus while the times of high water at Dover will coincide with those of low water at Land's End (and vice versa), one must expect deviation from theory over an area of instability, as shown in Fig. 13, and it would be reasonable to assume maximum interference midway between the times of low and high waters (when tidal flow is strongest)—that is, four times a day, i.e. of a quarter-diurnal nature.

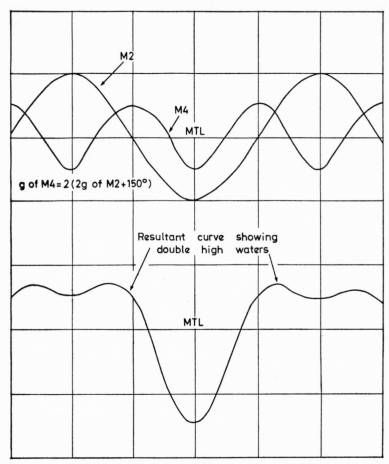

Fig. 10. The principle of a 'double' or prolonged high tide
MTL. Mean tidal level; M2. harmonic curve of semi-diurnal variety;
M4. harmonic curve of quarter-diurnal variety.

It is well known that when the harmonic curves of a semi-diurnal (M2) and quarter-diurnal (M4) variety are combined, they will produce a double high water of an elementary character if the initial phase differences between the constituents are 180° or near (Fig. 10). Fig. 11, showing synchronous tidal curves at Havre, Honfleur and Southampton, indicates that such a situation does occur across this section of the English Channel. It should, however, be noted that the duration of the ebb along the French coast is much longer than that of the flood, whereas the situation inside the Isle of Wight at Southampton reverses this relative duration. The reason for this will be discussed later. It is also interesting to note that

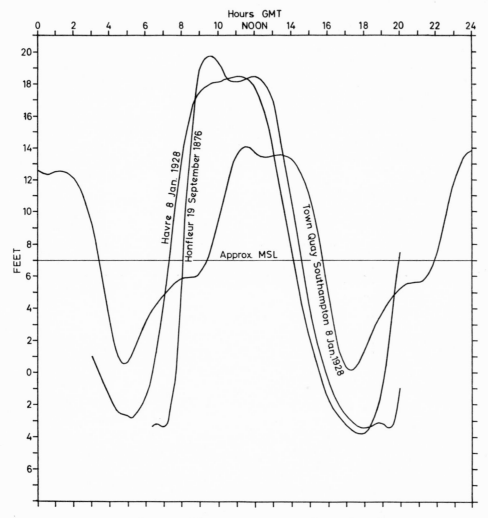

Fig. 11. Synchronous tidal curves at Havre, Honfleur and Southampton
MSL. Mean sea-level, related to the Newlyn Datum.

where the M_2 and M_4 constituents start initially in phase (that is, where the latter is displaced by only three hours from the relation shown in the former example), double low waters result (Fig. 12), as in the case at Portland.

Two further phenomena can be noted from examination of the cotidal chart (Fig. 9). In the first place, from its entrance to the English Channel, tidal undulation is normal (at right angles) to the Channel axis until its interruption by the Cherbourg peninsula, causing the elementary double high water produced in the manner described above. But the result of this asymmetrical constriction of flow and convergence is to build up the range towards Dover, and to produce a large area lying eastward of a line joining Portsmouth Harbour

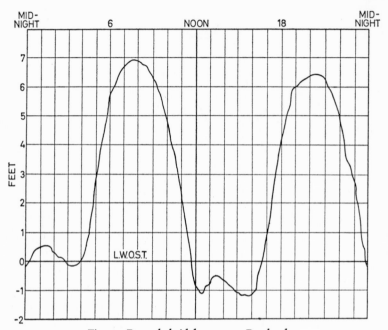

Fig. 12. Recorded tidal curves at Portland
L.W.O.S.T. Low water ordinary spring tides.

entrance and Dieppe, over which the times of high waters are almost simultaneous. In the second place, tidal ranges tend to build up almost dramatically on the French coast. This is mainly a result of the earth's rotation (the Coriolis effect), which causes a deviation to the right of rectilinear motion in the northern hemisphere. This effect is accentuated by the obstruction to up-Channel flow provided by the Cherbourg peninsula, and it is notable that at St. Malo, Cancale and Granville the normal spring ranges (heights above low water) are $35\frac{1}{2}$, 44 and 43 feet respectively. By contrast, spring tidal ranges on the English coast, between Land's End and Dover, do not exceed 20 feet.

The Tidal Régime within the Isle of Wight

It is clear that while the formation of the English Channel provided an eastern entrance to the Solent, via the much widened section of the mouth of the old 'Solent river' (see

p. 48), the Chalk barrier across what is now the western inlet must have successfully resisted the intensive battering by storm-waves for a considerable time after the main marine transgression. The Needles still remain as a witness of such resistance, and the Bridge Reef farther to the west, probably the base of vanished stacks, has shown little evidence of substantial diminution over the last two centuries. Authorities vary as to the chronology of the final break-through, but it could have been as late as 3000 B.C.; some even place it still later.

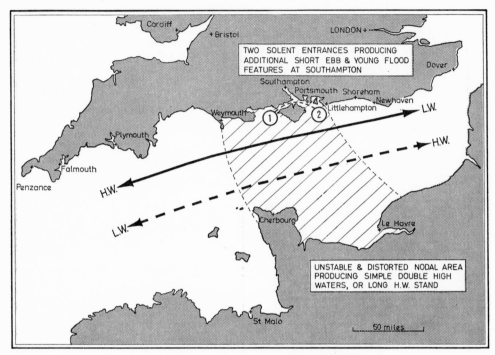

Fig. 13. Degenerate nodal area in the English Channel

While it has been shown that a pattern of simple double high water has occurred over the 'degenerate' nodal area (Fig. 13) since the formation of the English Channel, it is obvious that the tidal curves observed outside the Isle of Wight reveal remarkable divergences from those recorded at Calshot and Southampton, as can be seen from Fig. 14. For example, the Honfleur curve has a flood duration of only $2\frac{1}{2}$ hours, as compared with an ebb duration of 7 hours, and the Havre spring flood period occupies $4\frac{3}{4}$ hours, with the following ebb $6\frac{1}{2}$ hours.

To a seaman the longer the tide is standing or rising and the shorter the length of the ebb, the better he is pleased when navigating in shoal or harbour areas. The Southampton curve is indeed providential, and certainly exceptional, for it rises on the flood from low to high water at springs over a $6\frac{3}{4}$-hour period, with the remarkable interruption of a slack water stand lasting nearly two hours near Mean Tide Level, a phenomenon known locally as the 'Young Flood Stand'. In addition, the double high water period following covers 1¾ hours, but the subsequent ebb occupies only 3¾ hours of the total 12½-hour tidal cycle. These phenomena would not prevail if the eastern entrance to the Solent alone existed, for in such a case the situation outside the Isle of Wight would be more or less communicated to the Solent—namely, a short flood and a long ebb.

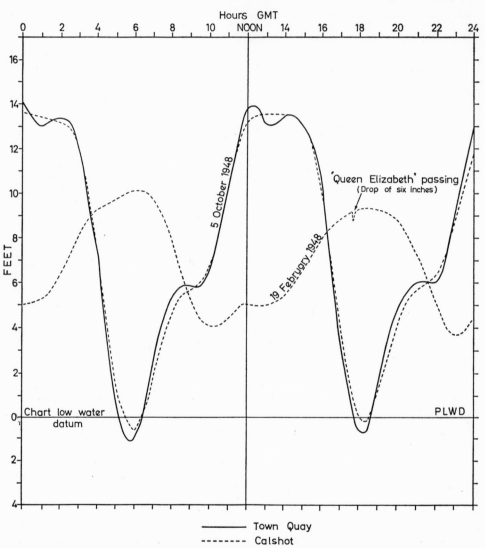

Fig. 14. Tidal curves at the Town Quay, Southampton, and at Calshot
PLWD. Port Low Water Datum (see Fig. 18).

An examination of Fig. 15 shows that the tidal stream flowing within the Solent, with its two entrances, is not in phase with the tidal rise and fall outside the Isle of Wight. It is determined by the varying hydraulic gradient prevailing at any given time between the Needles and Spithead. Thus at spring high water, which occurs at the Needles and Spithead within an hour of each other, the semi-ranges (or heights above Mean Tide Level) are $3\frac{1}{2}$ and $6\frac{1}{2}$ feet respectively.

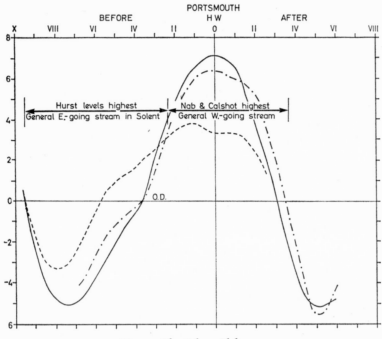

Fig. 15. The Solent tidal stream

The tidal stream over the high water period must therefore flow from east to west, the result of this 3-foot 'head'. The reverse situation occurs at the time of spring low water, the differences in ranges making the Needles low-water level about 3 feet above that at Spithead, causing an east-going stream in the whole Solent. When the Spithead level overtakes that at the Needles, as the tidal levels rise simultaneously at each end of the Solent, the direction of flow is reversed, following a very short period of slack water. There is little doubt that the existence of these two Solent entrances reverses the normal phase relation between the quarter-diurnal (M4) and diurnal (M2) tidal constituents, in such a manner as to cause long flood and short ebb periods, as well as the pause at the Young Flood Stand.

In the *Admiralty Manual of Tides*, the Southampton phenomena are regarded as probably due to the two entrances to the Solent, with their hydraulic implications, and the sixth-diurnal tidal constituent is considered to be the feature to which some of the unique characteristics of the tidal curve are due. It is instructive to note that the tidal model of the Solent and Southampton Water, constructed in 1958 for the Southampton Harbour Board, confirms this theory.

Summing up, it is abundantly clear that while simple double high-water phenomena prevail in the unstable area across the Channel between Portland and Chichester on the English side and Cherbourg and Dieppe on the French side (Fig. 11), the remarkable tidal features shown in the Southampton tidal curve are undoubtedly due to modifications brought about by the existence of two entrances to the Solent.

SOUTHAMPTON WATER

It is clear that a remarkable combination of natural features has favoured Southampton Water (Plate IX). These may be summarised as follows:

(i) The unique tidal régime, where for $8\frac{3}{4}$ hours the water level is either rising or standing, and the ebb lasts only $3\frac{3}{4}$ hours.

(ii) The 'halt' on the flood tide in Southampton Water, occurring from $1\frac{3}{4}$ to $3\frac{1}{2}$ hours after low water, and averaging a useful level of from 1 to 2 feet below Mean Tide Level, with little horizontal tidal movement off the Docks, where such movement is in phase with changes in vertical tidal movement.

(iii) The protecting and sheltering barrier of the Isle of Wight.

(iv) The lay-out of Southampton Water in a south-easterly direction across the dominant south-westerly direction of strong gales, with consequent freedom from powerful wave action. This feature has made Southampton Water a great attraction to ships of all sizes, seeking refuge from the storms of the English Channel, from pre-Roman times to the present. In addition, the short fetches result in freedom from wave erosion within Southampton Water. It is significant that the only wave-erosion occurs in the Hook area below the Hamble entrance, the result of west-south-westerly winds blowing over the maximum local fetch of 13 miles along the axis of the western Solent from the Needles Narrows off Hurst.

(v) The relatively small tidal range and the correspondingly small tidal streams in Southampton Water, which, while large enough to be useful, dispense with the need for lock-gates at the docks.

(vi) The incidence of dense fog (see p. 85) in the Southampton and Calshot (Figs. 28, 29) areas rarely exceeds an annual aggregate of 15 days. This value is considerably less than that prevailing even at the Needles entrance, or to the east of Spithead.

(vii) As the bed of Southampton Water and the Calshot submarine plateau was only recently submerged, the clays and gravels enable relatively permanent channels to be dredged easily as required to accommodate vessels of increasing draught (Figs. 16, 17). It is significant that there is no maintenance problem outside Calshot Castle, while the annual dredging programme of the thin alluvial 'dressing' over the clays in the main channel between Fawley and the Dockhead does not involve more than 200,000 cubic yards.

An incidental feature of economic importance is the heavy accretion of shingle in the area immediately south-west of the Needles, forming around Pot Bank a submarine shoal area with a crest about six fathoms below Mean Low Water Springs. The combined effects of the relatively small tidal range outside the Needles, the long tidal stand and the continuous easterly movement of shingle on the bed of the English Channel, together with a northerly component (due to occasional strong southerly to south-westerly gales), result in a build-up and continuous supply of clean shingle at this site, with a corresponding wastage to the eastward. This phenomenon provides a source of valuable building aggregate, now in

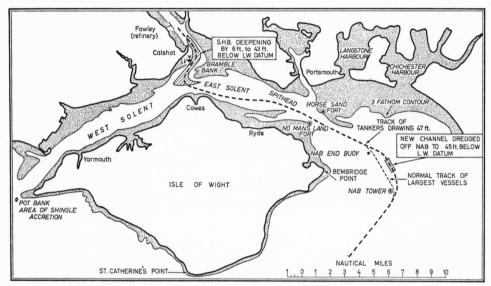

Fig. 16. Dredged channels off Calshot and The Nab
Based on original drawings by the Southampton Harbour Board (S.H.B.).

increasing demand. A number of suction hopper dredgers (some constructed specifically for this purpose) are now exploiting this, and by the use of variable suction devices are able to select material of specified diameter immediately available for use.

(viii) The excellent holding-ground for anchoring the largest ships in the world is a special feature of Southampton Water and the Solent generally, where tenuous sticky clay is characteristic. The 17-ton anchor of the *Queen Mary* can enter for 5 to 6 feet below the sea-floor in such material with a tenacity that would part her 4-inch diameter cable before dragging.

(ix) The situation of the Solent, and especially Southampton Water, enables a large ship to avoid the tortuous routes, buoyed channels and long prevailing periods of poor visibility incidental to berthing at the ports of Liverpool, Bristol and London. Ships can arrive safely within the shelter of the Solent, half-way along the English Channel, where passengers and cargo are within easy reach of London.

HYDROGRAPHIC SURVEYS

Lord Kelvin once said that 'science is measurement', and the science of hydrography is the precise measurement of all the phenomena of submarine areas related to the safe passage and reception of the largest and deepest-draught ships using them. Scientific hydrographic surveys really commenced with Captain James Cook, R.N., during the eighteenth century, and some rather superficial work on the south-eastern coast of England was carried out by his redoubtable first lieutenant, Captain Bligh, after his unfortunate experience in H.M.S. *Bounty*. The development in the eighteenth century of Hadley's sextant made it possible for the first time to carry out accurate triangulation of the shore objects which must be available to control the accurate movement of the survey vessel, and enable it to plot its course and the position of the soundings it takes.

Lieutenant Murdoch McKenzie, R.N., made the first reasonably accurate survey of Southampton, both as to adjacent shore features and the positions and values of the soundings and contours. They are given on his plan dated 1783. Since that date, Admiralty charts presenting surveys of increasing detail of the Southampton and Solent areas have appeared with increasing frequency, especially after the 'iron and steam' revolution which developed apace during the middle of the nineteenth century. It can be said, however, that the seaward limit of detailed soundings in estuarine areas and their approaches did not extend much beyond the 5-fathom contour; soundings in deeper waters were not necessary because of the light draught of ships, which did not exceed 20 feet for a long time. Moreover, the laborious method of sounding by lead and line made progress both difficult and slow.

The need for detailed surveys because of the increasing draught of ships has now extended beyond the 10-fathom contour. This requirement is met by the latest techniques of echo-sounding and of electronic devices for the accurate location of ships engaged in survey, developed over the last three decades, especially under the stimulus of the War of 1939-45.

MODERN DEVELOPMENTS IN SOUTHAMPTON WATER

The remarkable scientific advances of the last century included the change of ship construction from wood to steel, and, almost simultaneously, from sail to mechanical propulsion, with a correspondingly dramatic increase in the size of ships regularly plying the North Atlantic. Design, reflected in the increasing length and draught of such ships, is largely dependent upon the terminal facilities available, and, as has been shown, Southampton Water is most favourably situated. Under the aegis of Parliament, statutory powers were exercised by the Southampton Harbour Board in deepening and widening the approach channels, as the laying down of the keels of liners of ever increasing dimensions proceeded apace; the *Oceanic*, *Majestic*, *Teutonic* and *Adriatic* all made Southampton their European terminal in 1907. In 1909 the keels of the *Olympic* and the ill-fated *Titanic*, and soon after the *Aquitania* and the *Mauretania*, were laid. The approach channels to the Docks were accordingly deepened from 30 to 35 feet below Mean Low Water Springs between the years 1893 and 1913. Between the two World Wars further widening and deepening proceeded, notably in preparation for the *Queen Mary* in 1936. The favourable nature of the bed of Southampton Water and its approaches from the Solent is reflected in the uniquely low maintenance dredging requirements already stressed.

In 1950 further dredging was undertaken in the approaches to Southampton and the Docks, the spoil amounting to 3½ million cubic yards. On this occasion the Calshot Spit was shaped to a 4000-foot radius curve to fit the turning tracks in shallow water of the Cunard 'Queens', each over 1000 feet in length. These vessels can now negotiate what used to be a dangerously acute turn with relatively small easy helm (5° to 10°) and no requirements of drastic engine assistance. The berm, or dredged margin, of the new curve (composed of clay, gravel and shingle) has retained its dredged contours.

The largest project ever for dredging the bed of the Solent off the Nab and Calshot

Fig. 17. Southampton Water Based on the Southampton Harbour Board's map on a scale of 1:29,256 (1952), with revisions. PLWD. Port Low Water Datum (see Fig. 18); bn. beacon.

Fs

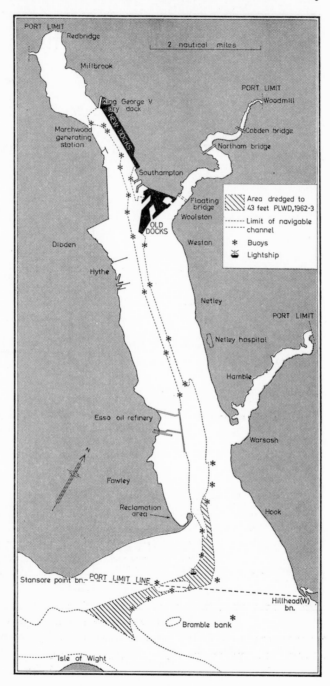

PORT LIMIT
Redbridge
Millbrook
2 nautical miles
PORT LIMIT
Woodmill
King George V dry dock
NEW DOCKS
Cobden bridge
Marchwood generating station
Northam bridge
Southampton
Floating bridge
Woolston
OLD DOCKS
Dibden
Weston
Hythe
Netley
Netley hospital
Hamble
PORT LIMIT
Esso oil refinery
Warsash
Fawley
Reclamation area
Hook
Stansore point bn.   PORT LIMIT LINE
Hillhead(W) bn.
Bramble bank
Isle of Wight

Area dredged to 43 feet PLWD, 1962-3
------- Limit of navigable channel
✳ Buoys
⚓ Lightship

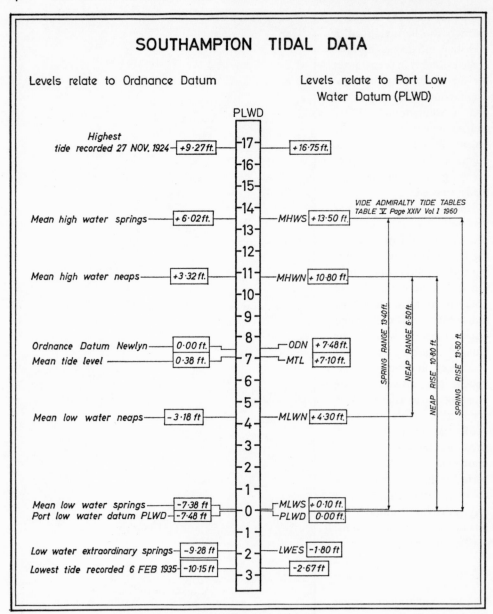

Fig. 18. Southampton tidal data

Based on (i) *Admiralty Tide Tables*, vol. I, table V, p. xxiv (London, 1960); and (ii) Southampton Harbour Board records.

The Hydrographer of the Navy has decided to lower the Port Low Water Datum by 1·5 feet as from 1 January, 1965.

commenced in 1962, where it was required to accommodate tankers of over 100,000 tons displacement and drawing 47 feet at the Fawley installation (see p. 265 and Plate XXVIII). Model tests at the National Physical Laboratory (Teddington) indicated that in shallow approach channels these vessels would trim by the head, and increase draught by as much as 3 to 5 feet at speeds of 10 to 12 knots respectively. Accordingly, the requirements aimed at providing dredged channels 45 to 43 feet below Mean Low Water Springs off the Nab and off Calshot respectively (Fig. 16). The problem was to determine whether the large flints and shingle, 2 to 3 feet thick, covering a hard sand base in the Nab Channel, would remain stable after dredging to the specified depth, in view of the large swell values of up to 10 feet in strong winds, rising to values of 12 to 15 feet during exceptional southerly gales over the 90-mile fetch from the French coast. Fortunately, the rotary anti-clockwise tidal streams prevailing at the site naturally favoured the project after the channel had been deepened beyond 50 per cent of the required sectional area. The annual accretion, estimated as being less than 500,000 cubic yards, was accepted as being within economic limits for the maintenance costs involved in operating the 1500-foot wide channel. Subsequent surveys have much reduced this estimate.

Accordingly, as the Nab investigation proved favourable, the approach channels leading from the Solent off Calshot to the Fawley installation were deepened by 6 feet below their present bed level, to 43 feet below Port Low Water Datum (Fig. 18). This bottom level now gives depths at high water of 55 and 53 feet at springs and neaps respectively; the work was completed in August 1963.*

It is certain, however, that the exhaustion of marine possibilities in the Solent and Southampton areas is not yet in sight. Notwithstanding the demanding pressures of the twentieth century, the ideal concentration of varied natural features here provide an ocean terminal towards which science and technology must increasingly devote their attention and direct their skills.

BIBLIOGRAPHICAL NOTE

(1) A. T. Doodson and H. D. Warburg, *Admiralty manual of tides* (London, 1941), pp. 224-6.
(2) R. C. H. Russel and D. H. Macmillan, *Waves and tides* (London, 1952).
(3) *The Channel pilot*, vol. I (14th edition, London, 1957), especially pp. 204-27.

* The first large tanker, *Esso Lancashire* (drawing 47 feet 5 inches), arrived at the Fawley Marine Terminal on 29 August, 1963, bringing 78,300 tons of crude oil from Marsa el Brega, Libya.

V

SOILS

THE first investigations into the soils of the Hampshire Basin and its chalk rim date from the beginning of the nineteenth century. Both Vancouver (1810) in his *General view of the agriculture of Hampshire including the Isle of Wight* and Stevenson (1815) in his report on Dorset's agriculture included maps which drew the broad distinction between the soils of the chalklands and those on the Tertiary deposits. As a rough outline of the pattern of soils in the region, their maps and accounts, though produced from an agricultural point of view, are still useful. Nearly a century later Luxmoore and his colleagues (1907) analysed soils from Dorset, using the techniques of agricultural chemistry available at the time. As in the case of other soil surveys at that period, no soil map was produced, for it was assumed that the correlation between geology and soil was sufficiently close for the geological map to reveal the main outlines of the soil distribution.

During the last forty years the study of soil morphology, as demonstrated by the soil profile, has become the foundation for mapping soils, and a few areas within the region and near its boundaries have been surveyed in detail by this method. The basic mapping unit is the *soil series*, which classes together those soils occupying similar sites, having developed from a common parent material, and with profiles revealing a similar history of development. Each series generally takes the name of the locality where it was first mapped.

In the Hampshire Basin F. F. Kay (1939) surveyed on the 6 inches to a mile scale the soils of the strawberry-growing district to the east of Southampton Water to see if there were any relation between soil conditions and diseases of the strawberry crop. Later K. L. Robinson (1948) carried out a reconnaissance survey of the soils of Dorset, and recognised on the Eocene and Cretaceous rocks of the county many of the series already established by Kay in Hampshire.

On the Chalk, Kay carried out a small survey near Andover (unpublished, but reproduced in part by Green, 1940) and recognised several new series, as well as some she had already mapped in Berkshire (1934). Other areas on the Chalk were surveyed by Robinson.

Since the War of 1939-45 a small area on the Isle of Wight has been surveyed in detail, while the Forestry Commission has recently carried out limited studies in the New Forest and on the Dorset heaths. Land classification work in parts of the region (e.g. Wiltshire) has also involved a certain amount of soil reconnaissance. The Soil Survey of England and Wales, however, is not yet mapping any of the 1-inch sheets in the region.

Thus, including Robinson's reconnaissance of the Dorset soils, less than a third of the region has been surveyed in any detail; no satisfactory review therefore can be given until more of this mapping is completed and further pedological research initiated. The work of Dimbleby (1962) and Gill (1955) on New Forest podzols under heath and forest is of interest in this direction. In the present account it is only possible to indicate broadly some of the soils found in the region and the factors which have caused their formation.

SOIL FORMATION WITHIN THE REGION

Soils develop as a result of physical, chemical and biological processes acting upon parent materials. Many of these materials are derived from the weathering of rocks *in situ*, so that the main properties of the resulting soils are closely tied to the physical and chemical characteristics of the underlying rocks. Several soil boundaries therefore coincide with geological divisions, but each outcrop can, through variations within its beds and in hydrologic condition, produce a considerable range of soils. Also within the region broad spreads of drift deposits occur on the higher ground, and colluvial and terrace deposits on slopes and in valleys. These materials, of Pleistocene and Recent age, generally have more variable compositions than the solid formations exposed over the rest of the region. Soil patterns under these conditions tend to be complex.

Other factors controlling soil formation can further complicate the picture. Relief influences the development of some soils, both by allowing the erosion and accumulation of soil materials and also by creating a variety of drainage conditions down a slope, as can be seen in some catenary sequences. Climate is another important factor in soil formation, while in some soils a change of vegetation or a modification of the natural conditions by man must be given due consideration, especially in those parts of the region with a long history of settlement.

Soils in the Tertiary Basin

Most of the soils developed in the Hampshire Basin can be assigned to three major groups: the *podzolic* soils, the *brown earths* and the *gleys*. Podzolic soils most often form on the acid and coarser-textured parent materials. With a low base status and high permeability, they have been least able to resist the effects of the loss of exchangeable cations by leaching. The soils are generally associated with a vegetation cover whose leaf-fall and residues are insufficient to maintain the base status, and they have a soil fauna which does little to reincorporate surface organic material into the mineral part of the soil.

The typical podzol profile as seen in the New Forest and Dorset heathlands consists of a horizon of decomposing leaf litter and spongy raw humus (the A_0 horizon), resting on a grey A_1 horizon with mineral particles stained by organic substances. This grades into a bleached A_2 mineral horizon. The B horizons are enriched by some of the materials lost from the A horizons. In the most strongly podzolised soils, a B_1 horizon rich in organic matter may lie above a B_2 horizon with a rusty colour derived from its ferric oxide accumulation. A compact iron pan may develop and so impede drainage (Plate XII).

Although the podzol is closely associated with the heathlands of the Hampshire Basin, other more useful agricultural soils are to be seen. Some of these less podzolised and less acid soils form a second major group, the brown earths, especially where the parent materials have a rather better supply of bases and are of a finer texture. Podzols on lighter materials in some instances have, however, been turned into soils resembling brown earths.

The typical brown earth profile consists of an A horizon of a dark-coloured intimate mixture of organic and mineral matter, which passes into a B horizon containing less organic matter and with a colour similar to or browner than that of the parent material. These soils have developed for the most part under a cover of deciduous forest, for which reason they are sometimes termed *brown forest* soils. The forest cover maintains the base status of the soil by its annual leaf-fall, and the soil fauna incorporate the organic matter with the upper part of the mineral soil into a *mull* humus. The brown earth is a delicately balanced soil and podzolisation (to a podzolic brown earth and eventually a podzol) can result from the removal of the forest cover and its replacement by heath. On the other hand, removal of the forest for purposes of cultivation affects the soil less radically, producing an 'agricultural brown earth' in which the topsoil is more sharply differentiated from the subsoil.

These soils form under conditions of free drainage. Those which have developed features of poor drainage are termed *gley soils*, a group containing a variety of soils related to both podzols and brown earths, all of which are characterised by orange or grey mottling in the profile. For example, there may be some drainage impedance in the subsoil of a brown earth, producing a *brown earth with gleying*. A *surface-water gley* may develop on the heaviest parent materials such as a clay, and intense podzolisation can create a pan leading to the development of a *gley podzol*. Frequently gleying is related to the relief, as in alluvial soils, where the ground-water table is near the surface (a *ground-water* gley). In the wettest gley soils, plant residues are not well incorporated and a peaty A horizon is found. In time this may thicken to give a more highly organic soil, and peats of this type occur in some New Forest bogs.

Scattered examples of very youthful soils occur in the Hampshire Basin. These include river alluvium, the characteristics of which vary greatly according to its situation and age, salt-marsh muds and gleys, and raw sand soils developing on blown sands, as around Poole Harbour.

Within this broad frame a wide variety of soil series develops. Kay, in her survey of 50 square miles in the Swanwick area, mapped twenty series, apart from undifferentiated alluvium, on less than the full range of geological outcrops encountered across the whole Basin.

Two podzol series are particularly noteworthy. The Southampton series is a humus-iron podzol characterised by sub-angular flints, which develops widely on the platforms of plateau-gravels in the New Forest, behind Bournemouth, to the east of Southampton Water and in parts of Dorset. It is frequently found under conifer woodland or *Erica* and *Calluna* heath, which help to account for its strongly podzolised condition. Where it is cultivated, as in the eastern part of the Basin, the raw humus (A_0) layer is absent, having been mechanically incorporated with the underlying grey mineral horizon.

Broad areas of the sands of the Bagshot and Bracklesham Beds give rise to the Shirrell Heath series, a podzol resembling the Southampton series but lacking the sub-angular flints and much of the induration of the B horizons. The series is found on the northern side of the New Forest and has also been mapped widely in Dorset. Other podzol series, as yet unnamed, have developed on the Barton Sands in the New Forest area and are well seen around Lyndhurst.

Associated with each of these podzols are gley soils developed on the same parent materials. The Sarisbury series often forms alongside the Southampton series, where water is held up either by induration or by more clayey underlying material. Soils similar to these

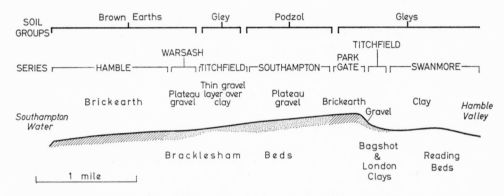

Fig. 19. A sequence of soils on Tertiary and later materials

Based on soil series mapping by Dr. F. F. Kay.
Superficial deposits of brickearth are indicated by diagonal shading, plateau-gravels by stippling.

can be seen in the Bolderwood Grounds in the New Forest, where a layer of plateau-gravel overlies Headon Clay.

The occurrence of podzols on these coarser materials does not preclude the existence of brown earths on the same formations and indeed often alongside the podzols. In the Swanwick area, Kay mapped the Warsash series on the plateau-gravels, and found other brown earths (e.g. the Shedfield series) on the Bagshot Sands. Both have also been mapped by Robinson in Dorset. These coarse-textured brown earths are generally under cultivation for market gardening and arable farming, which perhaps partly accounts for their fertility. Good soils also form on the belt of valley-gravels bordering the Avon and the Stour, providing a vivid contrast in land use to that of the New Forest and Dorset heaths on either side.

As might be expected, many clays and loams of the brown earth and gley groups are found on the materials of finer texture, especially those on the London Clay and Reading Bed outcrops which fringe the Basin, and on the Oligocene marls and clays on the Isle of

Wight. Considerable areas with poor drainage are under pasture and oakwood. Even so, their presence creates a belt of more useful land stretching from the east of Southampton Water into Dorset. Calcareous material washed from the chalk downs helps to improve soil conditions in some of these districts.

Brickearth deposits near Portsmouth (the Hamble series), at Eastleigh and on the coast provide fertile and stoneless soils for arable use. Unfortunately, much of this land is now built over and lost to agriculture.

Fig. 19 shows a sequence of some of these soils, as found to the east of the Hamble river. The brickearth gives rise to both brown earths and gleys, the gravels provide brown earths, podzols and gleys, whilst the underlying clay formations produce various types of gleys. Sandy parent materials, not included in the sequence in Fig. 19, can give rise, like the gravels, to soils in all three groups.

Similar complexes, mainly of gleys and brown earths, occur in the Purbeck district and on the southern side of the Isle of Wight. An intricate pattern of soils ranges from the heavy clays on the Wealden materials, through lighter loams on the Greensands, to shallow calcareous soils on the chalk ridges, all within the space of a few miles.

Soils on the Chalk Rim

The Chalk outcrops over about 60 per cent of the region and provides a homogeneous parent material over considerable areas. Most of the soils found there belong to the calcareous group. The *rendzina* which develops on the Chalk is a shallow soil, with an A horizon of less than 9 inches of dark grey or brown friable loam, overlying a C horizon of highly calcareous loam or chalky brash. This passes into the weathering rock at less than 15 inches below the surface.

Variations result, however, from the effects of soil creep and the downwashing of both fine-textured calcareous materials from the chalk slopes above and of non-calcareous materials from the superficial deposits, such as the Clay-with-Flints, which cap some upland parts of the Chalk. Many downland areas therefore display soil catenas passing laterally from shallow rendzinas to *brown calcareous* soils deepened by downwash. At the upper end of the catena there may be a brown earth soil derived from the remains of the Clay-with-Flints.

The Upper Chalk forms by far the broadest outcrop of the three divisions of the Chalk. The rendzinas developing on it, together with those on the Middle Chalk, are assigned to the Icknield and Andover series, though the narrow fringe of the Lower Chalk produces a clay loam soil classed as the Wantage series. Being retentive of moisture, though not ill-drained, it is less liable to summer drought than the soils of the Icknield and Andover series. The profile of the Icknield series consists of a dark grey turfy loam, often flinty and decalcified, lying over a whiter calcareous loam rich in chalk fragments which increase in number and size down the profile. Soil depth varies according to relief and to the amount of erosion. Whilst the Icknield series is typically developed under grass, Kay mapped the Andover series on arable land. Here the soil is lighter in colour as a result of the loss of organic matter, but it is less decalcified since cultivation brings chalk fragments up into the topsoil. The Icknield series is commonly separated from the Andover by field boundaries, affording a good example of soil differentiation resulting from the effects of cultivation.

While erosion has prevented the development of soils of greater depth on the higher surfaces and slopes, the colluvial soils on lower slopes and in valley bottoms (e.g. the Coombe series) have deeper, more leached profiles and finer textures. They often reveal the beginnings of a cloddy B horizon, so that they superficially resemble brown earths, but they are still calcareous and therefore must be classed as such.

Superficial deposits of Clay-with-Flints and brickearth, which originated under peri-glacial conditions, cap some of the chalk ridges. They occur more frequently in Hampshire

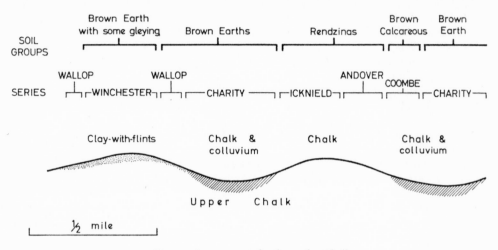

Fig. 20. A sequence of soils on the Chalk

Based on soil series mapping by Dr. F. F. Kay.
Superficial deposits of chalk downwash and colluvium are indicated by diagonal shading, Clay-with-Flints by stippling.

than in Dorset or on Salisbury Plain, and give rise to several series which are mainly classed as brown earths. On the variable Clay-with-Flints, perhaps itself a relic of a soil formed under sub-tropical conditions, the soil is mapped as the Winchester series. These profiles are characterised by a compact yellow-red clay layer which lies near the surface and is often flinty; the fine texture can cause gley features. Elsewhere the deposit is less flinty and appears to be partly loessic in origin. With a loamy horizon lying above mottled clay, these soils belong to the Batcombe series. As the Clay-with-Flints cappings thin out, Chalk enters the lower part of the soil profile, giving soils which have been assigned to the Wallop series. Here textural characteristics of the soil are largely derived from the clay cover, and yet it possesses a neutral reaction and greyness which it owes to its chalk content.

In downland valley bottoms resorted superficial and calcareous materials often occur. Common amongst the soils developed are the free draining, but acid, brown earths of the

Charity series. Many of the valley soils are gleyed and in some peaty alluvium forms over calcareous material. Fig. 20 shows a sequence of some of the series developed on Clay-with-Flints and Chalk on a 2-mile transect 8 miles north of Winchester.

BIBLIOGRAPHICAL NOTE

(1) G. W. Dimbleby and J. M. Gill, 'The occurrence of podzols under deciduous woodland in the New Forest', *Forestry* (1955), vol. 28, pp. 95-106.

(2) G. W. Dimbleby, *The development of British heathlands and their soils*, Oxford Forestry Memoir, 23 (1962).

(3) F. H. W. Green, *The report of the land utilisation survey of Britain*, Part 89, Hampshire (London, 1940), pp. 322-32.

(4) F. F. Kay, 'A soil survey of the eastern portion of the Vale of the White Horse', *University of Reading Bulletin*, 48 (1934), pp. 26-38.

(5) F. F. Kay, 'A soil survey of the strawberry district of south Hampshire', *University of Reading Bulletin*, 52 (1939).

(6) C. M. Luxmoore, *The soils of Dorset* (Reading, 1907).

(7) D. A. Osmond, 'The soils of Gloucestershire, Somerset and Wiltshire', in *Bristol and its adjoining counties* (Bristol, 1955), pp. 67-72.

(8) Reconstruction Research Group, *Land classification in Gloucestershire, Somerset and Wiltshire* (Bristol, 1947).

(9) K. L. Robinson, 'The soils of Dorset', in R. A. Good, *A geographical handbook of Dorset flora* (Dorchester, 1948), pp. 19-28.

(10) W. Stevenson, *General view of the agriculture of the county of Dorset* (London, 1815), pp. 35-43.

(11) C. Vancouver, *General view of the agriculture of Hampshire including the Isle of Wight* (London, 1810), pp. 11-40.

VI

WEATHER AND CLIMATE

THE coastal districts of central south England are noted for their warm, sunny summers and generally mild winters. Indeed, the popularity of the coastal resorts for holidays and retirement to a large extent depends upon this agreeable climate. The usually mild conditions of the winter half-year are reflected too by the rarity of snowfall and a long growing-season. The climate of the area is transitional between the maritime conditions of the South-west Peninsula and the relative continentality of south-eastern England. The general decrease of rainfall eastward across Britain, together with the configuration of the uplands in Dorset and Wiltshire, limits average annual totals to 760 mm. (approximately 30 inches) within the core of the area and along much of the coast (Fig. 21). Summer maximum temperatures at the coast are almost identical with those along the southern coast of Cornwall and Devon, though in winter average maxima and minima are a degree or so lower along the Hampshire coast than in the south-west. The climate of the coastal fringe is, however, far from uniform since the section from Lymington to Portsmouth is sheltered by the Isle of Wight from southerly air flow. Several climatological features testify to the existence of a marked climatic gradient inland. There is, for example, a steady increase away from the coast in the frequency of days on which snow falls during the year, and in both summer and winter a greater mean daily range of temperature. In summer afternoon maxima are usually higher and in winter night minimum temperatures are lower inland than at the coast. Southampton itself is effectively an inland station in many respects (Tables II, III).*

Climatological averages for the year or for individual months can be quite misleading unless the year to year variability is taken into account, as the severe winter conditions of 1962-3 in southern England clearly demonstrate. Correspondingly, monthly averages have to be interpreted in terms of the weather situations of individual days. For this reason, the climatic characteristics of various pressure patterns are discussed in the first half of this chapter to provide an outline of the 'synoptic climatology' of the area. A complete analysis of the synoptic climatology has not yet been undertaken and accordingly the study is restricted to temperature and precipitation for January and July, 1921-50; other climatic elements are examined in the second part of the chapter. Daily averages of maximum and minimum temperature have been determined for different types of pressure situation at ten stations in the region, and of precipitation for twelve stations; the data for the major types are presented in Tables II and III. Those stations not included (owing to lack of space) are Ryde, Totland Bay and Marlborough for temperature and precipitation, and Fordingbridge for precipitation only.

* Tables II-VII are on pp. 89-92.

SYNOPTIC CLIMATOLOGY IN JANUARY

The character of our winter weather depends upon the relative strength and position of the Azores High Pressure and the intensity, frequency and path of Atlantic depressions. Sometimes, however, high pressure over central or northern Europe exerts a dominant control over the country, particularly in late winter. These factors provide the basis for a classification of the daily synoptic weather-map which has been developed by H. H. Lamb for the British Isles. The classification recognises five major types, which are named

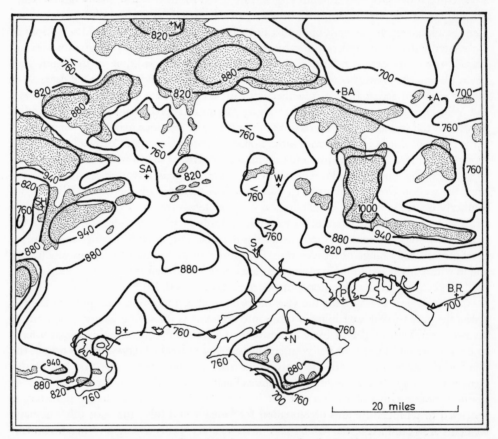

Fig. 21. Average annual precipitation, 1916–50, for the Southampton region

Based on 'The Average Rainfall Map of Britain', 1916–50, reproduced by courtesy of the Meteorological Office and the Controller of H.M. Stationery Office.
Land over 400 feet O.D. is stippled. Figures relating to isohyets are in millimetres, at 60 mm. intervals. Abbreviations are as follows: A. Alton; B. Bournemouth; BA. Basingstoke; B.R. Bognor Regis; M. Marlborough; N. Newport; P. Portsmouth; S. Southampton; SA. Salisbury; SH. Shaftesbury; W. Winchester.

according to the direction from which the air flow comes, and two further types which refer to the predominance of either high or low pressure over the country.

The most common weather-map pattern (40 per cent frequency for January) is the *Westerly type*, when high pressure remains to the south-west or south of the country, and the eastward passage of depressions brings relatively mild, changeable weather. Not infrequently the depression track lies along the English Channel and widespread rainfall occurs over southern England, lasting for six hours or more. Table I shows that the average 24-hour precipitation over most of the region with Westerly type, and with Westerly cyclonic sub-type, is 2·5 to 3·4 mm. The higher figure at Selborne indicates orographic intensification over the South Downs. Daily maximum temperatures for Westerly type are 9 to 10°C at coastal and lowland stations and 8 to 9°C on higher ground, while the respective averages of daily minima are 3 to 5°C and 2 to 3°C. Both maxima and minima are 1 to 2°C above the mean values in January (Table II). The high minima indicate a tendency for persistent cloud cover at night with Westerly flow. However, since the Westerly type may be associated with air of Maritime Tropical or Maritime Polar origin, the actual temperature conditions can depart radically from the calculated averages. A study of wind direction and cloud amount at Andover and Worthy Down (Winchester) for the winters of 1922-33 finds with west winds a one in three probability of 8/10 to 10/10 of low cloud at 1300 hours, decreasing to less than 6/10 of low cloud at 1800 hours. Actual wind directions cannot be equated directly with pressure-pattern types, but these results suggest that low cloud may disperse in the evening and cause lower minima on some occasions of Westerly flow.

Another major contributor to January weather is the *Cyclonic type* (12 per cent frequency). The designation refers either to periods of very frequent depression passages across Britain or to a slow-moving low-pressure area lying over the whole country. Average minimum temperatures for Cyclonic type are about a degree above the mean minima for January as a result of high cloud amounts, but average maxima are near the mean values (Table I). However, these averages may conceal high variability, arising from the changeable wind directions within depressions. For example, the standard deviation of the average maximum with Cyclonic type is between 2·5 to 3·3°C at ten stations, compared with 1·7 to 2·2°C for Westerly types. Considerable rainfall is likely with these synoptic situations, for the average daily amount is of the order of 4 mm. Similar high daily averages of rainfall occur on days which are 'Unclassified' (Table II), because these cases mainly represent complex synoptic situations with a depression affecting only part of the country.

A variant of the Westerly type occurs whenever a northward extension of the Azores anticyclone causes depressions to approach Britain from the north-west. Such rather infrequent *North-westerly* situations (4 per cent in January) bring cold air from the neighbourhood of Iceland in the rear of the depressions. Daily precipitation amounts average only 0·5 to 1·5 mm., although over high ground precipitation may take the form of snowshowers. Average daily maxima and minima with North-westerly flow are close to the January averages at each station, with many occurrences of night air frost over high ground (Table II).

Similar, but more extreme, conditions pertain to *Northerly* air flow, when high pressure over the North Atlantic extends in a south to north wedge between 40° and 65°N. latitude (3 per cent frequency in January). Average maxima with Northerly flow are 4 to 5°C at lowland stations and 3°C on higher ground, while minima are −1° to 1°C and −2°C, respectively. Despite the low day temperatures, little cloud cover is usually associated with Northerly flow and the winter sunshine provides some compensation for the cold air.

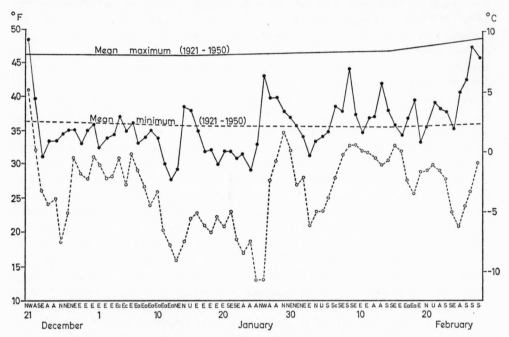

Fig. 22. Daily temperatures at Southampton, winter 1962-3
Based on information supplied by the Southampton Weather Centre.
The solid line indicates daily maximum temperature, the pecked line indicates daily minimum temperature. The letters indicating the air flow type on each day are: NW. North-westerly; N. Northerly; NE. North-easterly; E. Easterly; Ea. Easterly anticyclonic; Ec. Easterly cyclonic; SE. South-easterly; S. Southerly; Sc. Southerly cyclonic; A. Anticyclonic; U. Unclassified.

Northerly flow is essentially unstable, but showers are only light over southern England due to the long passage of the air over land. In view of the low temperatures, many showers are of snow, for snow is more likely than rain when the surface air temperature is below 2°C.

Easterly air flow has given rise to some memorable winters, but it is generally rather infrequent in January (8 per cent occurrence, including the Easterly cyclonic and anticyclonic sub-types). Easterly spells usually develop with the establishment of a blocking anticyclone over Scandinavia, which may subsequently extend westward, thus excluding depressions from the area of the British Isles. This situation can become persistent, as in the severe winter of 1947, and the conditions of January 1963 provide a further example, which is illustrated for Southampton in Fig. 22. The temperatures fell considerably below the calculated average maximum of 3·7°C and average minimum of − 1·0°C for Easterly type at Southampton (Table II). Average daily precipitation is about 2 mm. with Easterly type, although on occasions moderate falls of snow may occur.

Cold weather in January occurs most frequently with the high pressure or *Anticyclonic type* (10 per cent frequency). Average maxima and minima for these cases are 3°C below the respective monthly averages, and night frosts are common, even at exposed coastal stations. The low averages of daily maxima reflect the development of frequent winter anticyclones in cold Polar Continental air from central or northern Europe, or in Polar Maritime air from the area between Greenland and the Faeroes. Radiation fog is most common with Anticyclonic type, and in winter may persist during much of the day (Fig. 29). Precipitation falls occasionally on days which are classified as mainly Anticyclonic, but amounts are small (Table II).

Southerly flow (11 per cent frequency in January) is usually associated with anticyclonic blocking over Britain and the North Sea, or over central and northern Europe. The weather tends to be cloudy, with an average daily precipitation (generally rain) of 3 to 4 mm. The calculated temperatures are close

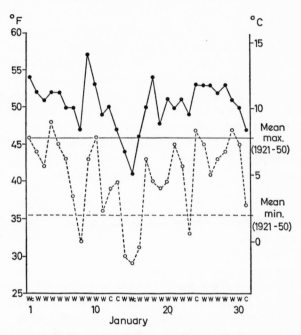

Fig. 23. Daily temperatures at Southampton, January 1921
Based on data supplied by the Meteorological Office Archives. The solid line indicates daily maximum temperature, the pecked line indicates daily minimum temperature. The letters indicating the air flow type on each day are: W. Westerly; Wc. Westerly cyclonic; C. Cyclonic.

to the averages for January (Table II), although the values conceal considerable variability, since a spell of Southerly flow may alternate either with Westerly or Easterly flow, giving rise to rather different weather conditions over southern England. Fig. 22 illustrates the latter case during February 1963.

While the averages of daily precipitation and daily maximum and minimum temperatures provide in general a useful indication of the climatic characteristics for particular types of synoptic pressure patterns, it must be recognised that non-characteristic conditions may be associated with any synoptic type over at least part of Britain. For example, January 1942 was much colder than average in central south England, despite the occurrence of ten days of Westerly type during the month. The low temperatures were not related to any single flow type, and in fact were below average even on days of Westerly flow. Nevertheless, the very warm Januarys of 1921, 1932 and 1944 can be ascribed to an incidence of twenty or more days of Westerly type in each month. Temperatures at Southampton during January 1921 (Fig. 23) were well above the monthly mean values on all except a few days. The very cold weather in central south England during the Januarys of 1929, 1940, 1941 and 1945 was associated with mixed spells of Northerly, Easterly, Anticyclonic and Southerly types, rather than with a single type.

The predominance of particular synoptic types in wet or dry months shows similar diversity. The area experienced above average precipitation in January 1936, 1939 and 1943, and each of these months had eight or more days of Cyclonic type, though with spells of Westerly flow and with the Unclassified and Southerly types also prominent. The extremely wet January of 1937, with 172 mm. recorded at Southampton, had seventeen days of Westerly type and seven days of Southerly type. In contrast, Southampton received little precipitation in January 1949 and 1950, despite a high proportion of days with Westerly and Southerly flow, while Anticyclonic conditions were primarily responsible for the low precipitation in the area during January 1934.

SYNOPTIC CLIMATOLOGY IN JULY

The major controls of summer weather in England are still the Azores High Pressure and travelling depressions from the Atlantic, although the former is now stronger and lies further north; consequently, Atlantic depressions tend to move eastward in rather higher latitudes and are less intense than in winter. Occasions when high pressure develops over Europe are usually associated with extensions of the Azores High. There are no new synoptic types in July, but the climatic characteristics and frequencies differ considerably from January.

Westerly type remains the most frequent synoptic pattern (31 per cent) in July, and although its overall predominance is less marked than in January, there are only two July months in which fewer than five days of Westerly flow occur. In contrast to January, below-average maximum temperatures accompany this air flow as a result of its maritime origin. Average maxima are 19 to 21°C throughout the region with Westerly type, and average minima range from 13°C at lowland stations to 11°C on higher ground. Night cloud cover keeps the minima close to the mean monthly values. Rainfall may be widespread, but daily amounts average only a little over 1 mm. (Table III). The Westerly anticyclonic sub-type gives mainly dry, sunny weather with above-average day temperatures, although clear night skies give cooler than average minima. The Westerly cyclonic sub-type results in rather cool, dull weather, generally with rain. Average falls (1·5 to 3 mm.) are less than in January, but still provide an important contribution to summer rainfall totals.

Cyclonic situations in July (19 per cent) are of increased frequency compared with January, and average rainfall amounts are again considerable; some of the precipitation occurs with thunderstorms. Daily values are 3 to 4 mm. at lowland stations and approximately 5 mm. at Selborne, Shaftesbury and Marlborough, where orographic influence increases the amounts.

IX   Southampton Water, looking north-west, with Fawley on the left and the mouth of the Hamble river on the right

X   The Lymington estuary, looking south-east towards the Isle of Wight. Note the extensive *Spartina* swards on the mud-flats at the mouth of the river

XI   Slumping along the cliffs near Barton-on-Sea (*N.G. ref.* SZ 2493)

XII   Podzol soil-profile above current-bedded Barton Sands in old sand-pit, New Forest (*N.G. ref.* SU 9140)

Spells of Cyclonic type in the July of 1922, 1939 and 1950 made significant contributions to monthly totals, which at Southampton exceeded 100 mm. in each of these three months. Temperature averages are similar to those with the Westerly cyclonic sub-type.

North-westerly (6 per cent) and *Northerly* (4 per cent) situations are slightly more frequent in July than January. The characteristics of the two air flows are similar, for each brings relatively cool, fresh air and light showers interspersed with periods of bright sunshine. Northerly type gives, on average, the lowest maxima and minima, which are 2° to 3°C and 2°C respectively below the mean values for July (Table III).

Easterly type is infrequent in July (3 per cent occurrence), largely as a result of the low frequency of blocking anticyclones over Europe. Nevertheless, the type merits comment in view of its contrasting climatic characteristics in summer and winter. Temperatures, especially minima, are above average when Easterly flow from the Continent does occur in July, although August 1947 provides the best example of a very warm month as a result of Easterly situations. Daily rain amounts with Easterly type in July exceed those in January, averaging 3 to 5 mm., except further west at Shaftesbury. However, many days are dry and the rain occurs mainly as thundery showers.

Southerly flow is also less frequent in July (5 per cent of days). Temperature conditions are almost identical with those for Easterly type, though rainfall is less. Average daily falls range from 1·5 to 3 mm., except where the orographic influence of the South Downs increases the figure to 4·5 mm. at Selborne (Table III).

The warmest days in July occur under *Anticyclonic* situations (15 per cent frequency) at all stations (except Ryde and Sandown), and in some cases the average maxima are 3°C above the mean July maximum. Actual values are several degrees lower at coastal stations than inland, owing to the development of sea breezes on many occasions. July and August 1949, with a high proportion of Anticyclonic days, illustrate the agreeable summer weather which usually accompanies high pressure in summer. The mean daily maxima for July and August of that year were 24·7°C and 24·1°C at Southampton. Average minimum temperatures with Anticyclonic type in July are close to the monthly mean minimum.

The 'Unclassified' category accounts for 5 per cent of days in July, as in January, although a much smaller proportion of the month's precipitation falls on these days. Average temperatures are also closer to the monthly mean values (Table III).

The typical features of the synoptic patterns in July are not necessarily found every year, as has been demonstrated for January conditions. In July 1921 and July 1934 high average maxima and dry conditions were experienced at Southampton, and two-thirds of each month was dominated by Westerly and Anticyclonic types. Similarly, there were eighteen and twenty days, respectively, of Westerly flow during July 1923 and July 1933, occurring in long spells, and both were dry months, with temperatures well above average at Southampton. The July minima in these latter cases were the two highest at Southampton during the period 1921-50. In July 1922, on the other hand, there were fifteen days of Westerly type, four of the Westerly cyclonic sub-type and seven days of Cyclonic type, but at Southampton the average daily maximum and minimum temperatures were well below average, and the rainfall total of 109 mm. was the third highest for 1921-50. The Westerly

Gs

days in this month, however, did not constitute a long spell and the occurrence of a similar sequence in July 1936, again a very wet, cool month at Southampton, emphasises the need to take into account not simply the total frequency of a type but also the duration of particular spells and their relation with other synoptic types.

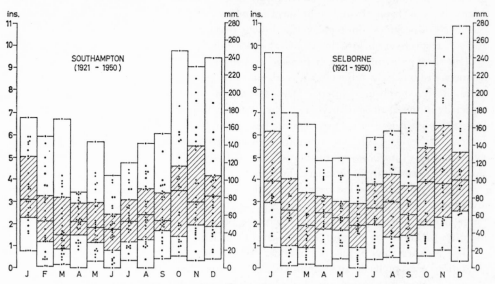

Fig. 24. Monthly precipitation at Southampton and Selborne, 1921-50

Based on data supplied by the Meteorological Office Archives.
Each dot represents the precipitation in the particular month for a single year. The shaded portion indicates the central 50 per cent of the monthly values.

CLIMATIC ELEMENTS THROUGHOUT THE YEAR

Other climatic elements and their seasonal variations in the area will now be treated in a more standard climatological analysis, owing to the lack of detailed information about their relationships with the synoptic types.

Precipitation

Average annual totals of precipitation (1916-50) range from 700 mm. (27·6 inches) between Portsmouth and Selsey Bill to over 940 mm. (37 inches) on high ground in Dorset and at the western end of the South Downs. The distribution of annual averages (Fig. 21) reflects broad features of the relief in the area, with the high ground which encloses the area, including St. Catherine's Down (Isle of Wight), receiving an average total exceeding 880 mm. This figure is also achieved over the northern part of the New Forest. The effect of orography for particular synoptic patterns appears to be most important at Selborne for

Southerly and Cyclonic types in July and Westerly and Cyclonic types in January (Table II). The sheltering influence of the high ground is evident in the areas inland which receive less than 760 mm., and a similar effect east of the Isle of Wight is probably responsible in part for the low totals along the coastal strip to the east of Portsmouth. Certainly Southsea and

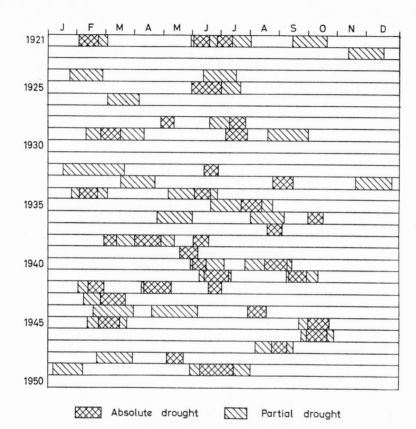

Fig. 25. Droughts at Ventnor, Isle of Wight, 1921-50

Based on data in successive volumes of *British Rainfall*, 1921-50.
Absolute drought: fifteen successive days, each with less than 0·25 mm. rainfall.
Partial drought: twenty-nine days, each with an average daily rainfall of less than 0·25 mm.

Bognor Regis have lower daily averages of precipitation than Sandown for Westerly types in both January and July (Tables II, III).

Stations in the area have between approximately 160 to 190 rain days (greater than 0·2 mm. in 24 hours) per year, of which nearly 75 per cent are wet days (greater than 1·0 mm.), as Table III shows. Comparison of the annual average rainfall and number of rain days at Southampton and Selborne shows that there is a greater increase of rainfall amount than number of rain days with increased elevation.

The months October to January receive most rain, with over 75 mm. in each month throughout the region and more than 100 mm. in November, December and January at many upland stations. Nevertheless, large departures from average may occur in individual months, as the dispersion graphs show (Fig. 24). If the median value is adopted, October is the wettest month (1921-50) at Southampton and December at Selborne, though monthly mean values (1916-50) show November as the wettest month throughout the region (Table III). This month has high frequencies of Westerly and Cyclonic types, although on rare occasions Anticyclonic and Easterly or Northerly spells give a mainly dry November in the area, as in 1933 and 1942. The lowest monthly averages are in June at almost all stations in central south England, though March to June are all relatively dry months and April and June in particular also show low variability (Fig. 24). It may be noted that the decrease in average monthly totals in spring and summer is relatively greater than the decrease in the number of rain days (Table III), indicating low average falls in these seasons.

Droughts are most common in spring or summer and may occur in two years out of three at this time of year, as Fig. 25 indicates for Ventnor. The dryness of spring and early summer is characteristic of all of Britain and is in part related to a low frequency of Westerly flow. Anticyclonic type is particularly frequent in May and June, while Northerly flow and to a lesser extent Easterly flow are relatively important in April and May.

The low average rainfall of spring and early summer coincides with long hours of sunshine, amounting on average to 44 per cent of the possible latitudinal total of sunshine at Southampton in May and June. The combined effect frequently leads to a deficit of soil moisture in summer. The average water loss, during April to September, by evapotranspiration from a grass cover adequately supplied with water ('potential evapotranspiration') exceeds the average rainfall for the same months by 50 to 75 mm. in northern parts of the area and by 125 to 150 mm. on the Isle of Wight, on the mainland adjacent to the Solent and Spithead and in coastal Sussex. Consequently, irrigation may be necessary in the latter areas to obtain full growth of crops in at least nine summers out of ten, although soil differences may modify or exacerbate the importance of the purely climatological factors.

Snow

Both the frequency and amount of snowfall are very variable from year to year. There may be no snow over much of the area even in January or February in approximately one year in three (Table V), yet snow flurries occur at Southampton in many years on one or two days in April. These late falls occur especially with outbreaks of cold, unstable Northerly or North-westerly air flow. The figures in Table V suggest that the effect of 300 to 400 feet of elevation increases snowfall frequency by only the same amount as does the change from a coastal to a low-lying inland locality. In most years, snow lies on low ground in the area for a very short time (Table VI), and even at Larkhill the average duration is only just over two days in January and February. It is, however, important to note that data of snow frequency are greatly affected by exceptional winters. For example, snow fell at South-ampton on twenty-nine days during the period January to March 1947 and lay on the ground for seventeen days, although it persisted for thirty-eight days during the same period at Larkhill. During the more severe winter of 1962-3, snow lay continuously at South-ampton from 26 December to 8 March.

Thunderstorms

Recent investigation of thunderstorm distribution over Britain during 1955-9 shows that there is a high annual frequency over the eastern half of the Isle of Wight and the area immediately east of Southampton Water, with an average of approximately eighteen storms per year. The number decreases quite rapidly westward to between six and twelve per year in Dorset. Seasonal frequency shows the usual July-August maximum, when thunderstorms often originate over France or the Channel and travel north or north-eastward to cross the south coast about mid-day. In winter, however, many of the storms occur during the evening or night. Thunderstorms tend to be associated with Cyclonic situations at any season, but they may also be associated with Southerly or Easterly flow, especially in summer, or with low pressure troughs in North-westerly or Northerly flow.

Temperature

The contrasts of temperature between coastal and inland areas have already been outlined. The magnitude of the difference in summer may be illustrated by comparison of the average July maximum of 21·5°C at Southampton with the corresponding figures of 19·9°C at Bognor Regis and 20·5°C at Sandown. The difference between Sandown and Southampton is greatest for Southerly and Anticyclonic types (Table III); the higher value at Southampton with Southerly flow is indicative of sheltering, and with Anticyclonic situations the frequent development of sea breezes in spring and summer limit maxima near the coast. In January the average minimum temperature at Southampton is 1·1°C less than at Sandown and this difference occurs to a greater or less extent with the average minima for all the synoptic types (Table II). The average January maximum at Sandown is slightly higher than at Southampton, although the difference is greatly reduced with Westerly and Cyclonic types owing to the generally dull, rainy conditions.

The effect of elevation on temperatures appears to be most marked for minimum values, if figures at Southampton and Porton are compared. Annual mean maxima and minima at Porton are respectively 0·7°C and 1·8°C lower than at Southampton. The difference between the minima is 1·7°C in January and 2·0°C in July, whereas that between the maxima is 0·8°C in January and 0·2°C in July. The height difference between the stations would only produce a mean temperature difference of 0·6°C, and inland location itself is not responsible since Porton and Marlborough have lower average minima than Shaftesbury (680 feet). These differences indicate the important influence of actual station sites, particularly on minimum temperatures.

The range of temperatures experienced at Southampton between 1921-50 is shown in Fig. 26. The characteristic pattern of smallest departures of the lowest monthly minima in summer and of the highest monthly maxima in winter is clearly demonstrated. The extremes recorded during 1921-50 were − 11°C (12°F) in February 1929 and 34°C (93°F) in August 1947.

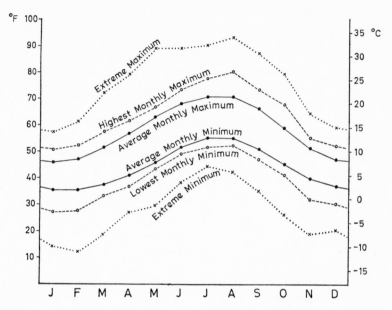

Fig. 26. Temperatures at Southampton, 1921-50

Based on *Averages of temperatures for Great Britain and Northern Ireland, 1921-50*, M.O. 571 (London, 1953).

Ground Frost

Ground frost occurs on approximately ten days per month from December to March, even at exposed coastal stations. More important from the point of view of agriculture is the fact that June to September is frost free and even May and October escape ground frost in about one year in three (Table VII) near the coast. Southampton has slightly more ground frost than coastal stations, but stations further inland show greatly increased frequencies. Larkhill (431 feet) can expect ground frost, on average, every other night during December to March and the risk remains high even in May. Frosts in June and even August were by no means unknown at Larkhill in the 1920's and 1930's and there was an isolated occurrence on 1 July 1924, although no ground frosts occurred during these months between 1937 and 1950.

Winds

The prevailing winds over the area are from south-west or west, and it is from this sector that gale-force winds are most common. Important differences of direction are observable at different hours of the day in summer as Fig. 27 demonstrates for Calshot. There is a significant increase in the frequency of winds with a southerly component during the afternoon, whereas winds with a northerly component decrease in frequency from 0700 to 1200 GMT. Many of these cases arise from the reversal of the gradient wind by the development of a sea breeze. South-westerly winds at Calshot are over-represented owing to wind channelling along the Solent. Nevertheless, the data at 1200 GMT in July undoubtedly underestimate the frequency of sea breezes, since the necessary conditions may not occur until mid-afternoon if there are opposing gradient winds of 10 to 15 m.p.h., or if the air mass is stable. Their development is dependent upon the temperature over the land exceeding that of the adjacent sea surface; the excess required is determined by the pressure gradient and the stability of the air. The reversal of wind direction takes place gradually if the air is stable. The necessary conditions for sea breezes occur mainly between May and September, although they may develop earlier in the year when the sea surface is cold, should a day of warm weather cause temperatures to rise markedly over the land. In addition to modifying or reversing the wind direction, the onset of a sea breeze produces in many cases a marked fall of temperature and a rise in humidity. These effects may be perceptible even away from the coast as the landward boundary or 'front' of the sea breeze, which is sometimes marked by cumulus clouds, moves slowly inland, penetrating on some occasions for 30 to 40 miles by 1800 or 1900 hours. However, the effect of sea breezes is only of real climatic significance along the coastal fringe.

A further small-scale feature of the wind régime is the nocturnal land breeze, which may reverse a sea breeze or a light southerly gradient wind. The coastal plain of eastern Hampshire and western Sussex is a preferred area for these winds because of the katabatic drift of air down the slope of the South Downs. They may develop at any time of year when the sky is clear, commencing two to four hours after sunset.

Fog

Poor visibility is of great concern in the activities of sea- and air-ports of the region, and consequently considerable interest attaches to fog data (the official definition of fog is visibility below 1100 yards). Fog is most frequent in the autumn and winter months and, although sea fogs are not uncommon on summer mornings, radiation is the major cause even near the coast. This seasonal régime may be contrasted with the spring and early summer maximum along the coasts of the South-west Peninsula where advection fogs predominate. Pollution at Southampton and Portsmouth helps to increase the frequency and intensity of fogs in the Solent area in autumn and winter, and the effect is detectable at Calshot when the wind direction is between north-west and east (Fig. 28). There are marked diurnal variations of fog occurrence (Fig. 29); the maximum frequency at Calshot is

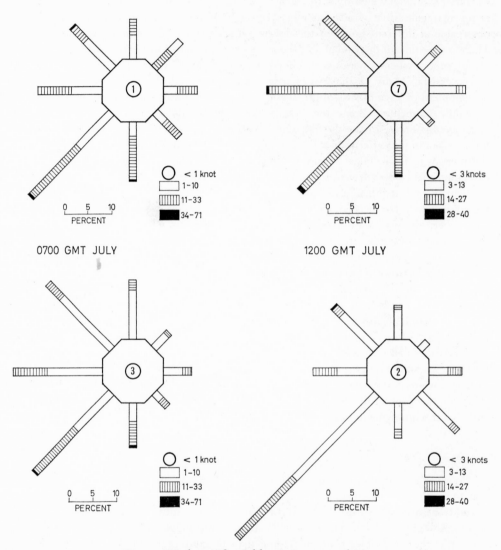

Fig. 27. Wind-roses for Calshot in January and July

Based on data in *Weather in home waters and the north-eastern Atlantic*, vol. II, part 3, 'The English Channel', M.O. 446b. (3) (London, 1940).

The period of observation for 0700 GMT January and July is 1921–39, for 1200 GMT January and July is 1921–34. The roses show percentage frequency of winds of given force and direction, with calms and winds of less than 3 knots given in the centre circles.

approximately one to two hours after sunrise throughout the year, though in December and January fogs often persist for much of the day. The nocturnal winds discussed earlier may delay the onset of fog in the eastern coastal section, or even disperse fog or mist which has formed. However, in the coastal area of western Hampshire, where there are no nearby hills, it may be expected that radiation fogs will be rather more frequent.

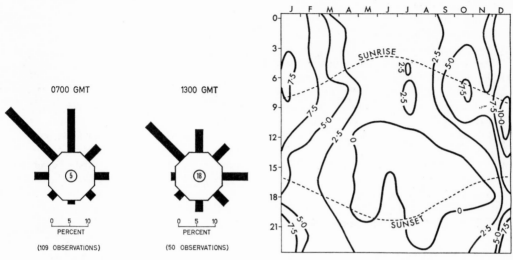

Fig. 28. Poor visibility and wind direction in autumn and winter at Calshot, 1926-35

Based on data in *Weather in home waters and the north-eastern Atlantic*, vol. II, part 3, 'The English Channel', M.O. 446b. (3) (London, 1940). The figure shows frequency of visibility below a half nautical mile, with wind from a given direction expressed as a percentage of all cases of visibility below a half nautical mile for the period September–February, 1926-35.

Fig. 29. Diurnal variation of fog throughout the year at Calshot, 1953-60

Based on data supplied by the Harbour Master, Southampton Harbour Board, to the Southampton Weather Centre.
Isolines indicate percentage frequency of visibility below 1100 yards. Figures in the left margin indicate time of day on the 24-hour system. Times of sunrise and sunset are indicated by pecked lines.

Rather limited pre-1939 data indicate more frequent morning fog for inland stations than at Calshot; the difference is small in winter, but for June to August, 1927-36, the fog frequency at 0700 is 2 per cent at Calshot, compared with 7 per cent at Boscombe Down and 5 per cent at Worthy Down. The importance of radiation, causing lower minimum temperatures, is clearly demonstrated. It is of interest to note that poor visibility (below $2\frac{1}{4}$ miles) in winter at Worthy Down and Andover has been shown to occur most often during calms or with light winds from between north-east and east, which bring smoke as much as 60 to 70 miles from the Greater London area.

BIBLIOGRAPHICAL NOTE

The author wishes to express his gratitude for assistance from the Director and staff of the Computer Laboratory of the University of Southampton; Mr. H. H. Lamb of the Meteorological Office; Mr. T. E. Oliver of the Meteorological Office Archives; and the staff of Southampton Weather Centre, High Street, Southampton.

(1) H. H. Lamb, 'Types and spells of weather around the year in the British Isles: annual trends, seasonal structure of the year, singularities', *Quarterly Journal of the Royal Meteorological Society* (1950), vol. 76, pp. 393-429.

(2) Meteorological Office, M.O. 446b (3), *Weather in home waters and the north-eastern Atlantic*, vol. II, part 3: 'The English Channel' (London, 1940), 179 pp.

(3) Meteorological Office, M.O. 521, *Percentage frequencies of various visibility ranges at certain places in the British Isles, between the years 1927 and 1936* (London, 1949), 52 pp.

(4) R. C. Miller and L. G. Starrett, 'Thunderstorms in Great Britain', *Meteorological Magazine* (1962), vol. 91, pp. 247-55.

(5) B. J. Moffit, 'Nocturnal wind at Thorney Island', *Meteorological Magazine* (1956), vol. 85, pp. 268-71.

(6) C. V. Ockenden, 'A comparison between surface wind and ground day-visibility at Andover and Winchester (Hants.) over the four years 1924 to 1927', *Quarterly Journal of the Royal Meteorological Society* (1928), vol. 54, pp. 337-40.

(7) R. T. Pearl (ed.), *The calculation of irrigation need*, Technical Bulletin No. 4, Ministry of Agriculture, Fisheries and Food (London, 1954), 34 pp.

(8) S. P. Peters, 'Sea breezes at Worthy Down, Winchester', *Professional Notes, Meteorological Office* (1938), vol. VI (6), 11 pp.

(9) S. P. Peters and C. F. J. Jestico, 'The variation of low-cloud amount from mid-day to early evening in winter at Worthy Down, Winchester', *Quarterly Journal of the Royal Meteorological Society* (1934), vol. 60, pp. 356-8.

(10) A. J. Watts, 'Sea breeze at Thorney Island', *Meteorological Magazine* (1955), vol. 84, pp. 42-8.

Table II. Averages of Daily Precipitation and Temperatures for Types of Air Flow in January (1921-50)

Types*	Height in feet	Nw	N	E	S	Wa	W	Wc	C	A	U	January Average
Number of cases		35	32	49	105	23	372	28	110	96	43	
Station		PRECIPITATION (mm.)										
Bognor Regis	24	0·84	0·84	2·69	2·77	0·28	2·94	2·62	3·96	0·56	4·01	
Bournemouth†	139	1·32	0·71	2·06	4·24	0·66	2·79	2·74	4·06	0·71	4·55	
Sandown	13	1·55	0·91	2·49	3·76	0·33	3·28	2·69	3·79	0·59	3·61	
Southsea†	7	1·15	0·64	2·37	3·43	0·28	2·92	2·54	3·68	0·56	3·69	
Southampton	65	0·96	0·56	2·39	3·76	0·54	3·30	3·38	4·24	0·61	3·91	
Selborne	400	0·94	0·91	2·77	4·06	0·18	4·29	4·77	5·38	0·56	5·23	
Porton	363	0·51	0·56	2·08	3·43	0·30	2·77	2·34	3·69	0·51	4·14	
Shaftesbury	680	0·91	0·94	1·81	3·56	0·76	2·87	2·82	3·56	0·66	3·59	
		MEAN DAILY MAXIMUM (°C)										
Bognor Regis		7·6	4·7	4·1	7·3	7·7	9·1	9·4	7·8	4·7	5·9	7·4
Bournemouth		7·9	4·9	3·9	7·7	7·8	9·6	10·0	8·1	4·7	6·1	7·8
Sandown		8·1	4·7	4·4	8·0	7·9	9·8	10·2	8·5	5·2	6·6	8·1
Southsea		7·9	4·7	4·3	7·7	7·5	9·4	10·0	8·3	5·1	6·1	7·9
Southampton‡		8·0	5·1	3·7	7·4	7·4	9·5	10·2	8·2	4·8	5·9	7·7
Porton		6·8	3·5	2·6	6·7	6·8	8·9	9·3	7·1	3·8	4·8	6·9
Shaftesbury		6·4	3·3	2·6	6·9	6·4	8·3	8·6	6·7	3·3	5·0	6·6
		MEAN DAILY MINIMUM (°C)										
Bognor Regis		2·2	−0·3	−0·1	2·4	1·8	3·9	4·6	3·6	−0·2	1·3	2·6
Bournemouth		2·6	−0·4	−0·6	2·0	1·3	3·8	4·1	3·3	−1·2	1·3	2·2
Sandown		3·1	0·2	0·6	3·3	2·3	4·3	4·7	3·8	0·3	2·1	3·1
Southsea		3·2	0·6	0·2	2·8	2·3	4·2	4·8	3·9	0·0	1·7	3·0
Southampton‡		2·1	−0·3	−1·0	2·1	0·5	3·4	3·8	3·0	−1·1	0·9	2·0
Porton		0·6	−2·3	−1·5	−0·1	−0·7	1·7	1·7	1·4	−2·7	−0·7	0·3
Shaftesbury		0·8	−1·6	−2·0	1·2	1·3	2·8	2·6	1·6	−1·9	−0·3	1·2

* **Nw**=North-westerly; **N**=Northerly; **E**=Easterly; **S**=Southerly; **Wa**=Westerly anticyclonic; **W**=Westerly; **Wc**=Westerly cyclonic; **C**=Cyclonic; **A**=Anticyclonic; **U**=Unclassified.

† 1926-50 only.

‡ No data for January 1941.

Note: Precipitation data are only significant to one decimal place.

Source: Average temperatures for January and July are derived from 'Averages of temperature for Great Britain and Northern Ireland, 1921-50', M.O. 571 (London, 1953).

Table III. Averages of Daily Precipitation and Temperatures for Types of Air Flow in July (1921-50)

Types*	Height in feet	Nw	N	E	S	Wa	W	Wc	C	A	U	July Average
Number of cases		52	39	26	43	37	293	46	176	137	48	
Station		PRECIPITATION (mm.)										
Bognor Regis†	24	0·79	0·54	4·32	2·89	0·35	1·15	1·70	3·84	0·59	1·62	
Bournemouth‡	139	0·74	1·67	5·03	2·59	0·64	1·20	1·47	3·15	0·59	2·03	
Sandown	13	1·14	0·64	5·18	2·84	0·47	1·27	1·90	3·79	0·61	1·65	
Southsea‡	7	0·74	0·56	4·72	2·87	0·30	1·10	1·57	3·13	0·56	1·70	
Southampton	65	1·10	0·71	2·79	2·69	0·91	1·15	2·01	4·42	0·64	1·15	
Selborne	400	1·45	1·02	4·42	4·50	0·96	1·40	2·59	5·41	0·66	1·67	
Porton	363	0·88	0·56	5·43	2·06	0·40	1·25	1·96	3·68	0·54	1·70	
Shaftesbury	680	0·69	0·76	2·34	1·72	0·40	1·42	2·97	4·65	0·37	2·15	
		MEAN DAILY MAXIMUM (°C)										
Bognor Regis†		19·3	18·1	20·6	20·1	21·6	19·7	18·4	18·7	21·6	20·6	19·9
Bournemouth		20·3	19·3	21·5	21·9	23·7	21·1	19·6	19·7	24·0	21·8	21·4
Sandown		19·9	18·9	21·0	20·7	22·6	20·4	19·3	19·3	22·1	20·7	20·5
Southsea§		20·1	18·8	22·2	22·2	23·3	21·1	20·0	20·0	23·5	21·7	21·3
Southampton§§		20·2	19·2	22·6	22·9	23·9	21·2	19·6	19·8	24·4	21·6	21·5
Porton		19·4	18·6	21·6	22·9	23·8	21·1	19·6	19·7	24·3	21·8	21·3
Shaftesbury		18·4	17·6	20·1	21·4	22·7	19·6	17·8	18·3	23·2	20·3	19·9
		MEAN DAILY MINIMUM (°C)										
Bognor Regis†		12·0	11·3	14·5	14·7	12·3	13·3	13·2	14·1	13·4	13·5	13·4
Bournemouth		11·6	10·8	13·6	13·6	11·4	12·7	12·6	13·2	12·4	12·7	12·7
Sandown		12·3	11·8	14·6	14·8	12·4	13·3	13·1	13·9	13·7	13·6	13·4
Southsea§		12·7	11·9	14·8	15·0	12·8	13·9	13·4	14·2	14·1	14·1	13·9
Southampton		11·4	10·7	14·1	13·9	11·6	12·7	12·3	13·3	12·8	12·7	12·7
Porton		9·5	8·9	12·6	12·1	9·0	10·5	10·6	11·5	10·5	10·9	10·7
Shaftesbury		10·3	9·6	12·1	12·2	11·2	11·3	10·8	11·5	12·1	11·2	11·4

* See footnote (*), Table II.
† No data for July 1923.
‡ 1926-50 only.
§ No data for July 1929.
§§ No data for 1 to 23 July 1941.

Table IV. Averages of Rainfall (1916-50) and Frequency of Rain Days and Wet Days (1921-50)

Southampton

	J	F	M	A	M	J	J	A	S	O	N	D	Year
(a)	18·1	13·0	12·8	13·0	12·9	11·0	12·9	12·8	13·3	14·7	16·5	16·5	167·4
(b)	24	26	27	23	23	21	22	21	25	26	27	27	203 (1927)
(c)	14·1	9·4	9·1	9·7	9·0	8·3	9·2	9·4	9·9	11·4	12·0	12·3	124·0
(d)	87·1	58·9	53·1	54·6	51·6	44·2	61·5	66·0	64·5	84·1	92·0	86·1	803·7

Selborne

	J	F	M	A	M	J	J	A	S	O	N	D	Year
(a)	19·8	14·6	13·1	14·5	13·4	12·2	14·2	14·5	14·4	16·8	18·4	18·4	184·2
(b)	26	24	24	23	23	23	28	26	23	26	27	28	212 (1927)
(c)	15·0	10·9	9·8	11·1	10·4	9·1	10·3	10·6	10·9	12·4	12·9	13·2	136·7
(d)	108·7	75·4	63·8	66·0	61·2	50·6	76·0	76·7	74·9	98·8	110·7	106·4	969·3

(a) Average number of rain days (greater than 0·2 mm.).
(b) Maximum number of rain days in any year.
(c) Average number of wet days (greater than 1·0 mm.).
(d) Averages of rainfall (mm.) for 1916-50 (based on 'Averages of rainfall for Great Britain and Northern Ireland, 1916-50', M.O. 635 (London, 1958)).

Table V. Number of Days with Snow or Sleet Falling (1921-50)

Southampton★

	J	F	M	A	M	J	J	A	S	O	N	D	Year
(a)	2·0	2·3	1·8	0·8	0·1	—	—	—	—	0·0	0·2	1·3	8·5
(b)	10	12	7	4	1	—	—	—	—	1	2	7	31 (1947)
(c)	10	10	11	16	26	30	30	30	30	29	26	14	—

Sandown

	J	F	M	A	M	J	J	A	S	O	N	D	Year
(a)	1·2	1·6	0·6	0·3	0·0	—	—	—	—	—	0·0	0·8	4·6
(b)	7	7	4	3	1	—	—	—	—	—	1	7	15 (1947)

Porton

	J	F	M	A	M	J	J	A	S	O	N	D	Year
(a)	2·8	3·2	1·8	0·5	0·0	—	—	—	—	0·1	0·3	1·7	10·6
(b)	11	10	9	3	1	—	—	—	—	1	3	11	26 (1947)
(c)	9	8	11	17	29	30	30	30	30	26	24	11	—

Larkhill

	J	F	M	A	M	J	J	A	S	O	N	D	Year
(a)	2·6	3·2	2·1	1·0	0·1	—	—	—	—	0·2	0·5	2·0	11·7
(b)	8	10	7	6	2	—	—	—	—	1	3	9	22 (1947)

(a) Average.
(b) Maximum number in any year.
(c) Number of years without snow falling.
★ December 1940–June 1941 missing. Annual totals based on twenty-nine years.

Table VI. *Number of Mornings with Snow Lying (1921–50)*

		J	F	M	A	N	D	Year
Southampton*	(a)	1·4	0·9	0·5	—	0·0	0·9	3·7
0900 GMT	(b)	9	8	6	—	1	7	17 (1947)
Larkhill	(a)	2·1	2·5	0·6	0·1	0·2	1·3	6·8
0700 GMT	(b)	10	27	6	2	4	6	40 (1947)

(a) Average.
(b) Maximum number in any year.
* December 1940–June 1941 missing.

Table VII. *Number of Days with Ground Frost* (1921–50)*

Southampton†

	J	F	M	A	M	J	J	A	S	O	N	D	Year
(a)	12·2	13·2	12·2	5·0	1·2	0·0	—	—	0·1	1·9	7·2	11·8	64·8
(b)	27	24	23	16	8	1	—	—	2	8	17	23	106 (1922)

Totland Bay‡

	J	F	M	A	M	J	J	A	S	O	N	D	Year
(a)	11·0	11·1	10·2	4·5	1·5	—	—	—	—	1·6	5·2	9·6	54·6
(b)	24	25	22	15	8	—	—	—	—	7	15	22	90 (1929)

Porton§

	J	F	M	A	M	J	J	A	S	O	N	D	Year
(a)	17·3	16·2	15·5	11·6	5·3	0·7	—	0·1	1·3	6·6	11·9	16·1	102·8
(b)	29	26	24	21	12	4	—	2	5	12	26	27	145 (1929)

Larkhill§§

	J	F	M	A	M	J	J	A	S	O	N	D	Year
(a)	15·5	14·9	14·7	9·7	5·2	0·6	0·0	0·2	1·6	5·9	10·7	14·8	94·1
(b)	28	27	22	21	14	3	1	2	4	11	22	29	119 (1929)

(a) Average.
(b) Maximum number in any year.
* Defined as reading of grass minimum thermometer less than −0·9°C.
† December 1940—June 1941 missing.
‡ 1921–47.
§ January 1922 missing.
§§ February–March 1949 missing.

VII

HYDROLOGY AND WATER SUPPLY

HYDROLOGICAL CHARACTERISTICS

NATURE has been kind to Hampshire in the matter of water resources, a fortunate situation in view of the ever increasing demands of its expanding population and growing industries. While the average annual rainfall is only about 30 inches, the Chalk deposits outcropping over a large part of the county form a most favourable factor. There is some minor folding (Fig. 5), but the general dip is to the south, which is the broad direction of surface drainage (Fig. 30). In the south of the county the Chalk is overlain by relatively impermeable Tertiary deposits. Stream flow in this region is subject to wide fluctuation; heavy rainfall causes a rapid increase in discharge with possible flooding, but after a short period of dry weather the flow is reduced to very meagre proportions.

Over a large area to the north, the Chalk (mainly the Upper subdivision) is exposed, and the landscape is characteristic of chalk upland country: gently undulating contours, large open fields, numerous dry valleys and a marked absence of drainage ditches. At lower levels springs break out, feeding the streams and rivers, the largest being the Test, Itchen and Avon, although the last is shared with Wiltshire and Dorset. These rivers are much cherished by fishermen on account of their constancy of flow and the presence of water weed conducive to fish-life; the dissolved salts emanating from the Chalk foster these desirable aquatic species.

Although chalk is a highly porous rock, in the block form it is relatively impermeable, water seeping through the material at only a very slow rate. However, fissures and well-defined bedding planes in the form of flint layers are normally well distributed throughout the formation. These have a most important role, since they serve as collectors and conduits facilitating the movement of ground water.

In those areas where the Chalk has only a thin soil covering, a high proportion of the rainfall infiltrates into the soil, and surface run-off is negligible except possibly on the steeper slopes. Moisture not returned to the atmosphere via evapotranspiration percolates downwards to the zone of saturation, the upper surface of which (the water-table) may be anything up to 300 feet below ground level. The water-table is not horizontal, but has a slight gradient in the direction of lateral ground-water movement. Water which has traversed these devious underground routes reappears at the surface at springs and seepage points, weeks, months or perhaps even years after it was precipitated.

Thus there normally exists in chalk strata a large store of underground water, which by contrast with a conventional surface reservoir costs nothing to provide, sterilises no land

and is virtually free from loss due to evaporation. As the greater part of river and stream flow is derived from this ground water, the time lag resulting from the slow rate of its movement has a most beneficial stabilising effect, greatly reducing the intensity of floods yet ensuring a well-sustained flow in dry weather.

Data obtained from percolation gauges and other evidence indicate that in a relatively dry summer there is little or no downward percolation to the water-table. Such rainfall as does occur dampens only the surface soil and is subsequently lost through evapotranspiration. Replenishment of ground-water storage is thus greatly dependent on the winter rainfall. In a typical year, then, water-table levels are highest in the late winter or early spring, and fall steadily throughout the summer to a minimum in the autumn. The stream and river flows exhibit similar behaviour, and are obviously directly influenced by the ground-water conditions.

In former times water for domestic and agricultural usage was drawn from wells, generally about 6 feet in diameter, but because of the limited means available only small quantities could be raised. Today the picture is very different. Almost every dwelling-house, farm and indeed field has its piped supply, the water being pumped from boreholes or in some cases from existing wells. Siting of the boreholes is important, for their diameter is often quite small, and a plentiful yield is dependent on the interception of a sufficient number of water-bearing fissures. At favourable sites the yield may be as much as three million gallons per day★ without excessive draw-down.

FLOW MEASUREMENT AND GROUND-WATER OBSERVATIONS

The three principal rivers in central Hampshire are the Test, Itchen and Meon, and the Hampshire River Board maintains a number of gauging stations on these and their tributaries (Fig. 30). Continuous autographic recorders are installed at the three most downstream stations at Broadlands (Test), Allbrook (Itchen) and Mislingford (Meon); these are in fact the nearest practicable measurement sites to the Tertiary boundary. Both the Broadlands and Allbrook stations are of the simple stage-discharge type, but as the stage (i.e. water level) is influenced by weed growth in the river, periodic calibration checks by means of a current meter are essential. A small standing-wave flume has been constructed at Mislingford, so that there is a direct and stable relationship between the upstream head and the discharge. At the remaining stations the discharge is measured at approximately monthly intervals, the only exception being at Broughton on the Wallop brook, a tributary of the Test, where a sharp-crested weir with continuous recorder is installed.

Many variable factors influence the relationship between rainfall and run-off, and for purposes of hydrological analysis comprehensive records extending over a lengthy period are most desirable. In common with most other parts of Britain, the gauging procedure in Hampshire has only been in operation for a brief number of years, although fortunately this period includes an exceedingly wet winter (1960-1) and some dry weather of appreciable

★ Waterworks engineers measure water quantity rates in millions of gallons per day. One million gallons per day is equal to 1·86 cubic feet per second (*cusecs*).

XIII   The river Test near Lower Brook (*N.G. ref.* SU 3429)

XIV   Sectional model of the structure of the Winchester pericline at Chilcomb (*N.G. ref.* SU 5128)

The vertical black lines represent three (of the five) boreholes sited along a line which runs almost north–south. The white layer, immediately below the surface, is the Chalk, underlain by Upper Greensand (pale-grey) and Gault (grey). The white layer below the Gault is sandy Lower Greensand and the dark band below is the Atherfield Clay. Below the latter are Wealden Beds which are coloured grey if clayey and white if sandy.

XV The Conduit Head, in the grounds of Nazareth House, Hill Lane, Southampton

XVI The intake pumping station on the river Itchen, at Otterbourne Waterworks (*N.G. ref.* SU 7032)

XVII The tidal mill at Ashlett Creek (*N.G. ref.* SU 6533)

duration (in 1959 and 1962). Consideration of the data has already revealed some interesting and important facts.

For instance, the highest recorded flows at Broadlands, Allbrook and Mislingford in the winter of 1960-1 were 1330, 450 and 220 cusecs respectively. These flows included a substantial amount of surface run-off. By contrast, the minimum flows (autumn recordings) derived entirely from ground water, were 220, 90 and 5 cusecs respectively. On this basis

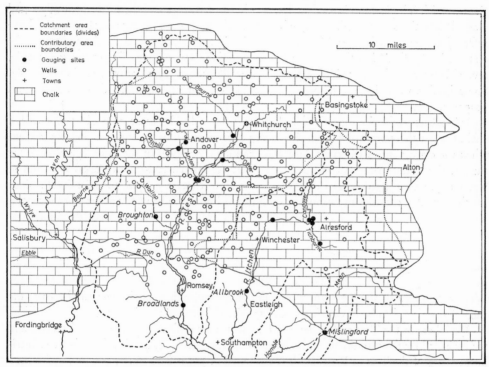

Fig. 30. The Test, Itchen and Meon catchments
Based on an original map supplied by the Hampshire River Board.

the ratios between maximum and minimum flow are thus 6:1, 5:1 and 44:1. In comparison with the vast majority of rivers in this country, these ratios are remarkably small, and in the case of the Test and the Itchen exceptionally so; they are a striking testimony to the effectiveness of an underground reservoir in regulating the discharge. The higher ratio for the Meon is due both to the configuration of the catchment, which is of relatively narrow width, and to its geological composition and structure. The Middle and Lower Chalk are exposed over a large portion of the catchment, and as aquifers these formations are inferior to the Upper Chalk. In particular, the marly nature of the Lower Chalk tends to seal the fissures, thereby reducing the degree of transmissibility within the aquifer.

Hs

For the Broadlands and Allbrook gauging sites, characteristic recession curves of base flow (i.e. dry-weather flow) have been deduced. With this information it is possible to forecast the minimum flow at the end of a dry summer, assuming that there is no replenishment of the aquifer. Proposals for direct abstraction for water supply or farm irrigation can thus be critically examined, with a view to ensuring that fishery, public health and amenity interests are adequately safeguarded.

The flow variation is normally much greater in the tributaries and near the sources of the rivers, which is logical in view of the lesser volume of storage and the movement of ground water below the stream bed. Many of the upland streams are of a seasonal nature and are referred to locally as *bournes*. The starting point in a valley is primarily dependent on the water-table levels within the aquifer; at the end of the wet winter of 1960-1, for example, several bournes broke out at higher levels in the valleys than were known to living memory. Some hardship and inconvenience were caused by the sustained flooding of roads and property.

It is common for the superficial and ground-water divides to be coincident, but with a chalk aquifer there are quite often significant differences. This became particularly evident when the catchment of the river Alre was examined. Analysis of the discharge records for the gauging station near Alresford showed that the annual run-off expressed as inches of water depth on the superficial catchment was almost exactly equal to the rainfall. Since for the southern counties the annual evaporation is known to be of the order of 18 inches, it was obvious that the effective contributory area was much greater than the superficial catchment. Indeed, the observed discharges of neighbouring streams, well records and geological conditions all pointed to the fact that the effective contributory area must extend much further in an easterly direction as far as the chalk escarpment, thereby adding about 28 square miles. Further confirmation was provided by the discharge data of the river Wey, a tributary of the Thames, which drains the adjoining catchment to the east; the run-off was found to be in deficit to an approximately corresponding extent.

Elsewhere in the Test and Itchen catchments minor differences have been detected, and are indicated by the catchment outlines shown in Fig. 30. Accordingly, the effective contributory area of the Test at Broadlands is estimated at 385 square miles, as compared with a superficial area of 403 square miles, whilst for the Itchen at Allbrook the corresponding areas are 169 square miles and 139 square miles respectively. The word 'estimated' must be emphasised, for the ground-water divides have not been precisely established. Indeed, there are indications of a small seasonal variation in some localities.

On the basis of the estimated contributory areas, the average run-off from the catchments comprising the Upper Chalk has been found to be slightly in excess of 1 cusec per square mile, while the maximum run-off is about 2·5 cusecs per square mile. Local variations are small and are attributable to physiographical and geological factors, such as the major joints induced by folding. It has not so far been practicable to make any comparable deductions for the Middle and Lower Chalk.

Movement of ground water within an aquifer is dependent on the permeability of the strata and on gradients of the water-table. The latter may be estimated from observations of the standing water level in wells; unfortunately, many have been filled in or slabbed over, but a reasonable number are still accessible. During the past few years the Hampshire River Board has made periodic observations on about 200 of these, their locations being indicated in Fig. 30. Since the seasonal fluctuation of level is often appreciable, measurements in an area of likely mutual influence are taken as far as possible within a short time of each other. In addition, a few autographic recorders with monthly charts have been installed at suitable sites.

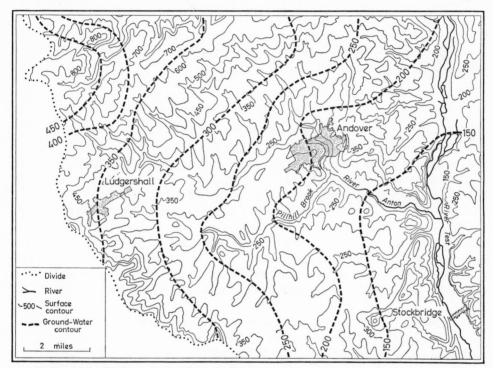

Fig. 31. Superficial contours and assumed ground-water contours of the Andover district
Based on an original map supplied by the Hampshire River Board. The main built-up areas are stippled.

For obvious reasons, the ground-water contours are much flatter than the corresponding topographical contours, but there is generally some resemblance, the highest ground-water levels and greatest depth to the water-table tending to occur beneath the highest ground, although there are many exceptions. A typical relationship is depicted in Fig. 31, a map of the Andover district with the estimated ground-water contours in March 1962 shown superimposed on the surface relief contours.

The well observations carried out to date indicate that the greatest variation of the water-table is at Vernham Dean (66 feet in 1961-2), and that some of the smallest variations are on the high ground in the Chute district, which is known to be a poor source of water supply. The winter hydraulic gradient west of the Test is of the order of 30 feet to the mile, but it is as high as 100 feet to the mile in the Chute district and as low as 15 feet to the mile north of Vernham Dean and west of Fullerton. Winter gradients to the east of the Test in the Overton district tend to be small (about 10 feet to the mile), while gradients to the west of Winchester are high (about 100 feet to the mile). For the greater part of the Test and Itchen catchments, gradients are on an average about 25 to 30 feet to the mile.

Thus a useful start has been made on hydrological studies of the chalk areas of Hampshire. In the course of the years, as further data become available, we can look forward to a more detailed knowledge and better understanding of local surface- and ground-water behaviour. At present, there are too many important questions for which the answers must necessarily be largely conjectural.

THE WATER SUPPLY OF SOUTHAMPTON AND THE NEIGHBOURING DISTRICT

Public water supply in Hampshire is the responsibility of a number of undertakings, the various statutory areas being outlined in Fig. 32. The Southampton Corporation undertaking serves the largest area in the county, 570 square miles, involving a population of 396,000 (1963). Southampton was one of the first towns in Britain to have a piped supply of water, the source of supply being springs in the plateau-gravels (Plate XV). In 1310 a monastic order in which rights were vested granted the use of the water to the inhabitants. About a century later, in 1420, the supply was taken over by the town, thereafter remaining in municipal ownership. This supply, with the later addition of springs in the Grosvenor Square area, was led to the water-house in Commercial Road, which is still in existence opposite the Gaumont Cinema. From there water was conveyed by a lead pipe, about 4 inches in diameter, past the Bargate to the Friary, situated near to God's House Tower adjoining the Town Quay.

Supplies from these local springs were adequate to meet water needs until the nineteenth century, when a marked increase in population was associated with the development of Southampton as a major port, while the simultaneous rise of Eastleigh as a railway centre created an appreciable additional nearby demand. In 1838 an attempt was made to obtain water from the underground storage in the Chalk by sinking a well and borehole on Southampton Common; a depth of 1317 feet was reached, but the yield was not satisfactory and the works were not proceeded with. In 1851 a pumping station (subsequently abandoned) was constructed at Mansbridge on the river Itchen between Southampton and Eastleigh. Then in 1888 a waterworks was established at Otterbourne adjacent to the Itchen upstream of Eastleigh, the pumps being capable of delivering up to 2 million gallons per day from wells and adits in the Chalk.

In 1921 Southampton Corporation acquired the adjoining undertaking of the South Hants Water Company, thereby adding two major additional sources of supply: the Timsbury pumping station near Romsey, and the Twyford pumping station about 2 miles north-east of Otterbourne. Increasing demands led to the enlarging of the Otterbourne works in 1925, and in 1942 to the commissioning of a pumping station, together with treatment plant, for the purpose of direct abstraction from the Itchen (Plate XVI). The authorising act stipulated a maximum abstraction of 10 million gallons per day, though the full pumping potential was not provided until later. This new source of supply was of

Fig. 32. Areas served by various water undertakings in Hampshire

Based on an original map supplied by the Southampton Corporation Water Undertaking.
The area of the Southampton County Borough is stippled.

great value in the early days of the 1944 invasion of France, when more than 100 million gallons of water were transported in tankers from Southampton Docks to the Normandy coast.

Since the War consumption has increased apace, rising from an average of 12 million gallons a day in 1945 to 19 million gallons a day in 1962. To meet this demand the Otterbourne and Twyford works have been further developed. Fig. 33 shows the present lay-out

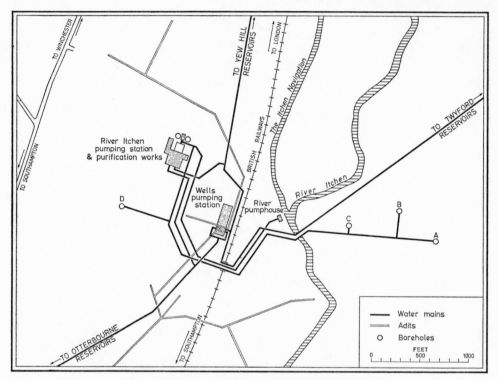

Fig. 33. The layout of the Otterbourne Waterworks

Based on an original map supplied by the Southampton Corporation Water Undertaking. The four main boreholes are lettered A to D.

of the former; the adits are situated about 100 feet below the surface, and the boreholes are up to 500 feet in depth. In addition to development of the sources, many miles of trunk main have been laid, together with the provision of reservoirs and ancillary works (such as booster stations) for peak demands.

In furtherance of the Government policy of amalgamation within the water industry, a number of the smaller Hampshire undertakings were in 1962 transferred to the Southampton Corporation. The enlarged area of supply (570 square miles) coincides approximately with the catchments of the Test and Itchen, with the exclusion at present of those areas which are supplied by the undertakings of the Winchester City and Winchester Rural District Councils. The distribution system is outlined in Fig. 32. There are twelve pumping stations, thirty-eight service reservoirs and water towers, and 1185 miles of mains.

For the immediate future, the continuing expansion of population and industry, and more particularly the oil refinery extensions and the new power-station at Fawley (see p. 265), have made it imperative to establish an additional major source of supply. To meet this need the Corporation are constructing a waterworks on the Test just upstream of the tidal limit, scheduled for completion in 1966. Ministerial approval has been given for the direct abstraction of up to 18 million gallons per day.

For the long term the Corporation are planning to meet a demand (excluding that of major industries) of 28 million gallons per day in 1970, rising to 46 million gallons per day in the year 2000. The aim is to establish an integrated system throughout the distribution area, linking the various separate networks and concentrating the sources of supply into the principal pumping stations. It is anticipated that the future demand can be met from local resources by the establishment of the new works on the Test and by further development of the boreholes. The hydrological studies referred to earlier will be of particular value in the latter respect.

BIBLIOGRAPHICAL NOTE

(1) *County Survey of Water Resources*, Report (1947), submitted to the Hampshire County Council by Herbert Lapworth Partners (unpublished).
(2) C. A. Bradley, 'The river Itchen supply', *Journal of the Institution of Water Engineers* (1948), vol. 2, pp. 333-57.
(3) J. Hawksley, 'Southampton's water supply', *ibid.*, pp. 369-76.
(4) A. T. Macdonald and W. J. Kenyon, 'Run-off of chalk streams', *Proceedings of the Institution of Civil Engineers* (1961), vol. 19, pp. 23-38.
(5) W. Matthews, *Underground water-levels in the Chalk in the valleys of the Test and Itchen*, Memoir of the Geological Survey on the Water Supply of Hampshire (1910).
(6) N. B. Webber, 'The base-flow recession curve: its derivation and application', *Journal of the Institution of Water Engineers* (1961), vol. 15, pp. 368-86.

Appendix

HYDROLOGY IN THE PAST

One of the problems which has to be taken into account in assessing underground water resources is the possibility of a falling water-table; in other words, is the available quantity of underground water actually diminishing? There is no convincing evidence of a decline at present, though clearly it was once much higher than it is now, and there is some evidence of a general fall in level over the past thousand years or so. General Pitt-Rivers, when excavating in the late nineteenth century on Cranborne Chase, which is also chalk country, concluded that there had been a fall of about 60 feet since Roman times. More recent archaeological work seems to support this general tendency. Normally in the past, during a prolonged drought when the wells dried up, well-diggers were sent down to deepen them until they struck the water-table. But a man cannot work in more than a foot or two of water in such conditions, so the actual depth of a well today is a fairly good indication of the lowest level to which the water-table has fallen since that well was first dug.

Saxon Charter Evidence

Unfortunately, reliable documentary evidence on this general question is very scanty, and in any case it goes back no farther than Saxon times; however, the surviving Saxon land charters for this area happen to be particularly valuable in this respect. For one thing, they seem to show that many streams broke out much higher up their valleys than they normally do today. According to the geological evidence afforded by the valley-gravels, the so-called upper Itchen, better described as the Cheriton brook, at an early stage in its history had its source at Lower Bordean, not far from the crest of the present chalk escarpment overlooking the western Weald. But the farthest point up valley that Saxon charters locate it is in the vicinity of the inn now called the West Meon Hut, where it is termed a 'beck'. Even this is more than 2 miles above the highest point at which it ever breaks out today. A reading taken in March 1958, in a disused well dug in the bed of this old stream, showed the rest level of the water to be 58 feet below the surface of the ground. Since this was at a time when the level was at its seasonal highest, it seems to indicate that a fall of some 60 feet has occurred here too. Incidentally, the beck in this valley was fed by a *floda*, which evidently came down the hillside from the direction of Privett. Now where the term *floda* can be identified with a Hampshire stream today it is of the intermittent variety, which flows only after exceptionally heavy or prolonged rain. But since our word 'flood' is derived from this, the implication is that the flow was considerable. It has survived as a place-name in various parts of the country, usually in the form of Whiteflood, though another form, Fulflood, has given its name to a suburb of Winchester. This latter is mentioned in Saxon charters as *Fulfloda*, the first syllable meaning 'foul' or 'dirty', and the stream appears to have flowed down the steep valley in which the station is situated. It flows no longer, its course having been severed by the railway cutting.

The Anomalous Alre

There is another sense in which these Saxon charters are valuable: the light they throw on the anomalous character of the Alre. It may come as a surprise to many people to learn that the stream that rises at Bramdean and flows through Cheriton is not really the Itchen at all, though it is so named on the Ordnance Survey maps. In Saxon charters it is invariably called the *Ticceburna*, which we recognise as Tichborne, the name usually applied nowadays only to the village on its banks, though some local people still use the Saxon name for the stream. On the other hand, the stream now called the Alre was in Saxon times known as the *Icene*, which is clearly the old form of Itchen. There has therefore been a transference of the name Itchen from one river to the other, and in order to discover how this confusion has occurred it is necessary to look into the place-name evidence.

The late Dr. Grundy once pointed out that Alresford meant 'the ford of the alder tree', and that it referred to a particular alder tree growing by the river at this point, and not to alder trees in general. One can well imagine how a little settlement—the one now known as Old Alresford—would grow at a fordable point on this quite substantial stream, and that it would take its name from such a feature. But at some subsequent date, perhaps not so long ago, someone apparently assumed that Alresford meant 'ford over the river Alre', just as Brentford means 'ford over the river Brent'. So, whereas in the case of Tichborne the river gave its name to the village, at Alresford the village gave its name to the river. If this assumption is correct we can understand how the Cheriton brook, which would be the obvious second choice, came to be regarded as the uppermost course of the Itchen. The Candover brook, although actually much longer than the Cheriton brook, would be ruled out because it joins the main stream just below the point where the Cheriton brook comes in. If confirmatory evidence were needed that the present Alre was recognised as the main headstream in early days, one need refer only to the fact that Bishop Lucy, at the end of the twelfth century, chose to dam it, rather than either of the other two head-streams, in order to provide a reservoir to keep his canalised Itchen navigable in dry seasons.

Water Mills

It will have been inferred from what has already been said that the rate of discharge of chalk streams does not fluctuate in the same way as does that of the streams draining the clay vales. An interesting illustration of this is the marked absence of mill-ponds along the valleys of the former. There is none along the Itchen or the Test, nor on any of their tributaries, to compare with Sowley pond, near Lymington, or others on the Tertiary outcrops. And it has already been shown that Alresford pond, the one apparent exception, was not originally a mill-pond at all, although its water has, in fact, been utilised for that purpose. All that one normally finds is a slightly widened portion of the mill-race, which has been cut along the valley side to create a head of water for the wheel. There is a problem here. If, away back in the Middle Ages, when the majority of these mill-races were cut, the water-table happened to be no lower than the level of their beds, there would have been no danger of seepage. But at Soberton, on the Meon, there has been trouble in recent years through the appearance of swallow-holes in the mill-stream bed. This is circumstantial evidence of a drop in the water table, and must mean that the mill-race is now 'perched'. Yet it is not likely that it would have been when first dug, otherwise, presumably, it would have been lined with puddled clay, of which there is plenty within easy reach, to prevent loss of water in this way.

Between Drayton and West Meon a problem of a different kind has arisen. Here there is temporary loss of water from the river itself where it flows over an outcrop of the more permeable Upper Chalk after leaving its upper catchment basin at East Meon, which is floored with the much less permeable Lower Chalk. This has, in the past, made milling somewhat precarious at West Meon, but the problem has been minimised by diverting all the available water along the valley side to the mill. As a result, enough water has generally been available to work it, even without the help of a sizeable pond. But it has led to the mistaken view locally that the present mill-race is the bed of the original river Meon. The same thing happened at Drayton Mill, and for the same reason. At Warnford, farther down the valley, the Lower Chalk comes to the surface again, and with it the water that has been working its way underground.

The fact that practically the whole of the water entering rivers in the chalk country is spring water has had an advantage of another kind. The temperature of the water as it issues from the rock is remarkably uniform throughout the year at about 10°C. It is this fact above all others that gives special value to the water-meadows and the watercress beds, for they can be flooded in early spring when the quantity of water available is at its maximum and when the air temperature may be well down. The stimulating effect of this relatively warm water also ensures the 'early bite' so essential for cattle at a time when fodder is scarcest. There would always have been a reluctance to sacrifice acres of these water-meadows to make mill-ponds, so it is fortunate that the need to do so has not arisen.

VIII

BOTANY

THE VEGETATION OF THE REGION

ALTHOUGH most of the region round Southampton is relatively densely populated and intensively cultivated, several large tracts of natural and semi-natural vegetation still survive. Among these, the New Forest, with its woodlands, heaths and bogs on Tertiary and Quaternary deposits, is outstanding; the unenclosed parts of the Forest are unique, at least in southern England, and have probably not undergone any drastic changes since early Bronze Age times. Moreover, the long sinuous coastline, with its mud flats, saltmarshes and shingle spits, is relatively undisturbed in many places and offers much of interest. On the Chalk farther inland, most of the old beechwoods and downlands have disappeared as a result of agriculture and forestry, but the fragments which remain are sufficient to give some idea of the former vegetation. Lakes are few and mostly artificial, but the valleys of the larger rivers flowing off the Chalk provide examples of freshwater vegetation, marsh and water meadow, while valley bogs occur at the heads of smaller streams draining from the sands and gravels. Thus, though the Southampton region lacks hill and moorland vegetation based on older and harder rocks, it possesses a representative range of most types of vegetation occurring in southern Britain. Unfortunately, few of the areas concerned have been studied adequately from an ecological point of view, and such information as exists about them is scattered and fragmentary.

Most of the remaining unexploited woodland consists of oak and beech, with more occasional areas of pinewood, birchwood, ashwood and alder carr. The richer soils of the region usually bear pedunculate oak (*Quercus robur*). For instance, in the New Forest, such oakwood occupies many of the better sands, clays and gravels, while oakwood with hazel (frequently coppiced) occurs on both Clay-with-Flints overlying the Chalk and on some of the Tertiary clays, both on the mainland and in the Isle of Wight. The range of soil tolerance of the oak is generally considered to be less than that of beech, but the former extent of selective felling is unknown, so that the real factors controlling the relative abundance and present distribution of the two species are obscure. Thus, evidence from pollen analysis of the soils of certain New Forest woods (Dimbleby and Gill, 1955) suggests that oak formerly occupied areas which are now beechwood; moreover, in various of the existing woodlands of mixed oak and beech, such as Denny Wait, beech is regenerating much more freely than oak at the present time.

In a few New Forest woods, notably Salisbury Trench and certain others in the north, the pedunculate oak is replaced by freely regenerating sessile oak (*Q. petraea*) on a corresponding range of soils. From the distribution and character of these woods, Anderson (1951) has in fact suggested that *Q. petraea* is the real New Forest native, which has been largely replaced by *Q. robur* as the result of selection by man.

The best and most extensive beechwoods of the region formerly occurred on the Chalk, and a few lay within the area covered by Watt (1925) in his classic studies on the native beechwoods of the South Downs. Since the time of his work, however, much felling and replanting have been carried out, and only fragments of the original woodlands now remain; these occur as typical beech hangers on scarp slopes with rendzina soils, and contain the usual calcicolous shrubs and sparse ground flora.

Beechwoods on acid soils are rather uncommon in Britain, but are a striking feature of the New Forest. They are characterised by the consistent presence of an understorey of holly (*Ilex aquifolium*) and by the occurrence of a non-calcicolous ground flora in the gaps and glades. Recent evidence from pollen analysis (Seagrief, 1955) suggests that beech entered the Hampshire Basin in late Boreal times (a much earlier date than for other parts of Britain) and it seems logical to regard the New Forest beechwoods as an extension of the Continental beech forests on acid soils.

Natural and semi-natural woods in which other trees are dominant are of lesser importance in the region. Scots Pine (*Pinus sylvestris*) is probably not native here, but since its eighteenth-century introduction into the Forest as a 'nurse' tree in plantations, it has spread considerably into the adjoining heaths and bogs, while *P. pinaster* similarly forms woods around Bournemouth. Ash (*Fraxinus excelsior*) occurs mainly as a seral stage when beech on chalk is felled. The silver birch (*Betula verrucosa*) similarly follows felling on other soils, but also appears to form more permanent woodland round the margins of oak and beechwood in the Forest. Lastly, there are several small alder carrs in the centres of some of the valley bogs, along the edges of streams where drainage is impeded and around certain of the artificial lakes; the alder is often mixed with sallow (*Salix cinerea*) and birch (*Betula pubescens*), and the alderwoods vary in physiognomy from quaking 'swamp-carr' with much *Carex paniculata* in the ground flora to a rather drier type of woodland on firmer ground.

As with the woodland, the amount of grassland in the region has been much reduced in recent years. For Hampshire as a whole, the Agricultural Return for 1881 gives the area under permanent grass as 199,100 acres; by 1962 this figure had dropped to 148,700 acres, largely as the result of ploughing or afforestation of chalk grassland. The situation is similar on the Isle of Wight, where again much of the former downland has disappeared. However, a number of isolated areas of chalk grassland still remain, especially on the steeper slopes; for example, Old Winchester Hill near Corhampton, which is now a National Nature Reserve (see p. 148), and Tennyson Down on the Isle of Wight, now owned by the National Trust, are both examples of residual grassland slopes which have been left unploughed.

The presence of typical chalk downland, rich in species, depends on continued grazing by rabbits or sheep, and the widespread reduction of the rabbit population by myxomatosis has recently affected the character of such vegetation to a marked degree. Not only have low-growing herbs been progressively ousted by the vigorous growth of grasses, but the seedlings of bushes like hawthorn (*Crataegus monogyna*) and juniper (*Juniperus communis*) are becoming established. Older examples of both hawthorn and juniper scrub can be seen in places, as on Old Winchester Hill. The juniper usually occupies the exposed steeper slopes, and the hawthorn the more sheltered areas and deeper soils, in the manner described by Watt (1934). Further progression would ultimately lead to woodland, and it is noteworthy in this connection that the juniper bushes often act as a 'nurse' for yew (*Taxus baccata*), so that yew woods sometimes result instead of the more usual beechwood of such chalk-based areas.

Of the other grasslands, perhaps the most interesting are the New Forest 'lawns'. These have developed as the results of felling, burning and grazing, and are maintained by pony and cattle grazing. The lawns may be derived from heathland, woodland or alder carr (Plates XVIII–XX), and though the swards are superficially similar in appearance, their dominant species differ according to the nature of the soil and the original vegetation. *Agrostis setacea* is common in lawns derived from heath, while in those from woodland or carr *Agrostis tenuis*, *Festuca ovina* and *Anthoxanthum odoratum* predominate, with *Poa trivialis* in shady places.

Heathland in the region is confined to the poorer sands and gravels, usually with a more or less podzolised soil. Such heaths are usually regarded as derived from woodland in pre-historic times, and podzolisation of the soil may well have accompanied, rather than preceded, the establishment of heathland species (cf. Dimbleby, 1962). Today, the extensive heaths of the New Forest are maintained by periodic burning by the Forestry Commission, but some areas which have been left unburnt for several years are showing rapid colonisation by pine.

Although the Forest contains excellent examples of heath vegetation at all stages of regeneration after burning, the actual floristic composition of these heaths is by no means uniform across the area. In the north-west, where there are large areas of plateau-gravels at 350 to 400 feet, the heaths are well drained by the comparatively steep valleys dissecting the plateau; such areas bear a typical dry heath vegetation, dominated by heather (*Calluna vulgaris*) with much *Erica cinerea*, and with bracken (*Pteridium aquilinum*) sparsely distributed throughout. In contrast, the south-eastern heaths lie on less elevated ground with shallower valleys, and the gravels possess a rather clayey matrix; these heaths provide a rather wetter facies, with heather still abundant, but now accompanied by *Erica tetralix* and *Molinia caerulea*.

Towards the valley bottoms, the heathland vegetation is usually replaced by bog. Such bogs are best developed in the shallower valleys where drainage is impeded, either by the general conformation of the land or by the accumulation of mineral and peaty alluvium. An excellent series of valley bogs occurs in the Matley and Denny Forest Nature Reserve to the south-east of Lyndhurst; these bogs show an almost diagrammatic zonation (cf. Rose, 1953) from wet heath along their margins, through typical bog communities of bog-moss (*Sphagnum* spp.), cotton-grass (*Eriophorum angustifolium*) and bog myrtle (*Myrica gale*), to a central alder carr with the tallest trees in the middle (Plate XXI).

The deepest bog in the Forest is Cranesmoor, west of Burley, and this has been intensively investigated by Newbould (1953, 1960). It lies in a basin at the confluence of a number of small valleys, with the narrow exit to the basin blocked by a plug of clay. The bog is formed over lake muds estimated from pollen analysis to have been laid down in early Boreal times, and the overlying peat is up to 15 feet deep in parts. The peat consists mainly of either *Sphagnum* or *Schoenus nigricans* remains, and the present surface vegetation shows a similar variation associated with hydrological differences in different parts of the bog.

Whereas the valley bogs are associated with streams draining from base-poor rocks, the larger rivers flowing southwards from the Chalk into Southampton Water support an entirely different type of freshwater vegetation. Most of the alluvial flats along their courses are drained and used as pasture, but areas of more waterlogged marsh occur in parts, with stretches of sweet-grass (*Glyceria maxima*), reed (*Phragmites communis*) and large sedges (mainly *Carex riparia* and *C. acutiformis*). For instance, the Winchester water-meadows, with their network of dykes, and other less extensive stretches near Mansbridge at Swaythling, provide good examples of this in the Itchen valley.

Where the entry of brackish water is restricted, even the tidal reaches of the rivers are sometimes bordered by great beds of reed, as in the Test north of Redbridge and in the Beaulieu river above the Beaulieu bridge. Such artificial impediments to tidal flow in fact often provide a sharp boundary between the reed and the exclusively maritime vegetation which fringes the coast.

Easily the most important coastal species is *Spartina townsendii* agg. This vigorous maritime grass forms virtually monospecific swards over the great stretches of mud bordering the coastline almost continuously from Hurst Castle to Chichester Harbour, and occupies similarly suitable sites on the sheltered side of the Isle of Wight. The interest of *Spartina* lies not only in its origin as a new species in Southampton Water nearly a century ago (see p. 109), but also in the rapidity with which it has taken sole possession of soft mud-flats previously unoccupied except by *Zostera*. Within the last thirty years, however, the swards have shown progressive signs of 'die-back', particularly in the Lymington and Beaulieu estuaries (Goodman, 1957, 1960; Goodman *et al.*, 1959, 1961; Braybrooks, 1957); this phenomenon is believed to be connected with the mode of build-up of the sward over the fine-particled mud, but it is difficult to predict at present the ultimate fate of these *Spartina* marshes (Plates X, XXII, XXIII).

More traditional saltmarshes are represented only locally round the coast, partly because the extremely soft muds are unsuitable for most saltmarsh plants, and partly because some of the older saltings on firmer sites, like Lincegrove Marsh at Bursledon, have already been invaded and virtually overrun by *Spartina*. However, a number of saltmarsh areas have been described by Perraton (1953) for Portsmouth and Langstone Harbours, and islands in the latter still show an excellent saltmarsh series ranging from *Aster tripolium* swards to mixed saltmarsh vegetation.

Finally, some mention should be made of the shingle areas (see p. 109). The drift is from west to east along the coast, and eastwardly directed spits are present at the mouths of many of the Hampshire rivers, notably at Calshot, Needs Oar Point and Hurst Beach. None of these areas, however, is vegetationally outstanding. Other shingle areas occur at Brown-down and on Portsea and Hayling Islands, but although these stretches in general possess a better range of species, the natural communities are for the most part disturbed.

The purpose of this account has been to provide a basic description of the main types of natural and semi-natural vegetation to be found within a radius of roughly 25 miles round Southampton. Only a fraction of the vegetationally important plants has been mentioned by name, and there are of course in addition numerous subordinate species which contribute to the total flora of the region. Even the inconspicuous plants are of interest to the botanist and others; and hence the subsequent contributions will briefly survey the main features of significance in the local distribution of representatives of the major systematic groups.

THE FLORA OF THE REGION

Vascular Plants

Because the Hampshire Basin, with its sheltered sea coast and fringe of chalk hills, offers such a wide range of habitats, the flora of the region shows a great diversity. The Isle of Wight, with its close succession of geological outcrops, also helps to make the South-ampton region one of the richest in the country in the number of vascular species to be found. Situated about midway along the southern coast, it shares the floras both of the south-east (as *Phyteuma tenerum* and *Aceras anthropophora*) and of the south-west (*Pinguicula lusitanica, Parentucellia viscosa, Wahlenbergia hederacea, Rubia peregrina*). With the rainfall much more limited than farther west, perhaps ferns are not to be seen at their best, but they are still present in good variety.

The sea coast possesses examples of most types of coastal environment at one place or another. The vestiges of sand dunes on Hayling Island and at St. Helens provide Marram Grass, Lyme Grass, the beautiful Sea Convolvulus, Sea Holly, and a good variety of Clovers; rarities to be looked for include *Poa bulbosa, Phleum arenarium, Teesdalia nudicaulis* and *Scilla autumnalis*. On the shingle beaches and spits, plants include Sea Kale, Sea Campion and Thrift, with the rarities *Frankenia laevis, Kohlrauschia nanteuilii, Geranium purpureum* and *Silene nutans*. Chalk cliffs are to be found on the Isle of Wight, with *Matthiola incana, Marrubium vulgare, Centaurium capitatum* and *Daucus gummifer; Cochlearia officinalis* and *Brassica oleracea*, however, seem to have vanished. The clay cliffs and slips of the Island have a very interesting flora; newly bared areas are rapidly colonised by Coltsfoot and Great Horsetail, while *Linum bienne, Melilotus altissima, Lotus tenuis, Blackstonia perfoliata, Epipactis palustris, Gymnadenia densiflora* and *Anacamptis pyramidalis* are frequent as the areas become more stabilised.

But saltmarshes and tidal mud-flats are the typical habitats of the Hampshire coast. These provide the one true Hampshire native, *Spartina townsendii*, first collected near Hythe in 1870 and believed to have arisen as a hybrid between the indigenous *Spartina maritima* and the introduced *Spartina alterniflora*. Other notable saltmarsh plants include species of *Zostera* and *Salicornia* (Ball and Tutin described their *Salicornia obscura* and *Salicornia nitens* from Hayling Island), *Inula crithmoides, Althaea officinalis* and, mostly behind the sea-walls, grasses such as *Polypogon monspeliensis*, *Agropyron littorale*, *Hordeum marinum* and the *Puccinellia* spp.

The scattered remnants of the woodland contain another range of interesting species. For instance, the woods of the clays and gravels of the north of the Isle of Wight and in the south of the New Forest are characterised by a typically Hampshire plant, the Long-leaved Lungwort or 'Cowslips of Jerusalem'. Wild Daffodils are to be found in many woods, and Butcher's Broom, Spurge Laurel and Tutsan are frequent. Columbine, Green and Stinking Hellebores, Lesser and Greater Butterfly Orchids, Bird's-nest Orchid and both species of Yellow Bird's-nest are occasionally to be found. *Carex paniculata*, *Carex pendula* and *Carex laevigata* are the most striking sedges of the wetter woodland (Plate XXIV).

The Hampshire rivers and water meadows are particularly attractive botanical 'hunting-grounds'. Most streams contain the Yellow Waterlily, Marestail, several species of Pond-weeds, the Stream Crowfoot (*Ranunculus pseudofluitans*) and the River Water Dropwort. Among the sedges and reedbeds of the river banks are to be found the Yellow and Purple Loosestrifes, Blue Skullcap, Yellow Iris, Valerian and, more rarely, Meadow Rue, Lesser Teasel and Flowering Rush. *Mimulus guttatus* and *Impatiens capensis*, both introduced species, are increasing along the river sides, while the Butterbur (*Petasites hybridus*), with its giant leaves, monopolises several stretches of bank. The characteristic plant of the meadows is Water Avens (*Geum rivale*).

The wet heathland and bogs of the New Forest contain several insectivorous plants; *Drosera rotundifolia*, *intermedia* and *anglica*, *Pinguicula lusitanica*, *Utricularia minor* and *intermedia* are all there (*Utricularia vulgaris* and *neglecta* are elsewhere in the area, at Christchurch and at Freshwater respectively). *Dactylorchis incarnata*, *Hammarbya paludosa*, *Eriophorum angustifolium*, *vaginatum* and *gracile* are other bog plants, while in and around the peaty gravel pools are *Lycopodium inundatum*, *Ranunculus lingua* and *tripartitus*, *Ludwigia palustris*, *Cicendia filiformis*, *Galium debile*, *Sparganium minimum* and *angustifolium*. The Coral Necklace (*Illecebrum verticillatum*), once very restricted in area, has spread widely on wet gravel rides and is now to be found close to the county boundaries to east and west, both near Woolsbridge beyond Ringwood and in the Southleigh Forest by Emsworth. In drier parts of the heathland *Lobelia urens* still persists (though it was nearly lost through afforestation) and *Gladiolus illyricus* is to be found under the bracken (Plate XXV). Two New Forest orchids, *Listera cordata* and *Spiranthes aestivalis*, have, however, disappeared, the latter now being extinct in Britain.

Although the old downland turf is fast disappearing from the hills around the basin, Man Orchid, Frog Orchid and the Fragrant, Pyramid, Bee and Fly Orchids are still to be found. *Filipendula vulgaris*, *Thesium humifusum*, *Cynoglossum officinale*, *Phyteuma tenerum*, *Cirsium eriophorum*, *Carex humilis* and *Nardurus maritimus* are others of the downland plants.

Even the large towns must not be overlooked by the botanist. Perhaps the most characteristic species there, all on the increase, are *Senecio squalidus*, *viscosus* and *vulgaris* (var. *radiatus*), while of more specialised interest are the casuals and aliens of the rubbish tips and the docks areas.

Several species, as well as those already mentioned, have special claims as Hampshire plants. The common Heath Spotted Orchid was first named, as *Orchis ericetorum*, by Linton from Bournemouth specimens. Bromfield's *Calamintha sylvatica* is still conserved in his original locality on the Isle of Wight. Townsend's *Arum italicum β neglectum*, now known to be widely distributed, was found near Ventnor, as also was the still more widespread *Epipactis phyllanthes* as its variety *vectensis*. In this district the striking *Melampyrum arvense*, 'Poverty Weed', once so common in the wheatfields that bread made from Island grain was black and bitter with its seeds, is now restricted to a single grassy bank. *Centaurium tenuifolium*, found in the north of the Island by Townsend, is now also very rare indeed. *Pulicaria vulgaris*, nowhere common, has perhaps its main distribution in this country in South Hampshire, as has the much more common weed *Misopates orontium*.

In spite of the large number of existing records of Hampshire's plants, new discoveries are still being made. Recent additions are the Northern Marsh Orchid (*Dactylorchis purpurella*), Variegated Horsetail (*Equisetum variegatum*) and Marsh Sowthistle (*Sonchus palustris*).

Mosses and Liverworts

An account of the distribution of mosses and liverworts in southern Hampshire is best considered by dividing the region into three parts. The New Forest area is very rich in mosses and liverworts and has been visited by many bryologists during the last 150 years. The chalk hills to the north of Southampton also have a rich bryophyte flora, which differs considerably from that in the New Forest; this area had not been so closely investigated until recent years. The remainder of the region, around and to the east of Southampton, has long been neglected by bryologists, and the paucity of species is very marked in this highly cultivated and extensively developed area.

Between 1957 and 1960, recording was carried on in a wide variety of habitats throughout the whole of the botanical vice-county of South Hants, and all records were related to 10-kilometre squares on the National Grid of the Ordnance Survey. By 1960 sufficient records had been accumulated to warrant the publication of the first Bryophyte County Flora based on the National Grid (Paton, 1961). As a result of this recording on the Grid many places not previously visited by bryologists were examined and many names were added to the total list of species. Thus in 1961 there were 416 species and varieties recorded in the vice-county.

In the older unspoilt woodlands of the New Forest a number of interesting bryophytes are present, often very local in their distribution, for instance *Bazzania trilobata* and *Saccogyna viticulosa* on sheltered banks. On tree trunks *Frullania fragilifolia*, *Dicranum montanum* and *Pterogonium gracile* occur scattered in the Forest, but the rare *Zygodon forsteri* is only known in one locality. Where afforestation has not been too extensive in woodlands on the Chalk, *Porella platyphylla*, *Eurhynchium schleicheri* and *Isopterygium depressum* are to be found about tree roots and on earthy banks, while on fragments of loose chalk on woodland banks or under scrub, several minute species are found such as *Fissidens minutulus*, *Seligeria paucifolia* and *Tortella inflexa*. Throughout the region elm, ash and elder trees in particular often have interesting bryophyte floras which include *Orthotrichum tenellum* and *Leptodon smithii*.

Undisturbed chalk downland is rich in species, especially where the ground is sloping or uneven and where the plants do not get buried by dead grass. *Weissia crispa*, *Neckera crispa*, *Entodon orthocarpus* and *Thuidium hystricosum* are scattered throughout the region, but *Scapania aspera* and *Weissia tortilis* are much more restricted. On disturbed soil a number of small ephemeral species are seen at their best in winter, including such rarities as *Aloina rigida*, *Phascum curvicollum*, *P. floerkeanum*, *Ephemerum recurvifolium* and several species of *Pottia*.

Most of the dry *Calluna* heaths are poor in species, though *Campylopus introflexus* appears to be spreading. Where the heaths are wetter characteristic species include *Sphagnum molle*, *Dicranum spurium* and *Campylopus brevipilus*. On damp peaty banks *Cladopodiella franscisci* and *Odontochisma denudatum* may be locally abundant. The valley bogs consist mainly of Sphagna, of which *Sphagnum magellanicum* is the most striking; these bogs are rich in hepatics, which frequently grow mixed together with the upper branches of the Sphagna. Here may be found the minute *Lepidozia setacea*, *Calypogeia sphagnicola* and *Cephalozia macrostachya*, while larger species such as *Mylia anomala*, *Cladopodiella fluitans* and *Odontoschisma sphagni* may occur mixed or in pure mats. The moss *Splachnum ampullaceum* also occurs in the New Forest bogs, but is always restricted to patches of decaying animal dung. Where the bogs become rather more marshy, such mosses as *Campylium stellatum*, *Drepanocladus revolvens* and *Acrocladium stramineum* are often found. In places where the Lower Headon Beds come to the surface the calcareous clay soils provide habitats suitable for a much larger number of species. Of these *Preissia quadrata* and *Drepanocladus sendtneri* are each only known in a single locality; *Mnium pseudopunctatum*, *Philonotis calcarea* and *Campylium elodes* are very local, but others such as *Trichostomum crispulum* and *Campylium protensum* are also characteristic of chalk downland.

On stream banks in the New Forest *Lejeunea lamacerina* var. *azorica* and *Hookeria lucens* are frequently found. Where the water flows from the Chalk a number of interesting species occur on the bases and trunks of trees beside streams and rivers, including *Tortula latifolia* and *Orthotrichum sprucei*. On the bases of walls and bridges *Fissidens crassipes* is frequent, and *Cinclidotus fontinaloides* and *Barbula nicholsonii* are more local in their distribution. On damp brick walls *Tortula marginata* and *Gyroweissia tenuis* often occur growing together, while on dry flint walls a wide variety of species of *Barbula* and several *Orthotricha* are to be found with *Tortula intermedia*.

The bryophyte flora of the coast is very limited because there are no good dune slacks and the Chalk does not reach the coast anywhere. *Cololejeunea minutissima* and *Ulota phyllantha* occur on scrub, and on the cliffs *Pottia crinita* and *Eurhynchium speciosum* have been recorded. *Pottia heimii* and *Eurhynchium megapolitanum* occur in saltmarshes, but all these species of maritime habitats are rare in Hampshire.

In terms of the vice-county as a whole, about fifty species are rare or very restricted in their distribution, and many, such as *Nardia geoscyphus* and *Ulota ludwigii*, have been recorded only once. In contrast, nearly fifty species are widely distributed throughout South Hants, and occur in most of the grid squares. Of these the following have been recorded in every square: *Ceratodon purpureus, Tortula muralis, Barbula convoluta, B. unguiculata, Bryum argenteum, Brachythecium rutabulum* and *Eurchynchium praelongum*. Many other species are nearly as widespread throughout the region, while others are common either in the New Forest or on the chalk ridge.

The wide variety of habitats present in the region enables a large number of bryophytes to thrive, but its climate and geographical position and the lack of rocky habitats limit the number of species that are able to survive. The mild, humid climate of the low-lying parts of the New Forest favours the growth of bryophytes and the more basic marshy areas are the richest in southern Hampshire.

Fungi

Our main source of imformation on the fungi of the region is largely due to two amateurs: the Rev. W. L. W. Eyre (1841-1914) who was rector of Swarraton, and J. F Rayner (1854-1947), a medical man who lived in Southampton. Eyre studied intensively the area in the neighbourhood of his rectory, especially Grange Wood and nearby Micheldever, but he also had a wide knowledge of the larger fungi of the whole region and contributed an account of them to the *Victoria County History of Hampshire* (1900). Rayner made a special study of the fungi of the New Forest and also prepared the first list of fungi for the Isle of Wight, making numerous additions by leading subsequent forays. This work was continued by E. W. Swanton (1870-1958), for fifty-one years the distinguished curator of the Haslemere Educational Museum, who published the most recent list in the *Proceedings of the Isle of Wight Natural History and Archaeological Society* for 1934. Both Eyre and Rayner published in the *Proceedings of the Hampshire Field Club* and Rayner also in the *Proceedings of the Bournemouth Natural Science Society*, his last supplement to the New Forest list appearing in the *Proceedings* of the latter Society for 1918.

The region under consideration may, for the present purpose, be conveniently divided into three districts: the mainland part of the Hampshire Basin; the chalk margins; and the Isle of Wight.

The first of these districts, with its Tertiary and Quaternary deposits, has two great tracts of forest land. To the south-east is the Forest of Bere (3000 acres), to the south-west the New Forest (of some 90,000 acres). Only the latter has been investigated mycologically, and here about 1000 of the larger fungi have been recorded. The deadly Death Cap (*Amanita phalloides*) is frequent and always associated with trees, mainly oak and beech, while the closely related and equally deadly *A. virosa* and *A. verna* are also present, though much less common. The rare *Hydnum erinaceum* (Plate XXVI) sometimes provides a magnificent sight, as, for example, an exceptionally fine specimen found in Denny Wait on 22 October 1960. Many species are also associated with the planted conifers, like the beautiful *Lactarius deliciosus*, with its deep carrot-coloured latex.

The Ascomycetes and other micro-fungi have scarcely been examined in this district, although they probably occur abundantly. For example, all the British species of the

Discomycete *Trichoscyphella* (with one doubtful exception) have been found in the New Forest in recent years by Dr. J. G. Manners in the course of his work on larch canker caused by *T. willkommii*. On the other hand, rust fungi are not well represented in the Forest, probably because the rainfall is relatively low and the area is poor in the type of damp, floristically rich habitat in which rust fungi are abundant.

For the present purposes, the chalk area may be taken as extending as far north as Basingstoke, and from Alton in the east to the county boundary in the west. It thus takes in the great exposure of open chalk downland, the soil of which is shallow and well drained, so that typical grassland toadstools like *Hygrophorus* (sections *Camarophyllus* and *Hygrocybe*), *Panaeolus* and *Stropharia* are for the most part poorly represented. The most noteworthy grassland species are the Field Mushroom, *Agaricus campestris* (not to be confused with the much less tasty Cultivated Mushroom, *A. bisporus*), and the equally edible St. George's mushroom (*Tricholoma gambosum*), so called because it is at its most abundant round about St. George's Day.

Woodland is sparse in this district, and except for Harewood Forest (2000 acres), woods are mostly quite small. The top soil is often derived from Clay-with-Flints and is thus water-retaining, or the Chalk may be overlain with a reasonably deep loam soil derived from Tertiary debris. Mycologically these small woods are very rewarding, yielding many of the really fine toadstools which are associated with beech and oak woods on chalk. Probably a number have disappeared with the destruction of many of the old beechwoods, but the following are still found: the edible *Amanita strobiliformis*; *Clitocybe odora*, with its blue-green cap and splendid 'anise' smell; *Inocybe patouillardii*, which is wholly white or cream but bruises bright red and is deadly poisonous; Horn of Plenty (*Craterellus cornucopioides*) whose black trumpets are delicious when fried and served on hot buttered toast; the large Fairy Club, *Clavaria pistillaris*; and *Boletus satanas*, attractive to look at but a powerful emetic.

The area round the rectory at Swarraton will always be remembered for two outstanding finds by the Rev. Eyre—namely, the Discomycete *Sarcosphaera eximia* with its violet hymenium, and the little toadstool *Melanophyllum eyrei* (*Lepiota eyrei*), remarkable for the very unusual bluish-green colour of its spores. Moreover, in Eyre's time the Summer Truffle (*Tuber aestivum*) was common in this district, equally on chalk and stiff clay, and under oak and fir as well as beech.

The Isle of Wight, which combines the geology of the two previous districts, also combines their fungus floras. The more southerly position of the Island, however, no doubt accounts for the presence of *Clathrus ruber* (*cancellatus*), a distinctly southern species, whose red-latticed beauty is marred only by its disgusting smell. Swanton, in his list already referred to, states that only a small area of the Island had been 'at all intensively examined'. Nevertheless, some 650 Basidiomycetes and 130 species in the other groups of fungi—mostly Ascomycetes—are on record, and there is no doubt that further search on the Island would easily bring the number of larger fungi up to that of the New Forest. Noteworthy toadstools are the Earth-star (*Geastrum* (*Geaster*) *triplex*), the rare *Lepiota emplastrum*, the strong-smelling *L. bucknallii*, and *Boletus parasticus* which parasitises earthballs (*Scleroderma*).

Marine Algae

The Southampton region is not characterised by large quantities of seaweed, since rocky coasts are infrequent. One rocky area is at Bembridge on the Isle of Wight, where ledges of limestone run well out to sea and, with the intervening channels, provide a habitat for quite a variety of marine algae. These include the usual larger brown seaweeds, among which are *Halidrys siliquosa* and *Cystoseira tamariscifolia*, while smaller specimens include *Asperococcus bullosus* and *Padina pavonia*. Many red algae can be found at low-water spring tides, including *Chylocladia verticillata*, *Furcellaria fastigiata* and abundant *Plocamium coccinium*. The green alga *Codium* is also conspicuous. Other rocky areas also occur on the coast of the Island, but probably none possesses a greater range of species than that met with at Bembridge, though Steephill Cove near Ventnor might be worth investigating.

On the mainland suitable sites are more restricted. The very numerous mud-flats have a conspicuous zone of *Enteromorpha* at certain times of the year, and this is likewise abundant on the lower parts of the saltmarshes, where *Fucus vesiculosus* may also be found. At the western end of the region, some seaweed occurs at Hengistbury Head, but otherwise very few appropriate habitats exist. Towards the east, however, just south of the Castle at Southsea, adequate anchorage is provided by the stone and concrete sea defences, with boulders and smaller stones on the shore below; but no pools are left at low tide and the variety of algae is limited. Species of *Laminaria* and fucoids are abundant, with the red algae *Rhodymenia palmata* and *Callithamnion tetragonum* epiphytic on the former. *Polysiphonia elongata* and *Gracilaria verrucosa* may be conspicuous on areas where rock is overlain by sand near low-water level.

A different type of environment is provided in the more sheltered waters of Portsmouth Harbour, where a causeway of concrete exists between Horsea Island and the mainland, and broken masses of concrete and many small stones are mingled with mud. The shore has a gradual slope on which small plants of *Fucus vesiculosus* are abundant, with good *Fucus serratus* at a lower level. The channel from the northern part of the harbour contains a small quantity of *Laminaria saccharina*, but it is not usually exposed at low water of any tide. *Halidrys siliquosa* and *Cystoseira tamariscifolia* are present in the quieter water west of this channel. Shallow pools draining to the sea are left at low tide and these contain an abundance of more delicate algae, including attractive masses of *Nitophyllum punctatum*, *Griffithsia corallinoides* and *Chondria dasyphylla*. *Dictyota dichotoma* and *Bryopsis plumosa* are also present, while drift specimens of *Cutleria multifida* have been collected.

Freshwater Algae

In contrast to the seaweeds, the freshwater algal flora of the area is both extensive and varied. In a single week in June 1947, N. Woodhead and R. D. Tweed of the University College of North Wales, Bangor, collected 476 different species and in addition 106 varieties; many of these were first records for the British Isles. In spring and early summer almost every pond, stream and woodland or farm puddle can be depended upon to produce a variety of specimens. The New Forest in particular is plentifully supplied with ponds and streams, all of which produce rich hauls. The Holmsley bogs yielded 206 species and varieties and Hatchet Pond 203, when investigated by the two botanists mentioned above. Elsewhere the distribution of suitable collecting areas is more sparse, but they nevertheless exhibit the same luxuriance. Unfortunately, this happy state of affairs is being interfered with by the reclaiming of land for agriculture and forestry, and by a general lowering of the water-table, resulting in the disappearance of ponds and streams.

All the common filamentous algae are represented and are widely distributed. Species of *Spirogyra*, *Oedogonium*, *Ulothrix*, *Cladophora*, *Chaetophora*, *Mougeotia*, *Zygnema*, and like forms can be found without difficulty in the spring and early summer. *Microspora* can be collected at any time of the year in certain localities. The Boarhunt pond will usually yield the rare *Cylindrocapsa geminella* Woole var. *minor* Hansg. The environs of the rivers Itchen, Hamble and Meon provide other uncommon species. *Volvox aureus* occurs in many woodland and urban ornamental ponds with quite surprising regularity. *Batrachospermum* is widely distributed; *Chlamydomonas*, *Eudorina*, *Pandorina*, *Tetraspora* and other *Volvocales* are of course common. *Hydrodictyon* is infrequent, but is found occasionally. The ponds and puddles of every farmyard can be relied upon to produce Desmids and several species of *Euglena*, *Phacus* and other *Euglenineae*. *Vaucheria* is especially common near the coast. The commonest alga of the brackish waters is, as might be expected, *Enteromorpha*; it occurs everywhere, reaching into streams seemingly as far as any salty water can penetrate, the exclusively freshwater *Spirogyra* for instance being found only a short distance away. Diatoms are of course to be found everywhere. The *Myxophyceae* are widespread and in great variety: *Oscillatoria*, *Arthrospira*, *Gloeotrichia*, *Tolypothrix* and *Aphanothece* are all common. The *Charophyta* occur with fair frequency, but are much more abundant just outside the area.

Even from this limited survey, there is no doubt that the region is of very considerable interest and deserves much more attention from freshwater algologists than it has so far received.

BIBLIOGRAPHICAL NOTE

(1) M. L. Anderson, 'Distribution of the sessile oak in the New Forest, Hampshire', *Forestry* (1951), vol. 24, pp. 79-113.

(2) E. M. Braybrooks, *The general ecology of* Spartina townsendii *with special reference to sward build-up and degradation* (Ph.D. thesis, University of Southampton, 1957).

(3) G. W. Dimbleby, *The development of British heathlands and their soils*, Oxford Forestry Memoir 23 (1962).

(4) G. W. Dimbleby and J. M. Gill, 'The occurrence of podzols under deciduous woodland in the New Forest', *Forestry* (1955), vol. 28, pp. 95-106.

(5) W. L. W. Eyre, 'Fungi', *Victoria County History of Hampshire and the Isle of Wight* (1900), vol. 1, pp. 82-87.

(6) P. J. Goodman, *An investigation of 'die-back' in* Spartina townsendii *H. & J. Groves* (Ph.D. thesis, University of Southampton, 1957).

(7) P. J. Goodman, 'Investigations into "die-back" in *Spartina townsendii* agg. II. The morphological structure and composition of the Lymington sward', *Journal of Ecology* (1960), vol. 48, pp. 711-24.

(8) P. J. Goodman and W. T. Williams, 'Investigations into "die-back" in *Spartina townsendii* agg. III. Physiological correlates of "die-back"', *Journal of Ecology* (1961), vol. 49, pp. 391-8.

(9) P. J. Goodman, E. M. Braybrooks and J. M. Lambert, 'Investigations into "die-back" in *Spartina townsendii* agg. I. The present status of *Spartina townsendii* in Britain', *Journal of Ecology* (1959), vol. 47, pp. 651-77.

(10) P. J. Newbould, *The ecology of Cranesmoor* (Ph.D. thesis, University of London, 1953).

(11) P. J. Newbould, 'The ecology of Cranesmoor, a New Forest valley bog. I. The present vegetation', *Journal of Ecology* (1960), vol. 48, pp. 361-83.

(12) J. A. Paton, 'A Bryophyte flora of South Hants', *Transactions of the British Bryological Society* (1961), vol. 4, pp. 1-83.

(13) C. Perraton, 'Saltmarshes of the Hampshire-Sussex border', *Journal of Ecology* (1953), vol. 41, pp. 240-7.

(14) J. F. Rayner, *A list of the fungi of the New Forest* (Southampton, 1906).

(15) J. F. Rayner, 'Guide to the fungi and mycetozoa of the New Forest', *Proceedings of the Bournemouth Natural Science Society* (1912), vol. 3, pp. 105-55.

(16) J. F. Rayner, 'A supplement to the guide to the fungi and mycetozoa of the New Forest', *Proceedings of the Bournemouth Natural Science Society* (1918), vol. 9, pp. 82-93.

(17) J. F. Rayner, *A supplement to Frederick Townsend's Flora of Hampshire and the Isle of Wight* (Southampton, 1929).

(18) F. Rose, 'A survey of the ecology of the British lowland bogs', *Proceedings of the Linnean Society of London* (1953), vol. 164, pp. 186-211.

(19) S. C. Seagrief, *A pollen analytic investigation of the Quaternary period in Britain* (Ph.D. thesis, University of Cambridge, 1955).

(20) E. W. Swanton, 'List of fungi found in the Isle of Wight', *Proceedings of the Isle of Wight Natural History and Archaeological Society* (1934), vol. 2, pp. 365-94.

(21) F. Townsend, *Flora of Hampshire including the Isle of Wight* (London, 1883).

(22) A. S. Watt, 'On the ecology of the British beechwoods with special reference to their regeneration. II. The development and structure of beech communities on the Sussex Downs', *Journal of Ecology* (1925), vol. 13, pp. 27-73.

(23) A. S. Watt, 'The vegetation of the Chiltern Hills, with special reference to the beechwoods and their seral relationships', *Journal of Ecology* (1934), vol. 22, pp. 230-70.

(24) N. Woodhead and R. D. Tweed, 'Some freshwater algae in southern Hampshire', *Proceedings of the Bournemouth Natural Science Society* (1947), vol. 37, pp. 50-67.

IX

ZOOLOGY

ECOLOGICAL interest in the area around Southampton is stimulated by the wide variety of habitat. Chalk downland and patches of beech woodland contrast with open heathland and with the mixed woodland areas and heaths of the New Forest. The rich valley floors and water-meadows are different again. The freshwater habitats are also varied; patches of bog and small ponds in the New Forest drain into somewhat acid streams that contrast sharply with the well-known chalk rivers such as the Avon, Test and Itchen. The estuaries of these rivers are in places bordered by saltmarshes. An extensive coastline lends further variety to the Southampton region. Much of the area has muddy sand and shingle, but there are sandy beaches and, on the Isle of Wight, some rocky shores.

The varied fauna accompanying such a diversity of habitat is far too rich for complete investigation. Attention has been concentrated therefore in turn on the marine fauna, which has been limited to Southampton Water; on hydrobiological studies; on some groups of invertebrates, mainly arthropods; and on birds and mammals. Some other important aspects of the animal life of the Southampton area are also referred to in connection with conservation in Chapter X.

THE MARINE FAUNA OF SOUTHAMPTON WATER

Although the rivers Test and Itchen flow into Southampton Water, the area as a whole cannot be regarded as estuarine. The reduction of salinity is slight, apart from the surface layers of the upper reaches, and fairly typical marine communities exist throughout the Water. Apart from the dredged ship channel, its bottom is characterised by extensive shallow banks of fairly soft mud. The benthic population of these banks changes relatively little from place to place throughout the region. Extensive beds of *Mytilus edulis* appear to be increasing, especially towards the northern end of Southampton Water, despite a considerable infection of *Mytilus* with *Mytilicola intestinalis* (cf. Hockley, 1951). Other bivalves include *Cardium edule*, *Tapes (Venerupis) decussata* and a few *Mya*. Perhaps the most interesting lamellibranch is the American hard clam, *Venus (Mercenaria) mercenaria*. This was first recorded in 1956/7, when a few large specimens were identified; a flourishing population is now known around the Marchwood area, and it is also extending along almost the whole of the east side of Southampton Water. Age determinations indicate that the very oldest clams may date even from the year brood of 1936, though exceedingly few clams are found older than the age brood of *c.* 1948. However, the presence of various age broods of *Venus* since that year suggests that several successful spat falls have occurred during more recent years (cf. Ansell, 1963). No artificial layings of this clam have been made in the south of England, and although the possibility exists of larval transport from Brittany, where clams have been imported, it is more likely that the adult bivalves have accidentally been brought into Southampton Water by American shipping. The comparatively warm water conditions, the result partly of industrial developments, have presumably enabled this species to spawn in at least some summers.

Crepidula fornicata, which has colonised so much of the eastern and southern coasts of Britain, is extremely common in the area. Another and more recent immigrant species is the barnacle, *Elminius modestus*. Whether this austral species, first noticed in this country at the end of the War of 1939-45 (Bishop, 1947; Crisp and Chipperfield, 1948), entered the Thames estuary and Southampton Water simultaneously is uncertain, but it is now the dominant species of barnacle in the latter, and rapidly settles on all new port and dock installations. Its larvae dominate numerically the plankton during most of the summer months, although as an essentially warmer water species it breeds later in the year than the two barnacles, *Balanus balanoides* and *B. crenatus*, whose nauplii are abundant in early spring.

The polychaete population of this area is comparatively restricted, both in species and in numbers. Only one intertidal flat is known where *Arenicola marina* is abundant, though *Audouinia* is plentiful in parts of the intertidal zone. *Nereis* (*N. diversicolor* and *N. virens*) are both common and are sought by bait diggers. Below low water-mark, *Sabella pavonina* is reasonably widespread.

A small number of *Saccoglossus horsti*, though more abundant near Lymington, have been recorded from Southampton Water. Of other benthic species, echinoderms are very poorly represented in this area; *Cucumaria elongata* is reasonably abundant just below low tide-mark and a few *Solaster* are taken, but *Asterias* is virtually unknown. Among decapod crustaceans *Carcinus*, *Eupagurus* and spider crabs, especially *Inachus*, are abundant, but the bottom macro-fauna is mainly characterised by an abundance of sea squirts. Several species of ascidians occur, of which one of the commonest is *Ascidiella aspersa*, but during the past two years the warm water species *Styela clava* has been reported in rapidly increasing numbers. Many of the estuarine species (*Eupagurus*, *Ascidiella*) show commensal associations, now under investigation, with smaller organisms.

The wood-boring marine invertebrates, *Limnoria* and *Teredo*, have been the subject of intensive investigation in this area during the past ten years (cf. Eltringham and Hockley, 1961; Jones, 1961). The relative abundance of *Limnoria quadripunctata*, and to a lesser extent of *L. tripunctata*, and the comparative scarcity of the more boreal species, *L. lignorum*, are notable. *Teredo navalis* is recorded in only small numbers in Southampton Water, though during the warm summer of 1959 a considerable, though temporary, increase in density was recorded.

Of the demersal fishes, *Gadus luscus*, *G. minutus*, *Pleuronectes flesus*, gobies and blennies are moderately abundant. Pelagic species are commoner, however; both sprats and herring occur from time to time, and especially conspicuous are the shoals of mullet and bass which follow the warmer water emanating from the outfalls of industrial water circulation systems.

A detailed zooplankton survey conducted over the past six years (cf. Raymont and

Carrie, 1959), has revealed the numerical abundance of cirripede nauplii, especially those of *Elminius modestus*, during most of the year. The copepod fauna is restricted in its number of species, but the genus *Acartia* is dominant and includes the widespread neritic forms *A. clausi*, *A. bifilosa* and *A. discaudata*. Conover (1957) reported the presence of *A. tonsa* from Southampton Water, this being the first record of the species in Great Britain, although this essentially American form had been previously reported from European estuaries. This copepod has since been taken here in considerable numbers during late summer and autumn. A single specimen of another species, *Acartia grani*, a warm water copepod first recorded in Britain by Norman and Scott (1906) at Plymouth, was found in 1956 in this area and was taken in small numbers again in 1958.

Of larger planktonic animals, several species of mysid occur fairly regularly in deeper waters, and the carnivorous forms *Aurelia aurita* and *Pleurobrachia pileus* form great shoals in Southampton Water during early summer. The timing of this invasion appears to be fairly strict; during May, June and early July, the heavy densities of *Aurelia* and *Pleurobrachia* cause a marked diminution of the copepod zooplankton, but outside this period numbers of these two predators are low.

Another marine animal which shows a fairly clear seasonal increase in numbers is *Sepia officinalis*. This cuttle-fish is moderately common about May and June, but dead shells then begin to appear in Southampton Water and few are taken alive outside these two months.

Changes in the faunal population of Southampton Water appear to have been taking place during the past ten to fifteen years. Some of the more recent changes, both among pelagic and benthic species, may be linked with the slight rise in temperature of the water noted in recent years. It is hoped that further investigations may assist in the elucidation of other factors which are also involved in these changes.

HYDROBIOLOGY

A variety of investigations has been conducted into the freshwater biology of the area under discussion, though perhaps more on the river Avon and its tributaries and in Dorset than on the two rivers of Southampton itself—the Test and the Itchen. The University of Southampton has naturally been in the forefront of this research, and in 1932 sponsored a survey of the Avon and its tributaries that was supported by local fishermen, laying emphasis on salmon biology. A considerable number of investigations was carried out by Dr. J. Berry and his colleagues, described in the annual reports (*Avon Biological Research*, 1933-9). In 1939 the administration of this project was taken over by the Freshwater Biological Association which, since the foundation of its Windermere laboratory in 1931, had wanted a branch on a southern river to provide an ecological contrast to the English Lake District. Before the war the Ministry of Agriculture and Fisheries maintained a small laboratory at Alresford on the Itchen, but this project ceased in 1940. Since the war the Zoology Department of the University of Southampton has carried out a number of research projects in the area, chiefly in the New Forest, some of which are mentioned in the account of invertebrates (p. 123). Dr. N. W. Moore of the Nature Conservancy studied several aspects of dragonfly biology on the Dorset heaths (Corbet, Longfield and Moore, 1960), and the Hampshire and the Avon and Dorset River Boards have developed their studies of the rivers in relation to drainage and fisheries (*Avon and Dorset River Board, Annual Report,* 1962). In 1963 the Freshwater Biological Association's long-laid plans came to fruition and a laboratory to study all aspects of chalk-stream biology was built at East Stoke on the river Frome. As well as these research projects based on organised laboratories, a number of both amateur and professional studies has been made in the area. Yet in spite of this valuable work, it can safely be said that in many groups there is still ignorance of what species are present, and the basic ecology and population dynamics of the principal aquatic animals and plants are still virtually unknown.

As the ecology of the freshwaters in any region is largely a reflection of its geology and land use, it is significant that the waters of the Hampshire Basin fall into two main groups, those of the Chalk and those of the Tertiary rocks. The Chalk is notable for its exceptional permeability and no natural still waters are to be found on it. But it does have one special type of artificial water, the dew-pond, of considerable biological interest. Dew-ponds have been made for stock-watering purposes all over the chalk uplands, and consist essentially of a waterproof pan of puddled clay or concrete that collects rain water (*not* dew) from an area considerably larger than the evaporation area of the pond itself, and thus maintains a supply of water throughout the year (Pugsley, 1939). They are completely isolated from all other waters, and their rich fauna and flora are a tribute to the dispersal powers of freshwater organisms. The water is also alkaline, and, if used directly by farm animals, rich with organic pollution. The fauna varies with the degree of pollution and the age of the pond; when neglected, dew-ponds tend to grow a succession of rooted aquatic plants and eventually dry up. The ecology of the water-bugs in dew-ponds has been described by Macan and Macfadyen (1941).

An interesting contrast to the dew-ponds is provided by the small natural and artificial ponds of the heathlands. Although they are often similarly formed over a clay pan, the water of these ponds is acid, and they contain characteristic species usually quite different from those in the dew-ponds. Some New Forest ponds have been known as localities for the medicinal leech (*Hirudo medicinalis*), which is scarce over the rest of England, and Moore (1962) has used the dragonfly (*Ceriagrion tenellum*) as an indicator species for heathlands when discussing their conservation.

Waters large enough to be called lakes or reservoirs are almost absent from the heathlands, as well as from the Chalk. There are, however, a few large artificial ornamental ponds, and the Little Sea at Studland is interesting, for its waters now contain small enough concentrations of sodium chloride to be considered fresh (Diver, 1933).

Although the Hampshire Basin may be poor in still waters, it is the classic home of the 'chalk-stream', and these rivers provide the region with a feature of outstanding interest for the freshwater biologist (Plate XIII). Famous for the trout-fishing which now makes each yard of their banks worth many pounds in rentals, they contain a rich and varied fauna and flora, show a high rate of biological productivity, and pose a number of unsolved ecological problems. Because their entire flow is derived from springs, and surface run-off is negligible, the rivers of the Chalk start in the main valley bottoms, and the area is devoid of those small headwaters of the type called 'becks' in the North of England. Even many of these valley streams are 'winterbournes', which dry up every summer when the general water-table in the Chalk falls below the level of their sources. However, in spite of their temporary nature these winterbournes appear to contain quite a rich fauna, including young trout, and obviously would repay detailed ecological study.

The spring-fed origin of the chalk-stream is also relatively constant in flow, and though floods do occur the seasonal fluctuations are much less violent than in most other rivers. The sources are also remarkably constant in temperature; the springs vary little from 7°C. throughout the year, so that the river water is warmer than the air in winter and early spring, and yet is cool enough for trout all summer. As it has percolated through the Chalk the water is clear, yet hard and rich in dissolved minerals, the pH is 7·5 to 8·0, the alkalinity equivalent to 150 to 250 parts per million of calcium carbonate, and other ions such as sodium and sulphate may be present in fair concentrations. Most of the chalk-streams in the area have so far been fortunate in avoiding any really harmful domestic or industrial pollution.

Chalk-streams have longitudinal profiles with remarkably constant slopes from source to mouth; as headstreams are absent, the whole length seems to belong to the middle reach of the classical river profile, to the 'grayling and barbel zones' of the continental river biologists. Variety is provided, however, by mill-weirs; the reach between each mill tends to have a profile of its own, steep at and immediately below the mill and nearly level in the next mill-head downstream. Because of this and also the complex network of irrigation channels provided by the now obsolescent water-meadow system (Moon and Green, 1940), species characteristic of becks and others typically found in ponds can occur within a few yards of each other along the whole length of a river; this may be one reason for the faunistic and floristic richness.

Their relative constancy of flow and temperature, variety in micro-profile and richness in plant nutrients may all be important factors in the ecology of chalk-streams, but their apparent high biological productivity cannot yet be explained with certainty. Primary production is undoubtedly considerable, mostly in the form of weed growths rooted in silt beds; *Ranunculus pseudo-fluitans* is perhaps the most characteristic of a number of plant species. Owens and Edwards (1962) recorded net carbon-fixation in spring at a rate of nearly 2 grams of carbon per square metre per day, equivalent to about 250 g./m.^{2} in a year (Westlake: personal communication). But little of this weed is directly consumed by animals, and fishermen resort to wholesale weed-cutting once or twice a year to provide space in which to cast their flies. Invertebrate production would appear to be at a high rate too, though it has not yet been measured. Certainly many of the fish that feed on these invertebrates grow well; for example, young salmon which in most British rivers take two or three years to reach smolt size, grow to this in only just over one year in the river Avon.

Perhaps the biological richness of chalk-streams can be explained by a more rapid turn-over in the alkaline water of the organic detritus that is the food of many invertebrates. It would seem unlikely, however, that the quantity of such detritus is any larger in chalk-streams than, for example, in those of the New Forest, which would appear to be abundantly supplied with dead leaves from the surrounding woodlands. These latter rivers on the Tertiary formations provide an intriguing contrast to the chalk-streams; though lower in productivity, they nevertheless contain many different and some unusual species (Butcher, 1938; Macan and Macan, 1940). Indeed, the main attraction of the whole region to the fresh-water biologist is this juxtaposition of such different types of water; perhaps advantage will be taken of this natural feature in the development of future studies on the basic problem of what factor really controls the productivity of waters.

THE INVERTEBRATES

Any picture of the invertebrate fauna of an area must be dominated by the arthropods, more especially the insects. Particularly is this the case in the Southampton area, which for the purposes of this account will be limited by the river Avon to the west, by the river Hamble to the east and by the line Salisbury–Winchester–Botley to the north. The richness and variety of the insect life of the New Forest are well known; clearly, any attempt at surveying it systematically would be inappropriate. Instead, attention will be concentrated on some of the less intensively studied groups associated with the New Forest and its streams, and with the chalk-streams of the region, particularly the Test, the Itchen and the Hamble.

Information on the Trichoptera of the area is surprisingly limited. There is no county list for Hampshire; many of the records are of captures of imagines, often with only approximate localities; and no detailed work has been done on the ecology and distribution of the larvae. It is not therefore surprising that recent collections from aquatic habitats have yielded larvae of a number of species not previously recorded from the area; of the 190 or so British species, some thirty-eight have been taken in the area.

Three groups of nematocerous Diptera, the Chironomidae, the Simuliidae and the Tipulidae, have been the subject of recent detailed ecological work. Some eighty species of Chironomidae have been taken; over sixty of these have been bred out and so can be associated with their larval habitats. Much of the work has been done on the three chalk-streams mentioned above. In parts of the Test the population densities of the Chironomidae were very high; the average was between 4000 and 5000 per square metre, though in certain parts the summer figures rose to 12,000 per square metre. It is of interest that two species of predaceous Tanypodinae formed roughly three-quarters of the population. Work on the Test and the Hamble indicates the presence of a considerable number of species of Orthocladiinae associated with aquatic weed; in some cases the larvae may form 50 per cent of the invertebrate population.

There is no general information on the Simuliidae of the region, but recently an ecological study of weed-masses in a chalk-stream, with particular emphasis on the simuliid population, has been carried out. Five species of the genus *Simulium* were bred out. Great variations in the population density of *Simulium* occurred throughout the season, and the much larger invertebrate populations found on *Carex* and *Ranunculus* were due entirely to the very large numbers of *Simulium ornatum* var. *nitidifrons* found on these plants.

The crane-flies (Tipulinae) have been the subject of some recent work, particularly in the area of Matley Bog. About seventy species have been recorded, some forty of which were members of the sub-family Limoniinae. Of the thirty or so representatives of the Tipulinae, some twenty-four belonged to the genus *Tipula*, rather more than one-third of the British total for this genus. Experimental work on the cold-hardiness of the larvae shows a correlation between this and the temperatures to which different species are exposed in their characteristic habitats. It also appears that the transpiration rates of certain adults are related to the dryness of the habitats in which they are found.

Recent studies have greatly increased our knowledge of the centipedes of the region. In the New Forest exists a variety of woodland habitats characterised by different types of litter layer; these differences are reflected in the centipede fauna. Seven species of Lithobiidae are found in Burley Wood, a typical beech-oak woodland characterised by the absence of herb and shrub layers. *Lithobius variegatus* is generally distributed throughout the litter, while the other common species, *L. duboscqui*, occurs in patches in the humus. *L. muticus*, *L. lapidicola* and *L. forficatus* all are represented as isolated colonies in the litter while *L. curtipes* and *L. melanops* are rare. Important factors determining vertical and horizontal distribution include sensitivity to extremes of relative humidity and of temperature, and ability to penetrate the lower layers of litter and humus.

In Nature Reserve 30 in the New Forest, which includes a variety of woodland types, some fifteen of the fifty-three British species have been taken. Three species, *Brachygeophilus truncorum*, *Geophilus carpophagus* and *Lithobius variegatus*, are particularly common and generally occur in all the woodland types. The largest populations appear where the litter layer is deep, the largest numbers and greatest variety of species being found in the sycamore woods. A factor affecting the distribution of centipedes appears to be their degree of tolerance to temporary flooding of their habitats.

Two branchiopod crustacea of some interest have been taken in the region. The rare *Triops cancriformis* has been recorded on several occasions from a temporary pond near Fordingbridge. The fairy shrimp, *Chirocephalus diaphanus* has been known in various localities within the area over a number of years. Its occurrences are, however, sporadic and frequently short-lived; recent work has been directed to elucidating some of the curious features of its biology.

ORNITHOLOGY

It is not possible, or indeed desirable, to give a completely detailed systematic list in a brief survey of this nature. It is more practical to propose some of the more interesting ornithological areas within easy reach of Southampton, and to mention some of the rarer and less common birds associated with each. It will be appreciated that, in the case of the rarer species, the localities, for obvious reasons, are left deliberately vague. Southampton itself, with its rapidly expanding boundaries, is ornithologically fortunate in possessing a considerable number of parks and open spaces, and many private houses with large gardens. These, together with the long and varied shore-line and the extensive river banks, provide the habitats for some sixty regular breeding species. The Common, through which runs the main Winchester road, even has a small breeding population of cirl buntings (*Emberiza cirlus*).

To the south-west of Southampton lies the New Forest, some 150 square miles of woodland and heath. The variety of this terrain provides the habitats of a number of the more interesting species of Hampshire birds. The gorse-dotted heathland is the haunt of the stonechat (*Saxicola torquata*) and, more rarely, the whinchat (*S. rubetra*). Until the severe winter of 1962-3, the Dartford warbler (*Sylvia undata*) had built up in such areas to a population of about 150 breeding pairs. Now, in the spring of 1963, it is certain that these warblers, together with a number of other resident passerines, have been sadly reduced in numbers to an extent not yet ascertained. The red-backed shrike (*Lanius collurio*) is a breeding species which has declined over the past years; some sixty pairs were located in 1961. Great grey shrikes (*L. excubitor*) are reported every winter. About thirty-five pairs of common buzzards (*B. buteo*) inhabit the Forest, fewer than the population before the virtual extinction of the rabbit by myxomatosis.

Honey buzzards (*Pernis apivorus*) have appeared in recent years, and the hobby (*Falco subbuteo*) is still a regular breeding species in spite of the depredations of egg-collectors; about fifteen pairs bred in 1961. Sparrow hawks (*Accipiter nisus*) and kestrels (*Falco tinnunculus*) are regular breeders, and Montagu's harrier (*Circus pygargus*) was just surviving (with two breeding pairs) in 1961. The redstart (*P. phoenicurus*), wheatear (*O. oenanthe*), woodlark (*Lullula arborea*) and nightjar (*Caprimulgus europaeus*) can be found breeding in fair numbers, and a few siskins (*Carduelis spinus*) appear to have bred in recent years. Crossbills (*Loxia recurvirostra*) are regularly found year by year in fluctuating numbers; there were some hundred pairs in 1960, though less than twenty pairs were reported in 1961. Most of the Forest streams have a pair of grey wagtails (*Motacilla cinerea*). The Forestry Commission, as the authority responsible for this area, makes every effort to safeguard both the habitats and the birds themselves by such means as the regulation of gorse burning and the constant vigilance of its officers (see p. 149).

North of Southampton, in the wooded areas around Ampfield, hawfinches (*C. coccothraustes*) can be found, and on the downlands around Winchester are corn buntings (*Emberiza calandra*). Somewhat rarer are the stone curlews (*Burhinus oedicnemus*), a few pairs only occurring on the wide open farmlands of this entire area.

The western coastline of Southampton Water is in the process of reclamation in some places and of industrialisation in others (Fig. 65). The early reclamation work created mud-pans which were excellent localities for waders, and the congregations, both in numbers and species, were ornithologically exciting. Unfortunately, the days when a little stint (*Calidris minuta*) could be compared with a Temminck's stint (*C. temminckii*) by observing them side by side have gone. However, some places, such as Dibden Bay and Ashlett Creek, still provide opportunities for seeing the ubiquitous redshank (*Tringa totanus*), with curlew (*Numenius arquata*), both godwits (*Limosa l.* and *lapponica*), greenshank (*Tringa nebularia*), spotted redshank (*T. erythropus*), knot (*Calidris canutus*), ruff (*Philomachus pugnax*), green and wood sandpiper (*Tringa ochropus* and *glareola*) and turnstone (*Arenaria interpres*). The little ringed plover (*Charadirus dubius*) has attempted to breed.

Needs Oar Point, at the mouth of the Beaulieu river, provides a similar list, with a probability of seeing more duck species. Garganey (*Anas querquedula*), gadwall (*A. strepera*) and pintail (*A. acuta*) occur, with scoter (*Melanitta nigra*) and eider (*Somateria mollissima*) on the sea.

To the west of Lymington, Pennington and Keyhaven marshes provide excellent wader habitats, and at Hurst Castle Spit sea-duck and occasional geese can be observed. Also recorded during most winters from this area are red-breasted mergansers (*Mergus serrator*), smew (*M. albellus*), Slavonian and black-necked grebe (*Podiceps auritus* and *caspicus*), and great northern, red-throated and black-throated divers (*Colymbus immer, stellatus,* and *arcticus*). In this general area are large breeding colonies of black-headed gulls (*Larus ridibundus*), though much molested by egg-collectors because these eggs are eaten. The shingle of Hurst Castle Spit is a breeding station of common/arctic Terns (*Sterna sp.*) and little terns (*S. albifrons*), with colonies of about a hundred pairs of the former and fifty pairs of the latter. The geographical situation of Hurst, jutting into the Solent, permits a seaward watch on the narrows between it and the Isle of Wight which is producing valuable data on the movement of sea birds along this coast, with records of roseate tern (*Sterna dougallii*) and sooty tern (*S. fuscata*) among the observed species.

Wintering white-fronted geese (*Anser albifrons*) are regularly found on the river Avon between Ringwood and Fordingbridge. Several hundred geese winter here on private land, where they are stringently protected and should be observed only from the road. If disturbed, they may be driven into unprotected areas, where some would undoubtedly be shot.

Space does not allow more than a mere reference to other important and interesting ornithological areas within reach of Southampton. Titchfield Haven, Langstone and Chichester Harbours, Farlington Marshes, Stanpit and Poole Harbour have all provided observers with numerous and valuable records.

In an average year southern Hampshire sees the recording of some 230 species, and among the more outstanding records during the last few years have been little egret (*Egretta garzetta*), white stork (*C. ciconia*), spoonbill (*Platalea leucorodia*), red-footed falcon (*Falco vespertinus*), goshawk (*Accipiter gentilis*), pectoral sandpiper (*Calidris melanotos*), Pomarine skua (*Stercorarius pomarinus*), desert wheatear (*Oenanthe deserti*), bluethroat (*Cyanosylvia svecica*), great reed warbler (*Acrocephalus arundinaceus*), Cetti's warbler (*Cettia cetti*), aquatic warbler (*Acrocephalus paludicola*), melodious warbler (*Hippolais polyglotta*), yellow-browed warbler (*Phylloscopus inornatus*), serin (*Serinus canarius*), Ortolan bunting (*Emberiza hortulana*) and Lapland bunting (*Calcarius lapponicus*).

MAMMALS

The British mammal fauna is well represented in the south of England generally, while the variety of vegetation in the Southampton region ensures that a considerable number of

XVIII   Typical New Forest beechwood with holly, in Denny Wood, New Forest (*N.G. ref.* SU 3306)

XIX   Typical New Forest heathland, on Matley Ridge (*N.G. ref.* SU 3207)

XX   Typical New Forest streamside 'lawn', near Whitemoor (*N.G. ref.* SU 3309)

XXI   Alder carr in Whitemoor Bog, New Forest (*N.G. ref.* SU 3309)

species occur. The largest wild mammals present are the deer. Fallow (*Dama dama*) are common in the New Forest, to the north-west of the main Bournemouth–Southampton railway, and elsewhere are evenly distributed, if less numerous. The red deer (*Cervus elaphus*) are nothing like so common, and apart from herds in parks are only to be found in the south-east of the New Forest. Roe (*Capreolus capreolus*) are numerous in south-western Hampshire and widely though less thickly distributed elsewhere. Sika (*Sika nippon*) are uncommon, being recorded from the New Forest and southern and western Dorset. Chinese Water Deer (*Hydropotes inermis*) appear to have escaped from two estates in northern Hampshire.

Of the carnivores, the fox (*Vulpes vulpes*) is common through the region, as is the badger (*Meles meles*). The latter is very abundant in some localities, particularly in the vicinity of Droxford in the Meon valley. In contrast, the otter (*Lutra lutra*) appears to be rather less numerous. Stoats (*Mustela erminea*) and weasels (*M. nivalis*) are not uncommon, although in many places, where land is used for sporting purposes, they tend to be rigorously trapped by game-keepers. A possible recent addition to the carnivores of the area is the mink (*Mustela vison*), which may have established itself, as a result of escapes, in the vicinity of the Hampshire Avon.

The small herbivorous mammals, many of which as a result of their small size and nocturnal activities are seen only infrequently, have numerous representatives within the region. The red squirrel (*Sciurus vulgaris*) has now been ousted from the mainland by the grey squirrel (*S. carolinensis*), in spite of attempts over the last twenty years to reduce the numbers of the latter. Colonies of the red squirrel still occur on the Isle of Wight. Its numbers having been very considerably reduced by myxomatosis, the rabbit (*Oryctolagus cuniculus*) is no longer as numerous as previously, although still ubiquitous. The brown hare (*Lepus europaeus*) is widespread. Both bank and field voles (*Clethrionomys glareolus* and *Microtus agrestis*) are common in suitable habitats, as is the long-tailed field-mouse (*Apodemus sylvaticus*). An interesting feature of the area is the relative abundance of the yellow-necked mouse (*A. flavicollis*), for which records are fairly numerous. The water vole (*Arvicola amphibius*) is locally very common along the banks of streams. The harvest mouse (*Micromys minutus*) occurs in cornfields and the fringing hedgerows, and it has also been found in comparatively large numbers in ricks in northern Hampshire and in the heathland at Studland. The existence of the dormouse (*Muscardinus avellanarius*) is far less certain; some may still persist in hazel coppice in the New Forest.

The Southampton region is one of the richest areas for bats in the British Isles. Species such as the serotine (*Eptesicus serotinus*), which is most common in the south-east of England, and the greater horseshoe bat (*Rhinolophus ferrum-equinum*) which is most numerous in the south-west, are both present here. Bechstein's bat (*Myotis bechsteini*), the rarest of the British bats, has been mainly recorded from Sussex and Hampshire. Of the twelve species of British bats, all but Leisler's (*Nyctalus leisleri*) have been recorded. The commonest are probably the pipistrelle (*Pipistrellus pipistrellus*) and the long-eared bat (*Plecotus auritus*).

The mole (*Talpa europaea*) is a common pest. The other insectivores, while quite common, are seldom seen and are not at all harmful. The water shrew (*Neomys fodiens*)

Ks

usually lives near streams and ponds, though it has been found at appreciable distances from them. The common and pygmy shrews (*Sorex araneus, S. minutus*), probably commonest in grassland, occur in most localities where insects are numerous and cover is available. The hedgehog (*Erinaceus europaeus*) is widespread and, from a survey conducted between 1952 and 1954 of the number of dead ones seen on the Hampshire roads, apparently quite common; comparatively large numbers were found in the less built-up suburbs of Bournemouth and Southampton.

Of the marine mammals, specimens of the porpoise (*Phocaena phocaena*), the common dolphin (*Delphinus delphis*) and the bottle-nosed dolphin (*Tursiops truncatus*) have been found stranded along the coastline. The common seal (*Phoca vitulina*) has visited these waters occasionally.

REPTILES AND AMPHIBIA

All six British species of reptiles are present, with the viper (*Vipera berus*), the grass snake (*Natrix natrix*), common lizard (*Lacerta vivipara*) and the slow worm (*Anguis fragilis*) all common. More local are the smooth snake (*Coronella austriaca*) and the sand lizard (*Lacerta agilis*). Amongst the amphibia the toad (*Bufo bufo*), frog (*Rana temporaria*), crested newt (*Triturus palustris*) and smooth newt (*T. vulgaris*) are widespread and abundant.

BIBLIOGRAPHICAL NOTE

The Marine Fauna of Southampton Water

(1) A. D. Ansell, '*Venus mercenaria* in Southampton Water, England', *Ecology* (1963), vol. 44, pp. 396-7.
(2) M. W. H. Bishop, 'Establishment of an immigrant barnacle in British coastal waters', *Nature* (1947), vol. 159, pp. 501-2.
(3) R. J. Conover, 'Notes on the seasonal distribution of zooplankton in Southampton Water, with special reference to the genus *Acartia*', *Annals and Magazine of Natural History* (1957), *Series 12*, vol. 10, pp. 63-67.
(4) D. J. Crisp and P. N. J. Chipperfield, 'Occurrence of *Eliminius modestus* (Darwin) in British waters', *Nature* (1948), vol. 161, p. 64.
(5) S. K. Eltringham and A. R. Hockley, 'Migration and reproduction of the wood-boring Isopod, *Limnoria*, in Southampton Water', *Limnology and Oceanography* (1961), vol. 6, pp. 467-82.
(6) A. R. Hockley, 'On the biology of *Mytilicola intestinalis* (Steuer)', *Journal of the Marine Biological Association of the United Kingdom* (1951), vol. 30, pp. 223-32.
(7) L. T. Jones, 'A comparative study of three species of the wood-boring isopod *Limnoria*' (Ph.D. thesis, University of Southampton, 1961).
(8) A. M. Norman and T. Scott, *The crustacea of Devon and Cornwall* (London, 1906).
(9) J. E. G. Raymont and B. G. A. Carrie, 'The zooplankton of Southampton Water', *International Oceanographical Congress, Preprints A.A.A.S., Washington* (1959), pp. 320-1.

Hydrobiology

(1) Avon Biological Research (1934-1938), *Annual Reports* (University College of Southampton).
(2) Avon and Dorset River Board (1962), *Annual Report for the year ended 31st March 1962* (Bournemouth).

(3) R. W. Butcher, 'The algae of the river' *Avon Biological Research* (1938), *Annual Report, 1936-7*, pp. 47-59.

(4) P. S. Corbet, C. Longfield and N. W. Moore, *Dragonflies* (London, 1960).

(5) C. Diver, 'The physiography of South Haven Peninsula, Studland Heath, Dorset', *Geographical Journal* (1933), vol. 81, pp. 404-27.

(6) T. T. Macan and Z. Macan, 'Preliminary note on the Ephemeroptera and Plecoptera of the Hampshire Avon and its tributaries', *Journal of the Society for British Entomology* (1940), vol. 2, pp. 53-61.

(7) T. T. Macan and A. Macfadyen, 'The water bugs of dew-ponds', *Journal of Animal Ecology* (1941), vol. 10, pp. 175-83.

(8) H. P. Moon and F. H. W. Green, 'Water meadows in southern England', in *The land of Britain, Part 89, Hampshire*, pp. 373-90 (London, 1940).

(9) N. W. Moore, 'The heaths of Dorset and their conservation', *Journal of Ecology* (1962), vol. 50, pp. 369-91.

(10) M. Owens and R. W. Edwards, 'The effects of plants on river conditions. III. Crop studies and estimates of net productivity of macrophytes in four streams in southern England', *Journal of Ecology* (1962), vol. 50, pp. 157-62.

(11) A. J. Pugsley, *Dewponds in fable and fact* (London, 1939).

Invertebrates

(1) J. B. Ford, 'A study of the biology and distribution of mud-dwelling chironomid larvae in a chalk-stream' (Ph.D. thesis, University of Southampton, 1957).

(2) H. Munro Fox, 'On *Apus*: its rediscovery in Britain, nomenclature and habits', *Proceedings of the Zoological Society of London* (1949), vol. 119, part III, pp. 693-702.

(3) R. E. Hall, 'The Chironomidae of three chalk-streams in southern England', *Verhandlungen XI, Internationaler Kongress für Entomologie* (1961), Band 1, pp. 178-81.

(4) R. E. Hall, 'On some aspects of the natural occurrence of *Chirocephalus diaphanus* Prevost', *Hydrobiologia* (1961), vol. XVIII, No. 3, pp. 205-17.

(5) H. Roberts, 'An ecological investigation of the arthropods of a beech-oak woodland, with particular reference to the Lithobiidae' (Ph.D. thesis, University of Southampton, 1957).

(6) S. Vaitilingam, 'The biology of the centipedes of some Hampshire woodlands' (M.Sc. thesis, University of Southampton, 1960).

Birds

Only one standard reference work exists on the birds of this region: *Birds of Hampshire and the Isle of Wight* (London) by J. E. Kelsall and P. W. Munn. This was published in 1905 and is considerably out of date. A new check-list is in preparation, but this has not yet been completed. The main published source of up-to-date information is the *Hampshire Bird Report* produced annually by the Ornithological Section of the Hampshire Field Club and Archaeological Society, whose headquarters are in Winchester. *Wildfowl in Hampshire* (Winchester, 1962), by J. H. Taverner, is an excellent survey covering the wildfowl records of the post-war years. G. E. W. is also indebted to his fellow-members of the New Forest Ornithologists' Club for the use of records.

Mammals

(1) J. Berlin *et al.*, *The New Forest* (London, 1960).

(2) J. L. Davies, 'A hedgehog road mortality index', *Proceedings of the Zoological Society of London* (1957), vol. 128, pp. 606-8.

(3) H. G. Lloyd, 'The distribution of squirrels in England and Wales', *Journal of Animal Ecology* (1962), vol. 31, pp. 157-65.

(4) F. J. T. Page, *Field guide to British deer* (Mammal Society of the British Isles, 1957).

(5) F. P. Rowe, 'Some observations on harvest mice from the corn ricks of a Hampshire farm', *Proceedings o the Zoological Society of London* (1958), vol. 131, pp. 320-3.

(6) E. Sandar, *A beast book for the pocket* (Oxford, 1937).

X

LAND USE, AGRICULTURE, FORESTRY AND CONSERVATION

THE fundamental division into the chalklands and the Tertiary lowlands, which forms such a striking feature of the structure and geomorphology of the Hampshire region, is obviously of major significance when considering land use. Moreover, the physical appearance of much of the county cannot have greatly changed during the centuries. In particular, the New Forest has for long occupied a vast area to the west of Southampton Water, and on the higher parts of the chalklands that surround the Forest much land remained for long uninhabited and uncultivated.

Enclosure took place first in the south-eastern parts of the county between Winchester and the coast, though much remained under forest, notably the Forest of Bere. Most of the cultivable parts were brought into use as a result of direct enclosure, a process that continued well into the seventeenth century. This may have been due to population pressure, to improved farm techniques or to the freer use of hired labour. It appears that only 6 per cent of the total area of the county was affected by the later eighteenth-century method of enclosure by Private Act of Parliament. There is some evidence that as early as Tudor and Stuart times demand for tillage had led to the enclosure of some of the wastes.

Two sixteenth-century inventories suggest that farming on the Chalk was mixed, with grazing of a variety of stock—cattle, sheep, pigs and poultry—and arable, producing wheat, barley, hay and vetches. The northern part of the county developed a reputation at an early date for the breeding of horses. In Henry VIII's time there was 'erected a noble studderie for breeding horse, especially the greatest sort, and for a time had a very great success with them'. In many parts the horse herds ran together over the common pastures, and various efforts were made to check the inevitable degeneracy that followed. Today, some of the finest stables in the country are to be found in the same area. Besides horses and sheep, the county was also famous for its hogs. In 1662 Thomas Fuller wrote 'Hampshire Hogs are allowed by all for the best bacon, being our English Westphalian and which, well ordered, have deceived the most judicious palates. Here the swine feed in the forest on plenty of acorns . . . which going out lean return home fat, without either care or cost to their owners. Nothing but fulness stinteth their feeding on the mast falling from the trees, where also they lodge at liberty (not pent up, as in other places, to stacks of peas) which some assign the reason of the fineness of their flesh. . . .' One of the common rights in the New Forest was that of pannage, the right to turn out swine during a limited period in autumn to feed on beech mast and acorns. The time was sharply defined in favour of the deer, for they sicken and die if fed on green acorns and mast, but thrive on them when they are really ripe and dry. Hence the prohibition of pannage by pigs in winter, during which deer could get the best feeding.

New methods of husbandry were introduced into the northern part of the county early in the seventeenth century. Turnips had appeared long before Townsend's time, and new types of grass, clover and sainfoin were firmly established, as well as wheat, barley, peas, beans and vetches. By the eighteenth century, large areas of downland had been converted from sheep walks into wheat lands, especially between Winchester and Salisbury. Defoe was much impressed by the downland sheep, but what surprised him more was 'how a great part of these Downs comes by a new method of Husbandry, to be only made Arable, which they never were in former Days, but to bear excellent wheat and great Crops too, tho' otherwise poor, barren land and never known to our Ancestors to be capable of any such Thing— for by only folding the Sheep upon the Plow'd Lands, those Lands which otherwise are barren, and where the Plow goes within three or four Inches of the solid Rock of Chalk, are made fruitful . . .', and grew crops of wheat, rye and barley.

When Arthur Young visited the district between Salisbury, Winchester and Alton in 1768 he found that, apart from the poor unenclosed chalk hills around Winchester, much of the land was enclosed, though most farms were smaller than a hundred acres. In the west a rotation was followed of fallow, wheat, oats, peas or beans, and vetches, and further east fallow, wheat, barley, clover and trefoil. Turnips were grown, and folded by sheep. On the eastern margin of the county hops were a profitable crop. It is evident that a cash economy was bringing prosperity to the area, with wheat, barley and hops, as well as wool, bacon and honey, for sale.

By contrast, the condition of the New Forest deteriorated during the eighteenth century, and it became necessary to set up a Commission to investigate the causes. Many trees were decayed, there was insufficient reafforestation, deer were overstocked, encroachments had been made within and around the Forest boundaries, rabbits and stock destroyed, young trees and the mature timber was stolen.

At the end of the eighteenth century, Charles Vancouver published his *General View of the Agriculture of the County of Hampshire*. Barley and oats were then widely grown; turnips had been introduced in the neighbourhood of Hayling Island; vegetables were cultivated for both local and more distant markets; and specialised crops, such as hops, lucerne and sainfoin were becoming increasingly important in the south-east. Vancouver, however, displayed little enthusiasm for Hampshire livestock, though he observed a measure of enterprise on the part of some breeders.

Hampshire was hit by the lean years following 1815, and depression characterised the agriculture of the county for the following twenty years. Nevertheless, William Cobbett found evidence of good farming practice in 1821-2, though admittedly some of the enclosures had not revealed much real success. By 1850 Henry Gawlor, W. H. Rham and Sir James Caird had each noted that while some improvements had taken place they were accompanied by too much labour, too many losses, insufficient machinery, inefficient use of feedstuffs and manure, and ill-planned farm buildings. Ten years later, the north of the county was still under small backward farms, with low cereal yields and poor quality of cattle. From the downlands, however, 300,000 Hampshire Down sheep were sold off annually at Weyhill and other fairs, while in the southern part of the county dairying to supply the ports and naval establishments was developing. Gradually improvements were introduced, drainage made the cultivation of vetches possible, swedes and mangolds were grown on the lighter soils, and clover was more widely introduced. The arable-sheep system persisted on the chalklands, though actually the number of sheep dropped by 16 per cent from 612,000 in 1874 to 512,000 in 1880. This rate of decline accelerated during the next few years, for by 1893 the numbers had dropped to 380,000. On the other hand, cattle had risen in the same period from 67,000 to 81,000. Later in the century, the 1893 depression resulted in a great deal of land going completely out of cultivation and being used only as sheep runs, especially between Winchester and Basingstoke.

MODERN AGRICULTURAL TRENDS

The graphs (Figs. 35, 36), based on the June returns to the Ministry of Agriculture, Fisheries and Food, reveal several of the general trends in agriculture from 1866 to the present day, and at the same time show the effects of the more striking influences, such as economic depressions and the two world wars. They also illustrate the general fluctuations in arable production, the remarkable growth of dairying, the tendency in arable cultivation towards barley, and the more general change towards cultivation of grasses and other feed crops. Perhaps the most striking changes have taken place in the last ten years, for farming is now a business rather than a profession. Fig. 34 shows the changes in size of farms. Throughout Hampshire the trend is towards larger units, so that today 80 per cent of the county is farmed by 18 per cent of the farmers, while on the other hand only 5 per cent of the land is worked by 60 per cent of the farmers. The very small units are mostly on the Tertiaries, around the New Forest and to the east of Southampton Water, and in the northern parts of the county to the north-east of Basingstoke. It will be seen that the decrease in the number of farms is derived mainly from the small units, while the increase in the number of farms is mainly in the larger units.

In 1950, 5188 farmers were working units of less than twenty acres, but by 1960 there were 4508, and by 1961 only 4216 (Fig. 34). Thus nearly a thousand of these small-holders had either gone out of business or had amalgamated to form larger units. To a lesser extent a similar sequence can be seen in holdings of from 20 to 100 acres. In 1961 these holdings accounted for 15 per cent of the land, and were being farmed by 20 per cent of the farmers, but in the period 1950 to 1961 the number dropped from 1794 to 1597. Even from holdings of 100 to 500 acres, which account for about half of the total farm area, 120 farmers either sold out of business or their lands were amalgamated into larger units. On the other hand, during the same period there was an increase of fifteen in the number of holdings between 500 and 1000 acres and of eighteen in the number of holdings of more than 1000 acres.

THE PRESENT AGRICULTURAL PATTERN

In a general way, farming in Hampshire today can be divided into, first, the chalkland farms which are devoted almost exclusively to barley production, usually with one other secondary enterprise; and secondly, the smaller and more varied enterprises away from the Chalk.

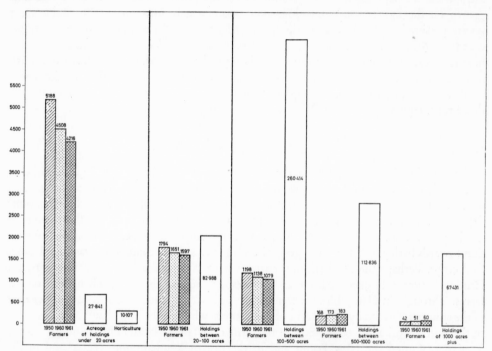

Fig. 34. Size of holdings and numbers of farmers in Hampshire, 1950–61

The left-hand section indicates holdings under 20 acres, the centre section holdings between 20 and 100 acres, and the right-hand section holdings over 100 acres, subdivided into 100–500, 500–1000 and over 1000 acres. The shaded columns indicate the numbers of farmers in each category for 1950, 1960 and 1961, according to the scale on the left. The white columns are drawn proportional to the total acreage in each category of size of holding (in thousands of acres) for 1961.

Since 1939 the acreage under barley has increased more than sevenfold from 21,000 to 150,000 acres (Fig. 37), and moreover it is now cropped continuously. A simplified farming system prevails, with large units growing barley to the exclusion of most other crops, thus developing almost a monoculture. It is in effect a kind of hydrogenic industry, for it has been discovered that the Chalk holds and releases moisture in an ideal way for barley, and the primary function of the farmer is to control the methods of cultivation and the application of fertilisers to take advantage of this fact. 'Procter' and more recently 'Baldrick' and

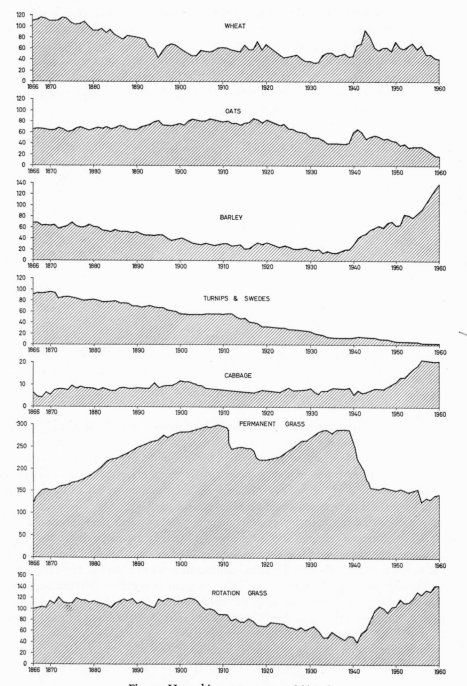

Fig. 35. Hampshire crop returns, 1866-1960

'Badger' breeds of barley now dominate on the chalkland farms. The crop is either sold for malting if the quality is right or is used on the farm for stock-feed. In addition, yields have doubled in the last ten years from 20 to 40 cwts. per acre, brought about, in part, by the destruction of rabbits by myxomatosis. There is usually one other enterprise, perhaps dairy cattle, sheep, pigs or occasionally poultry. But many farms have no livestock, and the secondary enterprise may be the production of herbage seed; the acreage under this rose from 2000 in 1956 to over 6000 in 1963.

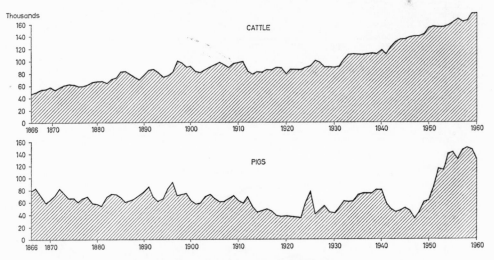

Fig. 36. Hampshire livestock returns, 1866-1960

Although some attempt was made after the War of 1939-45 to maintain the high acreage of wheat achieved during the war years (Fig. 37), barley production under the new mono-cultural system was obviously so much more profitable that from 1954 wheat steadily decreased in cultivation to less, in fact, than the 1939 acreage. A similar trend can be seen in the acreage of oats, though the causes are related more to the introduction of mechanisation to replace horses, and to new and better methods of stock feeding.

The sound economics of barley production, the trend towards simplification and the increase in size of units is reflected also in the changes in the farming of dairy cows (Fig. 36). For instance, while about 3000 farmers kept a dairy herd in 1950, by 1960 the number had dropped to less than 2000, though the actual number of cows had increased and the amount of milk likewise, until in 1961 a peak production of 50 million gallons was reached. At the same time, fewer people were working the herds, which themselves were much larger and the milk-yield per cow was higher. These changes were brought about by modifications in farm buildings, such as the development of 'herring-bone parlours', and by better mechanisation; in several districts one man is handling a herd of 80 to 100 cows. Neverthe-less, a slight downward trend in the number of dairy cows is becoming appreciable; this is probably linked both with the major movement towards the growing of barley and with the reduction in the number of small farm units in the neighbourhood of the New Forest.

A steady decrease took place in the total number of sheep from about a million at the beginning of the last century to 300,000 at the beginning of the twentieth, and to 15,000 in

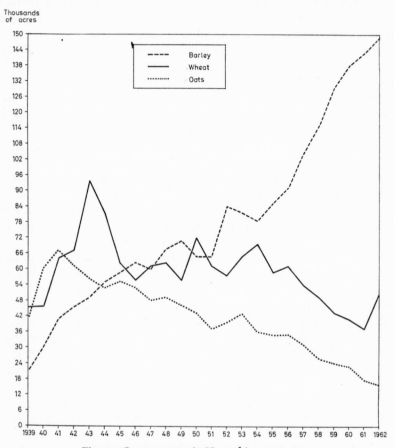

Fig. 37. Crop acreages in Hampshire, 1939-61

1949. But during the last ten years there has been a significant increase to 42,000 in 1962, and it appears that this is likely to continue. Formerly, the sheep were mostly Hampshire Downs, but now they are being replaced by Suffolks; once they were folded on roots, now they are fed on grasses. Their chief value, as formerly, is to improve the arable, and they are being introduced on the large barley farms to raise the yield.

Turnips which used to support the Hampshire Down sheep are now seldom grown. Potatoes, of which 20,000 acres were cultivated during the War of 1939-45, are now produced on less than 5500 acres, mostly in low-lying areas or on the Greensand. The sugar beet acreage has also declined from 3000 acres in 1954 to less than 1000 in 1963, partly because the nearest factory is at Kidderminster and the costs of transport have become prohibitive, and partly because it seems almost impossible to raise the sugar content of the beet in this district. For several years kale was introduced to supplement the animal feed, and its acreage rose to 20,000 in 1960, but improved techniques in the conservation and utilisation of grasses have reversed this trend, and are likely to continue to do so.

The trend towards larger units is also seen in the pig-rearing industry. While in 1947 there were only 3000 sows in Hampshire, by 1962 there were 91,000, tied mostly to the large barley farms and in large units; a farm might formerly carry twenty sows, but today from 300 to 500. The pigs are produced for three kinds of market and there are accordingly three types of development: for pork, for bacon and for heavy hogs, and production is tied closely to the large factories and to the supermarkets.

Similar trends towards large units have taken place in the poultry industry; in 1944 there were 55,000 laying hens, but in 1962 there were 1,100,000, and 80 per cent of these were being farmed in only thirty-five units. There has also been a sudden development of turkey farming, again dependent on the activity of only a few people, for while in 1943 there were 10,000 turkeys in the county, this figure had risen to over 300,000 in 1963. This increase was achieved in spite of the periodically devastating effects of fowl pest, though it is anticipated that inoculation will in due course stamp out this disease.

These fundamental changes towards monoculture on the Chalk, towards larger units, and towards dairying and poultry farming on a large scale could not have taken place without radical changes in the attitude towards the land, in the use of fertilisers, in the economic use of labour, and in improvements in mechanisation, farm buildings, transport and marketing. Practically all these, including the increasing of yields per acre or per animal, have been made with a declining labour force. In 1949 about 16,000 persons were working on the land, but in 1962 only 10,000. Improvements have been achieved, in fact, by the introduction of more mechanisation on the farms; in 1942 2800 tractors were in use, by 1956 over 11,000. It is, however, of interest and significance to observe that by 1958 the numbers had dropped somewhat to 10,000, because by that year many of the small farmers, each of whom had owned a tractor, had sold out to the larger units; and on these farms bigger but fewer all-purpose tractors were in use.

Today the main buildings on a large Hampshire farm are the grain drier and the storer. In some areas machinery syndicates deal with the needs of groups of farmers, and there are also building syndicates for grain drying and storage. About five large firms are responsible for the bulk supply of farm requisites in the county, and these also make themselves responsible for buying and marketing most of the farmers' surplus cereal products.

In Hampshire few livestock sales are effected at public cattle markets, for most selling is on a contract basis to large buyers and to the supermarkets. Some movement towards group organisation has occurred, so that groups of farmers create larger units of production and voluntarily guarantee both quantity and quality of supply to the factories and slaughter-houses. Thus, in addition to the machinery and building syndicates, there are buying and selling groups, and production groups who guarantee prime pork or quality bacon.

Other aspects of this move towards larger units are seen in the use made of soil nutrients and in soil treatment. Since the War of 1939-45, deficiencies in phosphates and potash have been gradually corrected, and in some areas on the Chalk there may even be a surplus of these two chemicals. Accordingly, full use can now be made of heavy applications of nitrogen. Furthermore, the liberal use of weed-killers and sprays, especially on growing barley, is now a routine activity which has contributed to the heavy yields. Fig. 38 shows the use made of the three primary soil nutrients during the past few years, achieving a steady increase in the application of nitrogen, phosphates and potash, much above the average for the country as a whole. In fact, applications of nitrogen have reached 76 per cent of the estimated optimum, phosphates about 64 per cent and potash 58 per cent.

LAND CLASSIFICATION

Since most of these trends are associated, under modern conditions, with the formation of larger farm units, and as for the most part the overall farming structure improves with an increase in the size of holding, it would appear that a method of land classification can

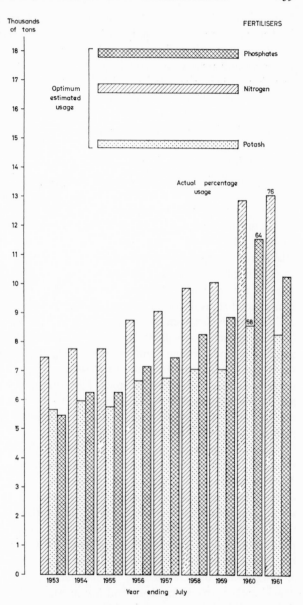

Fig. 38. Consumption of plant nutrients on Hampshire farms, 1953-61

The highest usage (percentage of optimum) of nitrogen was 76 (in 1961), of phosphates 64 (in 1960) and of potash 58 (in 1960).

be based on an evaluation related to farm size. Fig. 39 shows such an attempt to produce a land classification map, by applying information concerning size of farms to an agricultural production map. It will be seen that the urban areas of Portsmouth, Southampton and Bournemouth are of course agriculturally useless, with similar, though smaller, areas around Eastleigh, Winchester, Fareham, Alton, Basingstoke and Andover.

A second category of areas comprises land mostly non-agricultural, though not necessarily urban. This includes the New Forest and the adjacent commonland, which occupy a dominant part of south-western Hampshire. It also comprises part of the Western Weald, that part of the London Basin lying within Hampshire, parts of the Tertiary coast-lands, and the heathlands that extend beyond the river Avon. Of these, the New Forest is mainly Crown land, while north-eastern Hampshire is not only agriculturally poor but declining, and moreover is becoming more and more tributary to London and its overspill. The nature and size of the holdings in the Western Weald, apart from the commons and waste land, are determined to a considerable extent by rapid changes in relief and soils. Much of the coastal zone between the New Forest and the sea is residential, though inland it is interspersed with small but profitable, mostly horticultural, holdings.

The third category of areas consists of small and medium-sized farms, most of which must be regarded as at or below the national average of productivity, after allowance has been made for production performance and farming structure. These farms lie adjacent to the Test valley between the New Forest and the Chalk, they also flank the rich valley bottoms of the Avon valley, they occupy much of the western parts of the London Basin, and they extend between Southampton and Fareham towards the urban ribbon extension to the north of Portsmouth. Many of these farms are small; some concentrate on dairying, others on mixed arable and livestock. Few attempts have been made to amalgamate them and in any case they do not lend themselves to the kind of development that has taken place on the Chalk. In very few places is the profitability of these areas comparable with the majority of the chalkland farms.

The most profitable group is to be found, with one or two exceptions, on the Chalk, a zone clearly delimited on the south by a line a mile or so north of Eastleigh and Portsmouth. The northern boundary of the zone also follows the edge of the Chalk, though not so sharply defined. Here the holdings are large, with many of them of more than 500 or even 1000 acres. Most concentrate on barley production with the one other secondary enterprise, and their profitability is well above the national average after allowance has been made for production performance and farming structure. Outside the main belt of the chalklands a number of smaller areas is included in this group: the chalklands that protrude into Dorset at Rockbourne and Damerham, the northern flanks of Portsdown, some of the intensive 'truck' areas between Fareham and Southampton and between the Solent and the New Forest, and the lower part of the Avon valley.

LAND USE AND SILVICULTURE IN THE NEW FOREST

The New Forest forms one of the largest areas of unenclosed land remaining in the south of Britain. Within the 'Perambulation' or legal forest boundary (Fig. 40) lies a total area of

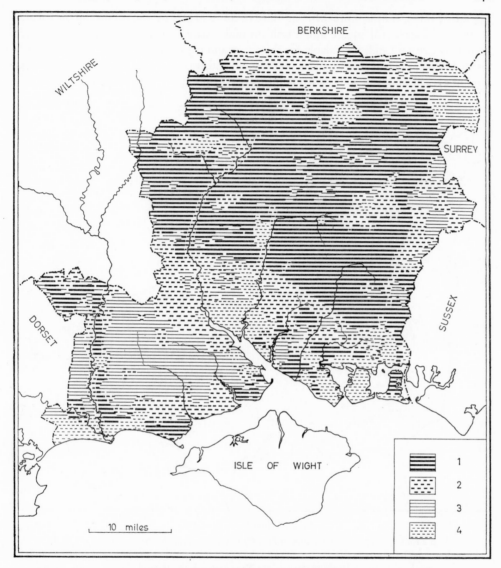

Fig. 39. Land classification in Hampshire

The numerals are as follows: 1. Land above national average of productivity. 2. Land of average productivity. 3. Land mostly non-agricultural. 4. Urban land.

144 square miles. A little more than one-third of this is in private ownership and the balance, about 65,000 acres (101 square miles) remains under state ownership. Nearly all the latter, known as Crown Land, is available for the access and enjoyment of the public, and can be divided into approximately 25,500 acres of woodland, 38,000 acres of open heath and 1000 acres of agricultural land and residential property (Plates IV, XVIII–XXI).

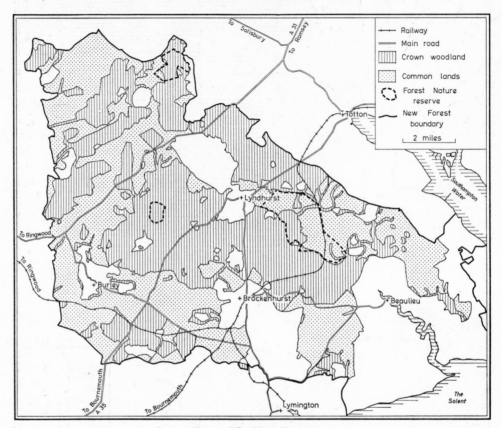

Fig. 40. The New Forest

Based on a folding map, scale 1:63,360, in *Forestry Commission Guide: the New Forest* (H.M.S.O., London, 1951).
The correct legal term for the boundary of the New Forest is the Perambulation. Areas left un-shaded within the Perambulation represent private freehold land.

This ancient Royal Forest is administered by the Forestry Commission, the direct successor of the Lords Warden appointed by the medieval kings to preserve their personal domains. Its principal officer is still known by the ancient title of Deputy Surveyor. The New Forest Commoners, who include descendants of men who pastured cattle and ponies on the Forest in prehistoric and Saxon times, still exercise their grazing rights. Disputes

XXII 'Channel die-back' of *Spartina* at Lymington (*N.G. ref.* SZ 3395)

XXIII 'Pan die-back' of *Spartina* at Lymington

XXIV   Tussock-sedge (*Carex paniculata*) and bog-moss (*Sphagnum*) in alder carr at Whitemoor (*N.G. ref.* SU 3309)

XXV   *Gladiolus illyricus*, a very rare New Forest plant

XXVI   *Hydnum erinaceum*, a New Forest fungus, growing on a beech near Knightwood

affecting these rights are decided by the Verderers' Court of Swainmote and Attachment, almost the sole survivor of the many powerful courts of forest law that once held sway over much of England.

During medieval times the Forest was managed primarily as a royal hunting-ground, with little or no regard for timber production. Increasing demands for timber for ship-building in the seventeenth century led to the 1698 Act, authorising the inclosure and plant-ing of 6000 acres. A further Act, in 1851, authorised the removal of deer from, and made the inclosure and planting of, a further 10,000 acres possible. The implementation of this latter Act, though beneficial to silviculture, caused much dissatisfaction among the Commoners, and the situation was altered by a further Act in 1877. This forbade further inclosure, and re-constituted the Verderers' Court; the number of Verderers was increased from four to seven, one Official Verderer was appointed by the Crown and the six others were elected by the Commoners and Parliamentary voters in the Forest. The powers of the Verderers were also increased, so as to give them effective control over matters affecting Commoners' rights.

In 1949 another New Forest Act was passed, under which the number of Verderers was increased to ten, five being appointed and five elected. The Official Verderer is appointed by the Queen, and one Verderer each by the Forestry Commissioners, the Minister of Agriculture, the local Hampshire planning authority, and the Council for the Preservation of Rural England; the remaining five Verderers are elected by the Commoners. For this purpose a Commoner is defined as an occupier (though not necessarily the owner) of not less than one acre of land to which common rights are attached. Of the total number of ten Verderers, only the Official Verderer and four others nominated by the Lord Chancellor can sit and adjudicate in the Court of Swainmote. All other matters are considered and decided upon by all the Verderers, except that in any division upon the question of allowing the Forestry Commissioners or the Minister of Agriculture to enclose lands in the Open Forest for purposes defined by the Act, the appointee of the authority concerned is not allowed to vote.

As a result of the 1949 Act, an atlas was prepared, based on the 1858 register, to cover all lands with common rights. Provision was made for a limited amount of reseeding in the Open Forest, to improve the grazing. The Act also authorised the temporary inclosure of areas of ancient and ornamental woodland, to secure their regeneration, and the inclosure of a further 5000 acres for silviculture. The responsibility of the Forestry Commission in regard to the open forest was defined more clearly than hitherto.

Today the principal concerns in the administration of the Forest are the Commoners' rights, particularly with regard to the grazing of animals, silviculture and timber production, public amenity, and the conservation of wild life; the last of these is discussed below (see p. 149). At the present time nearly 2000 ponies and 4000 cattle graze there, wandering unrestrictedly, and swine feed in autumn on the acorns and beech-mast (see p. 131). There are also estimated to be about 1000 fallow deer and 300 roe, but red and Sika deer are present only in small numbers. The animals add a characteristic charm to the Forest, but they create a major hazard on the unfenced roads which cross it, and many are involved in accidents each year. Immense numbers of people enjoy the unspoilt beauty of the Forest, and numerous camping and caravanning licences are issued each year. Yet even on a summer Sunday, when the main roads are thronged, those who know can walk for miles in near solitude. Unfortunately, the greatest single problem arises out of this huge increase in the number of the general public who visit the Forest, for many leave behind excreta and litter, cause fires, seriously disturb the wild life and commit acts of vandalism.

Open Forest (38,000 acres)

Through this area both the Commoners' animals and the public are free to wander at large. Four Agisters, employed by the Verderers, are responsible for the supervision of the Commoners' animals—that is, for seeing that they are properly marked, that the due fees are paid and that the Commoners comply with the by-laws which cover the conditions under which the animals may be turned out. The Forestry Commission is responsible for keeping the open forest free from coarse vegetation, for maintaining the 'passages' through the bogs and for necessary drainage. Some 2000 acres of coarse vegetation are burnt or cut annually in accordance with a plan agreed by the Commoners' Defence Association and by the Nature Conservancy.

Ancient and Ornamental Woodlands (6000 acres)

These areas are composed mainly of hardwoods (beech and oak), with a little natural Scots pine in places. The hardwoods are of great age and low timber value; many have been pollarded, a practice which was carried out up to 1698 to provide winter fodder for the deer and also fuel wood, but was brought to an end in that year by Act of Parliament. The ancient and ornamental areas are open alike to the public and to Commoners' animals, and as a result of the heavy grazing pressure regeneration is virtually impossible. Until the passing of the 1949 Act, the Crown was not entitled to fell and remove any timber other than that which was dead, dying or windthrown, but that Act made it possible to fell and restock, by planting or natural regeneration, blocks of up to twenty acres, arranged so that no two blocks were contiguous, provided that the Verderers first gave their approval. Some 391 acres have been so treated to date. Unfortunately, there is now a wide age gap between the ancient trees which are dying of decay and those in the new regeneration areas, the best of which are still only about 8 feet high.

The Inclosures (20,000 acres, including Freehold and Leasehold)

These are the areas, fenced against the Commoners' animals, where plantations are managed on a silvicultural basis, albeit with a high regard to amenity. There are 18,000 acres of these statutory inclosures, of which 16,000 acres may be inclosed at any one time. The balance may only be re-inclosed if any equivalent acreage is thrown open to grazing, the trees having grown large enough to be virtually immune from grazing damage. In addition, under the 1949 Act 2000 acres, out of a possible maximum of 5000, have been approved by the Verderers for inclosure and are at present in process of being planted.

Freehold

Certain plantations, a little agricultural land and numerous residential properties are Crown Freehold. Within the perambulation of the Forest exist many 'islands' of private freehold, which have been derived from the Crown during the ages for one reason or another. It is evident that quite large tracts may have changed little in character at least since Norman times. The need to preserve both these areas and the ancient and ornamental woodlands, together with the need to replant with a high proportion of hardwoods, has inevitably resulted in a very variable, even patchwork, pattern of forestry. The fact that all, or nearly all, tree species which grow reasonably well also regenerate freely, adds to the diversity of the pattern.

Silviculture

Down the ages the requirements of war have influenced silviculture greatly. Thus the need for yew for bows is possibly one of the reasons for the frequency of this tree on soils with which it is not normally associated. Wooden warships resulted in an era of open grown oak, with the object of producing the 'bends and knees' suitable for shipbuilding; many of them still stand today. They have a new value—amenity—which in monetary terms costs the Exchequer a not inconsiderable sum for loss of production of more marketable species producing a greater volume of timber per annum. During the War of 1914-18 the New Forest provided 8 million cubic feet of timber; many clear fellings were carried out and made good by subsequent replanting. During 1939-45 another 2000 acres had to be felled, providing $12\frac{1}{2}$ million cubic feet. It was these fellings, leaving 20 to 25 'mother trees' per acre, which led to a policy of natural regeneration of Scots pine.

By agreement, the ancient and ornamental areas and approximately 40 per cent of the inclosures must be stocked with hardwoods. Since time immemorial oak has been the principal hardwood; both the Sessile oak and the Pedunculate oak are present, the former being less common, but usually growing better. There is a very promising group of Spessart oak at Sloden. Red oak has been planted in odd groups, with one complete block of large timber, now no longer inclosed, at Freeworms Hill, while Turkey oak is present sporadically.

The proportion of the total woodland area occupied by beech was 16 per cent about forty years ago, but since then prolific regeneration, aided by considerable planting and underplanting, mainly during the 'thirties, has greatly increased this proportion. It is interesting to note that some of the New Forest beech is of good form and type, as at Woodfidley (which contains one of the largest beech trees in Europe), at Janes Hill, at Woodcrates and at Bramshaw High Beeches. Elsewhere, however, particularly at Emery Down, the beech is of a very inferior form. Sweet chestnut grows well on the lighter, better soils, though it is not free from 'shake', internal cracking in the wood which reduces its value as timber.

Other trees are of minor or negligible economic importance. Sycamore is present in a few areas, notably at Denny and Northerwood, where it is spreading rapidly. Ash is scarce and poor, and the elms are virtually absent, though common on alkaline soils to the west. Birch (mostly *Betula pendula*) is common as a native tree, and a few stands are managed silviculturally, while some of the alder, common in the bog 'carrs', is occasionally coppiced. Exotic species which have become naturalised include False acacia (*Robinia pseudoacacia*) which regenerates freely at New Park, and Snowy mespilus (*Amelanchia canadensis*), naturalised in the south-west.

Though yew is found in many areas, in recent years it has suffered considerably from die-back, the cause of which has not been determined with certainty. Scots pine, extinct since prehistoric times but reintroduced in 1776, is now the major conifer species and has colonised many parts of the open forest. In the plantations there is a preponderance of eighty- to ninety-year-old stands, with a great shortage of middle-aged trees and a large acreage of up to twenty-year-old stands resulting from the restocking of areas cleared during the War of 1939-45 by natural regeneration. Corsican pine (*Pinus laricio*), first planted at Knightwood where there is a magnificent stand, has been used fairly widely on the plateau-gravels; it regenerates to some extent, though rather sparingly. Weymouth pine (*P. strobus*), planted in Dames Slough, has regenerated freely, but the original trees have become subject to disease and many were removed in 1961. The only examples of Monterey pine (*P. radiata*), apart from some groups sown and planted within the last two years, are a fine tree at Northerwood and a tall avenue leading into Lyndhurst, together with a few in private gardens.

The European larch has proved very satisfactory, but Japanese larch is doubtful, for it suffers severely from drought, though there are some useful stands. Both the Norway and Sitka spruce are present and regenerate freely; the former seems to stand better the warm summers and spring frosts. Sitka spruce periodically suffers very severely from aphid attack, though some fine stands are at Knightwood.

The Douglas fir was first introduced about 1860 and many of the original trees still stand, the best examples being in Bolderwood; the climate of the New Forest is ideally suited to this species, which thrives and regenerates freely. The Silver fir (*Abies pectinata*) was planted at New Park at about the same time as the Douglas fir, and it too regenerates freely and so far has been free of disease; there is also regeneration in Puckpits. Other conifers are of only minor importance; there are a few small recent plantings of *Abies grandis*, a small stand of *Thuja* has been planted at Wilverley and a few groups of *Tsuga* are to be found. Some specimen trees of the redwoods, mostly *Sequoia sempervirens*, occur, and there are some plantings of Lawson cypress (*Chamaecyparis lawsoniana*).

The first record of a definite silvicultural system involving restocking by means of natural regeneration was in the 1920-30 plan, which mentions schemes for establishing oak by natural regeneration in Aldridge Hill and Salisbury Trench Inclosures; much of this has been very successful. In 1939-45 the natural regeneration of oak was again attempted in Holly Hatch, Broomy and Roe Wood Inclosures, thirty to thirty-five 'mother trees' per acre, evenly spaced, being left throughout each area. In Holly Hatch and Broomy regeneration failed, due to the dense growth of bracken so common on the Bracklesham Beds. In Roe Wood, on the Barton Clay, about 25 per cent of the 200 acres has been successfully regenerated, mainly on areas of grass and bramble. At the same period many areas of Scots pine were successfully regenerated by leaving twenty to twenty-five 'mother trees' per acre, while in Busketts Inclosure a strip system was employed, clear felled strips alternating with strips in which the trees were left standing. This too was highly successful, regeneration being profuse, even within the unfelled strips.

In 1946 a block of the Bolderwood Douglas fir was heavily thinned to promote regeneration; the resulting crop is excellent. A further block was opened up in 1958 and regeneration is occurring there too. In South Oakley and Shave Green Inclosures war-time fellings resulted in complete restocking by natural regeneration, the species being oak, beech, Douglas fir and Scots pine, with some European larch and Norway spruce in certain areas. There is much beech regeneration under oak in South Oakley and elsewhere, and under Scots pine in Knightwood. The main losses in natural regeneration are due to browsing by deer and the competition of grasses, rushes and bracken. Bramble is the least serious, for it gives some measure of protection against damage by deer.

Economic Value

The New Forest is well situated for the sale of round saw timber. There is a good demand by local sawmills for conifer timber, but economic sales of hardwood timber are generally limited to straight lengths of 4 feet by a foot quarter girth and over, while lower-grade material is sold locally, mainly for pit-props. The Forest has a high reputation for the production of telegraph poles; in fact, certain compartments of some inclosures are set aside especially for their production. The selected areas are high pruned and thinned with this object in view.

Wood wool, pit-props and pulpwood are produced and sold, although the haulage distances make the profits low. There is, however, a profitable local market for fencing and rustic material, and cleft oak piles of high quality are in good demand. Some hardwood material is sent to Sudbrook in South Wales, and charcoal is still burnt in the Forest.

CONSERVATION

The basic unit with which the conservationist is concerned is the habitat (or *ecosystem*). In Britain, most, if not all, ecosystems owe their present characteristics to human land use, to conditions of climate and to the physiographical features. Certain habitats, such as areas under arable cultivation or coniferous afforestation, obviously owe their origins to the direct intervention of man. Others, such as the chalk grasslands and the lowland heaths of Hampshire, have developed through less abrupt and more subtle changes. Gradual processes of woodland clearance, beginning in early times, together with the use of land for pasture, have evolved vegetative conditions best described as 'semi-natural'. Such areas of semi-natural vegetation normally support plant and animal species unable to survive under more intense agriculture. Because they are particularly liable at the present time to reclamation for agriculture, forestry and urban and industrial development, it is with such habitats that the conservationist inevitably finds himself most concerned. In Hampshire his particular interest is with the conservation of the chalk grasslands, the heaths in the north and in the New Forest, and the tidal and freshwater marshes along the coast.

The overall reduction in the area of semi-natural vegetation is a process centuries old, which may in general be regarded as an inevitable consequence of a steadily increasing population. This process has been accelerated during periods when rising market prices for arable produce resulted in an incentive to plough, as for example, during the Napoleonic Wars, the 1850's and 1860's, and again in the War of 1939-45. During the present century, and particularly during the past two decades, economic incentives to plough, together with the demands of housing, industry and forestry, have exerted unprecedented pressure on areas of semi-natural vegetation generally, and more especially on those in central and southern England.

The impact of these influences may be illustrated by the chalk grasslands of Hampshire. Here the extension of the arable, and to a lesser extent of afforestation, have reduced the sheep-downs, with their rich and characteristic flora, to the point where only small isolated fragments remain. Of these fragments few are grazed regularly, and with the decrease of sheep husbandry and with the destruction of the rabbit by myxomatosis most are reverting rapidly to scrub. It must be admitted that this process has happened before, under the stimulus of the rising prices of arable produce, but it is probable that never before has the area reclaimed been so extensive, and moreover it is doubtful whether it has ever had a greater prospect of permanency.

The problem which faces the conservationist on the chalk grasslands is therefore three-fold. Firstly, there is the actual acquisition of nature reserves, or the extension of some comparable form of protection. Secondly, there is the problem arising from the almost complete absence of grazing animals. Thirdly, there looms the question of whether these inevitably small sites are capable of supporting indefinitely many of the species they are meant to preserve. In Hampshire the Nature Conservancy has declared one National Nature Reserve on the chalk grasslands at Old Winchester Hill, and other sites are designated as 'Sites of Special Scientific Interest'. Negotiations are in progress by the Hampshire Naturalists' Trust, incorporated in 1960, for management interests in certain other sites. From the point of view of a voluntary body with only limited resources, however, inflated land values in the county are a major limiting factor.

At Old Winchester Hill, the suppression of scrub is one of the main features of management, a task which generally has to be undertaken manually, supported by some very limited winter grazing. At one Site of Scientific Interest, St. Catherine's Hill near Winchester, scrub clearance by voluntary bodies has also taken place. But at the present time, it cannot be claimed that the conservation of the relict sites of chalk grassland in Hampshire has proceeded beyond the very early stages. However, it is anticipated that with the growth and increasing influence of the Hampshire Naturalists' Trust, conservation measures will be extended to a much wider range of sites.

The problems inherent in the small size of sites, which at the present time do, or in the future will, receive varying measures of protection, can only be faced by a close study of the habitat requirements of the species of animals and plants which the sites are meant to protect, in order that such knowledge may be utilised to build up the maximum populations. Reserves and protected areas would thus function as 'reservoirs' for characteristic species, from which recolonisation of other sites, perhaps by deliberate reintroduction, might take place.

The conservationist is faced with similar problems in the heathlands of Hampshire, although in this county the overall reduction in the total area of heathland has not proceeded to the same extreme as in the case of the chalk grasslands. Large areas in the north of the county remain heathland because they are War Department property, while in the Hampshire Basin proper the New Forest, containing the largest area of lowland heath (Plate III) in Britain (about 38,000 acres) receives special statutory protection from reclamation or development (Fig. 40). The New Forest is the only really extensive area of semi-natural vegetation within easy reach of London with any prospect of relative ecological stability in the future. Within the general concept of the heathland is a veritable mosaic of habitats, the result of the very complicated history of land use in the area (see pp. 140-7). Perhaps mainly for this reason, perhaps also because of its very size, a wide range of species is present. These include most of those normally considered to be characteristic of the lowland heaths, some in fact occurring nowhere else in Britain, and a large number which are confined to 'waste and marginal land' generally. In the face of continued reduction in the area of heathland and 'waste and marginal land', birds such as the red-backed shrike (*Lanius collurio*) and Dartford warbler (*Sylvia undata*), and reptiles such as the smooth snake (*Coronella austriaca*) and sand lizard (*Lacerta agilis*), may be virtually limited to the Forest within the near future. In its size, its wide range of habitats and species, and its probable ecological stability, the New Forest therefore qualifies for special consideration as a conservation area. In an agreement with the Nature Conservancy in 1959, the Forestry Commission recognised the status of this important reserve. The interests of conservation, particularly with regard to the management of the heaths, are the subject of a close and sympathetic liaison between the Commission and the Conservancy.

Urban and industrial expansion mainly radiating from Southampton, Bournemouth and Portsmouth, the requirements of sites for power-stations and factories, and the more general impact of holiday-makers, have been particularly demanding on land within the coastal zone of the county. One main concern here of the conservationist is the provision of adequate refuges for wildfowl and other birds dependent on aquatic or semi-aquatic coastal feeding grounds. Despite the scale of development along the Hampshire coast, areas remain of outstanding importance in this respect. Most are designated by the Nature Conservancy as Sites of Special Scientific Interest; one is a proposed National Nature Reserve, while two others are proposed Local Nature Reserves. The Hampshire Naturalists' Trust has been particularly active in its efforts to extend conservation measures to many of these coastal areas.

Langstone Harbour, in the extreme east of the county, embraces the largest single area of tidal mudflats on the south coast of England, together with a number of islands which function as high-water concentration points for wading birds. The area is of major significance nationally as a wildfowl and wader feeding and resting ground, and in particular it appears to be the only area south of Essex capable of supporting substantial numbers of brent geese (*Branta bernicla*) in winter. The Harbour, together with Farlington Marshes, a peninsula of rough grazing and freshwater marsh in its north-western corner, constitutes a complex of marine, brackish and freshwater habitats of a category becoming sufficiently rare in England to merit preservation on these grounds alone; it has been scheduled, there-fore, as a proposed National Nature Reserve. In view of the likelihood of protracted negotiations over the establishment of this Reserve by the Nature Conservancy, the county Naturalists' Trust, with the close co-operation and support of the Langstone Harbour and District Wildfowlers' Association, concluded an annual lease on Farlington Marshes in October, 1962. A more informal agreement had already been entered into in respect of a large area of the Harbour itself, including the main islands, thus allowing a start to be made in active conservation. Control over shooting has found a ready response in the rising numbers of duck, mainly wigeon (*Anas penelope*) and teal (*Anas crecca*), using Farlington Marshes. Other immediate aims of management are the creation of suitable conditions for breeding birds and for waders at high water, and for the encouragement of a number of rare species of grasses.

Titchfield Haven, a freshwater marsh which owes its existence to the exclusion of salt water from the entrance to the river Meon, is a small but important duck marsh. The county Trust have, again, reached an informal agreement with the owner to maintain the existing ideal conditions.

On the Solent coast of the Isle of Wight, arrangements to declare Newtown Harbour a Local Nature Reserve are progressing favourably. Negotiations are being undertaken by the Trust either for the extension of certain measures of protection or for the establish-ment of nature reserves in two other areas of coastal marshlands. In the extreme west of the county, discussions are in progress for the establishment of a Local Nature Reserve at Christchurch Harbour.

A further major interest of the Hampshire Naturalists' Trust is the conservation of the tern colonies along the Solent coast. These colonies of common terns (*Sterna hirundo*) and sandwich terns (*Sterna sandvicensis*) are still substantial, but it is clear that those of the little tern (*Sterna albifrons*) reflect the decline in the species taking place generally in England; this is apparently the result of its tendency to colonise shingle beaches easily accessible to the public. Disturbance, both deliberate and unintentional, together with the wanton taking of eggs, is a major restriction on the breeding success of all three species. With the permission of Lord Montagu of Beaulieu, the terneries of the Beaulieu estuary have received the benefit of some degree of wardening by the Trust. At Hurst Castle Spit, with the permission of the Office of Works, a token fence was erected in 1962 round the colony of little terns, and this, together with a wardening system, has shown some positive results. The Trust's activities in 1962, however, were mainly in the nature of a preliminary survey of the size of the colonies and of the various factors imposing limits in their size, in order to decide what measures of protection were required and which could be regarded as practicable.

The role played by the Nature Conservancy on a broad, national scale needs to be supple-mented in detail within more limited local areas. In doing this, the work of the Naturalists'

Trust should therefore be of major importance in the conservation of its flora and fauna. The recognition of conservation, in itself too often a nebulous and ill-defined concept, as a positive force in the future planning of the landscape is necessarily protracted. It would be fair to say, however, that in terms of serious recognition by local government and other bodies responsible for the management of land and the planning of land use, conservation is beginning to emerge as such in Hampshire.

BIBLIOGRAPHICAL NOTE

L. E. T. would like to express his thanks to Mr. P. M. T. Jones, County Agricultural Advisory Officer for Hampshire, who discussed the present position of agriculture in the county and supplied the information for the maps and diagrams, and also to Mr. H. S. Dyer, Divisional Land Commissioner, who put at his disposal material for the compilation of the Land-Use map.

(1) H. L. Edlin (ed.), *Forestry Commission Guide. New Forest* (London, 1951).
(2) New Forest Committee, *Report* (London, 1947).
(3) J. R. Wise, *The New Forest, its history and its scenery* (London, 1895).
(4) L. E. Tavener, *The Common Lands of Hampshire* (Winchester, 1957); 'Dorset farming 1900-1950', *Proceedings of the Dorset Natural History and Archaeological Society* (1955), vol. 75, pp. 91-114; and 'Mid-century agriculture', ibid. (1961), vol. 83, pp. 130-7.
(5) *The New Forest. A symposium*, with contributions by ten authors (London, 1960).

XI

THE HAMPSHIRE DEVELOPMENT PLAN*

INTRODUCTION

THE main purpose of the County Development Plan, prepared under the Town and Country Planning Act, 1947, is to indicate the proposed allocation of land within the county for various uses and the stages by which any development should be carried out. It is intended, in fact, to provide a co-ordinated framework for the guidance of both public and private enterprise and of others concerned with the use of land.

Except in special cases where land may be designated for compulsory acquisition to secure its use in the manner proposed, the Local Planning Authority must rely largely for the implementation of the plan on its powers to grant or refuse permission for development proposed by others, subject of course to the determination by the Minister of Housing and Local Government of cases referred to him on appeal or otherwise. Thus the plan is filled in gradually as its execution proceeds, although it is never completely hard and fast at any stage. It may be amended at any time, and must be reviewed at least once every five years after its approval by the Minister, in order to bring it up to date should periodic survey indicate that this is necessary or desirable.

The Hampshire Development Plan was prepared during the years 1948 to 1951, submitted to the Minister in June 1952, and approved, with modifications, in June, 1955. Various additions have been made and approved in subsequent years, and the amendments constituting the first quinquennial review have been submitted in stages from August 1961. The Approved Plan relates to the period ending in 1971, but the review proposals extend its application to 1981.

The documents embodying the plan are the County Map, on a scale of 1 inch to 1 mile (1/63,360), and the Town Maps, on a scale of 6 inches to 1 mile (1/10,560), each of which is accompanied by a Written Statement and supporting survey material.

The County Map indicates the general framework of the plan, in terms of communications, green belts and areas of marked landscape value. It also shows major areas reserved for mineral workings, airfields, County Council smallholdings, use by Service and other Government Departments and by the Forestry Commission, ancient monuments and sites of special scientific interest. In addition, it forms an index to areas treated in greater detail on town maps on a larger scale.

The Town Maps, thirteen of which formed part of the original submission to the

---

* This Chapter was initially prepared under the direction of Mr. T. F. Thomson, County Planning Officer from 1945 to 1962.

Minister, allocate land for residential, industrial, commercial, educational, recreational and other purposes, in addition to indicating in greater detail items which also appear on the County Map. Four additional Town Maps have been submitted since 1955, and the current programme provides for the submission of a further eight maps, several of which are at an advanced stage of preparation (January 1963). In addition, proposals have been submitted for the redevelopment of certain town centres known as Comprehensive Development Areas.

BACKGROUND TO THE DEVELOPMENT PLAN

The Administrative County of Hampshire, which excludes the Isle of Wight and the three County Boroughs of Bournemouth, Southampton and Portsmouth, has an area of 929,952 acres and an estimated civilian population in 1961 of 744,670. It can be divided on a physiographic basis into four major areas, each of which presents its own distinctive planning problems; specific aspects have been discussed in detail in earlier chapters.

In the north, the county takes in the south-western fringes of the London Basin, where well-watered clay vales alternate with agriculturally unproductive sands and gravels. The latter give rise to extensive areas of heathland, especially in the east around Aldershot, Farnborough and Fleet, where the Service Departments maintain major establishments. The principal road and rail routes from London to the south-west of England pass through this area towards Basingstoke; their presence has led to an increasing demand for residential development to accommodate commuters to London, as have also the increasing restrictions against development in the Metropolitan Green Belt. This section of the county comprises about 14 per cent of its area, and contains 16 per cent of its civilian population.

In the centre of the county, the Hampshire Downs are characterised by large agricultural holdings and nucleated village settlements. The towns of the area—Winchester, Basingstoke, Andover, Alton, New Alresford and Whitchurch—have grown up as marketing centres on the main routeways across the Downs. This section of the county comprises 48 per cent of its area, but contains only 24 per cent of its population. Urban pressures have to date affected it relatively little, although Basingstoke now lies well within the sphere of metropolitan influence (see p. 158).

The central part of the eastern fringe of the county forms part of the Weald, and contains some of the county's most striking and varied rural scenery, as well as the small market-town of Petersfield. The Wealden area occupies about 5 per cent of the county area and contains 4 per cent of its population.

Finally, the county contains the major part of the Hampshire Basin, including the whole coastal belt between Bournemouth and Chichester Harbour. This area as a whole is relatively densely populated, containing 56 per cent of the inhabitants of the county on only 32 per cent of its area, but it exhibits within itself some considerable variations in character. East of Bournemouth, the residential and holiday towns of Christchurch, New Milton and Lymington form an almost continuous string of development along the coast to the south of the sparsely inhabited New Forest. The eastern boundary of the New Forest extends almost to Southampton Water, on the western bank of which have developed in recent years not only the oil refinery at Fawley (Plate XXVIII) with its associated industries and residential areas but also a large power-station at Marchwood. East of the Water, the whole of the Basin is semi-urbanised, and falls within the immediate spheres of influence of Southampton and Portsmouth. Other towns include Eastleigh (which grew up around the railway workshops established in 1894, but has now acquired other industries, as well as a residential character), Fareham and Havant (old market-centres which have added industrial and residential functions) and Gosport (an important naval victualling centre).

For local government purposes, the county is divided into nine municipal boroughs, six urban districts and eleven rural districts, which are grouped for planning administration into five areas (Fig. 41).

POPULATION AND HOUSING

In the hundred years between 1801 and 1901, the population of the Administrative County has increased by 240 per cent, rising from 157,480 to 377,204. By 1949, the date of survey for the approved Development Plan, there had been a rise since 1901 of 166 per cent to an estimated 627,380, of whom 578,610 were civilians. These rates of growth may be compared with percentages for England and Wales of 366 and 134 respectively in the same periods, which indicate that while Hampshire lagged behind in the nineteenth century, it has gained at the expense of the rest of the country since 1901.

Immigration has been most marked in the coastal belt around Southampton and Portsmouth, the Christchurch/Lymington area adjoining Bournemouth, and the north-eastern fringes between Petersfield and the Blackwater valley. All these districts have had influxes of retired people wishing to settle in congenial surroundings, and in the Southampton/Portsmouth area they have been accompanied also by those seeking employment in manufacturing industries and services of various kinds.

These tendencies were apparent before 1939, and were beginning to make themselves felt again when the Development Plan was in preparation. The bulk of house-building at that time was, however, being carried out by Local Authorities, who could restrict occupation to those with local qualifications and largely expected to do so; it was assumed that this would continue to be the case throughout the plan period to 1971. The plan as submitted therefore provided for a rate of growth of no more than about 7,600 persons per annum, as compared with 8,000 annually between 1931 and 1939. Over and above natural increase, some immigration was provided for, but this was expected to be concentrated particularly in areas around Southampton and Portsmouth, to accommodate 'overspill' from the two County Boroughs, and at Basingstoke, to which 15,000 Londoners were expected to move in accordance with the provisions of the Greater London Plan.

In fact, a net increase occurred in the ten years from 1949 to 1959 of some 152,000 through natural change and balance of migration. This was partially offset by the transfer to Southampton in 1954 of areas at Millbrook and West End, with a total population of 25,000, which had been substantially developed by the County Borough Council. This rapid growth of population may be accounted for partly by the unexpected rise in birth-rates nationally, which has led to successive upwards revisions by the Registrar General of

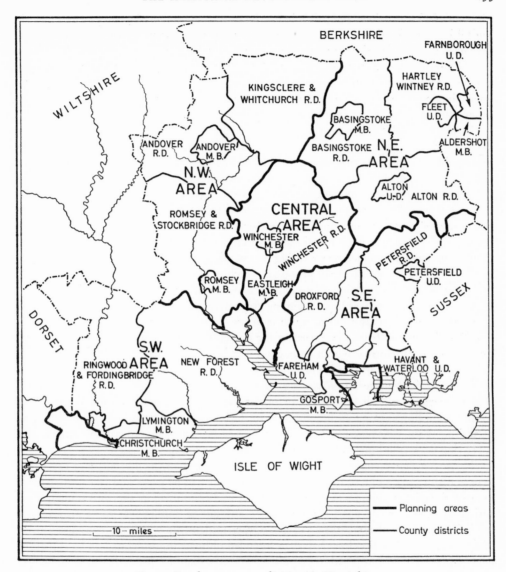

Fig. 41. Local government divisions in Hampshire

Based on Ordnance Survey, 'Administrative Diagram of Hampshire and the Isle of Wight',
scale 1:126,720.

M.B. Municipal Borough; R.D. Rural District; U.D. Urban District. This Figure indicates the
areas referred to in Table VIII.

his population projections, and partly by the increase in house-building by private enterprise which followed the abolition of building licensing in 1954. Private builders completed 600 dwellings in the Administrative County in 1949, 3,200 in 1954 and 7,200 in 1961, whereas Local Authority completions totalled only 2,700, 3,200 and 1,100 respectively. In terms of land use, complete figures are not available, but it is estimated that between 1950 and 1959 approximately 27,100 new dwellings were erected on 4,170 acres of land within the limits of the thirteen Town Maps approved in 1955.

By the mid-fifties, it was clear, in fact, that the pressures which had been operative in the years before 1939 had largely reasserted themselves and that, despite the best endeavours of the Local Planning Authority, there was a distinct danger that the whole of the coastal belt, with the exception of the New Forest, would become a continuous sprawl of urban development unless strong counter-measures were taken. The danger was not so particularly pressing where Town Maps were in existence—although some of them were already beginning to 'burst at the seams'—but rather in the 'white' areas around and between them which were not allocated for any specific form of development. Although the presumption was that in such areas existing uses would remain for the most part undisturbed, in practice it was difficult to resist proposals which, while individually of little significance, in aggregate were likely to have a prejudicial effect upon the coastal hinterland.

The County Council, as Local Planning Authority, therefore decided to define a coastal green belt (Fig. 42) to assist not so much in arresting the pressures for development, but in directing them away from those parts of the coastal belts which were as yet unspoilt, and towards those settlements, within or beyond it, where a measure of further growth could most satisfactorily be permitted. The Green Belt Amendment to the Development Plan was submitted to the Minister in November 1958, and inevitably aroused strong opposition in certain quarters, as well as support in others. Some 320 objections were received and considered, following a public inquiry in 1959. Although a final decision has not at the time of writing been received, the Minister in November 1960 announced his intention of approving the establishment of the green belt, illustrated in Fig. 42.

The green belt notation implies a very severe restriction on the purposes for which building (and the change of use of existing buildings) will be permitted, and in practice it limits residential development to that which can be justified in the direct interests of agriculture and forestry, apart from a limited amount of 'infilling' to meet proved local needs in a number of established villages. Other settlements which are considered to be capable of some expansion have had their intended ultimate limits defined on inset maps to the County Map. It is proposed to prepare programme maps to ensure their comprehensive development over a period of at least twenty years in relation to local needs, and the availability of such sewers and other public services as may be necessary.

The green belt notation has also been applied within Town Map areas, but, in order to keep the future amendment of the green belt boundaries to a minimum, the inner boundaries of the belt have been drawn so as to leave unallocated certain areas of land between these inner boundaries and the areas already shown for development on the Town Maps. These 'white' areas may later be allocated to meet demands for development beyond the present

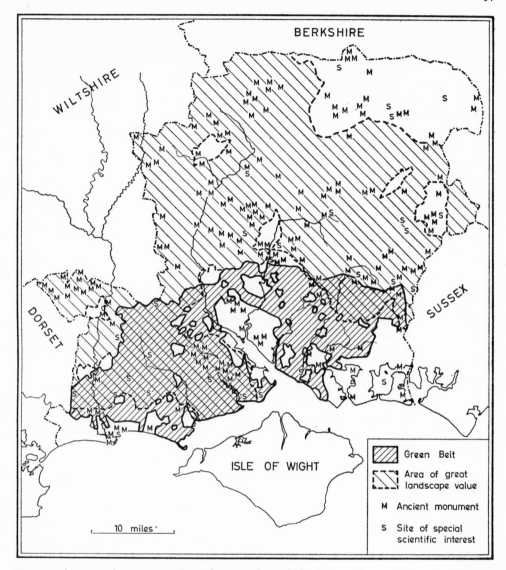

Fig. 42. The Hampshire Green Belt, with areas of specific landscape value, ancient monuments and sites of scientific interest

Based on *The Hampshire Development Plan*, with reviewed County Map (1961).

period of the plans on which they appear, or the green belt notation may be extended over them should it later appear that they should be kept open in the long term. But in any event only such development will be meanwhile permitted there as would be permissible within the neighbouring green belt.

An assessment made at the time of the submission of the green belt proposals to the Minister demonstrated that they would allow, at the base date of 1957, for the accommodation in Town Map and inset map areas of an increased population of upwards of 195,000. The Minister's proposed amendments to the green belt will extend the probable ultimate development areas, and hence their capacities, still further.

The green belt proposals were formulated as a matter of urgency, and enabled the position to be held in the southern part of the county while new policies were formulated for the first quinquennial review of the plan to meet the increased pressures already mentioned. Meanwhile, the London County Council, having been informed by the Minister that they could proceed with the promotion of a new town if they could find a satisfactory site somewhere in south-eastern England, in 1959 put forward a proposal to build a new town of 80,000 to 100,000 population at Hook, between Basingstoke and Fleet, to accommodate some of London's overspill. The Hampshire County Council objected strongly to this project, which would have extended the spread of almost continuous urban development, already reaching out from London as far as the Hampshire-Surrey border, and would have most seriously disrupted the existing pattern of urban spheres of influence in its vicinity.

The County Council did not wish, however, to adopt a purely negative attitude and therefore put forward a counter-proposal, which was accepted by the London County Council, for the large-scale expansion of the three existing townships of Basingstoke, Andover and Tadley. Basingstoke and Andover, as already mentioned, are old-established market towns and route centres, and the principle of receiving population from London, though on a much more limited scale, had already been accepted at Basingstoke. Tadley, on the other hand, has grown up since 1945 as mainly a residential settlement for workers at the adjoining Atomic Weapons Research Establishment situated on the Berkshire side of the county boundary. Here it is expected that the added population will be of great benefit in providing social diversification and justifying the provision of alternative sources of employment.

The Development Plan has been reviewed in the light of all these factors, and it is designed, firstly, to meet the need of accommodating the projected natural increase of the existing population, estimated at 87,300 by the Registrar General for the period 1959 to 1981. Secondly, it is designed to make allowance for some continuing decrease in size of the average household, which dropped by about 15 per cent between 1951 and 1961, and for the replacement of unfit and temporary dwellings.

Apart from these local needs, the Review Plan provides for the reception of some 70,000 Londoners at Basingstoke, Andover and Tadley, and for further overspill from the County Boroughs of Southampton and Portsmouth, although the long-term extent of this has not yet been determined. Finally, it allows for some further voluntary immigration. Assessments of the county's 1981 population potential are being continually revised as the various components of the plan come forward for review or are added as amendments, but it appears that an average increase over the period 1959 to 1981 of at least 18,500 persons per annum is probable. Table VIII indicates the distribution of civilian population by county district in 1959 and the anticipated minimum changes by natural increase and migration in the period to 1981 (or 1971 where no later estimates are available).

Table VIII. Hampshire: Anticipated Population Change, 1959 to 1981

AREA	ESTIMATED CIVILIAN POPULATION			
	1959	Change 1959 to 1981		1981
		Natural Change	Migration	Probable Minimum
	(1)	(2)	(3)	(4)
Eastleigh Borough	36,300	+ 4,400	+ 12,500	53,200
Winchester City	26,800	+ 1,200	+ 6,200	34,200
Winchester Rural District	43,200	+ 5,200	+ 11,700	60,100
Central Area Total	**106,300**	**+10,800**	**+ 30,400**	**147,500**
Andover Borough	15,500	+ 1,500	+ 29,800	46,800
Romsey Borough	6,500	+ 500	+ 3,800	†10,800
Andover Rural District	16,000	+ 2,600	+ 200	18,800
Kingsclere and Whitchurch Rural District	21,300	+ 3,100	+ 14,200	†38,600
Romsey and Stockbridge Rural District	20,700	+ 2,700	+ 22,400	†45,800
North-west Area Total	**80,000**	**+10,400**	**+ 70,400**	**160,800**
Aldershot Borough	29,500	+ 1,400	− 2,900	28,000
Alton Urban District	8,800	+ 1,300	+ 7,300	†17,400
Basingstoke Borough	23,100	+ 3,400	+ 48,800	75,300
Farnborough Urban District	26,100	+ 3,300	+ 7,300	36,700
Fleet Urban District	11,000	+ 800	+ 4,200	16,000
Alton Rural District	21,400	+ 3,200	+ 3,700	28,300
Basingstoke Rural District	17,300	+ 1,900	+ 4,600	23,800
Hartley Wintney Rural District	22,300	+ 2,200	+ 12,400	36,900
North-east Area Total	**159,500**	**+17,500**	**+ 85,400**	**262,400**
Christchurch Borough	24,800	+ 1,600	+ 9,500	35,900
Lymington Borough	25,800	− 100	+ 12,300	★38,000
New Forest Rural District	51,700	+ 6,900	+ 14,700	73,300
Ringwood and Fordingbridge Rural District	25,200	+ 2,700	+ 6,900	34,800
South-west Area Total	**127,500**	**+11,100**	**+ 43,400**	**182,000**
Fareham Urban District	54,600	+ 7,400	+ 23,800	85,800
Gosport Borough	58,800	+10,300	+ 5,800	74,900
Havant and Waterloo Urban District	68,100	+14,000	+ 16,900	★99,000
Petersfield Urban District	7,200	+ 300	+ 4,500	†12,000
Droxford Rural District	21,300	+ 2,600	+ 2,500	26,400
Petersfield Rural District	22,100	+ 2,900	+ 500	25,500
South-east Area Total	**232,100**	**+37,500**	**+ 54,000**	**323,600**
Administrative County Total	**705,400**	**+87,300**	**+283,600**	**1,076,300**

Sources: Columns (1) and (2): Registrar General through Ministry of Housing and Local Government. Columns (3) and (4): Development Plan provision, except figures marked †, which are County Planning Officer's estimates, 1 June 1963. Figures marked ★ refer to 1971 only.

Ms

In order that the land requirements to meet the needs described are kept to the minimum, the Written Statement accompanying the reviewed plan lays down, for the first time, as a general policy that where land is allocated for development in Town Map areas, it should be developed at the maximum density commensurate with the provision of adequate amenity for the future residents and the town as a whole; the location, character and environment of the site; the social problems involved; and the availability of transport, school facilities and other public services, including adequate sewers, so that development may be carried out without undue expenditure of public money. Development of mixed types will be encouraged, including development in the form of blocks of flats, both in areas ripe for urban renewal and in areas allocated for residential purposes but not yet developed. Certain areas have been defined for high density development within Town Map areas, and others will be defined from time to time as the need for the redevelopment of certain obsolescent localities becomes necessary.

Outside Town Map areas, in addition to the policy for land within the green belt which has already been described, it is intended that 'white' areas elsewhere shall generally be protected against all forms of development unrelated to the needs of the rural community. In a village, permission for a well-sited and well-designed house will normally be granted unless there is a definite planning reason to the contrary, but new houses will not normally be permitted in the open country unless, in the circumstances of the particular case, there is a special need.

INDUSTRY AND EMPLOYMENT

In terms of land use, Hampshire remains predominantly an agricultural county, although employment in this activity declined (because of increased mechanisation) by some 25 per cent between 1948 and 1958, and totalled no more than 14,300 in 1961. Further areas of agricultural land will inevitably be needed for various forms of development in the future, but it is intended that the land shall be conserved in so far as this is consistent with the other needs of the community. Areas for forestry and for the extraction of minerals will also be safeguarded in the Development Plan.

As far as the distribution of manufacturing industry is concerned, the general responsibility rests with the Board of Trade, whose certificate is required before permission may be granted for the development of over 5000 square feet of industrial floor-space by any single concern. The Board has consistently used its powers to steer industry, whenever possible, to the 'development districts' of persistent high unemployment, largely in the north and west of Britain, and away from the relatively prosperous south and east. The approved Development Plan recognised this and, while allocating some land for new industry, it provides for a measure of diversification in areas unduly dependent on particular sources of employment and for the needs of the expected additional population. Many sites are intended for the legitimate expansion or relocation of concerns already established in the area.

In only one significant case was large-scale industrial development provided for which would inevitably draw new population from outside the county. This was the petro-chemical complex at Fawley, the development of which was approved at Cabinet level on national economic grounds, and had given rise to employment totalling over 4500 by 1961.

The reviewed Development Plan introduces no changes in policy, although it makes clear that rural industries dependent on local, mainly agricultural or forestry, resources will be encouraged to develop, subject to proper regard to amenities and to the other needs of the community. It also lays down that as a safeguard for the future of towns where there is the slightest possibility of collapse of a major industry, as distinct from a general trade recession, suitable areas will be protected from development against such future emergency.

ROAD DEVELOPMENTS

The road system in Hampshire, the past development of which is discussed in Chapter XIX, may be said to be based on four major traffic routes (Fig. 43).

First, a route from London to the south-west of England, via Basingstoke and Andover. The Development Plan provides for the construction of a new length of motorway from the Surrey boundary north of Farnborough to join, to the south-west of Basingstoke, the existing road A30, for which other less extensive improvements are planned.

Second, routes from London to Bournemouth, Southampton and Portsmouth. As respects Bournemouth, a major improvement is planned to link it at Ringwood with the South Coast road, which will in turn connect with the London/Southampton road at Bassett. As respects Southampton, the principal improvement to road A33, which diverges from the A30 to the south-west of Basingstoke, will be a by-pass at Chandler's Ford and Otterbourne, linking with the existing Winchester By-pass. The Portsmouth road, A3, is to be improved largely upon its existing alignment, apart from by-passes at Liphook, Peters-field and Waterlooville.

Third, a South Coast road connecting the three County Boroughs and linking them with the other coastal towns on the east and west. The whole of the existing road A27, from a point west of Southampton to the Sussex boundary, is to be replaced by a new road to be built in several sections.

Fourth, a route to the north accessible from the three coastal County Boroughs. This road, A34, at present passes through Winchester, but it is to be connected to the northern terminal of the Winchester By-pass by a link from the junction of the Andover and Newbury roads. It will be improved elsewhere on its route to the Midlands and North of England.

This road improvement programme has suffered severely from restrictions on capital expenditure, and in the period up to 1959 only six major improvement schemes had been carried out. The reviewed plan includes a total of 91 schemes, and with the gradual release of more money a number is already in progress.

SOCIAL FACILITIES

The Development Plan makes provision, within Town Map areas, for sites for primary and secondary schools, health clinics, community centres, local government offices, places of

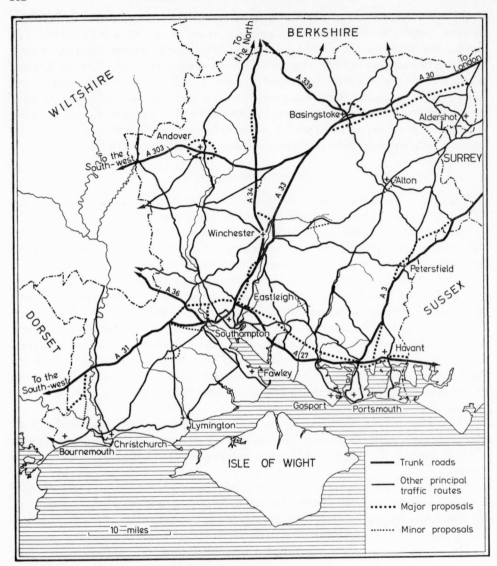

Fig. 43. The Hampshire road system

Based on *The Hampshire Development Plan*, with reviewed County Map (1961).

Only the most important of the numerous planned improvement schemes can be shown. The map illustrates the predominance of the north-east to south-west routes from London across the county.

worship and other social facilities, as well as for playing-fields and other public open spaces, allotments and cemeteries.

Excluding the coastal towns of Christchurch and South Hayling, where extensive areas of the foreshore are open to the public, the other eleven areas for which Town Maps were submitted in 1952 had an average of about 3·7 acres of public open space per thousand population in 1949. The Approved Plan provided for this to increase, by the addition of some 1,000 acres of land, to 6·0 acres per thousand in 1971. In fact, there had been a net increase of about 250 acres by 1959, and the reviewed plan, as submitted, provided for a further increase of 2,250 acres to raise the average to 6·4 acres per thousand by 1981.

Outside Town Map areas, the approved County Map indicated twenty-three towns and villages intended as centres for the social, educational and health services of the country-side (Fig. 44). These centres vary from established towns such as Alton, Lymington, Peters-field and Romsey, all of which have been or will be the subject of additional Town Maps, to 'key villages' such as Cadnam, Sutton Scotney and West Meon.

AREAS OF COMPREHENSIVE DEVELOPMENT

Although it was recognised that the centres of a number of towns in the county would ultimately require comprehensive redevelopment, no detailed proposals for this were incorporated in the approved plans. Plans for small parts of Fareham and Gosport, as well as for an 'outworn' residential area in Winchester, were, however, submitted as amendments to the Approved Plan.

The review proposals include an important scheme for the centre of Hythe, as well as far-reaching plans to remodel the centres of Basingstoke and Andover to equip them to serve their greatly expanded populations. This aspect of planning is becoming of increasing importance. The County Planning Department is itself engaged on the preparation of schemes for a number of additional towns, and still others are being worked out by consultants appointed by the County or County District Councils. All these are expected to be submitted to the Minister as amendments to the Development Plan within the course of the next few years.

AREAS OF SPECIAL INTEREST

The Approved Plan laid down no specific policy for the preservation and enhancement of amenities, but the Reviewed Plan defines large parts of the county as areas of great landscape value, within which it is intended to preserve and enhance the existing natural features, and to ensure that no development is carried out which would conflict with the special character of the areas concerned. Particular attention will be given to the form and siting of buildings in the landscape; a high standard of design will be required for new work and the extension of existing property, with especial regard to the colour and texture of building materials.

As respects architectural design generally, the Review Plan specifies that it is not possible to lay down rules defining what is good design and what is bad, since what is pleasing to the

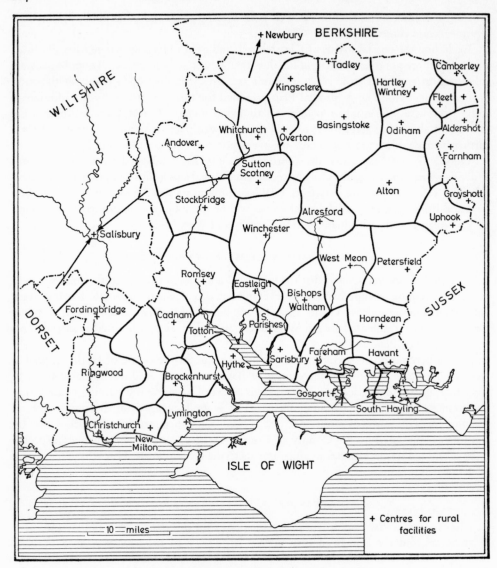

Fig. 44. Rural social service centres in Hampshire

Based on *The Hampshire Development Plan*, 'Analysis of Survey' (1952), map 9.
Major social facilities are to be provided largely in towns, but some villages in the less densely populated parts of the county have also been selected as centres.

eye, be it contemporary or traditional, is very much a matter of opinion, and much may in any event depend on the site. Even so, it is generally intended to require a high standard of architectural design, related to the character of the environment in which a proposed building is to be erected.

Proposals for development will be judged against these criteria. Every endeavour will also be made to preserve buildings and places of archaeological, architectural, historic and scientific interest, among which are sites scheduled under the Ancient Monuments Acts, nature reserves and other sites of special scientific interest notified by the Nature Conservancy, and buildings listed by the Ministry of Housing and Local Government as of special architectural or historic interest (Fig. 42).

PART II

THE HISTORICAL BACKGROUND

XII

THE CONCEPT OF WESSEX

THERE are several areas in this country which defy definition but which nevertheless have a strong regional characterisation. Yet none has an origin so romantic, so shrouded in mystery and so much the subject of controversy as Wessex. This part of England enjoys a double distinction in having served its regional apprenticeship under an illustrious king in the ninth century and then having been dragged out of retirement in order to serve the geographical needs of an illustrious novelist in the nineteenth. During the intervening thousand years Wessex lost its regional significance, so there is little doubt that much of the popularity which the name enjoys today must stem from Hardy's revival of it rather than Alfred's association with it. Yet Hardy made it quite clear that he had no intention of reviving the glories of Wessex. 'The series of novels I projected', he wrote, 'being mainly of the kind called local, seems to require a territorial definition of some sort to lend unity to their scene. Finding that the area of a single county did not afford a canvas large enough for this purpose, and that there were objections to an invented name, I disinterred the old one. The region designated was known but vaguely, and I was often asked even by educated people where it lay. However, the press and the public were kind enough to welcome the fanciful plan, and willingly joined me in the anachronism of imagining a Wessex population living under Queen Victoria. . . . Since then the appellation which I had thought to reserve to the horizons and landscapes of a partly real, partly dream-country has, by degrees, solidified into a utilitarian region which people can go to. . . . But I ask all good and idealistic readers to forget this, and to refuse steadfastly to believe that there are any inhabitants of a Victorian Wessex outside these volumes in which their lives and conversations are detailed'. Does the fact that this plea has been so flagrantly ignored mean that the inhabitants of the region lately desire some focus of expression which the name unintentionally supplies?

It is difficult to say whether Hardy awakened a dormant regional consciousness among the people of this part of the country or whether he actually created one. That some such feeling exists today must be conceded. It is evident in the frequency with which the name Wessex appears in the local press, and, as Fig. 45 shows, it has been taken up by a large number of firms whose distribution coincides rather strikingly with the historic kingdom of Wessex in its early days. Yet it would be unrealistic to assert that there is any strong fellow-feeling among the inhabitants of the area today comparable with that felt by the people of Yorkshire, Lancashire or Wales. May we not be dealing, then, with a paradoxical situation —a superficial sense of unity which in most people's minds is not causally related to anything more than a sense of belonging, but which is nevertheless rooted in an old and honourable historical tradition? After all, it is just as much an anachronism to apply the name 'Wessex' to any modern activity as it is to speak of a 'Wessex Culture' in the Bronze Age simply because it falls essentially within the bounds of historic Wessex. In both cases it must be regarded merely as a convenient 'gimmick' which has a useful geographical connotation but carries no necessarily historical implications, though of course it is to be welcomed as keeping alive a well-authenticated tradition.

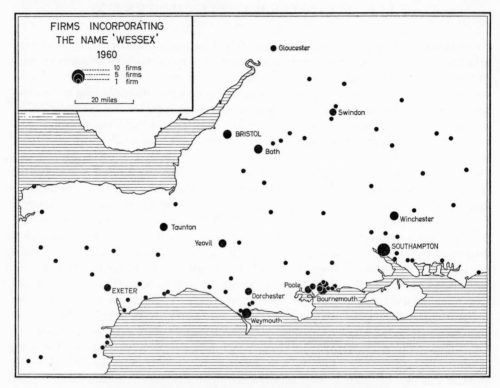

Fig. 45. The location of firms incorporating the name Wessex, 1960
Based on information extracted from the G.P.O. Telephone Directories, 1960.
The prominent position of Bournemouth should be noted because it has no history earlier than the nineteenth century, although it is the 'Sandbourne' of Thomas Hardy.

Today county loyalties are still noticeably strong in the region, fostered by the press, by sport and by various organisations, but if there is any semblance of true regional consciousness on a wider scale it expresses itself under the term 'West Country' rather than 'Wessex'. The reason for this may well lie in the influence exerted by the B.B.C. through its West Regional station at Bristol, which seems to have played some part in shifting the cultural centre of gravity of historic Wessex towards the west. Nor should the strength of Bristol's position in this respect be underrated, for in 1946 when the B.B.C. proposed to amalgamate the West Region with the Midland Region, the pressure of public opinion, forcibly expressed through local M.P.s, compelled them to abandon the scheme. It was claimed on that occasion that 'a separate region was necessary in order to preserve the special cultural, civic, agricultural and religious characteristics of the West Country.' But other factors are operating in the same direction. The eastern fringes of historic Wessex have materially gained but otherwise suffered from proximity to London, for the businessman-farmer and the middle-class commuter, together with naval influences permeating inland from Portsmouth and elsewhere, have introduced a degree of sophistication which is out of keeping with much of the traditional life of the area.

Is Hampshire then fighting a losing battle in its bid for recognition as the cradle of Wessex? If so, it is nevertheless a vigorous rearguard action. If the B.B.C. had set up a South Region based on Southampton there may well have been a strongly expressed desire to have it called the 'Wessex Region', just as there was an attempt to have the new University of Southampton designated the 'University of Wessex'. This failed partly because the neighbouring universities of Reading, Bristol and Exeter could all claim to have some association with Wessex, though they appeared less eager to do so. But this setback has not prevented the undergraduate newspaper at Southampton from continuing to be called *Wessex News*, its literary counterpart *Second Wessex*, nor the annual *Wessex Geographer*. Nor, for that matter, has it prevented local teams on the sports field from being urged on by their supporters to yells of 'Come on, Wessex!'

This raises the very pertinent question: is Southampton at all presumptuous in laying claim to any special association with historic Wessex? There is no simple answer. To seek it we have to grope among the tangled undergrowth of Dark Age history with little more than the flickering torches of the chroniclers to guide us. The result has been a quite astonishing amount of speculation resulting in several quite distinct viewpoints, not to say acrimonious disputes. Briefly, the problem is this: the *Anglo-Saxon Chronicle*, our main source, begins the story of the rise of Wessex by virtually apotheosising a small band of adventurers led by Cerdic (incidentally, of doubtful Saxon origin), who landed on the Hampshire coast at '*Cerdices ora*' (possibly near the head of Southampton Water) in A.D. 495. They and their descendants were held up, presumably by the Britons of Cranborne Chase, but after inflicting defeat on them at Sarum in 552 they crossed Salisbury Plain and fought another successful battle against British forces at Barbury, in northern Wiltshire, in 556. This victory seems to have opened the way for a penetration of the upper Thames valley, and we are led to believe that their successors in some way made themselves masters of this area. Then Ceawlin appeared as leader of the presumed Thames valley Saxons who carried out a series of conquests which extended considerably this 'West Saxon' territory. But there is a fundamental difficulty here which has not yet been resolved. The *Chronicle* tells us nothing about Saxons in the Thames valley; we are left to infer their existence from the quite considerable exploits of Ceawlin. But whence did they come? Long before archaeologists brought their techniques to bear, historians were already sharply divided among themselves on this issue. Apologists for the traditional 'southern entry' were challenged by those who envisaged a large colonising force moving up the Thames and becoming established around Dorchester-on-Thames which, because it became the seat of the first West Saxon bishopric, was thought likely to have been its first political capital as well. The two statues of Alfred, one at Wantage, his birthplace, and the other at Winchester, his capital, stand symbolically like sentinels guarding these two approaches to Wessex. Another statue is now needed to symbolise the startling and original view propounded by E. T. Leeds in 1925. Discounting entirely the *Chronicle* version, and working solely on archaeological evidence, he argued strongly that the upper Thames valley was first occupied by Saxons who landed on the east coast and made their way into the area along the line of the Icknield Way (Fig. 46).

Many pens have been transformed into sword blades for use, along with the slings and arrows of outraged historians, in attempts to ward off this attack from the north on their cherished preserves, with both sides calling up cultural reinforcements from every Saxon burial at home and abroad, and shifting their positions whenever a well-argued point strikes home. But it is no part of our task to enter the lists where so many protagonists have already suffered injury and defeat, though a few points are worth noting. For example, a powerful argument in the archaeologist's favour is the comparative scarcity of pagan Saxon remains in Hampshire and southern Wiltshire; and although a few significant additions have been made in recent years near both Salisbury and Winchester, it is difficult to envisage large-scale early colonisation via the southern entry. Yet it is inconceivable that the few shiploads of Cerdic and his followers referred to in the *Chronicle* could represent the total force entering Hampshire from the Channel, even at this early stage. To what date are we to ascribe the arrival of the Jutes who, although not mentioned in the *Chronicle*, are well attested by Bede? And must other landings be assumed in order to account for the *Gewissae*, the followers of Cerdic? Or is this the later name for a combined Saxo-Jutish population which became forged into some semblance of unity in the critical early days of the conquest? If by about 650 there was a see at Winchester, for whose benefit was it established? It pre-supposes a substantial population, to the existence of which the *Chronicle* gives no clue.

This difficulty has led to another interpretation which has been argued persuasively and which asserts that the southerners or Gewissae, together with the Jutes, never really became merged with the Thames valley Saxons, and that they retained their separate identity with Wilton as their capital. Furthermore, it is contended that Ceawlin was not a member of the family of Cerdic and that the clash in 591 at Wodenesbeorg, where the Icknield Way crosses the Wansdyke, was essentially one between Saxons in which Ceawlin was over-thrown; and that from then on the southerners asserted their overlordship of what was, in effect, a confederacy of two distinct peoples separated by an unattractive belt of chalk downland which, in all probability, was not finally colonised until a comparatively late date.

The process of expansion from the Thames valley received a serious check in the mid-seventh century with the rise of Mercia. As a result, all territory north of the Thames was lost to Wessex whose leaders thenceforth sought compensatory gains in other directions. But outlets were few. Any westward expansion was certain to be resisted by the still hostile Britons of Dorset and Dumnonia, so we may suppose that Saxons retreating from the

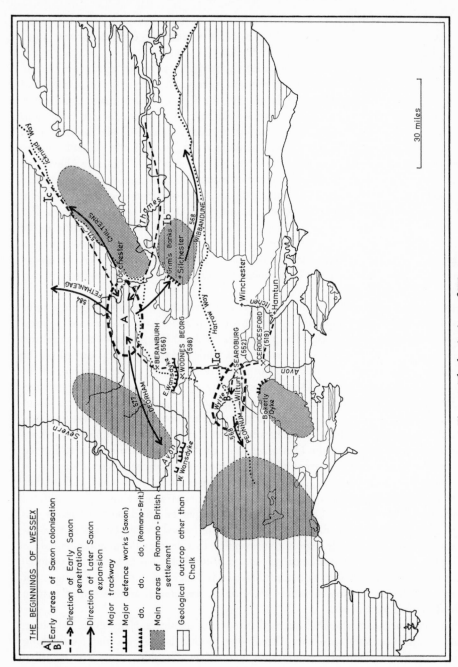

Fig. 46. The beginnings of Wessex

This shows the political situation to c. A.D. 600. Ia is the southern entry, Ib the Thames valley entry, and Ic the Icknield Way entry. There may have been some early penetration of Dorset via Poole Harbour, but the main westward expansion came after A.D. 600. The Wansdykes are now thought to have been defence works of the Wiltshire Saxons against Mercia.

Thames valley would seek first to establish themselves in the chalk country to the south, and this may be the time when this area was first colonised, though conditions were much less inviting here than in Somerset and eastern Devon.

The reasons for this probably late colonisation of the chalk valleys are worth considering. For one thing, the Saxons with their heavy ploughs were more interested in the loams and clays of the valleys than in the thin, light soils of the Chalk. Unfortunately, the rivers seldom cut down to the Lower Chalk which would have given them the soil conditions they preferred; the valleys are very narrow and steep-sided; arable soils are therefore confined to the tiny patches of Valley Gravel flanking them, because the valuable water-meadows would in any case have been kept for grazing and hay. The only alternative would have been to cultivate the downland as the Britons had done before them, and there is some evidence that this was done because a palimpsest of acre strips overlying the square 'Celtic fields' of earlier days can be identified, as on Fyfield Down, near Marlborough. But this must surely have been a last resort. Incidentally, by this time Saxon and Briton in the south had no doubt come to accept each other, and we may suppose that the two peoples became merged as the Britons forsook their downland settlements for the valley villages of their conquerors. That they were not exterminated by them seems clear from the surviving dark element in the population.

Whether this colonisation of the chalk valleys came from the north or whether it is to be related to fresh waves of immigrants from the south, it must have had certain political consequences, and it was then that the Hampshire area suddenly reappeared on the stage after having been relegated to the wings for many years while the spotlight was turned on the Thames valley and beyond. It was destined to play a double role. The transference of the bishopric from Dorchester to Winchester shortly after 650 gave it ecclesiastical prestige, and this may have had some bearing on its eventual choice as political capital of the kingdom. It was some time before peaceful conditions were restored, and it was not, perhaps, until Alfred's reign that true unity was achieved. Even then it was forced upon the Saxons by the unwelcome attentions of the Danes and was, to that extent, artificial. It is, in fact, very misleading to stress the apparent physical homogeneity of the region. Much of it certainly consists of chalk downland, and Salisbury Plain is a hub from which radiate, like the spokes of a wheel, the various chalk and limestone cuestas which must have facilitated communications with the rest of the country. But its general effect on the Saxons was centrifugal rather than centripetal. Salisbury Plain has remained to this day a thinly populated area right in the heart of the region, so preventing that degree of cohesion essential for the development of a strong regional consciousness. But what it has lacked at the regional level it has gained in another direction, and this, too, is associated with Alfred's reign. For many purposes Wessex was too unwieldy a region, so an internal administrative pattern was evolved to meet local needs.

Proleptic references have already been made to some of the shires. Hampshire, Wiltshire, Dorset and Somerset certainly date from Alfred's day, though there are grounds for thinking that the main outlines had already become clear before then. The shire names have no tribal significance; a town in each major subdivision of the region seems to have given its name to its territory (*scir*), and in three cases to its people (*sæte*). The amazing thing is that after a thousand years the shires of Wessex are still viable administrative units which do not call for serious modification to meet present-day needs. The question naturally arises as to whether they embody any fundamental principles which have enabled them to stand so well the test of time. It is true that they have not been badly disturbed by modern industrial development, but nor have other shires which are none the less the subject of major boundary adjustments.

When attempting to define a region it is customary to look first for a boundary which bears some relationship to its physical character as, for example, does C. B. Fawcett in his *Provinces of England*, where, for him, Wessex extends inland only to the edge of the chalk escarpment. But river basins and watersheds seem to have played comparatively little part in the 'shiring' of Wessex. Only a few short stretches of boundary coincide with watersheds; rivers are occasionally used, but as often ignored; dense woodland may formerly have played a larger part, but that, too, accounts nowadays for only short stretches. Nor is there geological homogeneity, as in many of the French *pays*. Unfortunately, it is impossible to know on precisely what criteria the delimitation of the shires was based. It would be reasonable to assume that if the intention had been merely to dissociate one area from another for purely administrative convenience, the lie of the land would have been taken into account and boundaries made to follow natural features wherever possible. But in actual fact this was rarely done. On the contrary, far from the shire being a homogeneous physical area it seems to have been formed with the intention of bringing together areas of marked geological contrast regardless of relief. Indeed, this tendency was so widespread as to constitute, it would seem, a deliberate policy. But why? The purpose is not clear, though there may be some significance in the fact that the shires were undoubtedly intended originally to be not only civil but military sub-regions, capable of acting independently in an emergency as, indeed, they sometimes did. At first sight this might appear to support a scheme for physical units defined by watersheds, rivers and woodland with some defensive value. But there is another possible factor: such a military force would need to be fed, and a geologically uniform area could not so easily provide a varied diet. So it is possible that the Saxons, with the uncanny eye for country which they displayed in the delimitation of their village lands (the later parishes) were showing more concern for logistics than for landforms. It is worth noting that in the fourteenth century, when military supplies were required for overseas expeditions, the shire was always the unit of purveyance and that its capacity to produce surplus grain, meat and other foodstuffs varied markedly from place to place within it.

There is much else of lasting value that can be attributed to Alfred and his age, but suffice it to say that under his vigorous direction it can be assumed that Winchester would flourish and Wilton decay; so the political centre of gravity was finally moved to the east and with it no doubt the economic activity in which *Hamwih* (see p. 205) would share. And although there were disastrous days to come, the die had been cast; what has been called 'the formative age of our race' would leave a legacy which may be but dimly perceived today, if at all. As Wessex expanded to include the whole country Winchester rose to be the capital of England, and it is to this era rather than to the controversial early stages of Saxon settlement that Hampshire must turn in order to justify its links with a heroic past.

BIBLIOGRAPHICAL NOTE

Of the vast literature on this subject, the *Anglo-Saxon Chronicle* must remain a principal source, supplemented by the studies of Sir Frank Stenton, *Anglo-Saxon England* (Oxford, 1943); R. H. Hodgkin, *A history of the Anglo-Saxons*, 2 vols. (Oxford, 1935); and J. N. L. Myres, *Roman Britain and the English settlements* (Oxford, 1936). On the archaeological side, see E. T. Leeds, 'The West Saxon invasion and the Icknield Way', *History* (1925), vol. X, pp. 97-109, and 'The Early Saxon penetration of the Upper Thames area', *Antiquaries Journal* (1933), vol. XIII, pp. 229-51; G. J. Copley, *The Conquest of Wessex in the sixth century* (London, 1954); and for a stimulating though highly speculative treatment, T. Dayrell Reed, *The rise of Wessex* (London, 1947). For the Saxons of Wiltshire, see G. M. Young, *Origin of the West Saxon Kingdom* (Oxford, 1934).

XIII

THE PLACE-NAMES OF HAMPSHIRE

THE central position of Hampshire on the south coast of England has had a striking effect on its place-name structure. To the west of the Hampshire Avon, Celtic place-names become increasingly more frequent, especially names of small streams, while to the east of the county and to the south of the Thames few pre-English names have survived. Similarly, Southampton Water forms the boundary of the zone of early settlement by Saxons and Jutes, on the evidence of *-ingas* and of heathen site names. Basically, most of the names of the county are of Germanic origin; the Norman manorial system has left its mark, though less than in the counties to the west.

The Earliest Names: the Pre-Saxon Element (Fig. 47)

Almost all the major rivers of the county—the Hamble is the only important exception —have pre-Saxon names. Stour probably means 'strong stream' and Loddon 'muddy stream', but many have names that are now difficult and sometimes impossible to interpret; Avon means simply 'river', and Test possibly has much the same meaning, while 'Itchel' and Itchen are names the meanings of which have now been lost, though they may be related to the tribal name *Iceni*. The alternative name, Ex, for the Beaulieu river seems to be a comparatively recent back-formation name, wrongly derived from Exbury near its mouth, which itself is derived from a personal name, *Eohhere*, so it has no link with the common Celtic river name. Its original Saxon name seems to have been the *Otere*.

Andover, Candover and Micheldever are now names of settlements, but they all are in origin the names of the rivers beside which they now stand, and all incorporate the British word *dubro*, meaning water. Lymington and nearby Everton have Saxon suffixes, but the first part of the names are those of Celtic river names, the former incorporating the Celtic word for 'elm' and the latter having the same origin as Yeovilton, for the earliest reference to Everton spells the name *Yveletona* (*Steptoe Charity Deeds* at Southampton, *c.* 1300).

Considerable intercourse between Celtic and Germanic peoples is indicated by the fifteen pre-Saxon river names and by twenty-one extant site names of Celtic origin. Four of the latter incorporate the word 'port', which seems to have been the Celtic name for the harbour where Portsmouth now lies. Not counted among the names of undoubted Celtic origin are four names marked on Fig. 47—Funtley, Havant, Boarhunt and Mottisfont—that incorporate the British loan word *funta*, a 'spring'; examples can also be found of names that utilise the word *cumb*, meaning valley, that is sometimes regarded as another word loaned from the British peoples. Names especially valuable as indications of Celtic survival are Melchet, 'a sparse wood', in which both elements are pre-Saxon, and Crow, meaning 'hovel'. Winchester and Portchester derive their modern prefixes from the Celtic, and it is possible that Silchester's prefix evolved from 'Calleva'. The names 'Clausentum' and 'Onna' are no longer used. A few names, English in origin, show contact with relics of the Roman past; thus the two places called Holbury may refer to ruined Roman buildings, and the examples of *Drakenhorde*, 'dragon hoard', in Crawley and Rockbourne probably indicate discoveries of Roman buried treasure. *Andret* in Domesday Book (*DB*) indicates the westward extent of the great 'Andredesweald' woodland.

Names of Earthworks

Hampshire contains many hill-forts, several incorporating in their names the element *bury*, 'a fort', as a suffix. Of these, Danebury and Norsebury through popular etymology now have names that seem falsely to link them with Scandinavian settlement. Butser and Tidbury are named from Saxon persons, and Bransbury from an Anglo-Scandinavian personal name. The name Buckland Rings means 'book land'—that is, 'land held by charter', and the second name, Rings, indicates that it is a multivallate earthwork. The name Winkle-bury means that it was used as a fort by men from 'Wiltshire; the name is not recorded before the mid-thirteenth century and may be evidence of a duty enjoined upon the men of Wiltshire to aid the men of Hampshire when invasion threatened; as late as 1545 there is a record of 1000 men being sent from Wiltshire to coastal Lymington. Old Winchester Hill near Meonstoke was so called late in the Middle Ages, though the name cannot now be explained. It would be of interest if early spellings could be found for Ladle Hill, famous because it was unfinished in the Iron Age, with the earth left in irregular mounds, for the name may be descriptive of its appearance. Although on a smaller scale, several barrows have names, such as those marked on Fig. 48, because they were and in fact still are used as New Forest bounds.

The Earliest Germanic Names

In the south of the county three place-names are folk-names of a type that must belong to the age of the earliest Germanic immigration, for they had in their earliest spellings the suffix *-ingas*. These are Hayling, Wymering and Eling. Their positions on the coast coincide with the traditions of the West Saxon royal house concerning the first invasions by its peoples; these traditions were used in Alfred's day by the compilers of the *Anglo-Saxon Chronicle*, which gives precise dates for various landings and battles. For instance, the *Chronicle* states that a man called Port, accompanied by his two sons, landed in 501 near Portsmouth; the coincidence of names is, of course, startling. Near Portsmouth are two of these *-ingas* names, Wymering and Hayling. Further west lies Eling, the position of which makes feasible the *Chronicle*'s story of a landing in 495 by Cerdic and his son at *Cerdicesora*, which may well be Ower near Calshot, followed by a battle in 508 close to Eling at Netley

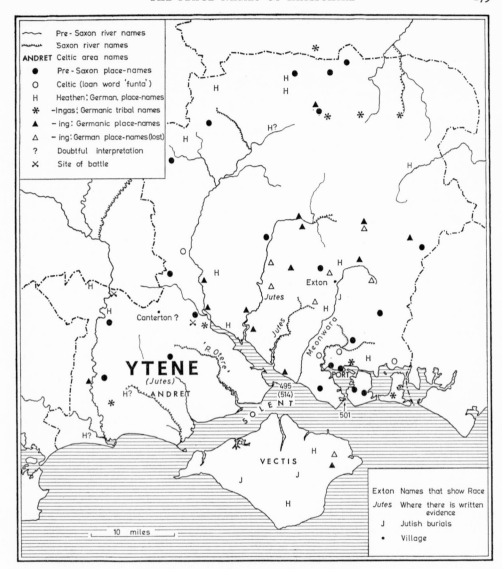

Fig. 47. The place-names of Hampshire

Most extant names of sites marked are given in the text. 'Lost' -*ing* names (*Brenting, Chittynge, Colynge, Twitaelingae, Walmerynge* and *Wopbincg*) have been marked in the parish areas to which they appear to belong. *Steynynge* in Southwick should be added. Existing -*ing* names as marked from left to right are Kittens, Waldron, Nursling, Swaythling, Sholing, Chilling, Hensting, Ripling, Hampage, Chitterling (in the north), Hayling (Meon), Swelling and Snailing. Pre-Saxon names not in the text include three near Portsmouth—Chark, Cams and Creech.

Marsh, where the British leader Natanleod and 5000 of his men were stated to have been slain. Ellingham, which appears to have been a daughter settlement of Eling, may exemplify infiltration westwards, perhaps half a century later, after the next recorded victory of the invaders, that at Salisbury in 552. If 'Murdinges', possibly Martin's in Sopley parish, is a tribal -*ingas* type of name, it is the most westerly example along the south coast of England, and shows that the Avon was used by the oared longboats of the very early Saxon raiders, whose burials have been uncovered in the Salisbury area, as well as at Iford on the Stour, near its junction with the Avon. Three other examples of the -*ingas* type are in the north, where settlers may either have come from the south via the Roman road or up the river valleys from the Thames; these are Worting, Basing and Poland (formerly Poling).

Names involving the singular suffix -*ing* are very difficult to distinguish. Only one example of this type has been found in the north of the county, but it possibly forms a link with the eight examples that once existed in Berkshire. Nine of the thirteen possible extant examples of the -*ing* type in Hampshire (some of which may indicate early Germanic settlement) lie near the four main rivers flowing into Southampton Water. This type of name is common in Kent, and it may be that the group in southern Hampshire confirms Bede's statement that the Jutes not only settled in Kent but on the Isle of Wight and the mainland opposite (see p. 172). In a separate passage he actually specified the settlers beside the Hamble as being Jutes. On the Isle of Wight only one example, Brading, exists of the -*ing* type, but Kentish style ornaments have also been found on the island. Objects of similar style were discovered in 1900 near Droxford, in the province of the *Meonwara*, who are known to have been ethnically distinct from the Saxons. The soil of the New Forest has not yielded any Jutish objects, but as late as 1100 the area was known to local inhabitants as *Ytene*, which means 'of the Jutes'. The name Canterton in the north of the Forest may show that a group of people direct from Kent made a settlement there at some later time, but insufficient early forms of the name exist to make the meaning certain. Other racial settlement names are marked on Fig. 47.

Hampshire has a greater number of names denoting heathen worship than have most counties. The names Frobury and Froyle, and possibly also Freefolk, show that the goddess Frig was worshipped in the extreme north of the county. Also in the north was the lost dlace *Tislea*, which means 'the grove of the war god, Tig'. A third deity, whose name is now given to the fourth day of the week, is Thunor; boundary charters show that he was worshipped at Millbrook and Droxford, both situated in areas that were probably peopled by Jutes. Two Grim's Dykes were named in thirteenth-century deeds and are now called by what seems to be Grim's alternative name, Woden. The names Weyhill and Wheely show that heathen shrines existed in the west and east of the county, for the names incorporate the word *weoh*, meaning 'heathen temple'. In the north-west, close to one Woden's Dyke, an early Saxon charter records the burial mound of a 'plunder lord', a designation that was probably derived from the time of the very early Germanic raids. Only a few miles to the south of the Dyke, in the bounds of St. Mary Bourne, another boundary charter mentions the burial mound of a man called Cerdic, who may indeed be that founder of the West Saxon Kingdom whose death in 534 is recorded in the *Anglo-Saxon Chronicle*.

Common Germanic Elements

The name Hampshire, like the vast majority of the place-names of the shire, is Germanic. It was called *Hamtunscire* in the *Anglo-Saxon Chronicle*, *sub anno* 755, a date that is now known to represent the year 757. Only three English shires are in fact mentioned at an earlier date. The abbreviation 'Hants' is surely derived from the spelling *Hantescire* in *DB*. In each case the letter *c* was probably pronounced like the letter *h* today. The name is from *Homtun*, meaning 'the water-meadow farm', though more commonly spelt *Hamtun*. The town acquired its defining prefix by 962 and this also became part of the shire name, used in some documents until Stuart times.

Over eighty Saxon land-charters that mention village names have survived; a number of village names also appear before *DB* on documents written in Latin. As one would expect, there is a proliferation around the cathedral city of Winchester, and a corresponding paucity in the south-west, to which belong only eight charters of Saxon times. The earliest of these is the royal grant to the Cathedral of Winchester in 735 of *Drucam* (*Thruhham* in 749 and *Truham*—the bishop's manor—in *DB*). This must have been the place, called *Thorougham* by William Leland about 1540, where he said Rufus had been killed. A reference of 1606 mentions 'Beauley Parke alias Throwgham', so if Leland's information is correct the Rufus Stone erected in 1745, over two centuries after Leland's time, stands very far from the correct spot.

Of place-names derived from personal names, Charford stands alone in historical significance, for it is derived from the founder of 495 of Wessex, Cerdic, whose name was actually Celtic in origin. The *Anglo-Saxon Chronicle* records a battle at *Cerdicesford* in 519. Hengistbury, an example of folk-etymology, has developed from *Hedenesburia* ('Heddin's fort'). J. E. B. Gover lists about 350 old English personal names used in the formation of Hampshire place-names; of these a few are derived from women's names, the most unusual being Worldham, for it combines a woman's name, Wærhild, with the early suffix -*ham*. Alice Holt is actually derived from a man's name, Ælfsige, though Alverstoke and nearby Elson are from women's names. The suffix of the last is -*tun*, the second commonest element in the place-names of the county, for there are some 110 examples. When these are mapped they give some idea of the areas of secondary settlement. For example, over twenty -*tuns* occur along the coastal strip from Lymington westward to Tuckton. One of these is Barton (*Bermintune* and *Burmintune* in *DB*), which is the only example of the common name Barton derived from a personal name. Of all the hundreds of place-names probably derived from personal names, the only one of any importance that still defies interpretation is Bransgore near Christchurch; so far the earliest reference to the name only dates from 1740. Perhaps it will be discovered that the name is not after all derived from a person.

The frequency of suffixes meaning 'wood' and of names compounded with plants affords some clues to the ecology of the county, most of which was under forest law in the thirteenth century. *Ley* is by far the commonest element in the county's names, for there are about 175 examples, as well as a dozen *holts* and about thirty *hursts*; these names all normally mean 'wood' or 'woodland clearing'. It is, however, possible that Hurst (where a castle was erected in Tudor times) may mean 'sandbank', for such is how the area was described when the castle was planned, and the word could have that meaning in the late Middle Ages, according to A. H. Smith's *English place-name elements* (1956). It is easy to compile a list of names that specify plants and trees. Lyndhurst, capital of the New Forest, and Holdenhurst, designated sometimes as 'the mother of Bournemouth' (for the latter developed within the parish of Holdenhurst), are derived from the lime and the holly respectively. Minstead is from mint, and Naish (like Ashley) is from the ash; St. Ives indicates ivy. Other vegetation names are evident in Appleshaw, Aldershot, Maplederwell, Ewhurst, Oakhanger and Privett. Bramshott and Bramshaw indicate bramble, though Bramley and Breamore are derived from the broom. Fern is the common element in the names Farley, Farnborough, Fareham and Vernham. A few names derived from occupations help to give the same picture of a well-wooded county; among these are Woodmancott, Fullerton ('enclosure of the bird-catchers') and Charlesford ('charcoal-burner's ford'). Wild creatures are well represented, from the wolf in the name Woolmer and the eagle in Arnewood, to the insects of Wigley, the swans of Elvetham, the doves of Culverley, frogs in Frogham and toads in Tadley. Evidence of the pleasures of the chase comes from such names as Durley (deer), Eversley (wild boar), Foxcott and Hounsdown. However, the meanings of Roeshot ('rough corner'), Boarhunt ('spring by the fort'), Buckholt ('beechwood'), Wolverton (possibly 'Wulfhere's farm'), Everton ('farm on the river Yevel') and Hound (a plant) should warn against too facile explanations. The significance of farm animals is attested by Tichborne, Tisted and Titchfield (kids), Rotherwick and Neatham (cattle), Keyhaven (a cow), Chawton (calves), Hursley and Studley (horses), Enham (lambs), Gosport (geese) and Andwell (ducks). The value of honey in the rural economy is shown by Beauworth (bees) and Empshott (a swarm).

A few names throw light on social behaviour or on local conditions. Warnborough means 'the stream in which felons were drowned', and the two Galley Hills may refer to the gallows. In the county four place-names incorporate the word *pleg* ('play') and thus indicate sites for games. Broadhalfpenny Down is probably a jocular description of the level space there for cricket. Sites where men congregated for more serious affairs were Mottisfont ('moot') and Shirley ('the grove of the shire'). The latter is near the *Hamtun* that gave its name to the shire. Close by is the 'look-out hill', Toot Hill. Rowner, Lepe and Hythe in various ways all indicate landing-places, and improvements at river crossings can be seen in the changing names of *Forde* to *Fordingebrige* (both in *DB*) and of the place once called 'reed ford' to Redbridge. Besides Christchurch (originally called *Tweoxneam* which meant ''tween the streams'), Cheriton and Whitchurch utilise the word 'church'. St. Cross, St. Denys, two St. Catherine Hills and Petersfield are named from various dedications. Penton and Pennington refer to 'penny payments', while Gollard ('gold')—'near the Roman Port Way—and Hordle ('hoard hill') indicate sites where treasure was discovered.

Scandinavian Names

Understandably, when one recalls that Viking settlements lay almost entirely north of the Watling Street, only three names extant in Hampshire definitely reveal Scandinavian ownership, with Bransbury making a possible fourth. These are Thruxton in the north-west, Ossemsley of Milton parish that is now in Lymington borough, and Colgrim's Mere near Beaulieu. The last named is probably of recent creation by someone conversant with the names of the medieval bounds of the Abbey estates; certainly it must be derived, though the final letter in his name has been changed, from that Colgrin who held one of the half-dozen *Truham* manors in *DB*. The Danes Stream at Milford is not derived from the Danes, but means 'valley stream'; nevertheless, the similarity of the names, combined with some burial mounds actually of the Bronze Age nearby, resulted in the inclusion of a battle symbol on the O.S. map.

Norman and French Names

The Norman Conquest introduced Hampshire's alternative name, the County of Southampton, which utilises the Norman-French word 'county'. In fact, this name ceased to be official only five years ago, in 1959. Excluding a considerable number of manorial sub-titles now little used, over thirty medieval owners have their patronymics perpetuated as additions to earlier names. There are three Hartleys defined from the names of their owners as Hartley Mauditt, Hartley Westpall and Hartley Wintney. Similarly there are three Hintons; that called Hinton Admiral, which lies close to the sea, obtained its secondary title from the Albamara family. The volumes of *The Victoria County History of Hampshire* and E. Ekwall's *Dictionary of English place-names* list early references to the manorial owners who have left their names attached to the twin examples of Barton, Hurstbourne, Newton, Penton, Sherborne, Stratfield and Weston. Fifteen names prefix the title or name of the manorial lord, especially King, Abbot and Bishop. For instance, Awbridge means Abbot's ridge and the family of Martyr owned Martyr Worthy. Family names have also survived as uncompounded place-names; among these are Skidmore, Fife Head and Tiptoe. The earliest document so far known that mentions this last-named place is dated 1555, but a few medieval deeds refer to the Tibetot family in connection with Barton-on-Sea, which is in the next parish. In a few instances the manorial name has replaced an earlier name, as is the case with *Scherperyxe*, which became Lisle Court (near Lymington) from a family famous in Stuart times that owned Moyles Court, itself named from a still earlier owner.

The biggest concentration of names derived directly from the French language occurs on the estates of the Abbey of Beaulieu, a name that has itself retained its French spelling, though the pronunciation has been Anglicised to 'Bewley'. Farms on the estate where the Abbey's sheep and oxen were kept are still called Bergerie and Beufre. Not far from Beaulieu is the separate part of Dibden known as Dibden Purlieu. An obvious example from the French language in the north of the county is Beaurepaire ('fine retreat'). Bure Homage was so designated, with two other places, in the Christchurch Priory Cartulary, but it alone has retained the subsidiary title Homage.

The use of Latin elements today is even rarer in the county's place-names. Districts of Romsey ('Rum's island') are called Infra and Extra; another example may be Cocum Farm at Barton Stacey, for the owner of an estate there in Edward II's reign was the King's cook.

The New Forest and Its Place-names in Domesday Book (Fig. 48)

Despite recent reiterations by some scholars of the eighteenth-century concept that the Forest existed in Saxon days, the name 'New' was first used in *DB*. This fact, combined with the loss between 1066 and 1086 of 106½ hides in assessment for tax and of approximately £247 in value, as the land could no longer be cultivated fully, points to an actual creation by William I. Certainly most medieval chroniclers wrote of William I as the king responsible for placing the area under forest law, though a few blamed Rufus. It is difficult to accept suggestions that the Conqueror merely extended an existing Forest.

DB includes about 360 manorial sites in mainland Hampshire, with a further 101 on the Isle of Wight. Just as it is difficult to arrive at accurate figures, owing to some sites having common names, so the position of a number will probably never be known. This is especially true of manors within and near to the New Forest. However, some manors left unidentified or wrongly identified by J. H. Round, in *V.C.H.*, vol. I, can now be ascribed with some certainty, and suggestions can be made for others. Certainly, an attempt to map the sites in their Hundreds is needed, if the significance of forty-five manors reduced to nothing in value is to be realised. J. H. Round's figures of money value lost (*V.C.H.*, vol. I, p. 411) are misquotations from the Rev. R. Warner's erroneous figures (*Topographical remarks*, 1793, vol. I, p. 189.)

Since 1791, when the Rev. William Gilpin suggested that *Truham* might be Fritham, near the Rufus Stone, this identification has been generally accepted, but that identification is incorrect, for *Truham* is the area now called Park Farm, Beaulieu. *V.C.H.*, vol. I, p. 511, offered two suggestions in an attempt to identify *Bermintune*, and the Rev. R. Warner had previously suggested another. However, three of the twenty-five medieval deeds in the Winchester College archives that pertain to this manor prove that it is actually Barton-on-Sea. *Wigarestun* appeared as 'Wygeston' in a survey of 1578, and was near Sowley. There is possibly a link with 'Whiskars' named in 1670, and the eponymous owner of the *DB* manor definitely gave his name to the place now called Vicar's Hill.

Fourteenth-century documents help the suggested ascriptions of *Cildeest* to a lost place in Brockenhurst, of *Alwinetune* to Allum Green and of *Godesmanescamp* to Godwinscroft; the last named was in *Rodedic* Hundred and could not have been Godshill near Fordingbridge, to which it has been ascribed on O.S. maps. Foxlease, south of Lyndhurst, was originally known as 'Cockslease', so *Cocherlei* is tentatively sited there. *Bortel*, mentioned in the Christchurch Priory Cartulary in a charter of 985, is probably Bosley Farm close to the Priory. As there are two places called Langley and two called Ower in Redbridge Hundred today, *Langelie* and *Hore* could be at either of the places which lie just outside the Forest and were consequently not drastically reduced in value.

One would expect a settlement at Burley, for there the land is more fertile than in some other parts of the Forest and Fig. 48 would otherwise show a big gap in that area, so *Bile* has been marked there; the Norman clerk may have misheard the name, as is also implied by the suggested identification of *Slacham* with Sloden. *Oselei* has been put between *Bedeslei* and *Truham*, because that is how it is recorded in *DB*. Buckholt, from *Bocolt*, has not been sited precisely, though J. R. Wise stated that it was just north of Dibden (*The New Forest*, 1863, p. 50). E. Ekwall's dictionary identification with Buckholt 10 miles north of the Forest is impossible to accept. *Oselei* is probably the *Osanlea* of 984, but ought not to be equated with Ossemsley.

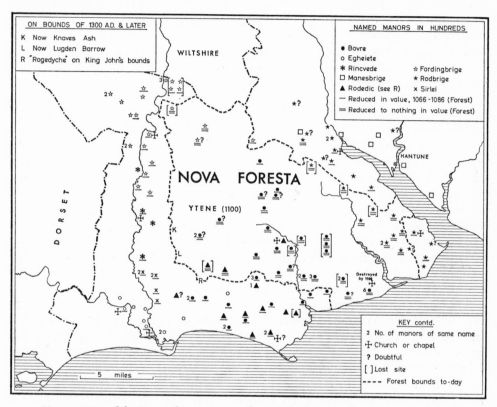

Fig. 48. Map of the Domesday manors, under Hundreds, in south-western Hampshire
The New Forest bounds have probably changed little since 1086. Reasons for marking nine manors under different Hundreds than they appear to be in *DB* are given in the text, as are reasons for suggested identifications that differ from those in *V.C.H.*, vol. I. Added to these is *Beceslei*, which has been marked as Batchley. Plate XXVII is a photograph of the meeting place of *Rodedic* Hundred, stated to be unknown by O. Anderson in *The English Hundred-Names* (Lund, 1934-9). p. 175.

J. R. Round identified *Titegrave* with Tidgrove in the extreme north of the county, though the manor was stated to be in *Rodbrige* Hundred. The entry is at the top of a fresh page, but the clerk had been very careful with Hundredal headings on the previous side. It may have been near a place called 'Tyttebrok', named on early perambulations, or close by at Tutt's Bridge in West Wellow. A marginal note, not mentioned in *V.C.H.*, adds that its name had once been *Middeltone*. There is a gap in the text beside *Pisteslei*, obviously left for the Hundredal heading, *Bovre* (folio 51a, ii); the six manors that follow this gap are put in Bovre Hundred on Fig. 48. Beside *Utefel* is a gap that may have been left for a similar purpose, though this is masked by words added from the previous entry (folio 51b, ii). The reference to Brockenhurst (which possibly means 'broken woodland') is the next named manor after *Utefel*. Both appear in *DB* under the heading *Rodedic* Hundred, but Brockenhurst is remarkably isolated from the rest of that Hundred; the inference is that a gap was left beside *Utefel* for the name *Bovre* Hundred, which would make more sense of the next entry, that of Sway, which is put in *Bovre* Hundred by the *DB* clerk when he recorded the place-name on three other occasions. Below the Sway reference the last three entries on the page are very cramped as the *DB* clerk tried to complete the New Forest entries. On Fig. 48, therefore, Minstead has been entered under *Bovre* Hundred and Bisterne and Crow under *Rincvede* Hundred.

The Brockenhurst entry is unique in another way, for it is the only manor known to be within the Forest bounds that did not have its value reduced to nothing. Instead, its value was doubled, and it was the only completely afforested place to keep its church. The reason must be that it was the centre from which the king hunted, and that the manorial owner held the estate for the *ministerium* ('service') of providing the king with lodging for himself and his steeds, though this service was not defined until 1212 (*V.C.H.*, vol. IV, p. 627.) The fact that two documents witnessed by Rufus at Brockenhurst have survived shows the significance of the place, but this is insufficient reason for T. A. M. Bishop and P. Chaplais to state that the King was actually killed at Brockenhurst (*Facsimiles of English Royal Writs to A.D. 1100*, Oxford, 1957, opp. Plate XVI).

Since John's time the bounds of the Forest have changed very little; in places the boundary banks and ditches remain very obvious today (Plate XXVII). *DB* alone can signify what was the original area, and its evidence seems to point to a similar conclusion, one of very little change. Since W. Faden's map of 1791, the only significant diminution of area seems to be in the north-east, where the manors of Bartley and Canterton have bitten into the bounds. Presumably this was after 654 cases of alleged infringement of the bounds were examined in 1801. Comparison of the names on the boundary at different times reveals some unlikely origins of modern place-names; for instance, *Wykeneshull* of 1300 became Vicar's Hill when Boldre vicars began to live there and *Wytehyndesburgh* of 1300, written *Albam Bissam* in the boundary list of 1279, became Whitelimeborough in 1670.

Newer Names

In *DB* three boroughs are mentioned—Winchester, Southampton and Christchurch. Before 1300 several settlements were given borough status, notably by the bishops of Winchester and the earls of Devon. In some cases, as at New Alresford and New Lymington, this involved additions to existing names, though this distinction is now lost at Lymington, which seems to have begun as a site on the hill west of the church, and not, as is usually assumed, beside the river. Newtown, close to the Berkshire border, never prospered in rivalry with Newbury. The area west of the Chewton stream in south-western Hampshire was also called Newtown, though without borough status, from the time of Elizabeth I at least, yet it adopted the name Highcliff(e) from the castle nearby less than seventy-five years ago; already knowledge of the former name has almost been lost.

Although Bournemouth is not recorded as having an inhabited house till 1812, apart from that shown on W. Faden's map of 1791, the site is referred to as early as 1407, when an 18-foot fish was washed up at *la bournemowthe*. This occurs in the Christchurch Priory Cartulary (*Tib. D* VI, ii, folio 134r), on the same folio as a list of Forest bounds. A second reference, not hitherto noticed, is on the unpublished map in the British Museum, compiled at a time when Henry VIII feared an attack from France, so it is the earliest detailed map of the district (*Cott. Aug.*, i, 31-33). On it are shown a blockhouse and a beacon beside the words *bowurnemothe wer ys feyer landyng*. Between the mainland and the Isle of Wight a long islet is named *chalke Roke*, a name that also appears on maps of 1588 and 1791, though in the plural.

Close to Portsmouth two place-names indicate links with the battle of Waterloo. In 1826 the Marquis of Anglesey, who had lost a leg in that battle, founded Anglesey (also called Angleseyville) south of Gosport; Waterlooville, north of Purbrook, took its name from an inn called 'The Heroes of Waterloo'.

For some years after the railway reached Southampton in 1840, the station now called Eastleigh was known as Bishopstoke. Eastleigh was merely a tiny farm, though listed in *DB*. New Milton is probably unique in that it received its defining element from the suggestion of the owner of a small shop. The railway station had opened in 1888 with the common name of Milton, which was causing confusion, so the railway adopted the name by which Mrs. Newhook distinguished her sub-post office near the station from the earlier office half a mile away in the old village centre. One contemporary estate agent's brochure tried to foist the name 'Milton-by-the-Sea' on the district. Nearby, the owner of estates in Milford reverted to *DB* for his sale brochure, calling it 'Melleford-on-Sea'. Like the name 'Montagu Town' for Buckler's Hard, these last two suggestions did not receive popular support, and the latter is now Milford-on-Sea. This addition of '-on-Sea', mainly since the end of the War of 1914-18, to the names of so many coastal resorts anxious to attract visitors, is itself evidence of the changing social patterns of behaviour in this present century. Since the War of 1939-45, the hamlet of Enham near Andover has become Enham Alamein. In such ways as this, place-names continue to mirror the history of both the county and the country.

BIBLIOGRAPHICAL NOTE

(1) J. E. B. Gover generously made available the typescript of his forthcoming volume for the English Place-Name Society, *The place-names of Hampshire*.

(2) E. Ekwall, *English place-names in -ing* (Lund, 1923); *English river names* (Oxford, 1928); *The Concise Oxford Dictionary of English place-names* (4th edit., Oxford, 1960) (this contains 500 references to Hampshire names).

(3) R. Welldon Finn, *An introduction to Domesday Book* (London, 1963), pp. 207-11; *The Domesday geography of south-east England*, edited H. C. Darby and E. M. J. Campbell (Cambridge, 1962), chapter VII, pp. 287-363.

(4) G. B. Grundy, 'The Saxon land charters of Hampshire, with notes on place and field names', *Archaeological Journal* (1921-8), vols. 78, 81, 83, 84 and index in vol. 85.

(5) H. Kokeritz, *The place-names of the Isle of Wight* (Uppsala, 1940).

(6) A. H. Smith, *English place-name elements* (Cambridge, 1956), Pts. I and II (this quotes 350 examples from Hampshire); 'Place-names and the Anglo-Saxon settlement', *Proceedings of the British Academy* (1956), vol. 42, pp. 67-88.

(7) Sir Frank Stenton, Presidential Addresses, *Transactions of the Royal Historical Society* (1939-41, 1943).

(8) J. H. Round, 'Introduction to the Hampshire Domesday' (pp. 399-448), and 'The text of the Hampshire Domesday' (pp. 449-516), *The Victoria County History of Hampshire and the Isle of Wight*, vol. I (now Oxford, 1900).

(9) *The Victoria County History of Hampshire and the Isle of Wight*, vols. II to V, lists early spellings of most place-names.

XIV

SETTLEMENT IN PREHISTORIC AND ROMAN TIMES

THE PALAEOLITHIC PERIOD

(before c. 7000 B.C.)

THE geography of southern Wessex during this long period, which may have lasted at least 100,000 years, bore little relation to that of today except perhaps for the river systems. The distribution of land and sea fluctuated within this period between the glacial and interglacial phases (see p. 47).

The Lower Palaeolithic period is represented mainly by Acheulian hand-axes and associated implements, which have been found in large numbers at Dunbridge, Kimbridge, Timsbury and elsewhere in the gravels of the river Test and at Warsash on the lower Hamble (Fig. 49). A smaller number has come from the gravels of the Salisbury Avon, the Wylye and the Nadder, particularly in the vicinity of Salisbury and around the Stour–Avon estuary in the Bournemouth region.[1] Many have come from the terraces of the Stour valley, especially at Canford and Corfe Mullen (*DCM*).* A few have been found at Southampton and Shirley,[2] and in various localities in the Isle of Wight.[3] They often occur between 80 feet and 150 feet above the present sea-level. The same general areas have yielded Pleistocene fauna, such as teeth of *elephas antiquus* and *elephas primigenius*.

The only known Upper Palaeolithic site within the region is an open site on Hengistbury Head, recently excavated by Mrs. A. Mace following earlier work by others. The flint assemblage includes backed blades, tanged points and gravers. It differs from the Creswellian industries in that trapeze forms are absent from Hengistbury, and tanged points do not occur on Creswellian sites (*BM* and *CRHM*)[4]. 'Laurel-leaf' implements from Havenstreet and elsewhere in the Isle of Wight (*CarCM*), hitherto claimed as Solutrian, are probably

---

* Abbreviations in brackets refer to the following Museums:

BM	British Museum	*DCM*	Dorset County Museum, Dorchester
BRCM	Bournemouth (Russel-Cotes Museum)	*DM*	Devizes Museum
CarCM	Carisbrooke Castle Museum	*Poole M*	Poole Museum
ChiCM	Chichester City Museum	*PRM*	Pitt-Rivers Museum, Farnham, Dorset
CMAE	Cambridge Museum of Archaeology and Ethnology	*SalM*	Salisbury Museum
		SthM	Southampton Museum
CRHM	Christchurch (Red House Museum)	*WM*	Winchester Museum

The small figures refer to references listed in numerical order at the end of this chapter. To assist location, the National Grid reference is given for many sites.

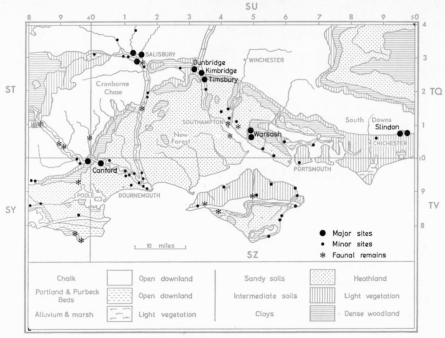

Fig. 49. The Palaeolithic period

Note. Since this map was completed, Mr. D. Roe has supplied the author with a list of Palaeolithic sites, which includes additional major sites at Bournemouth, Southampton, Romsey, Lavant (near Chichester), and Shide and Rew Street in the Isle of Wight, together with numerous additional minor sites.

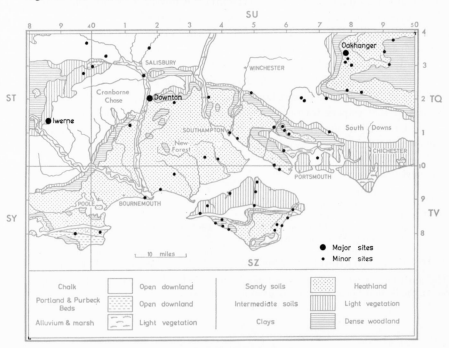

Fig. 50. The Mesolithic period

Neolithic, similar examples having been found stratified at the Neolithic site at Hurst Fen in Suffolk.[5] A probable fragment was found associated with Neolithic pottery in a pit at Southbourne near Bournemouth.[6]

THE MESOLITHIC PERIOD
(c. 7000 – 3200 B.C.)

Within this period, perhaps around 5000 B.C., occurred the final separation of England from the continent (see p. 48), and since then progressive encroachment of the sea along the south coast has continued.[7] A conjectural map showing the geography of the Solent area during part of this period, with Mesolithic sites added, has been published by the late W. F. Rankine,[8] based on the work of the Geological Survey. The main occupation period of Rankine's extensive Mesolithic site at Oakhanger near Selborne (SU 773346) has been shown by radio-carbon dating of carbonised hazelnut-shells to be about 4340 B.C., c. ± 120 years.[9] The perforated 'mace-head' of sarsen (SthM) found in 1883 on the site of the Ocean Dock, Southampton, about 20 feet deep in the peat, is probably of the same general period.

Mesolithic sites (Fig. 50) so far located in the region under review are mostly distributed on the sandy heaths of the New Forest and eastern Hampshire, and in the Greensand areas elsewhere; but a few have been identified in deposits of Clay-with-Flints capping the chalk downs, as on Old Winchester Hill (SU 640206) and Butser Hill (SU 720200). Some are located near coasts and rivers; a few sites between Freshwater and Brighstone Bays are related to the course of the former extension of the West Yar river. These distributions largely reflect economic factors, particularly hunting and fishing activities.

A Mesolithic site excavated in 1957 at Downton, Wiltshire[10] (SU 180211), contained both a 'light' microlithic industry and a 'heavy' industry of core-scrapers and other artifacts (CMAE), as well as a series of stake-holes best interpreted as the remains of a shelter or shelters. Finally, an antler engraved with rows of chevrons (BM), found near Romsey, is probably of the Maglemosian culture within this period.

THE NEOLITHIC PERIOD
(c. 3200 – 1850/1800 B.C.)

During the fourth and third millennia B.C., the climate of Britain became warmer and drier, resulting in a reduction in woodland. This was assisted by the introduction by Neolithic immigrants from the Continent of domesticated cattle and, later, sheep. These immigrants also brought with them a knowledge of the cultivation of cereals and the art of pottery-making.

Very few habitation sites of this period are known in Britain, but of these Wessex has its full share, although they are all unspectacular (Fig. 51). Those of Windmill Hill culture have been located at Corfe Mullen near Poole (SY 970980), Southbourne, Michelmersh near Romsey (SU 3526) and Selsey (pottery in ChiCM). Evidence of Secondary Neolithic (Peterborough) habitation has come from Downton south of Salisbury (SU 180210),[11] and

Os

from the sites of Bronze Age round barrows on Arreton Down and Niton Down in the Isle of Wight (*CarCM*).[12] The nearest causewayed enclosures of this period to the Southampton region are at Whitesheet Hill (ST 802352), Hambledon Hill (ST 849121), the Trundle (SU 878110) and Barkhale (SU 976126), the last two being in western Sussex. The precise function of these enclosures is uncertain; they have hitherto been regarded as essentially pastoral, but it has recently been suggested that they might have been for fairs where trading and other forms of social activity were practised.[13] Evidence of some industrial activity during this period is provided by the flint mines on Easton Down (SU 237358) and at Martin's Clump (SU 251390) near the border of Wiltshire and Hampshire, although certainly the former and probably the latter were worked mainly during the Beaker period. Of the flint mines on the Sussex Downs, those at Stoke Down (SU 831096) and Long Down (SU 931092) are in the region under review. A clear picture is now emerging regarding the distribution of stone axes to southern Wessex from the working-sites in the areas of igneous rock in Brittany and western and northern Britain. Ceremonial axes of jadeite and related material were imported from Brittany and have been found at Southampton (*SthM*), Bournemouth (*CRHM?*), Breamore (*DM*), Sturminster Marshall (*PRM*), Winterslow and the Stonehenge area (*SalM*); this would suggest Hengistbury to be the main port of entry. Axes of Cornish origin came into this area in quantity, but occur mostly west of the Salisbury Avon. Axes of preselite (the Pembrokeshire bluestone of Stonehenge) have been found at Bournemouth (*BRCM*), Stockton Earthworks to the west of Salisbury (*SalM*) and Worthy Down near Winchester (*SthM*). Implements of Graig Lwyd rock (North Wales) have come from Badbury Rings (*PooleM*), Bournemouth (*CRHM*), North Sway near Brockenhurst (*SalM*), Lee-on-the-Solent (private collection) and Stockbridge (*WM*). The Lake District working-sites of Great Langdale produced axes found at Broadstone (*DCM*) Bournemouth (*BM*), Southampton (*SthM*) and many sites in Wiltshire. Finally, the Whin Sill quartz-dolerite of Northumberland is represented by implements from Southampton (private collection) and Gorley near Fordingbridge (*SalM*).[14]

With regard to ceremonial sites, Stonehenge and Woodhenge are outside the area under review and are outside the scope of this chapter. The most important ceremonial site in the region, probably Neolithic, is the Dorset Cursus, a linear earthwork which extends from the two long barrows on Thickthorn Down (ST 972123) to the three or four long barrows on Bokerly Down (SU 040192), incorporating in its course other long barrows on Gussage Hill and Oakley Down; this appears to provide strong circumstantial evidence for a Neolithic date for the cursus. The latter is really two—the south-western or Gussage cursus, and the north-eastern or Pentridge cursus, which Professor R. J. C. Atkinson considers to be the later in date.

The Neolithic period is represented in the sepulchral record by the long barrows, which were essentially communal burial-places; in Wessex they are distributed on the chalk downs, with only two exceptions. The first of these is the Holdenhurst long barrow (now destroyed) on a gravel-spread beside the river Stour, which seems to connect the prehistoric port at Hengistbury with Cranborne Chase and its remarkable concentration of about thirty long barrows; the second is the Long Stone long barrow at Mottistone (Isle of Wight), sited on the Greensand to the south of the chalk ridge in order to make use of local stone slabs in its structure. An unusual characteristic of several of the long barrows on and around Cranborne Chase is that they have U-shaped ditches which enclose one end but not the other.

The general period of the earthen or unchambered long barrows is indicated by recent radio-carbon datings. That from burnt wood of the third phase of the structure within the east end of the Nutbane long barrow (SU 330495) near Andover, gave 2721 ± 150 B.C., and Windmill Hill ware occurred in a primary context.[15] That from the Fussell's Lodge long barrow north-east of Salisbury (SU 192325) is 3220 ± 150 B.C.[16] These datings accord well with that from a Neolithic occupation surface beneath the bank of the outer ditch at Windmill Hill (2950 ± 150 B.C.), and with that from the primary silting of the ditch (2570 ± 150 B.C.).[17]

The general distribution pattern for this period shows settlement predominantly on the chalk downs, but stone and flint axes and other implements sometimes occur elsewhere, especially along the coast and in the Bournemouth region. The importance of the river Stour as a means of entry from Hengistbury to Cranborne Chase is suggested not only by the concentration of Neolithic (and Bronze Age) material in the Bournemouth area, but also by the (destroyed) long barrow at Holdenhurst, the evidence of settlement at Corfe Mullen and such artifacts as the fine jade axe from Sturminster Marshall.

THE COPPER AND BRONZE AGES

(c. 1850/1800 B.C. – 500 B.C.)

During this period a warm dry climate continued until the Late Bronze Age (about 850 B.C.), when it rather suddenly turned cool and wet.

The Copper Age (c. 1850 – 1650 B.C.)

Recent research on the earliest metal implements used in Britain has shown that there was, after all, a Copper Age (roughly 1850 to 1650 B.C.) when the only metals known to have been used in this country were copper and a little gold.[18] The first part of this period, called *Copper I*, is characterised by bell-beakers (type B beakers) with a curve below the rim, associated with wrist-guards, barbed-and-tanged flint arrowheads and copper tanged flat daggers, knives and awls. A settlement of this period has recently been identified at Downton (Wiltshire),[19] and there are suggestions of others in the Bournemouth area.[20] Crouched interments associated with bell-beakers have been found beneath round barrows Tarrant Launceston 5 and Worth Matravers 3 (both in Dorset);[21] interments with no trace of any barrow have been found at Latch Farm and Boscombe, both near Bournemouth.[22]

The *Copper II* period is distinguished mainly by thistle-shaped 'necked' (or type A) beakers, barbed-and-tanged flint arrowheads, and flint daggers. Flint mines and settlements of this period have been identified on Easton Down (SU 237358), and a probable settlement has been recognised near Chale (Isle of Wight). Crouched burials with type A beakers are known from round barrows Tarrant Hinton 20b and Tarrant Launceston 7 on Cranborne

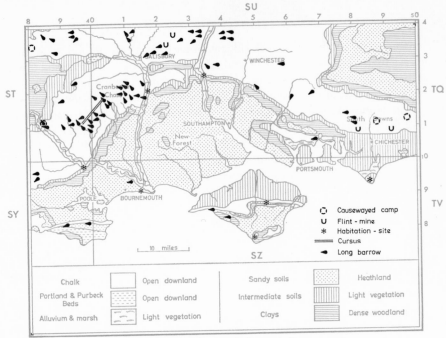

Fig. 51. The Neolithic period

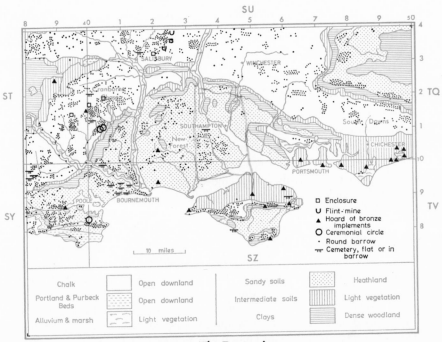

Fig. 52. The Bronze Age

Note. Since this map was completed, Mr. D. Britton has supplied the author with a list of Bronze Age hoards in southern England, which includes several not shown on this map, although they do not seriously affect the distribution pattern.

Chase,[23] and Gob's Barrow on Portsdown.[24] The crouched interment with handled cup from a round barrow at Studland can also be referred to this period.[25] Burials with no trace of any barrow have come from Weeke near Winchester,[26] and probably the Bournemouth area, Freshwater, and near Carisbrooke. Barrows II and IX on Beaulieu Heath, which contained mortuary chambers, are likely to belong to this period.[27]

Knowledge of comparable structures elsewhere justifies the provisional inference that the ceremonial earthen circles at Knowlton (Cranborne Chase) and the Rempstone stone circle (Purbeck) belong to the Copper Age. It is strange that no ceremonial circles have yet been identified in eastern Wessex, unless the two circles north of Horndean (SU 707154 and SU 717171) come within this category.

The Early Bronze Age (c. 1650 – 1400 B.C.)

This period is here represented by the *Wessex Culture*, which can be divided into two phases shading into one another, but for brevity they are here treated together. This culture shows the development of far-flung trading connections. Irish contacts provided imported Irish bronze implements, such as the hoards of flanged axes, tanged spearheads and grooved daggers from Arreton Down and Totland in the Isle of Wight. Contacts with Brittany are shown by grape-cups and Aldbourne cups; Breton-type flint arrowheads with squared barbs and tang; perhaps a continued use of jadeite axes; six-riveted bronze daggers; and probably imports of gold, tin and copper. Other objects of foreign trade include amber beads from the Baltic, and segmented faience beads ultimately from Egypt. Most of these objects occur among grave-groups in round barrows, as on Oakley Down (SU 017172), Hengistbury barrow I, Stockbridge Down, Arreton Down (Isle of Wight), and many others (Fig. 52).

Settlements of Wessex culture do not yet appear to have been identified. The burial rite in the earlier phase was inhumation, usually crouched but occasionally extended, and in the later phase cremation. The barrows are always round, and include not only bowl-barrows but also 'fancy' types of which the commonest are bell-barrows (for men) and disc-barrows (for women); fine examples of both of these exist on Cranborne Chase, in the New Forest, and along the chalk ridge of the Isle of Wight. During this period human occupation spread from the chalk downs over the sandy heaths of Thomas Hardy's 'Egdon', the New Forest and elsewhere.

Two of the Neolithic stone-axe working sites continued to be active in the Early Bronze Age, when they changed their products from axes to axe-hammers and battle-axes. The working sites on the Presely Hills in Pembrokeshire (Group XIII) produced axe-hammers which have been found at Fifield Bavant and Wilsford in southern Wiltshire, and the working sites on the Great Whin Sill in Northumberland produced battle-axes and axe-hammers which have been found at four sites in southern Wiltshire. The factory in the Cwm Mawr-Hyssington area, on the Shropshire-Montgomeryshire border, was working only during this period, its sole products being battle-axes and axe-hammers, one of which has been found at Shirley near Southampton (*SthM*).[28]

The Middle Bronze Age (c. *1400 – 850* B.C.)

A fusion of Copper Age and Early Bronze Age elements resulted in the formation of a Middle Bronze Age culture in Wessex, though shorn of most of the earlier foreign contacts and comparatively unimpressive in its surviving content. Its first phase (c. 1400 – 1200 B.C.) is represented by very occasional settlements, as on Stockbridge Down and Gore Down (Isle of Wight),[29] and by a rather dull series of round barrows with cremation as the almost invariable rite, accompanied by urns but by few other grave-goods. By this time bell-barrows and disc-barrows were going out of fashion. In its later phases (c. 1200 – 850 B.C.) there flourished what has usually been called the 'Deverel Rimbury Culture' (till lately supposed to be Late Bronze Age).[30] Of its various regional groups, that covering Hampshire and the Isle of Wight (with Wiltshire and the Berkshire Downs) is the one represented best on Cranborne Chase, from the excavations of Pitt-Rivers. The Stour-Avon river system was still of dominant importance for trade, and Hengistbury was the main port of entry. Among the objects imported were Irish gold torcs such as those found on St. Catherine's Hill north of Christchurch (SZ 145955) and at Moordown near Romsey.[31] Evidence of settlement occurs at Thorny Down near Salisbury, and includes stock enclosures on Cranborne Chase and elsewhere, field systems, and linear earthworks such as the Grim's Ditch on Cranborne Chase. Round barrows tend to diminish in size, and were now of less importance than cemeteries, several of which have been discovered in the Bournemouth area, the Isle of Wight and elsewhere.

The Late Bronze Age (c. *850 – 550* B.C.)

The agricultural and pastoral activities of the Middle Bronze Age continued into this period, but the 'Deverel-Rimbury Culture' declined. Lead replaced tin as the chief alloy with copper used to make bronze implements. Founders' hoards occur frequently along the south coast, in this area especially between Portsmouth and Bognor.

To this general period belong some remarkable imported objects, the most important being the bronze shaft-hole axe of Sicilian type (around 850 B.C.), fished up off Hengistbury Head in 1937 (*BM*). Among other objects are a double-looped bronze palstave of Iberian origin from Bournemouth (now lost), and Breton type square-sectioned axes of bronze or (more often) tin, such as a hoard of about thirty from Ventnor (5 in *CarCM*). It is uncertain whether Italian boat-brooches from Hod Hill and Bitterne were imported in this period or (more probably) in Roman times. Most of these Late Bronze Age imports show the continued use of the port at Hengistbury.

THE IRON AGE
(c. *550/500* B.C. – A.D. *43*)

The transition from the Late Bronze Age to the Iron Age was marked by a change to a cool and wet climate. Visible remains of this period consist mainly of evidence of settlement;

barrow-burial was exceptional, for most of the dead were placed in flat graves and cemeteries. The distribution of the chief field antiquities is shown in Fig. 53.

Iron Age A and B (c. 550/500 – c. 100 B.C.)

Iron Age A is basically Hallstatt and Iron Age B basically La Tène culture, names derived from type-sites in Austria and Switzerland. Invaders from Gaul landed along the south coast of Wessex, establishing beach-heads at Bindon Hill (SY 835803) and at the Double Dykes on Hengistbury Head (SZ 165910), still the key port for its hinterland.

The most conspicuous field monuments of this period are the great hill-forts, in Iron Age A usually univallate and in B usually multivallate, often with ramparts added to the univallate examples of Iron Age A. They are too numerous to describe in detail, but the univallate hill-forts include Spettisbury Rings on the Stour; Penbury Knoll, Rockbourne Knoll, and Clearbury Ring on Cranborne Chase; Chilworth Ring north of Southampton; St. Catherine's Hill south of Winchester; Old Winchester Hill above the Meon river; the Trundle in western Sussex, and the low-lying Tourner Bury on Hayling Island. An unfinished example known as Five Barrows occurs on the chalk ridge of the Isle of Wight. Multivallate hill-forts include Hod Hill and Hambledon Hill, Badbury Rings, the Whitsbury Castle Ditches, Danebury near Stockbridge, Buckland Rings and Ampress in the New Forest, and Tatchbury near Southampton (SU 330145).

Farms and other minor settlements, showing little trace on the ground until they were excavated, are known on Purbeck, where some are associated with the exploitation of Kimmeridge Shale. They are also known on Cranborne Chase (including Rotherley and Woodcuts excavated by Pitt-Rivers), Little Woodbury south-west of Salisbury (SU 150279), Meon Hill west of Stockbridge, around Winchester and elsewhere. The area devoted to agriculture probably increased progressively throughout the Iron Age, though the resulting field-systems have been omitted from the *O.S. Map of Southern Britain in the Iron Age* (1962) because few have been dated, and most of them continued in use into the Roman period.

Sepulchral evidence in this period is scanty. A small round barrow near Hatchet Pond in the New Forest yielded fragments of wood, bronze and iron, which have been interpreted tentatively as the first known Iron Age cart-burial found in this country; there are several Continental parallels. Spettisbury Rings has a war cemetery resulting from the clash with the Roman invaders about A.D. 45, and flat interments have been discovered on Purbeck, near Ventnor, and on Portsdown.

Iron Age C (c. 100 B.C. – A.D. 43)

From about 100 B.C., waves of immigrants from Gaul landed along the south coast, especially around 50 B.C., following Caesar's conquest of Gaul (57-51 B.C.). They established in the area under consideration two *oppida* (major defended settlements)—one where now is Winchester, a cemetery for which has also been found, and the other at Selsey, where the large number of ancient British coins found suggests a mint. Chichester Dykes, some

12 miles to the north, may have been outer defences for this *oppidum* and its surroundings, defending them from the Iron Age A and B survivors on the downs of western Sussex. A few farms and minor settlements of this culture have been identified, such as those at Sud Moor, Ventnor and Newport in the Isle of Wight; that at Sidlesham on the Selsey peninsula; and on the Hampshire Downs at Corhampton, Bentworth, Horndean and Rowland's Castle.

Evidence of their material culture has also been found at some of the Iron Age A and B hill-forts; for example, Bulbury near Poole (an iron anchor and chain and other objects from which are in *DCM*), Hod Hill, Buckland Rings, Great Woodbury, Old Sarum and several hill-forts along the Grovely Ridge to the west, and the defended site at Hengistbury. Their influence was also felt at some of the earlier farms and minor settlements, including several on Cranborne Chase, in the Bournemouth area, around Poole Harbour, at Armsley near Fordingbridge and on Worthy and Twyford Downs near Winchester.

The development of coinage on a tribal basis has enabled tribal regions to be identified during this period. In this region the main concern is with the Belgic *Atrebates* in eastern Hampshire and western Sussex, and with the *Durotriges* (comprising native Iron Age A and B stock, slightly Belgicised) in Dorset, western Hampshire and southern Wiltshire. At Hengistbury the *Durotriges* had a mint for casting debased bronze coins with silver wash for local use only, and apparently of the period A.D. 40 to 70. The finding of currency bars and coins of the *Dobunni* (whose tribal area comprised the Cotswolds and the Forest of Dean) at various places in the Stour valley attests the continued existence of the trade route along this river to the port at Hengistbury.[32] Trading with Gaul is indicated by Armorican (Breton) coins from the Bournemouth area, the Isle of Wight, Portsmouth and Selsey. A number of autonomous ancient Greek coins from the fourth century B.C. onwards, including several from Sicily, mostly found around the Stour valley and collected by the Rev. Thomas Rackett, F.R.S., rector of Spettisbury, between 1780 and 1840, suggests some Mediterranean trade. These indications of foreign trade are supported by imports such as the bronze figure of a bird (Italian?) from St. Catherine's Hill near Winchester, Arretine and Gallo-Belgic tableware, and stamped amphora-handles implying the import of foreign wines.

Sepulchral evidence in this period is slight. A small circular mound, one of two on Sud Moor in the Isle of Wight, has been shown to be of Belgic date, but may not have been a barrow. A Belgic cemetery has been found beneath Hyde Street, Winchester, and flat interments have come from Bitterne, Horndean (Snell's Corner) and Chillerton and Shanklin in the Isle of Wight.

THE ROMAN PERIOD

(c. A.D. *43* – c. *410*) (Fig. 54)

The development of trade between Gaul and Britain, noted in the last section, was accompanied by increasing political relations. About 52/50 B.C., Commius, chief of the Gaulish *Atrebates*, fled in the face of Caesar's conquest of Gaul to southern Britain, landing probably at Selsey, where he may well have founded the *oppidum* before moving northward

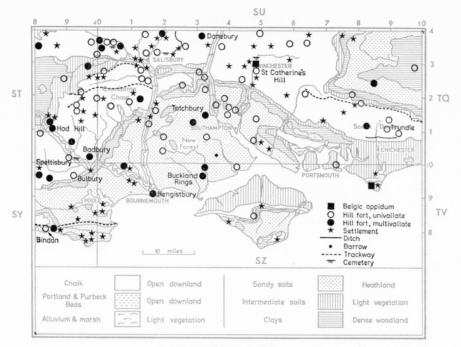

Fig. 53. The Iron Age

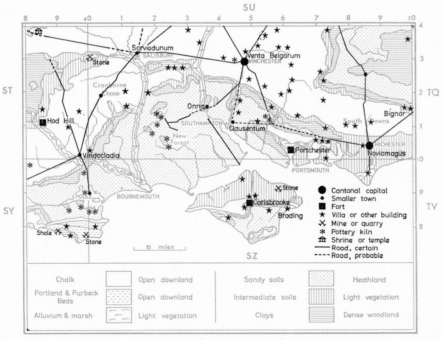

Fig. 54. The Roman period

to establish *Calleva* (Silchester). Reports of Britain's wealth in minerals and other material, and of feuds between the tribes of southern England, contributed first to Caesar's expeditions of 55/54 B.C., and then about 15 B.C. to Augustus' establishment of friendly relations with Commius' son Tincommius, whose dynasty was threatened by hostile rivals from beyond the Thames. It was their expulsion of his eventual successor Verica, who fled to seek Rome's protection, that led to the Claudian invasion and conquest of A.D. 43/5. Claudius replaced him by Cogidubnus, as king of the Regnenses centred on West Sussex, and thus cleared the way for a south-western advance by the Second Augustan legion commanded by Vespasian, later emperor.

Recent excavations near the top of Chichester Channel at New Fishbourne (SU 842049) have revealed the foundations of an extensive military timbered storage building dating from the years immediately following A.D. 43, which might well have belonged to the base from which Vespasian and his legion began their operations, a short time after the initial landings had been made at Richborough and perhaps elsewhere.[33] In due course Vespasian captured the Isle of Wight and vanquished the *Belgae* and the *Durotriges*, capturing in the process more than twenty hill-forts, the results of the conquest of two of which are reflected the war cemeteries uncovered at Maiden Castle and Spettisbury Rings.

A 'valleyward movement' from the Iron Age hill-forts had started in Iron Age C. St. Catherine's Hill was abandoned in favour of a site near the river Itchen for a Belgic *oppidum*, which after the Roman conquest became *Venta Belgarum*, the cantonal capital of the *Belgae* (now Winchester). The massacre at Maiden Castle was followed by the founding, near the river Frome two miles to the north-east, of *Durnovaria*, the cantonal capital of the *Durotriges* (now Dorchester). In West Sussex the Trundle hill-fort was first rivalled by the Belgic *oppidum* at Selsey, and later they were both superseded by *Noviomagus*, the cantonal capital of the Regnenses (now Chichester). It is of interest that all these places still play a major role because of the natural advantages of their siting. A system of fine metalled roads was constructed within a few years of the Roman conquest, connecting the cantonal capitals and other major inhabited sites.

Clausentum (now Bitterne, in the eastern part of the County Borough of Southampton) was founded as a port about A.D. 70, when roads were built connecting it with Winchester and Chichester. Its early phases (first and second centuries A.D.) are attested by much imported Samian ware, and by two lead pigs bearing the name of the emperor Vespasian, found near Bitterne Manor in 1918 and probably derived from the Mendip lead-mines. That *Clausentum* had a special function in the earlier Roman period for exporting lead is indicated also by the Neronian (A.D. 54-68) lead pig found in the river Test at Bossington (SU 337306) in 1783, presumably lost on its way to *Clausentum* for shipment; and perhaps by another Neronian lead pig from St. Valéry-sur-Somme. Both these pigs are probably from lead-mines in Flintshire or Shropshire.[34] Other evidence of the use of *Clausentum* as a port includes slabs of marble believed to be from Tuscany, and two Italian type bronze brooches which, although made about the seventh century B.C., were probably imported during the Roman period.[35] Third-century occupation is attested by several inscribed stones, including milestones of the period 238-73.

Towards the end of this century, during the reigns of the usurpers Carausius (A.D. 286-93) and Allectus (A.D. 293-6), the character of *Clausentum* appears to have changed from being primarily a port to a fort, functioning together with the magnificent fort at Portchester and possibly another at Carisbrooke as part of a system of coastal defences.[36] Strong reasons have recently been advanced to suggest that these forts (or most of them) were originally built by Carausius to defend his British separatist empire from Rome, and that not until between A.D. 350 and 400 were they adapted for defence against Saxon and other pirates, and named the Saxon Shore.[37] In any case, Carausius moved his fleet from Boulogne to the Solent. The question whether *Clausentum* had a coin-mint under Carausius and Allectus, represented by coins bearing the mint-marks C, CL and (according to Stukeley) CLA, has been debated for more than two centuries, and expert opinion is still divided between *Clausentum* and *Camulodunum* (Colchester) for these coins.[38] After Boulogne was recaptured for Rome in 293, Carausius was murdered by his finance minister Allectus, who then succeeded him as emperor of Britain. In 296, while Constantius Chlorus was emperor in Rome, his commander Asclepiodotus moved his troops from Boulogne to the Hampshire coast during a fog and recaptured Britain for Rome. Of the later history of *Clausentum*, it is enough to say that the stone-built town wall was constructed late in the fourth century, perhaps around 370, to replace Portchester as part of the Theodosian reorganisation of the Shore.

The main industries in the region during the Roman period can be briefly described. The limestones of Bembridge and Quarr in the Isle of Wight were worked and used in building the local villas and also at Portchester and possibly *Clausentum*, though the actual quarries do not seem to have been identified. The Purbeck marble quarries were worked extensively between A.D. 43 and 150, and also between about 350 and 400. Stone from them has been found in Roman buildings at Chichester, Cirencester, *Verulamium*, Colchester and elsewhere. Exploitation of the Kimmeridge shale outcrops of southern Purbeck, already worked during later prehistoric times, continued throughout the Roman period, especially for table-legs, armlets and many small articles.

The main groups of pottery kilns in the region were situated near Poole harbour and in the New Forest. The former used the clays of the Bagshot Beds, on which the modern Poole potteries also depend. The dated kilns range from the first to the third century A.D. The distribution of the products of the Purbeck–Poole area was facilitated by the Roman road from Hamworthy to Badbury Rings, where it was linked with the main road-system of the west country. A small port developed at Hamworthy to replace that at Hengistbury, which by the early Roman period had been relegated to local needs only. That Hamworthy had exports and imports as well as trade with its hinterland is shown by a fine quern of Niedermendig lava from the Rhineland (*BM*). Available evidence suggests that the New Forest replaced the Poole area as the main source of pottery in southern Wessex from the third century onwards. Distribution of the products was effected by local Roman roads which linked with the general road system.

During the Roman period, the chalk downs fringing the Southampton area were inhabited almost entirely by descendants of the native pre-Roman stock. Their slightly

Romanised 'native' farms were often of pre-Roman ancestry, as at Rotherley, Woodcuts, Gussage Hill and elsewhere on Cranborne Chase, and on Corhampton Down near the Meon valley (SU 576201). Their economy was mainly arable during the first half of the period, but during the second half it became more pastoral, as shown for example by instances of abandoned fields being used for pastoral enclosures, as at the Soldiers' Ring on Cranborne Chase (SU 082176). Around Winchester this partial replacement of tillage by pasture was possibly connected with the setting up of an Imperial weaving establishment.

The Roman villas were the centres of estates based on the local economy. Commonly they were sited near the foot of the chalk downs, as at Downton south of Salisbury; East Grimstead and West Dean east of Salisbury; Bignor north of and Fishbourne south of the West Sussex downs; and Carisbrooke, Newport and Brading in the Isle of Wight. The villas at Bignor, Brading and Newport can still be seen; the first two are among the most notable in Britain. At New Fishbourne, west of Chichester, recent excavations have revealed some fine mosaics dating between A.D. 75 and 100, apparently the earliest so far found in Britain.[39] Temples and shrines (other than those in towns) have been found at Maiden Castle and on Jordon Hill near Dorchester, at Chanctonbury and Lancing in Sussex, and probably at Cold Kitchen Hill (ST 833388).

Evidence of Roman sepulchral monuments is slight in southern Wessex. The three round barrows beside a Roman road west of Badbury Rings (ST 959030), formerly thought by some to be Roman, are now known to be prehistoric; but a small round barrow at Woodlands on Cranborne Chase (SU 052073) covered a cremated interment of late first century A.D.[40] There was formerly a Roman 'cartwheel' mausoleum near Pulborough in West Sussex. These and other three-dimensional sepulchral sites in Roman Britain normally belong to the first half of the Roman period, when cremation was the normal rite. To this early period also belong a group of 'chieftain' cremations with rich grave-goods, from Avisford, Aldingbourne, Densworth, and Westergate near Chichester. Inhumation burials of the later Roman period in southern Wessex call for no special comment.

BIBLIOGRAPHICAL NOTE

The author is grateful to Professor C. F. C. Hawkes for commenting on the first draft of this text. For help in matters of detail he is indebted to Miss Jean M. Cook (Chichester City Museum), Mr. F. Cottrill (Winchester City Museum), Mr. Anthony Norton (Portsmouth Museum), Mr. John Pallister (Southampton Museum), Mr. H. de S. Shortt (Salisbury Museum), Dr. Isobel F. Smith (Avebury), Miss E. M. Samuel (Dorset County Museum) and Mr. Barry Cunliffe (Bristol University).

The substance of much of this chapter appeared in the author's *The Archaeology of Wessex* (1958), and references there given are not repeated here. The following references are numbered to correspond to citations in the text.

(1) J. B. Calkin and J. F. N. Green, 'Palaeoliths and terraces near Bournemouth', *Proceedings of the Prehistoric Society* (1949), vol. 15, pp. 21-37.

(2) A. D. Lacaille, *Man* (1960), vol. 60, pp. 103-4.

(3) H. F. Poole, 'The Stone Age in the Isle of Wight', *Proceedings of the Isle of Wight Natural History Society* (1939), vol. 3, part i, pp. 37-47.

(4) A. Mace, 'Excavation of a late Upper Palaeolithic open site on Hengistbury Head', *Proceedings of the Prehistoric Society* (1959), vol. 25, pp. 233-59. For a possible site at Langstone Harbour, see J. C. Draper, 'Upper Palaeolithic type flints from Long Island, Langstone Harbour,' *Proceedings of the Hampshire Field Club* (1962), vol. 22, part ii, pp. 105-6.

(5) J. G. D. Clark and others, 'Excavations . . . at Hurst Fen', *Proceedings of the Prehistoric Society* (1960), vol. 26, p. 226.

(6) J. B. Calkin, 'Neolithic pit at Southbourne', *Proceedings of the Dorset Natural History and Archaeological Society* (1948), vol. 69, pp. 29-32.

(7) K. P. Oakley, 'A note of the late post-Glacial submergence of the Solent margins', *Proceedings of the Prehistoric Society* (1943), vol. 9, pp. 56-59.

(8) W. F. Rankine, *The Mesolithic of southern England* (Guildford, 1956), p. 33.

(9) W. F. Rankine and G. W. Dimbleby, 'Further investigations at a Mesolithic site at Oakhanger, Hants', *Proceedings of the Prehistoric Society* (1960), vol. 26, pp. 246-62, esp. 252.

(10) E. S. Higgs, 'Excavation of a late Mesolithic site at Downton, Wilts.', *Proceedings of the Prehistoric Society* (1959), vol. 25, pp. 209-32.

(11) P. A. Rahtz, 'Neolithic and Beaker sites at Downton', *Wiltshire Archaeological Magazine* (1962), vol. 58, pp. 116-41.

(12) P. C. Ozanne and A. Ozanne, 'Report on the investigation of a round barrow on Arreton Down', part ii, The Pre-barrow occupation, *Proceedings of the Prehistoric Society* (1960), vol. 26, pp. 276-96.

(13) By R. J. C. Atkinson during the Prehistoric Society's conference on Neolithic field monuments, April 1962.

(14) E. D. Evens and others, 'Fourth Report . . . on the petrological identification of stone axes', *Proceedings of the Prehistoric Society* (1962), vol. 28, pp. 209-66.

(15) F. de M. Vatcher, 'The radio-carbon dating of the Nutbane long barrow', *Antiquity* (1959), vol. 33, p. 289.

(16) Information kindly supplied by Mr. Paul Ashbee.

(17) I. F. Smith, 'Radio-carbon dates from Windmill Hill', *Antiquity* (1960), vol. 34, pp. 212-13.

(18) C. F. C. Hawkes, *A scheme for the British Bronze Age* (1960). Duplicated typescript issued for the Conference on the British Bronze Age arranged by the Council for British Archaeology, 1960. A fuller publication is forthcoming.

(19) P. A. Rahtz, 'Neolithic and beaker sites at Downton', *Wiltshire Archaeological Magazine* (1962), vol. 58, pp. 116-41.

(20) J. B. Calkin, 'The Bournemouth area in Neolithic and Early Bronze Age times', *Proceedings of the Dorset Natural History and Archaeological Society* (1952), vol. 73, pp. 32-70.

(21) L. V. Grinsell, *Dorset barrows* (Dorchester, 1959).

(22) J. B. Calkin, as no. 20 above.

(23) L. V. Grinsell, as no. 21 above.

(24) L. V. Grinsell, 'Hampshire barrows', *Proceedings of the Hampshire Field Club* (1952), vol. 14, part iii, p. 365.

(25) L. V. Grinsell, as no. 21 above.

(26) G. Chapman, 'A beaker burial at Weeke, Winchester', *Proceedings of the Hampshire Field Club* (1957), vol. 19, part iii, pp. 276-8.

(27) C. M. Piggott, 'Excavation of fifteen barrows in the New Forest, 1941-2', *Proceedings of the Prehistoric Society* (1943), vol. 9, pp. 1-27.

(28) E. D. Evens and others, as no. 14 above.

(29) G. C. Dunning, 'A Bronze Age hut on Gore Down, Chale', *Proceedings of the Isle of Wight Natural History Society* (1933), vol. 2, part iii, pp. 207-10.

(30) C. F. C. Hawkes, as no. 18 above.

(31) C. F. C. Hawkes, 'The Towednack gold hoard', *Man* (1932), vol. 32, p. 184.

(32) D. F. Allen, 'The origins of coinage in Britain: a reappraisal', in *Problems of the Iron Age in Southern Britain* (ed. S. Frere), N. D. (1961), pp. 97-308; the same author in text of *Ordnance Survey Map of Southern Britain in the Iron Age* (1962), pp. 19-24 and Maps.

(33) B. Cunliffe, 'Excavations at Fishbourne, 1962', *Antiquaries Journal* (1963), vol. 43, pp. 1-14.

(34) R. F. Tylecote, *Metallurgy in Archaeology* (London, 1962), chapter 4.

(35) D. M. Waterman, 'An Italian brooch from Bitterne?', *Proceedings of the Hampshire Field Club* (1945), vol. 16, part ii, pp. 189-90; another (unpublished) is in *SthM*.

(36) M. A. Cotton and P. W. Gathercole, *Excavations at Clausentum* (London, 1958); review by I. A. Richmond in *Journal of Roman Studies* (1962), vol. 52, pp. 271-2.

(37) D. A. White, *Litus Saxonicum: the British Saxon Shore in scholarship and history* (Madison, U.S.A., 1961).

(38) H. Mattingly, 'Carausius: his mints and money system', *Antiquity* (1945), vol. 19, pp. 122-4, and *Roman Coins* (2nd edn., London, 1960), p. 119, states the case in favour of there having been a mint at Clausentum. The identification of the C and CL mint with Colchester is favoured by M. R. Hull, *Roman Colchester* (London, 1958), pp. 275-6, and apparently also by R. A. G. Carson, 'Mints and coinage of Carausius and Allectus', *Journal of the British Archaeological Association* (1959), 3s, vol. 22, pp. 33-40.

(39) B. Cunliffe, 'Excavations at Fishbourne, 1961', *Antiquaries Journal* (1962), vol. 42, p. 15.

(40) P. J. Fowler, 'A Romano-British barrow, Knob's Crook, Woodlands, Dorset', *Proceedings of the Dorset Natural History and Archaeological Society* (1960), vol. 81, pp. 99-100. The same author's investigations at the barrows west of Badbury Rings are shortly to be published.

XV

THE HISTORY OF SOUTHAMPTON

THERE appears to be no definable relationship between Roman *Clausentum* (see p. 200) and the Saxon (or more probably Jutish) settlements that grew up in the vicinity. *Clausentum* disappeared from the map before the end of the fourth century, and the nodal area only re-entered history under the new name of Bitterne in the late eleventh century, when this site was occupied by the manor house of the Bishop of Winchester. The manor itself appears to correspond in large measure with the eastern (or trans-Itchen) portions of the Saxon vil of (South) Stoneham. Some other settlements—riverine in character, as might have been predicted—may well be represented by ancient local names preserved only in the town's ancient perambulations. These include Hilton (?*Healh-tun*) on the river bank at Swaythling, Blackworth near Belvedere Wharf (Northam) and Itchenworth on the site of the ancient Itchen ferry terminal. There also occurs a galaxy of *port* names, of which the only survivor on the modern map is Portswood. Formerly, however, in pre-Conquest and early medieval records, one could recognise Portsbridge (*Portesbricge*) and Portford (*Porte-froda*), both apparently concentrated on the St. Denys shore or abutting on to the Bitterne peninsula. The location suggests a connection with the Roman town nucleus.

The Saxons (or Jutes) were more attracted to the peninsula between the Test and Itchen estuaries, for reasons which become clear when the early physical character of the area is considered. Its reconstruction by the late Dr. O. G. S. Crawford shows that here, as at Calshot and Hurst, a narrow spit had been formed by currents, shingle having been swept round the tip of the peninsula and carried eastwards and north-eastwards for nearly a mile into the Itchen estuary until checked by the scouring action of the tides. The source of this spit is marked today by Canute Road and Cross House Road. Behind it a sheltered harbour was formed and ships could originally sail almost to St. Mary's church. The obtrusion of this spit into the estuary caused the Itchen to flow close to its eastern bank, thus eliminating mud-flats and creating a 'hard' at Woolston, which in fact has made possible the ferry crossing at this point.

Throughout the eighth, ninth and tenth centuries there were in common use two distinct place-names, *Hamtun* and *Hamwic* (or *Hamwih*), which do not necessarily refer to the same place. Owing to widespread unawareness in this country of the researches currently taking place into town origins in Germany and elsewhere on the Continent, the significance of the relationship between a *bourg* or *burh* and its commercial suburb, or *wik*, has been inade-quately grasped. The name *Hamwih* appears as early as A.D. 720 in the autobiographical

Life of St. Willibald, in which the saint describes how he set sail from *Hamlemuth* (Hamble) near the famous mart (*mercimonium*) of *Hamwih*. This led Crawford to examine two early land charters for South Stoneham which made mention of the 'Wic shore' and the 'minster at Wic', which he identified with St. Mary's (formerly collegiate) church. He was able in fact to indicate the line of Chapel Road as the quayside of the port of *Hamwih*. Subsequent excavations by Maitland Muller, Aberg and Pallister have amply substantiated the large area of the *mercimonium*, which presumably served the West Saxon capital of Winchester. Its inhabited area extended northward beyond the line of Northam Road and westward nearly to that of Palmerston Road. Eastward it rested on the Itchen shore. Its trade links appear to have extended to the Baltic Sea, and even into the Mediterranean. But it would appear to have ceased altogether for a time to function as a port after the heavy Danish raids of the early eleventh century.

The picture of *Hamwic* is so clear and self-contained that we are liable to overlook the significance of the separate name of *Hamtun* occurring alike in documents and coin legends. Despite the early importance of Winchester, Hampshire, first recorded as *Hamtunscire* in A.D. 755 (see p. 181), is named from *Hamtun*; how else can this be explained save on the assumption of the prior establishment by the invaders of the latter settlement? The occurrence in this neighbourhood of the place-name Shirley affords additional evidence of Southampton's being the original 'capital' of the embryonic shire.

Of outstanding importance is the problem of the location of the original settlement of *Hamtun*. Until comparatively recently it has been taken for granted that, since the only known Saxon remains have been found in the St. Mary's district, that district must perforce represent the original Hampton. In the *Burghal Hidage* of the early tenth century, *Hamtun* is recorded among the Wessex *burhs* with a maintenance hidage of 150. One variant text affords data for calculating the perimeter as roughly 206 yards, which suggests its being a strong point, perhaps on the margin of a settlement. The physical character of *Hamwic* precludes any suggestion of a strong point in this flat and featureless neighbourhood. Attention is therefore directed, by default, to the medieval town site and the low plateau-ridge, on the southern terminal of which it stands. It will be observed that after the mid-tenth century (coinciding strikingly with the first phase of the decline of *Hamwic*) there is the first mention of the name of Southampton. It is customary to attribute this fact to a newly felt need to distinguish the town from Northampton, also under the Wessex hegemony; but it would appear on balance more plausible to apply this name to a suburb, perhaps developed to accommodate the former inhabitants of *Hamwic* (then being displaced by the Danes' new practice of wintering here), occupying the southern flank of old Hampton.

Such considerations focus attention on the hitherto neglected area north of Bargate as potentially the site of the parent settlement of Hampton. Suggestively, this district incorporates a large plot of land formerly known as 'Hampton Field', and in this vicinity excavations carried out in recent years successively by Wacher and Aberg have revealed evidences of considerable settlement here in the years immediately following the Conquest. Such a settlement would have been small—though not as small as the *Burghal Hidage* enclosure— and it may have been linked with *Hamwic* by a road roughly along the line of modern

XXVII   Section of the bank marking the perambulation of the New Forest, near East Close, Hinton
(*N.G. ref.* SU 2298)

XXVIII   The Fawley Oil Refinery and Marine Terminal on Southampton Water

XXIX   The Bargate

XXX   God's House Tower and Gateway

Pound Tree Road and South Front. This is suggested partly by the density of archaeo-logically ascertained population in the northern parts of *Hamwic*, and partly by the fact that what was probably the road's western continuation became in the Middle Ages the town's traditional (and sole) outlet towards the west. It was called Canshut—later Windmill—Lane, and occupied modern Regent Street, Clifton Terrace, lower Manchester Street and the Western Esplanade.

The sudden decline in the fortunes of *Hamwic* led directly, *c.* A.D. 960, to the establish-ment of South Hampton, which must have been in the neighbourhood of the later Castle. There are indeed strong reasons for associating this phase with the area represented by that part of the traditional parish of All Saints that lay within the walled town (as shown on Fig. 55). East Street must represent the principal link between *Hamwic* and South Hampton.

To complete the picture, it may be advisable here to sketch in the immediately sub-sequent (i.e. post-Conquest) developments, following on the vitally important establish-ment of the King's castle and quay, safeguarding his communications with Normandy. The Domesday Survey records two colonies, of sixty-five French-born and thirty-one English-born householders, in addition to the original inhabitants. The survival of the names of French Street and English Street (now High Street) suggests the locations for these colonies.

We may thus summarise by saying that pre-Conquest Hampton must equate with the ancient parish of All Saints, stretching from the Castle's northern flank to the southern boundary of the present Common; that the original nucleus is in the Above Bar district; and that a brief southern extension, later incorporated within the walls, corresponds with the pre-Conquest suburb of 'South-hampton'.

The recorded history of pre-Conquest Southampton is monotonously preoccupied with Danish raids, understandably a matter of life-and-death urgency to the local inhabitants. The culminating moment was the proclamation of Cnut as King of England by the Witan assembled here. Cnut, one of the great mythopaeic figures of history, has certainly left his mark on local place-names. While we must perforce recognise the absurdity of the name Canute's Palace as applied (by Englefield, in the first instance) to the twelfth-century mer-chant's house in Porters' Lane, yet, of all reputed settings for the King's classic rebuke to his courtiers, the double high-tides of Southampton (first recorded by Bede) at least afford a suggestion of plausibility to an otherwise naïve and pointless anecdote.

A site which almost certainly dates from before the Conquest is Cut-thorn mound, the medieval place of assembly of the Court Leet, still functioning annually (see p. 257), albeit in the more sophisticated venue of the Civic Centre. In view of the mound's location at the northern extremity of the Common (on the medieval town's northern boundary) the site's earliest associations as a moot place were probably not with Southampton at all, since the Common was only acquired in 1228. It appears to represent a moot-place, possibly the *Shire-ley* suggested by the name of a neighbouring manor. The writer is also inclined to suspect its identity with the *Thunres lea* of Millbrook land charters, dated A.D. 956 and 1045. As to the age of the rectangular mound itself, Crawford's suggested analogies with similar structures at Calbourne (Isle of Wight) and Nursling, of presumed Iron Age origin, indicate that we may well have here a site of great antiquity.

Ps

MEDIEVAL SOUTHAMPTON

All the great ports of Britain have suffered setbacks in the course of history owing to circumstances beyond their control, such as wars and embargoes. But these have almost invariably been temporary in their effects, and conditions have generally been restored within a short time. Southampton, on the other hand, has been subject to much greater vicissitudes, and although it has enjoyed periods of considerable prosperity it has also endured long periods of depression bordering on decay. Those in medieval times have hitherto been ascribed to the long struggle with France and to the loss of the Italian trade in the sixteenth century following the opening up of the Cape Route to the Indies; but this is an over-simplification.

Southampton received a modest legacy of continental trade links from Saxon days and enjoyed an unearned increment in the extensive cross-Channel traffic which grew up with Normandy following the Conquest, when it rose to be one of the leading ports in the country, surpassed in 1203-5 only by London and Boston. The loss of Normandy shortly afterwards dealt a heavy blow, compensated only in part by the growth of the wine trade with Gascony and by participation in the expanding wool trade with Flanders and Italy. Then came war with France, beginning in 1336, and the great French raid on the town two years later directly and indirectly reduced its importance for a long time. The rise of trade with Italy in the fifteenth century restored its fortunes, and by the end of the period it could be said to have regained its former prosperity.

So the story of Southampton during the Middle Ages is one of adjustment to changing circumstances, but its fluctuating fortunes should not be too readily attributed to external conditions, important though these have been. A reappraisal of the available evidence shows that other factors of a more subtle nature have been involved.

Industry and Power

One of the outstanding characteristics of the town has been its curious seeming reluctance to develop manufactures on any appreciable scale. Even today it stands apart from all other comparable ports in this respect. The phenomenon is so striking that one is bound to inquire whether there is any inherent reason for this or whether it is purely fortuitous; and it is in the Middle Ages that an answer must be sought.

The port had great natural advantages in its sheltered roadstead and prolonged high tides, and it is not surprising that in early days its enterprising young men should have found the lure of the sea irresistible. But the majority of these men, like the inhabitants of all the new towns that were springing up, were drawn from the countryside, as many of their names reveal. By seeking their fortunes in the towns they were gaining freedom from the irksome obligations of feudal life, but they were losing the security which that way of life afforded. It is understandable, then, that they should band together in their new abode in order to obtain collectively the security which they could not acquire individually in the competitive conditions of urban life. That is how the gilds began, and it is not surprising

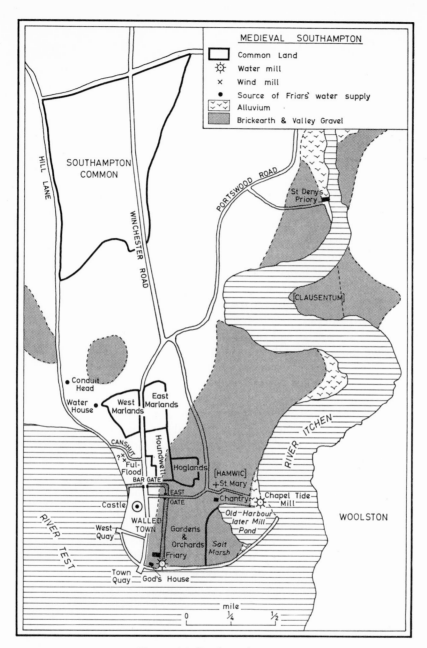

Fig. 55. Medieval Southampton

The common lands are shown in roughly their present form, but those adjacent to the walled town were formerly more extensive. Note that Clausentum, St. Denys Priory, *Hamwic* and parts of the original common lands (mainly arable) occupied the more attractive cultivated soils, whereas Southampton Common (pasture) did not. Another wind-mill stood on the shingle spit near the point where it changes direction.

that in Southampton the body so formed should have been a gild of merchants. So, although the town appears to have had the usual complement of craftsmen, they tended to be dominated from the start by the shipowners and merchants who pursued a much more lucrative, if dangerous, calling and rose to be men of substance and authority. But not only were the main energies of the townsfolk drawn off into commerce. A combination of circumstances in the fourteenth century destroyed any chance that the local craftsmen might have had of establishing themselves in comparable positions of affluence and power, as craft gildsmen did elsewhere. In the first place, the later decades of the century were a critically important period in the country as a whole, witnessing the first great upsurge of industrial activity based on the manufacture of woollen cloth. But for part at least of this period Southampton was semi-derelict and virtually bankrupt, and so unable to participate in the development. Secondly, even if these paralysing conditions had not prevailed it is most unlikely that the town would have become important as a manufacturing centre, because cloth-making came to depend more and more upon water-driven fulling mills in which the material was processed after being woven; and there was no suitable site in the immediate vicinity of the town for this purpose. It is significant that after the discovery of the Cape Route had sounded the death-knell of the Italian trade, Southampton enjoyed a belated, though temporary, period of manufacturing prosperity, but this was due to immigrant Walloons. And as though to underline the impossibility of permanent success in this direction, a fulling mill erected at the time in the Salt Marsh (Fig. 55), of all places, was very short-lived.

The problem of mechanical power was never really solved locally during the Middle Ages. The tiny rivulets which flowed from beneath the gravel capping of the Southampton plateau could never by themselves be very effective. The storm waters which gashed its western side and which led to the district west of Above Bar Street becoming known as Fulflood ('dirty intermittent stream', according to Dr. G. B. Grundy) could not be harnessed, for there was no space for the construction of a pond. So from an early date millers had to have recourse to other forms of power, and the town's flour was ground in the early thirteenth century with the aid of the tide. It appears that when the old harbour was abandoned owing to silting, a dam was built across it from the end of the shingle spit to a point near Trinity Chapel. By means of sluices the tidal flow was controlled and a mill (very similar to the one shown on Plate XVII) was at work there until the nineteenth century, its derelict remains being removed only in 1960. But a tide-mill could operate for only a few hours each day, so a windmill, one of the earliest recorded examples in the country, was built on the shingle spit some time before c. 1225. Another tide-mill was erected over the town ditch just outside God's House Gate, but only a small quantity of water could be ponded here, although the flow was augmented by the diversion of one of the Houndwell springs into the ditch for purposes of defence. Even these two mills proved insufficient to meet the town's needs, so two more windmills were erected on high ground overlooking the western shore, though their sites cannot be identified precisely. They gave their names to Windmill Lane (alias Canshut) and Windmill Field, but disappeared, like the one on the shingle spit, before the end of the eighteenth century. One further attempt to set up a water mill was made in the sixteenth century by diverting some of the Houndwell water along the northern ditch and under the Bar Gate to drive an overshot wheel near Catchcold Tower; but it was abandoned in the face of opposition, fears being expressed that the conduit would endanger the Bar Gate and by lowering the water-table would be a threat to the springs in the neighbourhood.

The Civic Authority

The town's affairs were originally conducted along two parallel lines: the borough-mote or court leet concerned itself essentially with civic matters, the merchant gild at first only with those relating to commerce. The former doubtless had its origin in Saxon times, when the chief dignitary appears to have been a reeve appointed by the king (the original *burhs* being royal foundations), but later—perhaps after the Conquest—elected by the burgesses. The merchant gild, on the other hand, with its alderman and bailiffs, is of later date. It may have been established soon after the Conquest by men trading with Normandy, but it is not recorded until the reign of Henry I (1135-54). Although perhaps at first somewhat exclusive, the gild appears later to have opened its doors to local craftsmen as well. But since Southampton never became a manufacturing town, its wealth was always concentrated in the hands of its merchants. Small wonder, then, that the effective government of the town fell under their control and that the gild ordinances came to be expanded into a set of regulations for the conduct of local affairs in general.

Throughout the second half of the twelfth century, Southampton was paying a considerable though fluctuating fee-farm rent to the Crown, which suggests a prosperous community, and it was in all likelihood the members of the gild who in 1199-1200 purchased the fee-farm from the Crown. This seems to have been the first important step towards the town's independence. In 1217 mention is first made of a mayor, but after 1270 the title of Alderman of the Gild appears to have been synonymous with that of mayor of the town. By 1300 the merchant gild and the Court Leet seem to have been completely merged, though it is clear that the mercantile element predominated. The functions of the court leet became progressively restricted, while those of the gild expanded; but this is not surprising in view of the social structure of the town. Some light is thrown upon this by the lay subsidy returns of 1327 and 1332, when levies of one-twentieth and one-tenth, respectively, were made on the value of assessed movable goods. These returns must be treated with considerable caution because they exclude the poor people, and of course the clergy, and are therefore quantitatively unreliable, while the basis of assessment seems not to have been consistently applied on the two occasions. Nevertheless, they do give the names of men who can be traced in other contemporary documents; and they enable comparison to be made with Winchester, which is illuminating.

The total amounts paid on the two occasions are almost exactly the same for both places, yet Winchester had many more taxpayers than Southampton, more than twice as many in 1332. This means that the average *per capita* wealth in Southampton was roughly double that in Winchester at that date.

Table IX. The Lay Subsidy Returns of 1327 and 1332

Assessable goods	1327		1332	
	Southampton	Winchester	Southampton	Winchester
£30 to £40	3	—	1	1
£20 to £30	2	3	5	3
£10 to £20	4	4	6	3
£5 to £10	8	12	13	5
£1 to £5	50	81	34	78
£1 and below	65	97	51	135
Total taxpayers	**132**	**197**	**110**	**225**
Tax paid	**£26 7s. 0d.**	**£26 12s. 10d.**	**£51 2s. 4d.**	**£51 3s. 5d.**

These figures also show that Southampton's taxpayers with more than £10 worth of assessable goods outnumbered those of Winchester on both occasions, whereas the reverse was true of people in the lower categories. Those with goods valued at over £20 in both years can easily be identified as men who were not only actively engaged in various commercial pursuits, for which there is abundant evidence, but who also held high office as mayor, bailiff and parliamentary representative. Indeed, the way in which these wealthy merchants exchanged offices among themselves makes it clear that the town was being run on oligarchical lines.

The association of mercantile wealth with civic authority runs right through the history of local government in Southampton during the Middle Ages, but it is only fair to record that much of the wealth was devoted to charitable causes. It played its part in the foundation and endowment of God's House and the leper Hospital of St. Magdalene, whilst St. Denys Priory and the Friary owed much to local support of this kind. These institutions looked after the sick and needy and thereby relieved the town of this christian duty. It was only after the breakdown of the voluntary system in the sixteenth century that the responsibility was thrust upon the townsfolk as a whole through the introduction of a compulsory rating system which still forms the basis of local taxation.

The second great leap forward in the town's civic development took place in the mid-fifteenth century. In 1445 the borough secured its charter of incorporation; in 1447 it was made into a county, whereupon the office of sheriff was instituted; in 1461 justices of the peace were appointed who took over certain of the bailiffs' juridical responsibilities. But the earlier gild ordinances with their restrictive practices continued to exert a stranglehold over the economic life of the town, and it is another of Southampton's misfortunes that long before their abolition in 1835 their enforcement had done much to ensure the prolonged ebb-tide of the town's fortunes during the seventeenth and early eighteenth centuries.

Trade

Much has already been written on the subject of Southampton's overseas trade, so it is only necessary to summarise the broader aspects of a markedly fluctuating activity which was at the mercy of changing political circumstances. Systematic accounts of foreign trade were not kept before 1275, and only shipments of wool and hides were registered until 1303, when a regular duty was first levied on alien general merchandise. But from other sources we know that throughout the thirteenth century merchants from Spain, Gascony and Flanders were actively engaged locally, many even taking up their abode in the town. Imported Spanish produce consisted mainly of wool, leather, iron, wax and fruit; the Gascons brought wine; the merchants of Picardy brought woad; the Flemings exported English wool and hides.

Italian contacts were of two kinds. At first their merchants exported wool in the vessels of other nationals from Southampton to the Low Countries for transport overland to Italy. Then, in 1319, soon after the Venetians had begun sending their fleets direct to Bruges, a number of their galleys came to Southampton. But their crews received such a hostile reception that this promising development ended abruptly. Then the outbreak of war with France in 1336 interrupted the trade with Bruges, and the Italians made attempts to establish themselves at Bristol and elsewhere, though without success. Meanwhile, as we have seen, the middle decades of the fourteenth century were a bad time for Southampton, though an Act passed in 1378 brought about a welcome transformation by permitting the Italians to ship direct to Italy, from Southampton and other ports, staple commodities such as wool, hides and tin which they had hitherto been required to export via Calais. Southampton's geographical advantages now began to tell and there is no doubt that this Act ushered in the town's 'golden age' which lasted until the end of the medieval period.

No small part of Southampton's early commercial prosperity derived from its relationship to an extensive and easily accessible hinterland. Centrally placed along the south coast, roughly equidistant from Bristol and London, and with no serious physical barriers to hinder movement, the town was bound to enjoy considerable transit trade.

Communications

It is customary to emphasise the difficulties of transport and communication in medieval England, but this can be very misleading because although conditions were generally bad in wet weather, the roads were capable of carrying cart traffic for most of the year. For example, the concentration of wine imports here led to Southampton becoming a distributing centre for this commodity over a wide area as early as the thirteenth century (Fig. 56). In the fourteenth century it was the natural outlet for the wool of Hampshire and Wiltshire, and in the fifteenth, thanks largely to Italian activity, its economic catchment area included the Cotswolds as well. The Brokage Books of the fifteenth century show that incoming raw materials spread out inland to serve more particularly the cloth manufacturing districts of the Midlands and the West Country. But perhaps the most significant deduction to be made from Fig. 58 is the extent to which Southampton at such an early date became an outport for London as, indeed, it still is.

Southampton was well served by a radial pattern of roads, though of course its peninsular position meant that the estuaries had to be bridged for east-west traffic. Redbridge on

the Test and Mansbridge on the Itchen were the main crossing points, and problems sometimes arose when they needed repair. Redbridge had been built by charity and was maintained by alms; Mansbridge, on the other hand, was maintained by a group of neighbouring
settlements: Allington, Botley, Woolston, Shirley, Sidford, Chilworth, Stoneham and
Eastleigh, the inhabitants of which could be called upon to undertake repairs, though in the

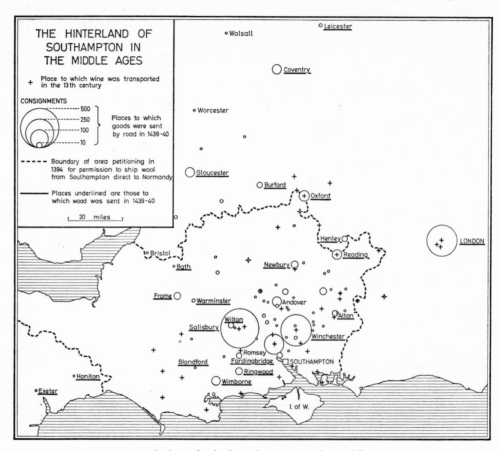

Fig. 56. The hinterland of Southampton in the Middle Ages

mid-fourteenth century they managed to shift the responsibility on to the Abbot of Netley
on the plea that he was the most frequent user by virtue of holding Townhill manor nearby.

The route to London ran through Winchester and the notorious 'Pass of Alton', the
lurking dangers of which were responsible for the clause inserted in the Statute of Winchester (1285) requiring the clearance of brushwood for a distance of 200 feet on either side
of a highway. Southampton also enjoyed the advantage of proximity to one of the earliest
canals in the country as an additional link with Winchester. The pond at Alresford, now

largely silted up, was constructed as a reservoir by Bishop Lucy in the twelfth century to maintain an adequate flow in dry weather. Even so, the canal fell into disuse, but when an attempt was made to restore it a century or so later it was resisted by the then bishop on the plea that any interference with the river's course would upset the working of his several mills between Bishopstoke and Winchester. So the importance of this waterway must not be exaggerated. The transport of building stone is a good index of this. It was carried by water wherever possible, but although some stone for Winchester Cathedral may well have come by water all the way from Caen, the Isle of Wight, Purbeck and Beer in Devon, this cannot be said of oolitic limestone used both at Winchester and in several churches to the north and west of the city; nor of Isle of Wight limestone in Saxon and Norman churches in remote places which could have been reached only by long overland hauls. There is, indeed, abundant evidence that cart traffic predominated throughout the Middle Ages for most classes of goods.

In view of the great mercantile activity locally, Southampton's wharfage facilities in the Middle Ages seem to have been singularly meagre. There was a quay for unloading stores by the castle at an early date, and God's House had two quays in its possession in the fourteenth century. There also appear to have been a number of private quays, though these in all probability were merely 'hards' up which the smaller boats were dragged when not in use. For berthing foreign ships there was at first, it seems, only the West Quay, which in Speed's map of 1610 is shown as capable of accommodating only three or four ships at a time. The addition of the quay outside the Water Gate in the early fifteenth century improved matters, but it is clear that many, if not most, of the vessels calling at the port in earlier days moored offshore and had their cargoes ferried to and fro in small boats that could land almost anywhere. This would have given employment to a large number of the poorer townsfolk, and a high proportion of the dockers of those days no doubt earned their living in this way. Even so, the town was never really populous, even by contemporary standards. It had an estimated total of 773 inhabitants in 1086, compared with 6000 at Winchester, 2310 at Bristol and 17,850 at London; in 1377 the comparable figures were 1728, 2160, 9518 and 34,971.

To the modern visitor Southampton's most prominent single legacy from the Middle Ages is its walls (Plate XXXI), but there is also a fine collection of merchants' houses and underground vaults, one church with a rare imported black stone font (St. Michael's), the Wool House and a Norman chimney; a water supply which gives Southampton the distinction of possessing what is thought to be the oldest municipal water undertaking in the country (Plate XV); and an incomparable group of open spaces indicating the original layout of the common lands.

The Walls

The defences in Norman times seem to have consisted solely of the castle, which may have been built on the site of the Saxon *burh*. But this castle was partly demolished in the thirteenth century, and although a new keep was erected in the late fourteenth century it never became a significant factor in the defence of the town. The southward extension to the sea after the Conquest of the presumed Saxon town on the plateau (Hampton) raised the problem of defence in a new form, for whereas the Exchequer was normally prepared to maintain the castle because it was royal property, no provision was made for protecting civilian property, the responsibility for which was thrown entirely on to the local inhabitants. Even so, royal encouragement was forthcoming in the early stages by means of a direct grant in 1203, and later by murage grants which authorised the town to collect small dues on goods entering and leaving it. In this latter way the ability of the townsfolk to defend themselves became geared to their commercial prosperity. The construction of the Bar Gate (Plate XXIX), the adjoining portions of the northern wall, and the eastern wall, though not to its present height, followed during the thirteenth century. Then, when the political situation became tense in the 1330's, further steps were taken to extend the fortifications on the south. But before anything at all effective could be done the town was raided in October 1338 by fifty galley-loads of French and Genoese, who not only burnt much property (including three churches), but destroyed over 70 tons of wool and seized nearly 200 tuns of wine. In the following spring, with government aid, the southern wall was built, albeit mainly of earth with wooden ramparts. Then, before the western wall could be tackled the danger of invasion had receded, following the victories of Sluys (1340) and Crécy (1346); but the recurrence of trouble later in the century led to a further spurt. At that time a number of stone houses stood close to the shore along the West Hithe, and as an economy measure the seaward sides of these houses were incorporated into the wall, where they can still be seen (Plate XXXI) in this uniquely fossilised form. The southern wall was rebuilt in stone, the eastern wall heightened, the South Gate was rebuilt as the Watergate and God's House Tower (Plate XXX) was constructed, in part over the ditches which had been dug to give extra protection along the eastern and northern walls of the town.

The Medieval Town

Until recently the street pattern within the walls had changed little since Norman times. At first there was no continuous thoroughfare southward from the Bar Gate to the shore because Holyrood church formerly stood slightly to the west of its present position, thus blocking such a north-south route anyway. When the church was rebuilt in the fourteenth century in its present position, the first Audit House was erected on the old site, so there was no through way until this building was pulled down in the eighteenth century.

The northern half of the present High Street seems to have been lined with the shops of the petty traders and craftsmen, within what was almost certainly the older part of the town clustering around the castle, whereas the post-Conquest extension, along with neighbouring streets, came to be occupied by the dwellings and warehouses of the merchant class. The dual character of the new part of the town, as revealed by the Domesday Survey, seems to be symbolised in the names English Street and French Street.

The extension of the town's built-up area brought with it a threat to its limited water resources. The restricted catchment area of the ridge not only meant a small run-off; it also reduced underground supplies for domestic uses to a minimum. It was probably on that account that the Friars sought and obtained permission in 1290 to go right outside the town and take water from a spring (*le conduit hede*) in what are now the grounds of Nazareth House, in Hill Lane (see p. 98 and Plate XV). The original stone chamber enclosing the spring is still there, and in Commercial Road there is also the Water House where there was another spring and a reservoir from which the flow to the Friary could be regulated through leaden pipes. In 1310 the Friars made their supply available to the inhabitants of the town by constructing a stone basin outside the wall of the Friary from which they could help themselves. But a century later the Friary was impoverished and unable to maintain the system in a proper state of repair, so in 1420 the Friars granted their water rights to the mayor and commonalty of Southampton who have held them ever since.

There is another part of the medieval heritage which, though not obvious to the casual observer, is of great current significance. Southampton enjoys a unique position among English towns in retaining almost intact its original common land from which its main food supply was originally drawn. But we must distinguish carefully between the common arable fields with their acre strips held by individual burgesses and the common pastures which were held by the Corporation on behalf of the burgesses as a whole. The former included West Marlands, East Marlands and Houndwell; the latter comprised at first mainly the Salt Marsh, but this was liable to flooding and perhaps for this reason the present Common was acquired from the neighbouring manor of Shirley in 1228. The Hoglands were probably the original swine pasture, but were divided into acre strips at a later date.

It was clear that as the town expanded the temptation to use these valuable spaces for building would increase, and some land was lost in this way during the Middle Ages. But the first really serious threat did not come until 1832, with the granting of permission by the Corporation for the railway company to develop part of the Salt Marsh on which the Terminus Station was later built. This was seen rather as a matter of principle, because the marsh, owing to its liability to flood, was of little real value to the townsfolk. But it was the only open space in the immediate vicinity of that part of the town where expansion was most pronounced, viz. to the south of East Street. In the end a sensible and rather ingenious compromise was effected by the Marsh Act of 1844, which allowed the Corporation to lease most of the marsh for building purposes and to apply the proceeds to the compulsory purchase of all the remaining holdings in the common fields. By this date a certain amount of enclosure had taken place, and the fields had shrunk to the following sizes:

West Marlands	16 acres
Houndwell	18 acres
East Marlands	22 acres
Hoglands	11 acres
Total	**67 acres**

Even so, this amount of open space in what was rapidly becoming the centre of the town was a most significant addition to Corporation property and it has remained intact to this day as such, the only noteworthy change being the erection of the Civic Centre on the West Marlands field. Furthermore, the wording of the Act was most specific on the main point of contention, viz. that the land so acquired 'shall for ever . . . be devoted and kept . . . exclusively as open Spaces for the general and public Advantage of the Inhabitants of Southampton, and of all other Persons for the Time being interested in the same . . .'. So, paradoxically, the Middle Ages, though remote in time, are still in many respects very much with us. Properly understood, they can continue to contribute towards that combination of pleasing aspect and historical interest which gives Southampton its uniquely attractive character.

SOUTHAMPTON IN THE SIXTEENTH AND SEVENTEENTH CENTURIES

Southampton's Commerce at its Peak, 1500-30

The sixteenth century was to see the decline of Southampton from an important centre of European commerce to a decayed local port. But in the first decades of the century this lay hidden in the future. The town was at the very height of its commercial prosperity. The falling-off which had taken place in the visits of the Italian carrack and galley fleets had been more than offset, as far as the volume of trade was concerned, by new developments. The Mediterranean and Iberian trade remained the most valuable: it was now divided between Venetian state galleys which still visited Southampton on their way to the Nether-lands, Spanish ships, and, increasingly, English ships pushing vigorously through the Straits of Gibraltar to the newly established staple at Pisa and into the Levant to compete with the Venetians in the shipment of sweet wine and currants. Some of these ships belonged to Southampton burgesses; a few, like the *Regent* and the *Sovereign*, to Henry VII, who hired them to the merchants; most, however, to Londoners, using Southampton as a base. The imported spices and fruits, wine and alum, were largely sent on to London, causing busy traffic by road and by coastal shipping. Of the principal exports, wool came direct from the Cotswolds; tin, for which Southampton had been appointed staple in 1492, arrived in regular fleets from Cornwall to be stored in the municipal tin-house until it was exported or sent on to London.

Nourished by this valuable trade, then, Southampton was still during the first three decades of the century a busy international port. True, customs receipts fell off after 1509; but this could be attributed partly to the French wars of 1512-14 and 1522-5. And if the Venetian state galleys came only irregularly after 1509 and ceased altogether after 1534, lead-ing Southampton merchants such as Sampson Thomas, Henry Huttoft and John Mille were still extending their Mediterranean trade. They worked in close association with the remain-ing Italian residents—the Genoese de Marini family and Huttoft's Florentine son-in-law, Antonio Guidotti, making use of these men's Mediterranean contacts, learning their busi-ness methods and aping their tastes in clothes, furniture and building. It was on the profits of this trade that they built or enlarged the mansions that Leland was to admire. At the same time, the Gascon wine trade was reviving and there was a growing traffic with Brittany and with the Channel Islands, whose merchants were induced by petty custom concessions in 1515 to forsake Poole for Southampton. Some ships were sent to the fishing grounds off Newfoundland and, later in Henry VIII's reign, Southampton merchants and seamen like John Pudsey, Thomas Borey and Robert Reneger were among the pioneers of English trade with Brazil.

The Collapse of the Town's Trade, 1530-60

Southampton's early Tudor prosperity was, however, precariously based. It has been estimated that in the peak years 1505-9 about half the trade of the port was in the hands of Londoners, who used Southampton as their south coast outport for the Mediterranean and southern European trade in order to avoid the dangers of navigation round the North Foreland and in the Thames estuary. Quite suddenly, about 1530, they ceased to use Southampton and withdrew to the Thames, as a result, it seems, partly of improvements in the rigging and design of sailing ships and of the increasing reliability of Thames pilotage after it was placed under the control of Trinity House, Deptford, in 1513, partly of wider changes then taking place in the whole pattern of European commerce. The opening of the Cape route had diverted the spice trade from the Mediterranean to Lisbon and Antwerp, and in consequence the English government became reluctant to license exports of wool to Italy in contravention of statutes intended to reserve it for English clothiers. Exports of wool fell heavily in the 1520's. The cloth which took its place was already collected from all parts of the kingdom at Blackwell Hall, the London cloth market, and could most conveniently be exported from there, even to southern Europe. But the main markets for cloth lay in the Netherlands and central Europe; England's foreign trade flowed increasingly along the London–Antwerp route. The old basis of Anglo-Mediterranean trade was dissolving and what was left of it, chiefly the import of Levant wine and currants, was recaptured in the second quarter of the century by Venetian private shipping; English voyages to the Mediterranean fell off sharply in the middle decades of the century.

These changes profoundly affected Southampton. Following the withdrawal of the Londoners, the annual Cornish tin fleets ceased to visit the town after 1531. A further blow fell in 1535 when Antonio Guidotti succumbed to huge debts, involving his father-in-law, then mayor, and other leading burgesses. The repercussions lasted several years and marked the end of an epoch for Southampton. The fourth decade of the century, as Dr. A. A. Ruddock has remarked, was in every way disastrous for the town. A rough measure of the shrinkage of its overseas trade is given by the receipts of the royal customers in Table X (p. 220).

In the 1540's the town already showed signs of decay: some of the younger men and the more enterprising merchants migrated to London; the stream of newcomers from the Isle of Wight, the Channel Islands and neighbouring towns dried up. For thirty years the port's commerce remained at a low ebb.

Table X. Annual Average Royal Customs Receipts for
Selected Periods

(to the nearest £ (Year Michaelmas to Michaelmas))

	£			£
1453-9	4,534		1540-5	707
1485-90	5,450		1555-60	1,314
1490-5	8,580		1560-5	1,134
1504-9	10,342		1565-70	1,258
1515-20	6,096		1570-5	2,380
1535-40	1,313		1575-80	[2,975] *

* Estimated from incomplete returns.

Table based on figures given in A. A. Ruddock, *Italian merchants and shipping in Southampton, 1270-1600*, pp. 258-62; and in Mrs. J. L. Thomas's unpublished Southampton University M.A. thesis, 'The seaborne trade of Southampton in the second half of the sixteenth century', pp. 57-8.

The Sweet Wine Grant

The first result of the collapse of the town's trade was a financial crisis for the Corporation. Already suffering from a decline of the petty custom receipts, its main source of income, through the passing of trade from Italians to local burgesses and Londoners who were exempt, it was now unable to pay the annual fee-farm of £226 to the Crown. Mounting arrears, 'stalled' in the 1530's, were largely remitted in 1549. In 1552 the farm was cut to £50 during all future years in which no galley or carrack should visit the port and petty custom receipts should not reach £200. The town's obligations were thus brought into some relation to its shrunken revenue, but the problem of economic decline was more intractable.

Requests for more positive government assistance were sympathetically received. The decline of provincial corporate towns as a result of the rise of London was already causing anxiety on fiscal, military and social grounds. The events of 1549 in Devon and Norfolk, and possibly also in Hampshire, focused attention on the importance of walled towns as barriers to peasant revolt, and walls could only be maintained by wealthy communities with adequate local revenues. In Southampton's case there were additional reasons for government concern. The incorporation of Brittany into France, the union of Spain and the Netherlands, and the rise of French and Spanish naval power had made the strengthening of the south coast defences a condition of England's independence. When Henry VIII defied the Catholic powers in the 1530's, he hastily constructed new forts to guard the Solent and Southampton Water, and in 1545 the French attacked the Isle of Wight. When Philip of Spain arrived at Southampton in July 1554 to marry Mary Tudor he cannot have learned without concern that the best harbour on England's Channel coast, on the line of communication between the Spanish and Netherlands ends of his empire, was in decay.

Three weeks later, on 9 August 1554, a royal charter was issued providing that in future no one should export wool to the Mediterranean or import Levant wines into England at any other port than Southampton on pain of triple duty.

The aim of this grant was to force back into the port the Mediterranean trade which had formerly been the main source of its wealth and of the Corporation's revenue. But the Venetians who now controlled this much reduced trade preferred to land their malmsey wines at London. They resisted for several years and finally, in 1561, obtained a judicial decision that Southampton's grant was contrary to the laws, statutes and customs of the realm. The struggle was transferred to Parliament, and in 1563 a temporary Act forbade aliens (though not Englishmen) to land Mediterranean wines at ports other than Southampton on pain of 20s. per butt, half of which was to go to the Corporation. The Venetians again resisted on various pretexts until 1567, when a compromise was reached and Southampton, after thirteen years of heavy expense on lawsuits and lobbying, at last began to receive substantial payments. But the attempt to bring back the Mediterranean trade had failed; what resulted from the grant, made perpetual in 1571, was a mere subsidy, received by the town from alien importers and supposed to be spent exclusively on the upkeep of the fortifications.

Other proposals for reviving the town's former prosperity were advanced from time to time: to make it a 'free mart', for instance, or a base for colonising expeditions. Most of such schemes involved government intervention to force back into Southampton trades which strong economic forces were tending to concentrate in London, and the influence of the Londoners was too strong. But efforts to maintain a limited regional monopoly had more success. Under an Act of 1559 against customs evasion, no Hampshire quays except those at Southampton were licensed for foreign trade, and in 1572 the town successfully resisted attempts to open up Portsmouth. Strangers importing canvas or woad were compelled to sell to townsmen only and in 1608 the Corporation got the old chartered privilege of 'foreign bought foreign sold' confirmed by Act of Parliament. Other medieval practices also were more strictly enforced: the use of the town market-halls for tin, cloth and linen; the supervision of dealings by sworn brokers; and the sharing of bargains among burgesses.

Revival and Relapse, 1560-85

During Elizabeth's reign Southampton experienced two periods of real, if limited, commercial revival: the 1570's and the early 1590's. In 1561 the Corporation was insolvent and the town's trade, small in volume, was largely carried in ships of neighbouring ports. But in the next few years several wealthy shipowners and merchants moved from Poole and Salisbury, and in 1567 the prospect improved when a colony of Walloon Protestant refugees, including merchants and clothiers, settled in the town. From 1569 a growth in trade is indicated by a steep rise in the royal customs receipts, whose annual average in the early 1570's was almost double that in recent decades and, after a slight setback in 1575-6, rose still higher in the years 1577-9 (see Table X, opposite). The beginning of this boom is not easy to explain, since from 1569 to 1573 there was an embargo on trade with Spain and the Netherlands, following Elizabeth's seizure of Alva's treasure ships. These were, however, years of intense privateering activity in the Channel. Goods seized by English captains under cover of letters of marque from Orange or Condé, as well as by way of legitimate reprisals, notoriously abounded in the creeks round the Solent and may have contributed to Southampton's renewed commercial activity. The prosperity of the later 'seventies arose chiefly from the activities of a group of substantial merchants who traded to south-western France for wine, salt and Toulouse woad, to Portugal and Andalusia for wine, oil and fruit, and to the Azores for green woad. This trade required both more capital and larger ships than the cross-Channel traffic, and it also stimulated shipbuilding and ancillary trades. Between 1561 and 1579 the number of ships of over a hundred tons in the port rose from one to eight.

This prosperity collapsed after 1579, and the 1580's were a period of deep commercial depression at Southampton. The local writer of two anonymous memoranda which found their way into the files of the Secretary of State about 1582 attributed the slump to several causes: bankruptcies due to losses at sea and to neglect of their businesses by the principal merchants; the capture of the woad trade by merchants of Lyme, Taunton and Bristol and of the canvas trade by Salisbury men; the strictness of the customs farmers; and, perhaps most important, the discrimination practised by the Londoners who controlled the great chartered companies, notably the Spanish Company, founded in 1577. An attempt by Southampton men to open a new trade by investing in Sir Humphrey Gilbert's last New-foundland expedition in 1582 came to nothing.

War and Privateering, 1585–1604

On the outbreak of war with Spain in 1585, normal trade was disrupted further; but privateering, no longer illicit, became a major industry, highly organised, heavily capital-ised, and focused on the Atlantic routes between Spain, Portugal and America. Throughout the years 1585–1604, customs officers like Edward Cotton and Thomas Heaton, gentlemen like the Earl of Cumberland and the Shirleys, and, most important of all, London merchants, found Southampton, with its well-placed harbour, its shipping facilities and its easy access to London, the chief market for prize-goods, a convenient base for privateering expedi-tions. These brought work to local shipyards and provision dealers and opportunities for investing small sums in victualling shares, and they probably account for the short-lived boom in the general trade of the port in the early 1590's, when the customs receipts even exceeded, for a year or two, the level of the late 'seventies. But in the long run this wartime reversion to the role of London's outport probably did Southampton more harm than good. The risks of privateering were too great for the resources of even the biggest local merchants and several, like John Crook, were impoverished or ruined. The sugar and other prize-goods mostly went straight to London and did not, like the familiar wine, woad and canvas, nourish an extensive regional wholesale trade. Already in 1600, even before the war ended, the port's commerce had sunk to a mere trickle, the customs receipts being lower than at any time in the previous century.

XXXI   The Town Walls, incorporating some Norman houses

XXXII   Tudor House

XXXIII   The West Gate Tower, with a new block of flats on the Castle Mound

XXXIV   Lower Southampton, showing the High Street, the Bargate, the West and East Ring
Roads, and in the left background part of the New Docks Industrial Estate

Trade and Industry in the Seventeenth Century

Southampton in 1600 has been described by Mrs. J. L. Thomas as 'a regional port serving the Hampshire Basin for general trade and a rather wider area for a specialised trade in wine and woad'; and, except that the woad trade fell off, this probably remained true throughout the seventeenth century, though the records await detailed study. The town did not share the expansion which the growth of the American colonies and the revival of the Mediterranean and Iberian trades brought to western ports such as Exeter, Bristol and Liverpool. True, some Southampton ships sailed to Newfoundland to fish for cod and to Virginia for tobacco; and the Pilgrim Fathers of 1620 were not the only emigrants to embark at Southampton. But these activities were on a small scale. In 1619 the Corporation informed the government that only eight small ships and barques were now owned in the port; and some accounts of the petty customer for 1637-8, though they yield an incomplete picture, strongly suggest that the town's seaborne trade was mainly with France and the Channel Islands for the needs of the Hampshire area. Fish is scarcely mentioned. The principal commodities appear to be wine and vinegar, probably imported from France; linen and canvas brought from Normandy and Brittany in three-cornered voyages by the small boats that provisioned the Channel Islands; deal boards for shipbuilding, often bought from Scottish ships or from London; and corn. Other items were prunes, salt, oil, tar and occasional consignments of Newcastle coal. The town's coastal trade was much busier in 1687 than in 1628, but this may well reflect the increased volume of England's trade generally, rather than any great change in the nature or importance of Southampton's share in it.

Southampton's commercial decline was to some extent offset, towards the end of the sixteenth century, by the growth of the serge industry. Already in 1582 the anonymous memorandist considered the town, in spite of the slump in its overseas trade, to be more populous and its common people more prosperous than a generation earlier, largely owing to the employment created by the Walloon refugee clothiers. Throughout the seventeenth century cloth-workers (excluding tailors and drapers) comprised about one-fifth of all persons admitted to the freedom. The only other industries serving more than the town's own needs were brewing, for the supply of ships and of the Channel Islands, and shipbuilding. Arthur Pett and William Guath in Elizabeth's reign and Essau Whittif, James Parker, Edward Knowler and others in the early seventeenth century had small yards at West Quay, where they built and repaired merchant ships. Some of these family businesses lasted into the eighteenth century and spread to the Itchen shore. In the 1650's and again in the 1690's when the navy was expanding rapidly, several warships were built in the town, and though none was built there between 1660 and 1690, the growing naval activity at Portsmouth affected Southampton in other ways, such as the periodic conscription of shipwrights and the stimulus given to the trade in shipbuilding materials.

Population and Social Structure

There seems to have been little domestic building in Southampton in the seventeenth century, and no increase in the number of inhabitants. While England's population may

Qs

have more than doubled between 1500 and 1700, and London's may have increased tenfold to half a million, Southampton's probably fluctuated between about 3000 and 5000. The evidence points to a fall in the mid-sixteenth century and a rise in Elizabeth's reign, followed by heavy losses during the plague epidemics of 1583 and 1604, when the number of burials recorded in the French church register alone rose from an annual average of five to seventy-one and over 150 respectively. In 1596 the population was recorded as 4200, including 397 aliens; during 1665, when the town was again swept by plague, it was reported to have lost 1700 of its inhabitants.

The distribution of occupations in the town appears, from a study of the register of admissions to the freedom between 1614 and 1700, to have been much what one would expect to find in any market town of the period, except for the prominence of wine-coopers and the high proportion of clothworkers already noted. The rate of admission remained constant at about six per year, and the distribution of trades did not change markedly, except for the appearance in the later seventeenth century of some new occupations, such as tobacco seller, tobacco-pipe maker, a 'confektmaker', and a 'perruquemaker', At least three-quarters of the freemen had served an apprenticeship within the town and the proportion tended to increase; a sign, possibly, of immobility and conservatism.

For the proportions of employers, self-employed and wage-workers it is less easy to find evidence. If one adds some fifty resident burgesses and a few dozen gentlemen, clergy and farmers to the 413 persons recorded as paying the annual *stall and art* fee to the Corporation for the right to practise a trade in 1596, it appears that economically independent heads of households and their families may have comprised rather more than half of the population, the rest being presumably servants, wage-workers, seamen, charwomen and paupers. The records suggest an increasing number of wage-workers, especially in the cloth industry and perhaps also in shipping and domestic service, and a growing problem of pauperism and of overcrowding in slum tenements. The number of poor would have grown faster if the ward-beadles had not reported and the justices expelled newcomers who lacked means or seemed likely to fall on the rates.

The ruling group in the town consisted primarily of the bigger shipowners and merchants in overseas trade, together with individual grocers, drapers, chandlers and lawyers. It was only gradually in the seventeenth century that the serge-clothiers came to enjoy an influence proportionate to their wealth and the numbers of workers they employed, since many apparently retained alien status. The position of the Southampton bourgeoisie had undergone a change in the sixteenth century, when the decline of its merchants' fortunes had coincided with the movement of gentry families into former church properties in or near the town. St. Denys priory with its manors of Portswood and Northam, St. Mary's rectory to which most of the town tithes were attached, and Netley Abbey across the water, became gentry seats. As a result there were disputes over pasture rights, tithes, musters and precedence. But in the long run the influence of neighbouring gentry in town affairs tended to increase: already in the 1590's two members of county families, William Wallop and Thomas Lambert, were elected mayor without having climbed the usual ladder of office.

External Relations

In the later sixteenth century the town oligarchy, reduced in wealth and standing, found increasing difficulty in maintaining Southampton's extensive medieval liberties, especially its claim to levy petty custom and exercise admiralty jurisdiction throughout the limits of the port, from Langstone in the east to Hurst at the mouth of the Solent in the west. These claims, no longer enforced at Portsmouth, were constantly disputed by Lymington and by local landowners. More important, they conflicted with the trend towards centralisation in admiralty affairs. Already in 1581 the mayor and town clerk were rapped over the knuckles by the Privy Council for obstructing the enforcement within the port of orders made by the High Court of Admiralty; and after 1585, when the expansion of privateering made prize jurisdiction lucrative, the new Lord Admiral, Howard of Effingham, seconded by Sir George Carey, Vice-Admiral for Hampshire and governor of the Isle of Wight, rejected the town's claims to take view and inventory of prize-goods landed in the port and to confiscate the goods of pirates, and forced the mayor into a legal contest, apparently ending in compromise. At the same time the town was pleading inability to supply the three ships demanded by the government as a contribution to the Armada campaign, though it did eventually send one, which was used as a fireship.

The town also came up against the lords-lieutenant of Hampshire in military matters and, in James I's reign, against the powerful London-based Levant Company, whose claim to monopoly threatened to eliminate the alien importers from whom Southampton's sweet wine revenue was derived. Less conspicuously but more insidiously, by a process of encroachments and lawsuits which deserves study, Southampton's own claim to monopolise the foreign trade of the Hampshire region was gradually eroded. These disputes engaged a great part of the Corporation's attention and resources, and it was partly to secure powerful patrons that it began, from about 1570, to place one of its two parliamentary seats at the disposal of a great man and to shower honorary burgess-ships on others. In the 1580's it thought itself fortunate to have the ear of Walsingham, who was connected with the town by marriage and employed in his office at least one local boy, Thomas Lakes, later himself to become Secretary of State.

Town Politics and the Borough Constitution

Within the town, if not outside, Southampton's merchant oligarchy met fewer challenges as time passed; the constitution became more rigid. In the early Tudor period there was sometimes widespread opposition from small traders and craftsmen, as in 1517 against the enclosure of common land, and possibly in 1549. But when William St. John in 1558, and William Capelin in 1570-3, protested against aldermanic rule, they represented only a handful of junior burgesses, themselves lesser merchants who meant to exclude the manual crafts from influence and enforce more strictly the traditional craft boundaries and trade restrictions. The conflict was limited to certain issues, while fear of the growing numbers of poor, liable to riot in years of famine (such as 1596 or 1608) drove the two groups together.

The weakness of the oligarchy's position was that most of the powers conferred by the charters ran in the name of the 'mayor, bailiffs and burgesses', aldermen being scarcely mentioned. Rebel burgesses could thus argue that acts done without their formal consent were invalid and might even give ground for forfeiture of the town's liberties. It was probably with a view to bringing law into accord with practice that in 1640 an elaborate new charter was procured that was to govern until the municipal Reform Act of 1835. Its main innovation was the formal recognition of the dominant role played by the ex-mayors or aldermen in the government of the town and the fixing of the legislative power in a new body, the common council, of which the aldermen constituted the core. The main function left to the burgess body was the election of officers; but this had already been reduced by the practice of 'private nomination' to formal approval of a choice previously made by the mayor and aldermen, except that a choice was still allowed in the mayoral election, at least at the beginning of the century, between two candidates privately nominated. In practice, before 1640 as after, an inner group of ex-mayors (aldermen and justices of the peace) controlled the affairs of the town, together with the mayor, appointing its officials, managing its property and finances, conducting its external relations and exercising over its inhabitants a wide if ill-defined summary jurisdiction.

Social and Cultural Life

Much of the physical and institutional framework of the medieval borough remained throughout this period: the walls, gates, ditches and quays; the weigh-house, market halls, prisons and other municipal buildings; the town courts and officials such as constables, beadles and serjeants. The ancient conduits were supplemented by an additional water-supply; twice weekly removal of refuse was arranged. Prices and supplies of food, fuel and candles continued to be controlled, especially in times of scarcity, when the authorities did not hesitate to requisition grain cargoes in the harbour. Changes of emphasis occurred. In local finance rates, both regular and *ad hoc*, played a bigger role as the ancient dues on trade declined. Poor relief, care of apprentices and orphans, the management of charities and almshouses and, after 1632, of the workhouse, took more of the magistrates' time.

The Reformation reduced the numbers and wealth of the town's clergy. Chantry-priests disappeared; the rectory-houses of Holyrood and St. Mary's were leased to laymen; the remaining parsons sometimes had to eke out their inadequate livings by practising a craft. The supervision of morals and the suppression of vice, including cards, bowling and drunkenness, became increasingly the concern of the town council, whose outlook under Elizabeth seems to have been distinctly protestant if not actively puritan; in 1569 it founded a weekly divinity lecture. Education also was its responsibility as governing body of the Free School, which had been founded in 1554 under the will of William Capon, probably to replace earlier chantry schools. Henceforth, the council, having merged the school endowment into the Corporation's property, appointed, paid and dismissed the master. In the late sixteenth and early seventeenth centuries the school flourished, attracting boarders from outside and producing some eminent scholars and men of affairs. Its most distinguished master, Adrian Saravia (1572-8) was a member of the French Calvinist refugee congregation of St. Julian's, whose influence radiated widely, especially among the many townsmen of Channel Island origin.

The Revolutions of 1640 and 1688

In the revolution of the 1640's, Southampton, like other commercial towns, was predominantly parliamentarian in sympathy. It sent two of its leading merchants to the Long Parliament—an unwonted gesture of independence—and in 1642, after some internal conflict, it accepted a parliamentarian garrison from Portsmouth. During the Civil War it served as a base for supplying isolated garrisons further west and, during the brief royalist advance into Hampshire in 1643-4, for attacks on Hopton's flank. Perhaps the most conspicuous result of the interregnum was the establishment of strong Independent congregations whose ministers, ejected from parochial livings in 1662, were able to take with them many of their followers, including the father of Isaac Watts the hymn-writer, and to establish a nonconformist tradition which survived all the persecutions of Charles II's reign as well as the brief but equally dangerous patronage of James II, who in 1688 attempted to use the Dissenters to obtain control of the Corporation.

The revolution of 1688 did not remove, though it mitigated, the disabilities of the Dissenters; but it was followed by a liberalisation of the town's constitution in another way, for in 1689 the burgesses and 'scot and lot' inhabitants successfully challenged the old custom whereby the town's members of parliament were chosen by the town council. The result was not a democratic movement, only a different way of deciding which of the local gentry should represent the town. For Southampton was now at the lowest ebb of its fortunes, a local port and minor county centre, soon to become more noted for its scenery than for its trade.

SOUTHAMPTON IN THE EIGHTEENTH AND NINETEENTH CENTURIES

'[Southampton]', wrote its mayor and other leading worthies to the Secretary of State in 1683, 'has been a rich place, but is now quite the contrary. The late rebellion [i.e. the Civil War] despoiled the chamber of all public moneys, in the plague 1700 inhabitants died, the Dutch war robbed them of almost all their ships. . . . The public revenues are incredibly sunk, . . . by which the Corporation is under great difficulties to discharge the burden on the chamber and the great rent to the King, as also repairing the walls, bulwarks, quays and seabanks.' Thirteen years later Celia Fiennes, while she found it 'a very neat clean town and a good port', added that 'now the trade has failed and the town almost forsooke and neglected'. Bishop Gibson in 1695, Defoe a generation later and the Southampton-born traveller Bishop Pococke in 1757 all testified to the same effect. The town was still largely confined within the area bounded by its ancient walls, except for a straggle of houses Above Bar and another from the East Gate towards St. Mary's church, with a few buildings further afield at Northam and Chapel on the banks of the Itchen. The population in the first half of the eighteenth century seems to have shrunk considerably below its earlier maximum and may not perhaps have been more than 3000. A retrospective statement in the early nineteenth century, quoting no contemporary authority but precise in its details and according well with other evidence, gives a total of 3297 inhabitants for 1757, when increase had already begun again.

Nevertheless, the sweeping statements quoted above must be taken with some reserve. Houses were being built as well as crumbling down, and modest wealth could still be made in trade. It was to this period that the old High Street owed some of its most substantial merchants' houses, and in it the fortunes were built up which laid the foundations of Alderman Taunton's School and more remotely of the Hartley Institution out of which the University has grown. Southampton in fact possessed advantages which saved it from complete decline. In the early eighteenth century it ranked twelfth or thirteenth among the outports of the country, with a trade that was largely regional except for the coastal traffic in coal from the Tyne and Wear and the importation of wine from Portugal and Spain. It had maintained its ancient trading connections with the Channel Islands, to which it acted as a kind of staple port; and until at least the 1770's 60 to 75 per cent of its non-coastal trade was with them. The chief item in this commerce was the specially permitted export of raw wool, which returned to Southampton in the shape of coarse worsted stockings knitted by the islanders, though among other commodities some Portuguese and Spanish and a little French wine came to it through the Islands; and the exports were wheat, barley and various textiles. There was a trade with Ireland that was nearly all outward, in wheat, barley, bark and timber; some commerce with France which, after the former trade in French wines and luxury goods had been largely extinguished by prohibitive duties at the beginning of the century, consisted chiefly of the exchange of wheat and barley for brandy, Caen stone and prunes from Bordeaux; a little miscellaneous importing from Rotterdam, Amsterdam and other Low Country ports, as well as from Germany; and every year a few Scandinavian or Russian ships brought timber. Its share in the Newfoundland fisheries was now passing, or had passed, to Poole, but occasionally a vessel arrived from or left for North America, the West Indies or Newfoundland. There were only two quays, at the Watergate and the West Gate, which could be used by ships of any size, even with some difficulty, but the wharves at Northam a mile or two away could accommodate coastal vessels, colliers and a variety of small craft.

Among the south coast ports Southampton ranked fifth in tonnage of coastwise shipping registered (though this is by no means an exact criterion of importance), after Poole, Weymouth, Exeter and perhaps Sandwich. It traded with London in a wide variety of goods, and to a smaller extent with Bristol, which besides groceries, West-country cider, rum, tobacco and sugar supplied almost all the glass bottles used in the Southampton wine trade. On the south coast its most regular traffic was with Portsmouth, Cowes, Poole, Weymouth, Lyme, Exeter, Dartmouth and Rye. From this last a good deal of wool was obtained, mostly for export to the Channel Islands, though the town's meagre industries still included a little cloth-making. There were also manufactures of silk and paper, the latter in particular having been introduced by some of the Huguenot refugees who after the revocation of the Edict of

Nantes in 1685 had come to join the descendants of their sixteenth-century predecessors and swell the congregation of the 'French Church' at God's House chapel. This manufacture, however, was mainly carried on at a mill at South Stoneham outside the town, and after 1718 much of it was transferred to Laverstoke in the north of the county by Henri Portal, the founder of a distinguished Hampshire family. Sufficient shipbuilding, too, was carried on at and near Southampton to enable most of the town's small vessels to be built locally. Before 1690 the only shipyards at Southampton itself were near the West Quay, but when in the ensuing wars with France the Admiralty began to give contracts to civilian yards for some of the smaller ships of the Navy, sites were developed at Northam and Chapel. Naval shipbuilding, however, remained intermittent and limited to wartime, while the building of small merchant vessels seems to have gradually increased as the century advanced.

In the relatively rapid expansion of English overseas trade which began about the middle of the eighteenth century Southampton had little share, since the main developments were in the more distant trades such as the American or East and West Indian which as yet scarcely concerned it. But for eighty or ninety years it experienced a transient rise to prominence as a fashionable seaside resort and spa. Like Weymouth and Brighton, though slightly earlier, it owed this development chiefly to royal patronage. George II's ill-fated son Prince Frederick of Wales came frequently to Southampton for bathing while staying in the New Forest and developed a great liking for the town, which despite his early death seems to have been a main reason why by the middle of the 1750's it was being crowded during the summer seasons by 'great numbers of people of distinction'. The Prince's *penchant* for Southampton was shared by his three younger sons, the Dukes of York, Gloucester and Cumberland, who in the 1760's became the social patrons of the place; and the discovery of a mineral spring gave it the attractions of a spa as well as those of a bathing-resort. A natural and immediate result was that the townspeople set to work to reconstruct and add to their public buildings and enlarge the amenities of the town. Baths, new assembly rooms, a playhouse, banks and a newspaper came into existence, though the last was soon transferred to Winchester, and its successors did not appear until the 1820's and 1830's. Coffee-rooms and circulating libraries competed with each other, and many of the townsfolk fitted up their houses 'in the neatest and genteelest manner' to provide accommodation for the summer visitors. The old Audit House which blocked the middle of the High Street opposite Holy Rood church was taken down, enabling what was widely considered one of the finest streets in England to be seen to better advantage, and was replaced by a new one more conveniently situated. The narrow East Gate was also demolished to open a better way for carriages. Coach services to London, Bath, Bristol, Salisbury, Oxford and other towns increased in number and gradually in speed. The main coaching inns developed—the Dolphin (already old but rebuilt in 1775), the Star, Royal George, Coach and Horses, Vine and Fountain; and coach-building became the town's main industry and remained so until the railway age. One over-ambitious venture failed, however. A group of enterprising spirits, who felt that since Bath had its Royal Crescent and Tunbridge Wells its Pantiles Southampton must have something equally distinctive, embarked upon a project of building a Polygon on a site with commanding views three-quarters of a mile north of the town;

that is, a wheel-shaped *ensemble* to consist of twelve large houses with gardens behind them stretching back like spokes to a central block comprising a hotel, assembly rooms and shops. By the early 1770's, though most of the houses were still unbuilt, this central block was sufficiently complete to serve as the focus for a few glittering seasons of social activity under the aegis of the Dukes of Gloucester and Cumberland (the Duke of York having died). These years were the heyday of Southampton as a watering-place, the time when a writer who wished to praise a minor spa did so by claiming that it was growing as genteel as Tunbridge, Brighton or Southampton. But the promoters of the Polygon became bankrupt, the buildings and land were disposed of, and the area gradually turned, as the town crept out towards it, into an early nineteenth-century residential suburb. The royal brothers continued to visit Southampton intermittently for a few years, but then their patronage ceased.

But although this meant that the town henceforward saw less of the cream of high society, it continued to be visited by plenty of people of rank and fashion. Moreover, from the middle of the century onwards its attractions and those of its immediate neighbourhood were bringing more and more of the gentry and the well-to-do not merely to visit but to settle. A thickening fringe of gentlemen's seats appeared on the north and north-west of the town and to the east across the Itchen. Nearer at hand 'marine cottages' and villas 'commanding an attractive prospect' sprang up to meet a growing demand; while within the walls arose the genteel houses of Gloucester Square. In turn the prospects of employment or commercial profit opened up by the influx of visitors and new residents brought to the town numbers of people in all walks of life. Although we must discount the exuberant claim made in 1770 by a prominent burgess giving evidence before a parliamentary committee, that the population had doubled in the past twenty years, it seems to have been from about 1750 that it began the rise which far anticipated the age of railways and steamships and whose tempo was not accelerated but only maintained by it, as shown on Fig. 57. In 1774, when there were 705 houses enumerated (with a few outlying omissions), to which we may apply the ratio of slightly over six persons per house suggested by the earliest definite statistics, there were probably about 4500 inhabitants, perhaps representing a rise of as much as 50 per cent since the middle of the century; and on the same hypothesis the 7913 of the census of 1801 would represent a further rise of nearly 75 per cent over a slightly longer period.

During the Revolutionary and Napoleonic Wars, which amounted between them to twenty-two years of almost continuous conflict from 1793 onwards, the growth of the town continued, probably at an uninterrupted or even faster pace in the closing years of the eighteenth century and with only a slight slackening in the first decade of the nineteenth. On the one hand, until towards the end of the wars they do not seem to have caused much injury to what in 1810 could still be called Southampton's 'high reputation as a watering-place of elegant and fashionable resort'. On the other, the armies which were assembled in the neighbourhood, especially those encamped on Shirley and Netley Commons in the 1790's in preparation for campaigns which mostly proved abortive, needed to be fed, clothed, entertained and (during the winter at least) housed; and these needs gave still further employment to the growing numbers of merchants, manufacturers, bankers, shopkeepers, artisans and labourers, to say nothing of camp-followers and (to judge from the matrimonial announcements in the *Hampshire Chronicle*) match-making mothers. Even when for a few years after 1812 the town's social activities and popularity faltered and seemed to be declining, this caused no perceptible check in its general progress. In the post-war years as a whole trade increased, while still preserving the general pattern of a hundred

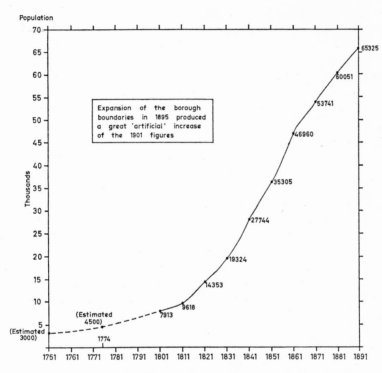

Fig. 57. Growth of the population of Southampton, 1751-1891

Based on (i) various assessments and street-plans in Southampton guide-books, 1768-95; (ii) evidence given before a Parliamentary Committee on the Paving of Southampton, 1770; and (iii) from 1801 the decennial Census returns.

years before; through passenger traffic to France, the Channel Islands and the Isle of Wight expanded, to Southampton's profit; and the economic depression of 1825 scarcely touched it. While banks elsewhere were tumbling like ninepins none of Southampton's failed and only one temporarily suspended payment. Yachting at Cowes and on Southampton Water, now all the rage among the fashionable world, drew more and more of that world to or through the town, added yacht-building to its industries and played a leading part in reviving for another fifteen years or so its vogue as a resort. Pre-war activities and pastimes were resumed or developed further—the annual race-meetings and regattas with their rounds of attendant festivities, the assemblies of the Royal Southampton Archers which had been outstanding social events in the early 1790's and now became even more so than ever. A new resplendent bathing establishment and new assembly rooms were built. Moreover, by this time the steamship, the means of Southampton's renaissance as a great port, had made its appearance, though only on a small scale.

In this transitional period, especially after 1820, the social and holiday attractions of Southampton on the one hand revived rather more and for a little longer than has perhaps been realised, while at the same time its modern expansion as a port was already beginning to get under way. And here, in this dual conjunction, surely lies the basic explanation of the long-puzzling fact that it was now and not twenty or thirty years later that the population figures spurted still faster. Furthermore, within this framework of events it is possible that, in view of the natural but perhaps excessive attention which has been paid to the liners of later days, the importance of the part played by the steam packets of the 1820's has been somewhat overlooked. Though Southampton Water presents difficulties to sailing-vessels, it has none for steamers, and so it was natural that its enterprising merchants and sea-captains (callings often combined in the same persons) should be among the first to appreciate and use the marine possibilities of steam. In the early 1820's steam packet services were established to the Isle of Wight, the Channel Islands and Le Havre. The vessels soon became faster, larger and more numerous; their competition cut down fares. The through passenger traffic that was already growing received a further stimulus, and Southampton began to vaunt itself as a thoroughfare to the Continent. In the last three years of the 1820's its steamboats alone were carrying more than 100,000 passengers a year, even though they did not yet run in the winter months; and the steamer interests were prominent in the rising local demand for improved landing facilities which led to the construction of the Royal Pier in 1833.

In the years that followed, a change that was relatively gradual and involved no interruption of the town's growth, though it completely changed its character, came over Southampton. On the one hand the tide of fashion began to ebb definitely and finally. As a watering-place and a residence for the leisured it now had too many competitors, some of them with advantages it did not possess. For after all it was hardly on the sea-side; it had no sandy beach; and its waters contained comparatively little salt. But this involved no more check in the overall progress of the town than the temporary decline of the eighteen-'teens had done. For some of the very factors—steam transport and the through traffic—which were bringing this phase of its history to an end were also among the strongest forces urging forward its further development and transformation. If more people were going elsewhere, as for instance to Cowes or other places in the Isle of Wight, they were often doing so by way of Southampton and its steamers, and so still bringing profit to the town. To increase this traffic was one of the motives of the group of local men who after informal preliminary conferences in 1830 formed the London and Southampton Railway Company in the following year. They also had larger aims of making Southampton again a great outport of London, as in the later Middle Ages, by enabling ships to discharge or load cargoes there which could be carried quickly to or from the capital by rail, thus avoiding the still difficult passage through the narrows of the Channel; but in this they were failing to foresee how the same power of steam which they were invoking in one form would in another reduce the hazards of that passage. They hoped in particular to attract to the port the West Indian and a greater share of the Mediterranean and other trades, but the event proved that it was not Southampton's destiny to become a great cargo port and that the development of the passenger traffic was to be the more important contributor to the future of the town.

When the railway, after some delay until strong financial backing could be obtained in London and elsewhere, had been completed in 1840 and renamed the London and South-Western, the docks were not long in being added. Already in 1803 an Act of Parliament had been obtained which established a board of Harbour Commissioners, empowered to construct a dock and pier and otherwise improve the port. But although the Commissioners had opened out the waterfront by demolishing the old Watergate and various buildings which were encumbering the quays, their lack of funds had prevented them from either building a pier (until they were goaded into it in 1833) or docks such as were then appearing in London, Liverpool and other ports. In 1836, however, a Dock Company was formed which by 1843 had built the first of the town's modern docks on reclaimed mudlands close to the new railway terminus (Fig. 70) and had followed it with a second by 1851. With the coming of the railway and the docks the foundations of Southampton's modern prosperity were completed. The growing industrialisation of the north-eastern United States and eastern Canada and the development of transatlantic mail and packet steamers enabled it to build on those foundations. The port was immediately chosen by the government as a mail packet and emigration station, and some of the most important of the new steamship lines began to base themselves on it—the Royal Mail Steam Packet Company, the Peninsular and Oriental, and a few years later the Union and the Castle lines (which presently amalgamated) and several others. But nothing could be further from the truth than to imagine that Southampton had now emerged from all its difficulties. Until the cargo space of steamships began to be increased after the middle of the century, the ships of the great companies carried chiefly passengers and a few valuable goods of small size, from which the port derived less advantage than would have accrued from a trade in bulky articles which needed warehousing. And a more lasting and indeed insurmountable obstacle to the high hopes which had been entertained of a vastly enlarged traffic in goods as well as passengers was that even in the railway age the town was too remote from the northern and midland manufacturing areas to make it easy to find return cargoes for ships unloading there. Nevertheless, by 1860 it had become the fifth port in the kingdom.

There were also serious administrative and social problems to be solved. Although the Municipal Corporations Act of 1835 had transferred the Borough Council to the broader basis of a ratepayers' franchise more smoothly in Southampton than in many other places, the government of the town continued to be divided between the Council and the Improvement Commissioners who had been set up in the late eighteenth century and were still responsible for paving and sewerage. Although there was a common element in the personnel of the two bodies, it was not sufficient to prevent differences of outlook and policy, especially when (as in the middle 1840's) they were controlled by different political parties. The position was further complicated by the fact that owing to the expansion of the town there were now a number of streets outside the area of the Commissioners' jurisdiction and indeed under no adequate control at all in matters of sanitation and maintenance. Necessary reforms and new amenities tended to be delayed by disputes, but in 1843 an Act was obtained for a much-needed borough cemetery on the Common, to relieve the pressure on the churchyards; in 1844 the Marsh Improvement Act enabled a large area on the eastern side of the town to be drained and developed for building, while in the same year the Improvement Commissioners' authority was extended over the whole borough. A serious cholera epidemic in 1848-9 led to the Council's becoming the local sanitary authority under the provisions of the Public Health Act of 1848, in which capacity it embarked on a programme of improving the drainage and water-supply. With the most pressing deficiencies in social services thus remedied, and more and more powers and functions being gathered into the Council's hands as time went on, increasingly efficient and centralised administration replaced the occasional checks and deadlocks of early Victorian days.

Meanwhile, the physical expansion of the town, governed by its peninsular situation, had at first mainly taken two directions and shown two different characters. Before the end of the eighteenth century the once fashionable districts behind the High Street had sunk in the social scale and were becoming slums, while Above Bar ranked as the genteel part of the town. Here in the early nineteenth century there developed a northward thrust of successive residential areas, marked by much good regency building in Portland Street and Portland Terrace and further afield beyond the Marlands in Brunswick Place, Bedford Place, Cumberland Place and Carlton Crescent, whose names reflected the period of their construction. Eastward and north-eastward there was another expansion which was chiefly artisan and industrial, linking the district of St. Mary's, once almost a detached hamlet, to the old town on one side and on the other to Northam. This last, with its kilns, foundries, developing shipbuilding and marine engineering, gasworks, working-class houses and small shops, was growing by the 1850's into an industrial centre. More directly to the east the coming of the railway and the docks, followed by the reclaiming of the marshlands, had led to the rapid urbanisation of the area about the Terminus station, which soon drew to itself more and more of the commercial bustle that had formerly centred about the old Town Quay at the foot of the High Street. In the second half of the century the northward expansion divided to creep around the Common on either side, aided, especially on the eastern flank, by the break-up and sale for building purposes of the estates surrounding the large mansions that had fringed the town in this direction. Streets of suburban houses now stretched out to take in the village of Portswood, which in turn began to spread northward towards Swaythling (still outside the borough boundaries) and uphill by way of rural Highfield to the eastern and north-eastern verges of the Common. On the north-west an extension of the borough in 1895 took in the former villages of Shirley and Freemantle with part of Millbrook, themselves much grown; while to the east the building of Cobden Bridge furthered the growth of Bitterne (though it could still be described in 1905 as a picturesque village two miles from Southampton) and prepared the way for its twentieth-century absorption into the borough along with Woolston, Sholing and other more out-lying areas.

The progress and prosperity of the port fluctuated somewhat in the latter part of the century. The good years of the early 'fifties, when the number of steamship lines which used it grew apace, gave way to a depression after the Crimean War. Nevertheless, it was then that the German lines which were entering into the transatlantic passenger traffic began to make their appearance here, and it presently became evident that though Southampton was making no great strides as a cargo port, it was the only one of the major British pas-senger ports which was not only a terminus but a port of call. There followed the halcyon decade of the 1860's, giving place in turn to the twenty years of the 'Great Depression' after 1873 from which the whole country suffered, made worse in Southampton by the with-drawal of the P. & O. Company from the port in 1878-9. Much of the dullness of trade was attributed locally, however, to the fact that the docks had not kept pace with the increas-ing size of ships and could not now provide adequate deep-water accommodation. In 1885 the Royal Mail Company threatened to follow the P. & O.'s example unless better facilities were forthcoming, and the Corporation put pressure on the Dock Company, which in turn appealed to the South-Western Railway. With money lent by the latter the Empress Dock was built and opened in 1890, but the Company still lacked capital to modernise its equip-ment sufficiently to attract more traffic. The Corporation now expressed willingness to buy the docks, but found that it also had not the money to do so, and in 1892 with its full approval they were sold to the Railway Company, which at once proceeded to spend large sums on improvement. This proved a turning-point; more docks were built, trade im-proved again and a great acceleration of progress followed. During the South African War the embarkation of nearly all the troops for the Cape took place from Southampton with a smoothness and despatch that foreshadowed the still greater achievements of the two world wars; and in the early twentieth century the transference hither of the White Star and then the Cunard Lines from Liverpool emphasised the town's position as the premier passenger port of Britain.

BIBLIOGRAPHICAL NOTE

Pre-Conquest Southampton
(1) L. A. Burgess, *The origins of Southampton* (Leicester, 1963).
(2) O. G. S. Crawford, 'Southampton', *Antiquity* (1942), no. 61, pp. 36-50.
(3) O. G. S. Crawford, 'Trinity chapel and fair', *Proceedings of the Hampshire Field Club* (1947-9), vol. XVII, pp. 45-53.

Medieval Southampton
(1) Rev. J. Silvester Davies, *A history of Southampton* (London and Southampton, 1883), remains the best general introduction.
(2) Various volumes of Southampton Record Society contain local material, e.g. *The Oak Book*, for civic government.

(3) The trade of the medieval port is covered by A. A. Ruddock, *Italian merchants and shipping in Southampton, 1270-1600* (Southampton, 1951).

(4) B. H. St. J. O'Neil, 'Southampton town wall', *Aspects of Archaeology*, ed. W. F. Grimes (London, 1951), deals with defence.

(5) See also *Collected essays on Southampton*, ed. J. B. Morgan and P. Peberdy (Southampton, 1958), and *Victoria County History of Hampshire*, vols. III and V.

Southampton in the Sixteenth and Seventeenth Centuries

(1) J. S. Davies, *A history of Southampton* (London and Southampton, 1883).

(2) A. J. Holland, 'Shipbuilding, mainly for the crown in the Southampton area, 1650 to 1820' (unpublished Southampton University M.A. thesis, 1961).

(3) J. B. Morgan and P. Peberdy (eds.), *Collected essays on Southampton* (Southampton, 1958).

(4) A. A. Ruddock, 'London capitalists and the decline of Southampton in the early Tudor period', *Economic History Review* (1949), second series, vol. II, no 2, pp. 137-51.

(5) C. F. Russell, *A history of King Edward VI School, Southampton* (privately printed, 1940).

(6) The publications of the Southampton Record Society (40 vols., 1905-41), and of the Southampton Records Series (1951-   ).

(7) J. L. Wiggs (Mrs. J. L. Thomas), 'The seaborne trade of Southampton in the second half of the sixteenth century' (unpublished Southampton University M.A. thesis, 1954).

(8) T. S. Willan, *The English coasting trade, 1600-1750* (Manchester, 1938), pp. 150-3.

Southampton in the Eighteenth and Nineteenth Centuries

(1) R. Davis, *The rise of the English shipping industry* (London, 1962).

(2) A. Anderson, 'Henry Robinson Hartley: his family, his life, and the establishment of the Hartley Institution' (unpublished Southampton University M.A. thesis, 1962, to which A. T. P. is particularly indebted for details of the trade of the town in the early eighteenth century).

(3) P. H. Morris, 'Southampton in the early dock and railway age, 1830-1860' (unpublished Southampton University M.A. thesis, 1957).

PART III

THE CHARACTER OF THE TOWN OF SOUTHAMPTON

XVI

THE SOCIAL PATTERN

THE site upon which the town of Southampton has developed is in certain respects highly individual. The medieval walled town (Chapter XV) occupied the tip of a low narrow plateau between the mud-flats of the Test estuary on the west and the extensive low ground bordering the Itchen on the east (Fig. 55). Since the Industrial Revolution these low-lying areas have followed their own separate courses of development as port, factory, railway and working-class housing zones. The centre proper has tended to move north from the walled town up the plateau; but here it has been restricted in width not only by the nature of the ground but also by the survival to the present day of a magnificent series of parklands. During the last century these parks have replaced the town's common-fields, and now occupy the whole eastern flank of the plateau for half a mile north of the walled town, eventually cutting right across the plateau near the critical point where the main approach roads from east and west converge upon the principal north–south artery (see p. 11). Only three-quarters of a mile to the north, the town's common pasture has been converted into a vast ordered wilderness (Southampton Common, 328 acres), and this 'green wedge' is continued less than half a mile to the north by the Sports Centre of 267 acres, unrivalled in the country for the imaginative exploitation of a wooded valley with terraced playing fields, golf-course and running track.

Between the 'green wedge' and the rivers Test to the west and Itchen to the east, the gently terraced plateau-slopes have afforded almost uninterruptedly favourable sites for the town's expansion. This part of the town can be seen to comprise a series of sectors, arranged more or less radially and focusing on the medieval walled nucleus. Along the Test water-front are the New Docks and the Millbrook Industrial Estate; then a large residential district is centred on Shirley, once an outlying separate hamlet; then the main 'central district' and the 'green wedge' culminate to the north in the high-class residential district of Bassett; next another residential district lies to the east, centred on Portswood; and lastly there is the Itchen waterfront industrial and port district.

The area of the town which lies east of the Itchen reveals a quite different arrangement. Here the fragmentation of the plateau-surface by a number of steep-sided valleys and the abrupt descent to the river have resulted in a more confused pattern of settlement. More-over, the negotiation of the Itchen estuary is a problem not even now satisfactorily solved (see p. 304). Three separate crossings have resulted in the development of three individual suburban centres on the eastern side: the Floating Bridge leads to Woolston; Northam Bridge to Bitterne; and Cobden Bridge to Bitterne Park. Further east large housing-estates have developed at Harefield and Thornhill (Plate LVI).

Rs

Those elements of this complex pattern which depend basically upon manufacturing industry and port activities are discussed in Chapters XVII and XVIII respectively. This chapter is specifically concerned with the central and residential districts, which for convenience are dealt with separately.

THE CENTRAL DISTRICT

The activities typical of the central district of a town are numerous and varied, but they have in common the fact that they are concerned in the broadest way with the life of the town as a whole and the region dependent on it. Attention will be focused on the analysis of the most highly centralised activities, business and shopping, and of certain others which are typically located on the margins of the central district: wholesaling, professional services and the accommodation of visitors. Figs. 59-60 provide some of the bases for such an analysis, and make it possible to trace the development of certain functional areas for just over a century. The scales of the maps for 1867, 1914 and 1962 have been adjusted in such a way that on each the whole town at the respective date occupies the same space as on the others. If the central district increased in area at the same rate as the town as a whole, as might reasonably be expected, then it would appear to occupy the same space on each of such adjusted maps, and the same would be true of the various component parts of the central district to be discussed in turn.

The Retail Zone

Shops and stores are the most obvious characteristic of the central district in Southampton, as elsewhere in Britain. The central shopping streets of Southampton appear from Fig. 60 to be neatly arranged in a 'ring' practically encircling the main central area of parkland; one can picture a 'ring' shopping expedition starting at the top of London Road and finishing only 200 yards away at the top of St. Mary Street. The various sections of this 'ring' are of quite different character. While the rateable value of Above Bar Street averages £220 per foot of frontage, East Street, St. Mary Street and London Road average £37, £24 and £34 respectively, values which may be compared with £39 and £42 for the shopping-centres in the principal suburbs. These three lower-value streets themselves in fact occupy differing niches in the central district. St. Mary Street, with St. Mary's Road, constitutes the local shopping centre of the dock-workers' district on the eastern side of the Itchen–Test peninsula. East Street contains a large popular department store (said to be the largest in the south of England) and a good many shops for fashionable working-class youth. London Road is the latest extension of the main 'spine', or central shopping street, which stretches from its junction with East Street to the point where it crosses the Parks. Along this 'spine' the frontages of highest value are found on the eastern side of the first 300 yards above the Bargate, and values fall off dramatically along the High Street below the East Street junction.

Comparison with the retail zones of 1867 and 1914 reveals the operation of two distinct

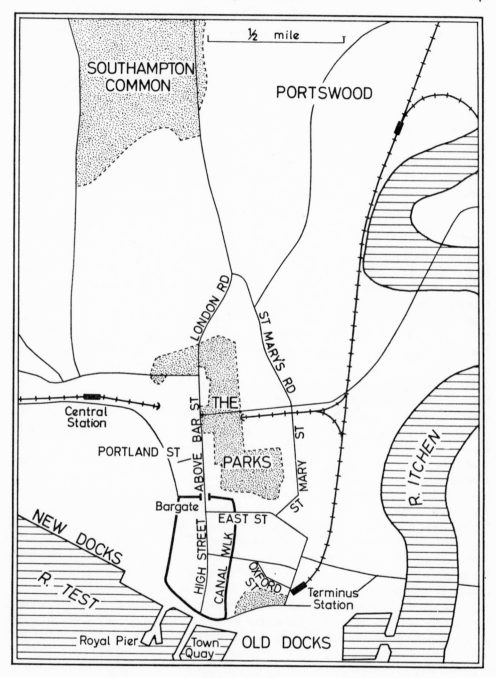

Fig. 58. Location map

This map locates the main features of the town involved in the analysis of functional zones.

tendencies. First, the retail zone has extended northwards, virtually reaching its present position by 1914. Second, there has been an actual retreat of shops from its southern end. In 1867 at the southern tip of the peninsula a complex of retail streets was based partly on the medieval town and partly on the main dock entrances, starting in Oxford Street and extending outwards by various connecting links towards High Street and East Street. By 1914 the High Street itself had ceased to count as a shopping street, and Canal Walk alone, then a narrow and somewhat lively 'sailors' paradise', connected the Dock Gate to the town. This street was destroyed by bombing in 1940, and the docks retail quarter was reduced to little more than Oxford Street. Fig. 58 shows, however, that the influence of the docks on the distribution of business activity extends, albeit with diminished intensity, well beyond this single street, though this quarter seems pitifully small for a port of Southampton's importance.

Subsidiary Central Functions

Figs. 59-60 illustrate the development of four functional zones which are usually located on the edge of the central retail zone of any town—business offices, lodgings (including hotels), wholesale establishments and professional premises. At the present time, the distribution of these activities in Southampton is quite distinctive. Wholesaling on a large scale is concentrated at the lower end of High Street and in the transitional area between the 'port' and the 'town' retail zones. Smaller firms are found diffused, largely in the 'run-down' zone just beyond the 'neck' of the peninsula. Offices are more closely linked to the retail zone, commonly occupying the upper floors of shops, but in addition to one side, as in Portland Street and along the terraces to the north of the parks. Architects, dentists and solicitors share this last district, though extending still further into the side-streets, while the main concentration of doctors lies further out near the Common. Lodgings are more widespread, though four typical locations can be picked out. First, the attractive old coaching inns in the High Street, notably the Dolphin, with its fine bow-windows (Plate XXXVI); second, the small boarding-houses in the vicinity of the Old Docks; third, a complete range of accommodation culminating in the three- and four-star hotels near the Central railway station; and fourth, largely converted property on the outer periphery of the central district, with local concentrations where circumstances have been particularly favourable.

The most noticeable feature of the development of these zones since the 1860's is, as implied above, the stability of their relative positions. The zone of wholesaling premises shows perhaps most change. Between 1867 and 1914 the chief concentration shifted from the immediate vicinity of the main retail zone (then in the High Street) to a specialised quarter at the lower end of the High Street and also between there and the Terminus station, while new locations north of the retail zone were already appearing by 1914. Offices have for the last hundred years been situated close alongside or actually above the retail zone. Some of the quarters established by 1867 are still favoured—in some cases, in fact, the actual buildings of that time survive. More striking, perhaps, is the way the office zone as a whole has adapted itself progressively to the general shift in the centre of gravity of the town.

The same can be said of the premises of architects, dentists and solicitors, and in fact their zones often coincide with the offices. Medical consultants, on the other hand, at each stage have kept well clear of the town centre, distinctly ahead of the members of other professions. Significant is the way in which the doctors' quarter of 1867 has become the dentists' quarter of 1914, while the doctors' quarters of 1914 are now occupied by architects and solicitors. The separate lodging quarters of 1962 have rather different histories. Those centred on the High Street, the Dock-gate and the Central railway station all show progressive decline *in situ* since their first appearance, but the peripheral quarter reveals not only repeated displacement towards the outskirts, but also expansion and some dispersion at the same time.

Summary

How big is the central district and what are the quarters within it? An attempt to answer the first question is made in Fig. 60 (last column). The area outlined covers (with the exception of wholesaling) the criteria used by A. E. Smailes to distinguish a major town. These comprise most of the equipment typical of a regional centre, and the area they characterise constitutes the Southampton of the country visitor, much as the City and West End constitute the London of the provincial. This central district during the Middle Ages was confined entirely within the town walls (Fig. 55). Since then a continual process of expansion and diffusion has taken place, almost entirely in one direction—northward. In 1867 there was only a tentative break-out beyond the Bargate into the immediately adjacent part of Above Bar Street. The situation in 1914 is most revealing, for while the walled town still formed an appendage of the central district, the centre of gravity now lay in Above Bar Street, and several functions had spread still further beyond, though always due northward. Today, while certain new 'bulges' can be seen to east and west, the main expansion is still to the north, where the University, the grammar schools and the medical specialists have moved to the margins of the Common and beyond.

Within and around the central district so outlined, most of the individual central functions are located in specific areas in such a way that a number of 'quarters' can be distinguished, each characterised by a different function or, more usually, by a complex of associated and inter-related functions. Eleven such quarters, with certain sub-divisions, are listed below, and shown on Fig. 61, to which the figures and letters refer.

(1) *The Dock Gate District*, with nautical shops, shipping and travel agents, eating- and lodging-houses.

(2) *The Wholesale Quarter*.

(3) *The Central High Street*, a discard quarter with relics of past centrality: the G.P.O., former coaching inns, head offices of banks and insurance companies.

(4) *The Core*, a typical south of England main street, with a particularly narrow and discontinuous fringe of offices and professional premises; (*a*) the Civic Centre.

(5) *The Growth Quarter*, with new smaller central-type shops, offices (older and more recent conversions and big new blocks), hotels; behind the main façades are professional

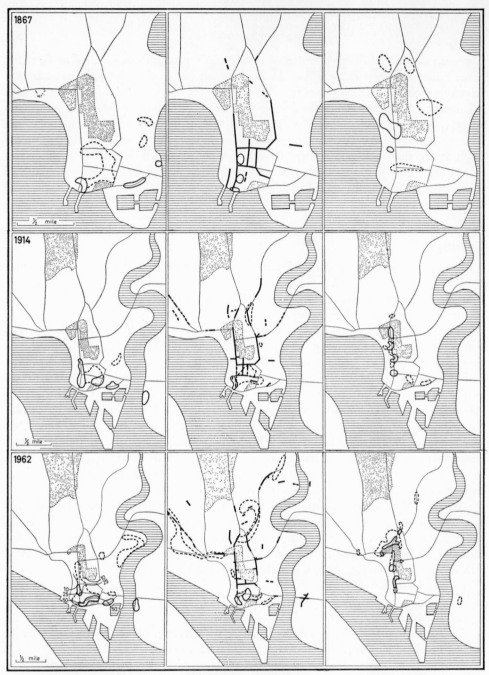

Maritime Activities | Wholesaling and Retailing | Business Offices

Areas of greater and less concentration are outlined. In the bottom map the numbered lines limit the areas where 50 per cent, 25 per cent and 10 per cent of retail activity was estimated in 1950 to be based on dock and port custom.

Areas of greater and less concentration of wholesaling are outlined. Streets exclusively and partially devoted to retailing are emphasised in continuous and pecked lines.

Areas of greater and less concentration are outlined.

Fig. 59

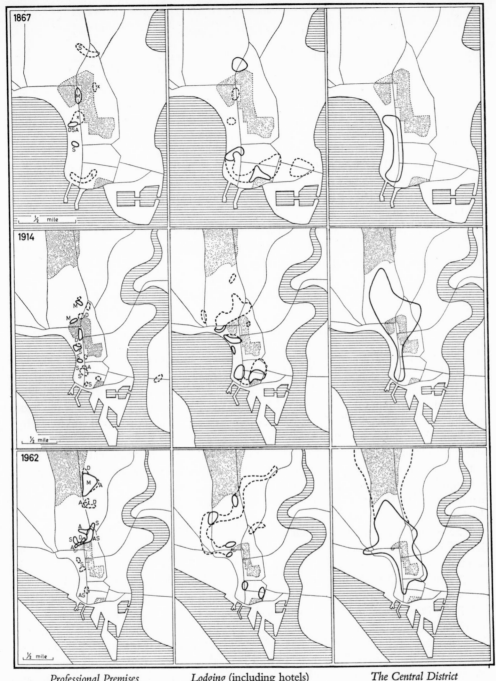

Professional Premises	Lodging (including hotels)	The Central District
Areas of greater and less concentration are outlined. Letters show preponderance of architects (A), dental practitioners (D), medical practitioners (M) and solicitors (S). X indicates a mixed area.	Areas of greater and less concentration are outlined.	Based on the location of activities characterising a major town. Central district outlined.

Figs. 59, 60. Functional zones in Southampton in 1867,
1914 and 1962

Water is lined, parks and other open spaces are stippled.

premises, wholesale establishments, lodgings and service back-streets; (*b*) Ordnance Survey Office and central Roman Catholic church, convent, college and school.

(6) *The Central Railway Station District*, with lower value shops, lodgings, restaurants, semi-wholesale establishments and hotels.

(7) *The 'Ring'* of lower value shopping streets; (*c*) specialised antique, art and book shops.

(8) *The Inner Diffuse Zone*, largely residential, with local concentrations of (*d*) lodgings; (*e*) hotels; (*f*) sports grounds and stadia; (*g*) professional premises; (*h*) motor-car sale-rooms and workshops; (*i*) wholesale emporia and small factories; (*j*) the central hospital; and (*k*) offices and semi-wholesale low-turnover shops.

(9) *The Outer Diffuse Zone* around Southampton Common, with grammar schools, the University and medical consultants' premises.

(10) *The Docks, Industry* and *Railyards:* (*l*) the Old Docks; (*m*) the New Docks and associated reclaimed land; and (*n*) the Town Quay and Royal Pier occupying the water front of the medieval town.

(11) *Residential Quarters*, with occasional shopping centres and through-streets devoted to miscellaneous commercial activity (unnumbered on Fig. 61; streets dotted).

THE GROWTH OF THE RESIDENTIAL AREA

The pattern of urban development since 1800 can be conveniently divided into three phases (Fig. 62). The first of these lasted until the early 1870's. By 1871, when the population of the borough had reached 53,741, the built-up area had spread out from the original medieval town within the walls until it filled the low-lying promontory between the Itchen and the Test and extended to the north-east into Bevois Town, Portswood and St. Denys. The bulk of the development in the down-town area took place along the Itchen riverside where the congested working-class housing contrasted markedly with that in the districts to the north, designed for the more prosperous sections of the community. Beyond the borough boundary to the west, a similarly spacious residential area was laid out in Freemantle, while in Shirley a township grew up which was predominantly working-class in character.

The second phase of development, between 1870 and 1914, included the incorporation of Freemantle and Shirley in 1895 and brought the population of the expanded borough by 1911 up to 119,012. It consisted chiefly of the extension of housing for the comparatively well-to-do in a zone running from Freemantle eastward to St. Denys and across the Itchen into Bitterne Park, with the latest and most imposing dwellings in Banister's Park, Winn Road and Westwood Road, adjacent to the Common.

Though Bitterne Park was incorporated in 1895, the main extension of the borough on the eastern side of the Itchen did not take place till 1920. Areas of working- and middle-class housing had already been built there around the older villages of Woolston, Sholing and Bitterne, contemporaneously with similar developments in Southampton, though on a much smaller scale. The main expansion of this part of the town began, however, after 1919; and this, together with similar development of private housing in Highfield and Shirley,

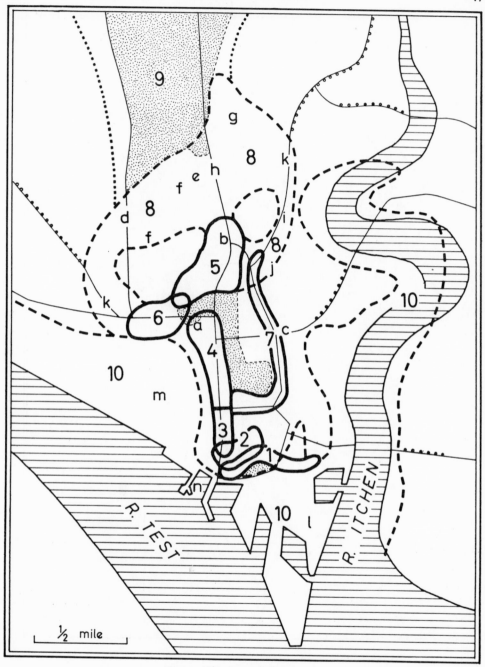

Fig. 61. The Central Quarters
The numbers and letters are listed in the text on pp. 243 and 246

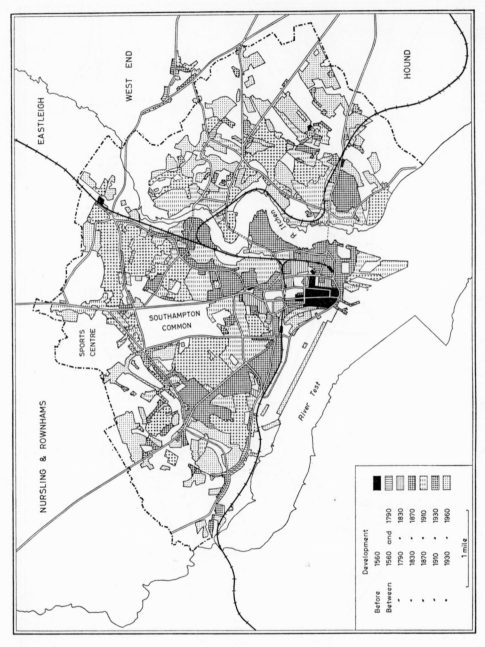

EASTLEIGH

WEST END

HOUND

NURSLING & ROWNHAMS

SPORTS
CENTRE

SOUTHAMPTON
COMMON

R. Itchen

River Test

Development

Before   1560
Between 1560 and 1790
         1790   "   1830
         1830   "   1870
         1870   "   1910
         1910   "   1930
         1930   "   1960

1 mile

Fig. 62. Phases of housing development in Southampton
Based on information made available by the County Borough Planning Office.

constitutes the third phase in the growth of the town. The expansion of these largely middle-class housing districts has continued to the present, at the same time as municipal housing schemes have been under construction on the edges of the town: before 1939 at Coxford, Burgess Road and Merry Oak, and notably since 1950 in the Millbrook, Thornhill and Harefield estates (Plates LV, LVI). Of the 63,000 dwellings in the borough, 30 per cent are now municipally owned, and of these almost three-quarters have been built by the Corporation since 1945.

POPULATION GROWTH

This residential development reflects the steady increase in the population of the borough and thus in the number of households requiring separate accommodation. From 160,994 in 1921, the population rose by 9·3 per cent to 176,007 in 1931, and thence to 181,000 by 1939. During the War of 1939-45, however, it dropped very rapidly to 122,000 as a result of recruitment for the Forces, enemy action and evacuation, rising again to its pre-war level by 1951, when it reached 178,343. Since then the population has risen further to 204,822 at the 1961 census, but as this figure includes some 11,000 people living in areas incorporated only in 1954, the real rate of increase during the decade was 7·8 per cent. Though above the national average of 5·3 per cent, this rate of growth was still appreciably below that of the county of Hampshire (21·2 per cent) and of adjacent coastal areas such as Fareham U.D. (37·1 per cent) and the New Forest R.D. (28·0 per cent). On the other hand, the increase of 13·4 per cent in the number of households in Southampton during the same period was slightly higher than that of the population as a whole, and this has been more than matched by an increase of 24·5 per cent in the number of dwellings. As a result, the ratio of persons per dwelling decreased during the decade from 3·77 to 3·05, and the excess of households over dwellings declined from 5700 in 1951 to a bare 274 in 1961.

Migration

Of the increase of 16,000 in the population of Southampton during the decade 1951-61, 12,620 is accounted for by natural increase, 1420 by demobilisation and 1960 by net migration into the town. This last figure, however, disguises the actual degree of population movement that has taken place. A more accurate indication of this movement can be gleaned from the results of a survey of every twentieth household in the borough in November 1961 which, in the absence of the complete 1961 census statistics at the date of writing, provide most of the statistical information used in the rest of this Chapter.★ This investigation showed that 16·3 per cent of these households had moved into the town since 1949, half of them during the period from October 1957 to November 1961. As the net migration

★ This survey of 2824 households was carried out by M. B. It was financed by Southampton Corporation and the computation of the data was undertaken by Leeds University Electronic Computing Laboratory. He is much indebted to Dr. P. A. Samet at Southampton and Dr. G. B. Cook at Leeds for this assistance.

into the borough was less than 2000, these figures suggest that probably some 28,000 people left the town in the period 1951-61, while 30,000 moved in.

No information is available concerning where these people have moved. A smaller study of 438 Corporation tenants who left post-war estates in 1959, however, showed that of those who had moved out of Southampton slightly more than half had left the district completely and the remainder had settled in adjacent areas, notably in Eastleigh and in the New Forest and Winchester Rural Districts.* Those informants in the larger survey who moved into the town between 1950 and 1961 came in the main from Hampshire (52·2 per cent), from London and other parts of southern England (23·5 per cent), from elsewhere in Britain (15·4 per cent) and from the colonies and dominions (6·2 per cent). This distribution broadly corresponds with information about where each householder's home was in 1945. There appears accordingly to be a considerable degree of movement both to and from neighbouring districts. In the sample population as a whole, furthermore, only 2·1 per cent had moved into the town from outside the British Isles, and the 1951 census also gave a similarly small percentage (1·5 per cent) as having been born abroad. Thus, though there is known to have been some immigration of foreigners into Southampton in recent years, no great concentration of foreign immigrants can be discerned in any particular part of the borough, which constitutes a feature of larger cities such as Liverpool and Manchester.

The majority of Southampton's population, on the contrary, is locally rooted. In 1951, 67·5 per cent were recorded as having been born in Hampshire, and the more recent inquiry indicates that in 62·1 per cent of the households interviewed, both man and wife (and in a further 7·4 per cent one or other) had been living in the borough continuously since before 1940. Nevertheless, within the town there has been a good deal of internal mobility; between October 1957 and November 1961, one household in every three had moved, a figure very close to the national average.†

The analysis of this movement shows two interesting characteristics. Firstly the majority of these moves were from one house to another in the same part of the town. This was particularly marked in the Shirley-Millbrook area west of the Common and in the downtown districts, where the percentages of local moves were respectively 45·2 and 48·7. On the Bitterne side of the Itchen, the corresponding figure was 39·2 per cent and in the Highfield–Swaythling area 30·3 per cent. The lower percentages in these two districts were no doubt due to the fact that new housing development was going on particularly fast in the Bitterne area, thus attracting purchasers from all over the town, and that Highfield and Swaythling, being high-status areas, tend to have a higher turnover-rate.

* M. Broady, 'A new trend in residential change: some Southampton data', *Housing* (1961), vol. 22, pp. 154-7.

† D. V. Donnison, 'The movement of households in England', *Journal of the Royal Statistical Society*, Series A (General) (1961), vol. 124, p. 61. Of a sample of 3137 housewives in England, 8 per cent had moved in the year ending July 1958. In general, however, Southampton households appear to be less stable than the average. In Professor Donnison's sample of housewives, 31 per cent had moved to their present homes before 1940, as against 22 per cent of householders in the Southampton sample; and 48 per cent had moved since 1949, as compared with 61 per cent in Southampton.

In the second place, it is possible to analyse the trends in residential tenure. The change in tenure among the people who moved during the four-year period is indicated in Table XI. This shows very clearly that the main direction of movement has been out of private tenancies and into ownership and Corporation tenancies. The further analysis presented in Table XII shows that the greatest degree of change has been occasioned by people moving from private into Corporation tenancies and into owner-occupied dwellings. There has also been a significant movement from both furnished tenancies and Corporation property into owner-occupation. Analysed by social class, these data show that with higher social status movement into owner-occupied property increases, while movement into Corporation property decreases. Thus, though there is now clearly some tendency for people from all social classes to become property owners, owner-occupation still remains a predominantly 'white-collar' characteristic.

SOCIAL ECOLOGY

The residential districts of Southampton form three broad zones defined primarily in terms of their social status; each zone may be further subdivided into sectors, each with its distinctive characteristics. Fig. 63 shows these divisions, the statistical basis of which is given in Table XIII. This zonal division is related broadly to the pattern of physical development of the town. Thus the working-class zone comprises the central down-town and riverside districts on the one hand and the outlying municipal estates on the other; the middle-class zone lies on the higher ground adjacent to Southampton Common in Shirley, Bassett, Highfield and Banister's Park; and between is the intermediate zone with a considerable mixture of both manual and white-collar workers.

In the *Working-class Zone*, sectors A and B constitute the pre-war and post-war municipal estates. The Corporation's housing policy, which has done so much to reduce slums and overcrowding in the town, has particularly benefited the local working class. Its effect has been to produce on the outskirts of the town housing districts in which the proportion of manual workers (over 70 per cent) is significantly higher than in any other part of the borough, and the demographic characteristics of which are also strikingly different. The proportion of people aged sixty-five and over is much lower there than elsewhere in the town (10 as against 20 per cent), and the proportion of families of five or more members rises to 34 per cent as against the borough's overall figure of 20 per cent. In the older-established pre-war estates, these large families typically consist of parents with children in their late 'teens or early twenties; in the post-war estates, the children tend to be more frequently of school age. Indeed, in these areas the proportion of householders aged under 40 (49 per cent) is nearly twice as high as in the borough's total population.

The other working-class parts of the borough comprise the down-town area, Woolston and Sholing and the older parts of Shirley, Bitterne village and Bitterne Park. These areas were all developed originally before 1914, and much of their present fabric dates from before 1870. For the most part the original dwellings still stand, though there has been a good deal of slum clearance and infilling of blitzed sites, particularly in the down-town area where large blocks of Corporation flats and houses such as those at Holyrood (Plate LI), Lansdowne Hill and Northam (Plate LIII) now accommodate some 40 per cent of the total population.

The demographic features of these older working-class areas are not markedly different from those of the intermediate and middle-class zones. By comparison with the municipal estates, however, they have much higher proportions both of people over sixty-five and of small elderly families. They have also experienced a greater influx of newcomers to Southampton, 8 per cent of householders in these areas having moved into the borough in 1957-61, as compared with 2 per cent in the municipal estates. It has been mainly from these older working-class sectors that people have moved out to the Corporation estates. This movement has affected the age-structure of the population, since it has been mainly the younger people with growing families who have gone, while the elderly have remained. The influx into these areas has accordingly been made possible both by the vacancies thus created and by the higher death-rate among an older section of the population.

Within these working-class sectors, however, the older parts of Shirley, Bitterne village and Bitterne Park stand out as having comparatively large numbers of elderly people (62 per cent aged fifty and over) and of long-standing residents. In old Bitterne, for example, two-thirds of the sample (65 per cent) have been living in the same house for over twenty years, as against an average of 22 per cent for the borough as a whole.

The Intermediate Zone of the town again can be divided into two separate sectors. There are, first, the areas in Freemantle, Hill and Portswood which were originally developed before 1914 as middle-class residential districts; and, second, the areas of post-1919 private housing in Shirley and, more extensively, on the Bitterne side of the Itchen. The older area has ceased to be as fashionable as it once was, and as its status has declined many of the large old houses have been converted into offices and hotels or subdivided into flats; one-third of all dwellings in this sector are in fact private flats or rooms. Though by no means as 'seedy' as rooming-house areas in larger cities often are, it is clear that this sector serves a function similar to theirs in catering for new arrivals in the town, of whom equal numbers were manual and non-manual workers. This is particularly true of Hill and Portswood, where the percentage of recent incomers to the town is 14, and about 20 per cent of the employed population had moved into Southampton between 1957 and 1961.

The more recently built districts in Shirley and Bitterne are areas in which house-ownership predominates, even among manual workers. The Shirley area was completely developed before 1939 and has a remarkably high degree of stability: 46 per cent of its householders have lived in their present houses since before 1940, and only 16 per cent of the houses have been occupied since October 1957. The Bitterne area, however, is more typical, for there housing development, begun mainly after 1919, has continued until the present time, when new sites within the borough are virtually non-existent. A surprisingly high proportion of dwellings on this side of the town (about 25 per cent) comprises bungalows, most of which have been built since 1945. The continuous process of housing development has brought into this district a stream of new residents (32 per cent arrived in 1957-61), most of whom, however, are Southampton people of long standing. In this

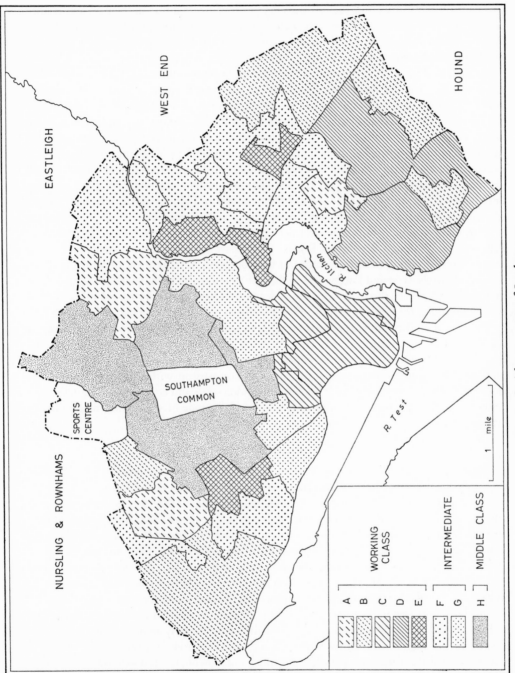

Fig. 63. Social status zones of Southampton
Based on a social survey of Southampton made in 1961.

part of the town a quarter of the residents (23 per cent) were living in their present houses, and 62 per cent within the borough, before 1940. The proportion of newcomers, conversely, is only 11 per cent, and these, by contrast with the Freemantle–Portswood area, are mainly middle- rather than working-class people.

In *the High Status Area*, adjacent to Southampton Common, the proportion of managerial, professional and senior office workers (29 per cent) is twice as high as in any other part of the town. It is well established that these categories of a population are residentially the most mobile. It is therefore to be expected that the percentage of people in this sector who were resident in Southampton before 1950 should be the lowest (56 per cent) and that of incomers to the town the highest (15 per cent, 1957–61) in Southampton. The demographic pattern of this zone as a whole does not differ strikingly from that of the intermediate zone, though for the most part the residents are owner-occupiers, living in dwellings built between the wars or else in new expensive houses and blocks of flats which have been erected in substantial numbers in the Bassett area in very recent years.

The main exception to this general pattern, however, is the area formed by Banister's Park and by Winn and Westwood Roads. This is part of the 'collar' of older middle-class districts created during the second phase of the borough's development, of which Hill and Freemantle to the west and Portswood to the east have already been described as part of the intermediate zone. In this area, too, the older houses have generally ceased to be used as private dwellings for single households, but have been subdivided into flats, which comprise 80 per cent of all dwellings, as compared with 10 per cent for Southampton as a whole. It is consequently also an immigrant's area. As many as 53 per cent of the population moved into it in the four years before the survey in 1961, while just over one-third (36 per cent) had only been living in Southampton since 1957. By comparison with the other immigrant's areas, the population here is almost exclusively middle-class and contains an unusually high proportion of single persons (19, against a borough average of 5 per cent), many of who are widowed.

CONCLUSION

Southampton has thus been growing steadily both in size and population over the past seventy years (Figs. 62, 64). In the course of this expansion an ecological pattern has developed, comparable in broad outlines with that of many other towns throughout the country. This basic pattern of social differentiation has, however, been modified by Southampton's topography, in which the Common blocked growth to the north and the river Itchen inhibited expansion into the Bitterne side of the town both before, and for some years after, it had ceased to be Southampton's eastern boundary. That this expansion will continue is not open to doubt. The general economic and social drift to the south of England is unlikely to be halted; and both the development of the port along the lines suggested in the Rochdale Report (see p. 291) and the recently announced plan to electrify the main line to London will foster the continued growth of the town. Already an increase in the population of the borough is planned for in the scheme, agreed in 1960, for the development of a new residential area for 20,000 people at Nursling and Rownhams, just beyond the borough

XXXV   The Mayflower Memorial on the Town Quay

XXXVI   The Dolphin Hotel in the High Street

XXXVII   The Millbrook Industrial Estate

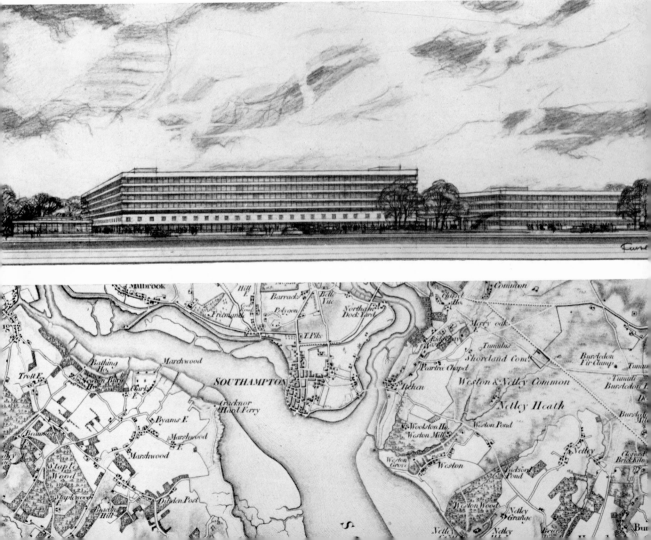

boundary (see p. 344). In a few years' time, therefore, it is likely to be even more desirable than at present to view the urban ecology of the town in the setting of the incipient conurbation which is growing up around Southampton Water.

Table XI. *Type of Tenure of a Sample of People who moved into or within Southampton, October 1957—November 1961*

(n = 806)

| | Type of tenure (per cent) | | | | |
| | | Tenant of: | | | |
	Owner	unfurnished accommodation	furnished accommodation	Corporation property	Total
Previous dwelling	18	44	18	20	100
Present dwelling	35	19	4	42	100
Percentage change	**+17**	**−25**	**−14**	**+22**	

Table XII. *Change of Tenure of a Sample of People who moved into or within Southampton, October 1957—November 1961*

(n = 806)

| Type of tenure of previous dwelling | Type of tenure of present dwelling (per cent) | | | | |
| | | Tenant of: | | | |
	Owner	unfurnished accommodation	furnished accommodation	Corporation property	Total
Owner	81	14	1	4	100
Tenant: unfurnished accommodation	29	31	2	38	100
Tenant: furnished accommodation	29	22	15	34	100
Tenant: Corporation property	18	3	0	79	100
Total	**35**	**19**	**4**	**42**	**100**

Table XIII. *Residential Zones: Occupation of Householders (per cent)*

| Type of occupation | Residential zones | | | | | | | | |
| | Working-class | | | | | Intermediate | | Middle-class | |
	A	B	C	D	E	F	G	H	Total
Non-manual	12	15	21	25	22	35	31	48	28
Foremen and skilled manual	39	47	20	31	32	27	24	15	29
Semi- and unskilled manual	29	25	32	21	14	15	14	4	18
Housewives: retired	18	10	23	21	31	21	27	29	22
Other	2	3	4	2	1	2	4	4	3

Ss

Appendix

THE BOUNDARY OF SOUTHAMPTON

The present boundary of the County Borough of Southampton is shown on Fig. 64, together with the constituent areas added at specific dates as the result of extension orders.

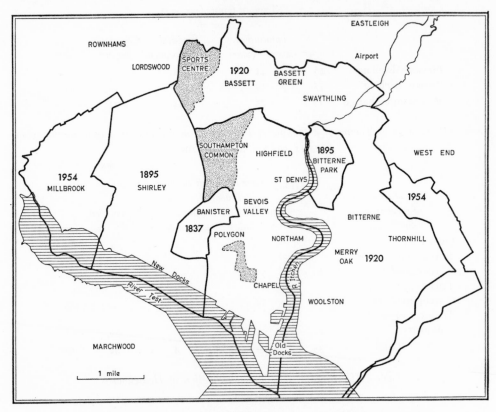

Fig. 64. The expanding boundaries of the County Borough of Southampton
Based on a map supplied by the Town Clerk's department, County Borough of Southampton.

The first extension of the ancient boundaries followed the Report of the Commissioner appointed by Parliament in 1837. This extension increased the number of councillors to thirty, six for each of five wards, and aldermen to ten. In 1895 the Borough was further extended by the incorporation of the Shirley and Freemantle Urban Districts and parts of the parishes of Bitterne, Millbrook and South Stoneham, all within the Rural District of South Stoneham. This increased the number of councillors to thirty-nine and aldermen to thirteen. In 1920 the Urban District of Itchen and parts of the parishes of Bitterne, North Stoneham and South Stoneham were added, again increasing the number of councillors to fifty-one and the aldermen to seventeen. The last extension was in 1954, when parts of the Romsey and Stockbridge Rural District and of the Winchester Rural District were added. There was subsequently an order of the Secretary of State following a review of ward boundaries, which fixed the number of councillors at fifty-four and of aldermen at eighteen. This constitutes the present Borough Council of seventy-two members.

Under the provisions of the Local Government Act, 1958, the Local Government Commission is to review the boundaries of all counties and county boroughs, and although the Commission have not, at the time of writing this information, visited Southampton, it is anticipated that their visit will take place in 1964.

These boundary extensions have of course affected markedly the official population totals of the Borough, as follows:

1831	18,670	*1920 boundary extension*	
1837 boundary extension		1921	160,994
1841	27,103	1951	178,343
1891	65,325	*1954 boundary extension*	
1895 boundary extension		1961	204,000
1901	104,824	1962 (June)	205,790 (Registrar General's
1911	119,012		estimate)

The growth in population within the County Borough will be curtailed on account of the small amount of building land available within the present boundaries, although this is, to some extent, offset by the increase in density by flat development in areas of renewal of low-density residential districts.

'Beating the Bounds'

In common with many other towns and cities, Southampton perpetuates the custom of 'Beating the Bounds'. This is done by the Sheriff of Southampton on 'Law Day', that is, the day of the meeting of Court Leet, the court of the Steward of the Manor of Southampton. This court is held on the first Tuesday in October.

The beating of the bounds ceremony takes place before the court sitting. It should in truth be stated that only the ancient boundary stones are visited at Chilworth Gate, at the Cutted Thorn (where traditionally King Canute is said to have been crowned) and at Crosshouse. The ancient custom was intended to impress on those present where the actual boundaries lay. The description of the present boundaries is read out in Court Leet by the Steward of the Manor, who, incidentally, is the Town Clerk, in the following terms, so that all present may be made aware of the town's boundaries:

'We present the Bounds and precincts of the Town and County of the Town of Southampton ought to extend from a point in Southampton Water opposite Netley Castle and from thence proceeding in a north-westerly direction along the River Test and up the Redbridge Channel, and thence along the railway leading to Salisbury, a distance of one thousand yards, thence in a north-easterly direction to Lords Hill, thence along the southern boundary of Lordswood to Winchester Road at Bassett, thence eastward to the River Itchen and south-eastward to Black House, thence south-westward near Townhill Park, thence south-eastward to Netley Common and from Netley Common along Tickleford Gulley in a south-westerly direction to the point of commencement in Southampton Water and the inhabitants in and about the said Town and County of the Town bounded as aforesaid do owe suit and service to and are within the jurisdiction of this Court.'

XVII

ECONOMIC ACTIVITY

SOUTHAMPTON, now a town with over 206,000 inhabitants, has developed on twin lines as a port, predominantly passenger, but with a significant cargo traffic as well, and as an industrial centre; the first development preceded the second by almost 2000 years. But it was not until the Industrial Revolution began towards the end of the eighteenth century that the potentialities of Southampton as a port in an industrial era began to be realised. The first industries to develop were those connected with the construction, repair and furnishing of ships; then followed those attendant on the shipping and shipbuilding industries, as, for example, firms supplying oxygen for welding purposes, marine engine manufacturers and carpet and other ships' furnishing manufacturers. Aircraft production came to the area mainly because yachtsmen had become enthusiastic about flying, and there were many local advantages for the manufacture and testing of seaplanes. In its early days an important 'growth' industry, aircraft manufacture conferred significant advantages on the region and greatly affected its subsequent industrial development, particularly during the War of 1939-45.

In 1945 Southampton was still very dependent on industries connected with its functions as a port and on aircraft manufacture, industries employing mainly men, so that the proportion of women in the labour force was below the national average. Since then, however, there has been an influx of new industry, partly the result of the residential attractions of the south of England, so that industries here have found the problem of recruiting personnel, particularly scientific staff for the science-based industries, easier than in many other parts of the country. Allied to this southward drift of population has been the desire on the part of industrialists to establish their industries in areas with large concentrations of consumers and adequate port facilities for handling imports and exports.

The main economic resources of Southampton have been developed by outside capital: the docks, the railways, the shipbuilding and repairing yards, and the shipping lines which operate from the port. These concerns have not developed from small beginnings by local inhabitants who amassed family fortunes and expanded their enterprises, but are large national organisations. Today the docks and the railways are publicly owned enterprises, and industrial leadership is provided by the executives of national concerns. This feature has become even more prominent recently with the development of a number of large undertakings, such as the Esso Petroleum Refinery at Fawley and the ancillary establishments in the vicinity of the refinery owned by companies with many other factories: the Monsanto Chemical Company, Union Carbide, International Synthetic Rubber Company and the Southern Gas Board. At Southampton itself, besides the shipbuilding and

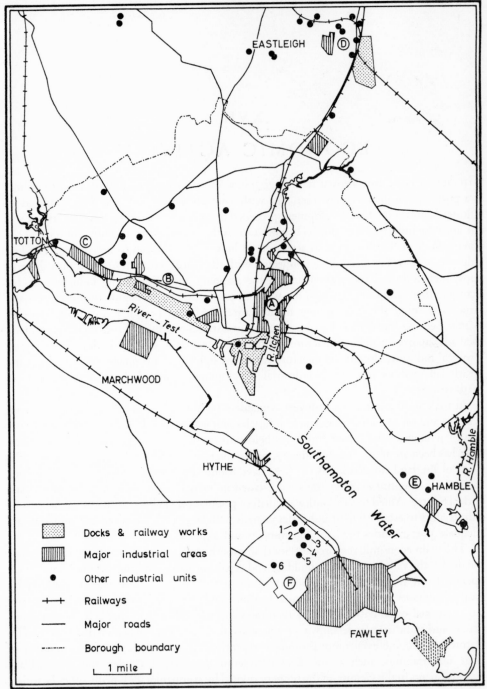

Fig. 65. The location of industry in and near Southampton

Based on a survey by M. J. Clark and J. Lewin.

The letters and numbers are as follows: A. Itchen Waterfront; B. New Docks Industrial Estate (see Fig. 66); C. Millbrook Trading Estate (see Fig. 67); D. Eastleigh; E. Hamble; and F. Esso Petroleum Co. Ltd., Fawley Oil Refinery, with present main area of development shaded.

Associated industrial units on F.: (1) Union Carbide Ltd.; (2) International Synthetic Rubber; (3) Monsanto Chemicals; (4) Air Products (G.B.) Ltd.; (5) Southern Gas Board; and (6) Esso Bulk Plant.

repairing firms of Harland and Wolff, J. I. Thornycroft and the British Railways Marine Engineering Department, all of which have establishments in other parts of the country, the most important employers are Vickers Armstrong and Folland (both until recently engaged in aircraft manufacture), the Pirelli General Cable Works, Mullard Southampton Works, the Ford Motor Company, and A.C.-Delco, a division of General Motors of the U.S.A.

For the purposes of the statistical analysis in this chapter, Southampton is defined as the employment exchange areas of Southampton (including Woolston), Eastleigh and Hythe, and five centres of industry may be distinguished (Fig. 65). Within the boundaries of the County Borough itself, industry is largely concentrated in two localities. Ship-repairing, shipbuilding and heavy engineering are located in the Old Docks and along both banks of the river Itchen. A newer development since the 1930's, characterised by modern light industry, is the New Docks and the Millbrook Trading Estates along the northern bank of the river Test between the centre of Southampton and Redbridge (Figs. 66-7, Plate XXXVII). Three other important centres of industry lie within a few miles of the boundaries of the County Borough. Eastleigh, to the north, began industrial development with railway workshops, and has since added a number of other industries. The Hamble area to the south-east of Southampton specialises in boat-building and repair and, a more recent development, in aircraft. Finally, the Hythe area, which includes Fawley and Marchwood, on the western shore of Southampton Water, has developed rapidly since the War of 1939-45 as a centre of the petroleum and petro-chemicals industry, and of the generation of electricity.

Despite these more recent developments, employment in the Southampton area is still to a very large extent dependent on the port. Table XIV gives the distribution of employed persons among the main industry groups in 1952, 1957 and 1961. 1952 is included as a year which, although well advanced in the post-war period, roughly separates the earlier period of reconstruction and consolidation of existing industries from the later period of technological revolution and innovation associated with the Government's policy of fostering oil-refining in Britain, the emergence of petro-chemicals as a new source of industrial raw materials, the spectacular growth of the electronics industry and the expansion of the motor vehicle industry, all developments which have greatly affected this region. 1957 has been included, since statistics are available on the same basis as for 1952, thus affording a more accurate indication of the pace of change and of the dynamic character of industry in this area than can be obtained by attempting to make a direct comparison of 1952 with 1961, particularly when the statistics are not strictly comparable because of changes of classification. In Table XV, however, the statistics for 1961 have been arranged to show the division of the labour force between the more progressive industries and those of lesser growth potential. This Table enables us to assess whether the structure conforms to the pattern of current demand, and whether the industries in the region are those which, on recent showing, have the greatest likelihood of growth.

In the Southampton area, industry is mainly 'heavy'—that is, the worker usually needs physical strength to do his job, so that a high proportion of male workers is employed. Almost half the employed males are in large, 'heavy industrial' establishments, as is brought

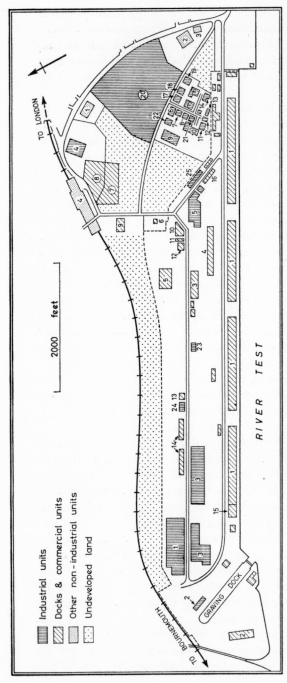

Fig. 66. Industrial and other units on the New Docks Estate

Based on a survey by M. J. Clark and J. Lewin.

The numbers are as follows:

A. *Industrial units*: (1) A.C.-Delco Ltd. (General Motors)—motor vehicle components; (2) John I. Thornycroft & Co. Ltd.—marine engineers; (3) Standard Telephones & Cables Ltd.—trans-ocean submarine telephone cables; (4) Southern Electricity Board—generating station; (5) Joseph Rank Ltd.—Solent Flour Mills; (6) W. & R. Jacobs & Co. (Liverpool) Ltd.—biscuits; (7) Pirelli Tyres; (8) Gillone Electric Ltd.—electrical components (radio); (9) Southern Electricity Board—depôt; (10) Power Brakes Ltd.—brakes; (11) Pinchin, Johnson & Associates—paints, varnishes, insulatings, etc.; (12) Andrew Weir & Co. (Liverpool) Ltd.—sacks & sack-cloth; (13) R. W. F. Thorn Engineering Ltd.—structural and ventilating engineering; (14) vacant; (15) Ferodo Ltd.—brake linings (also W. T. Clark Ltd.); (16) A.E.I. Lamp & Lighting Co. Ltd.—'Mazda' electrical products; (17) Ocean Trading Co. Ltd.—ships' stores and fancy goods; (18) Remploy Ltd.—light manufacturing, employment for disabled; (19) Itchen Transport Co. Ltd.; (20) Pirelli General Cable Works Ltd.; (21) Benson-Lehner (G.B.) Ltd.—processing equipment makers; (22) Bell & Nicholson Ltd.—textile distributors; (23) Durastic Ltd.—roofing materials; (24) Stewarts & Lloyds Ltd.—steel tubes; (25) Solent Canners Ltd.

B. *Docks and commercial units* (including depôts, warehouses, etc.): (1) passenger and cargo sheds; (2) Renault car depôt; (3) Montague L. Meyer Ltd.—timber depôt; (4) rail sheds; (5) G.P.O. depôt; (6) Southampton Motor Auction Mart; (7) Waterworks depôt; (8) garage; (9) H. J. Heinz & Co. Ltd.—canned food depôt; (10) garage; (11) Firestone Tyre & Rubber Co. Ltd.—tyres; (12) Denmark Bacon Co.—bacon depôt; (13) Rowntree Ltd.—depôt; (14) Ministry of Transport—sea transport offices; (15) International Cold Storage and Ice Co. Ltd.—cold store; (16) G. C. Hilbert Ltd.—Solent Wines and Spirits.

C. *Other non-industrial units*: (1) old swimming pool; (2) new swimming pool; (3) ambulance station; (4) Central railway station.

N.B. The representation of individual factories is necessarily diagrammatic on this scale.

out by the data in Table XVI. Some 29 per cent of the larger establishments (those employing 100 persons and over) actually employ 500 persons and over; the United Kingdom proportion is only 18·9 per cent. Southampton has a very high proportion of the large establishments employing 1000 persons and over. In addition to these, over 400 establishments employ 20 to 99 persons each.

In 1952 the group of industries closely connected with the sea employed 22,324 males, or approximately 1 in 4 of the male population; 7792 men, or almost 1 man in 10, was a seaman, although many of these of course lived outside the area. 2445 men, or 1 man in 30, was employed on port and inland water transport, 1887 or 1 in 40 was employed in the docks, while shipbuilding and ship-repairing employed 10,210 men or 1 in 8 of the total labour force.

In 1952 aircraft manufacture and the production of aircraft components was important, affording employment for 5000 men and 1000 women, the largest firms being Vickers Armstrong Ltd., Folland Aircraft Ltd. and Fairey Marine Ltd. Even in 1952 several of these firms combined other engineering with their aircraft work, and this general engineering was later greatly expanded; motor vehicles, accessories and components were other prominent manufactures. A.C.-Delco, first established in the New Docks Estate in 1937, employed some 700 persons. In 1952 the two factories of Pirelli-General Cable Works Ltd., one at Eastleigh and the other at Southampton, employed nearly 3000 persons, of whom about one-quarter were women. Eastleigh is sometimes described as a railway town because of the presence of two large works owned by British Railways, one a locomotive works and the other the British Carriage and Wagon Works, which between them provided employment for 3600 men.

The light industrial establishments were relatively small in 1952, except for the factory of the British American Tobacco Co., with a labour force of approximately 700 women and 400 men. The products of this group also included electronic apparatus, machine tools and plastics. These industries between them employed, mainly in small establishments, only 2 per cent of the total labour force in 1952. The service trades included in Table XIV cater mainly for the needs of the local population and to a lesser extent for industry in the area. Nearly 27,000 employees, or almost one-quarter of the labour force, were in this group, distribution being the largest industry with over 13,000 employees, one-half of them women.

By 1957 significant changes had taken place, and the total labour force had increased by 15 per cent, largely on account of immigration. Among the large industries two (electric cables and tobacco) had declined during the five years, though this was the result of temporary factors, as there has been subsequent expansion. Sea transport and dock and harbour services both increased by 23 per cent. The more significant advances, however, are those which reflect the main changes in industrial structure in the five-year period. Mineral oil-refining had increased by 37 per cent, consequent upon the enlargement of the refinery at Fawley, a process which in fact had started in 1950. Motor-car manufacture expanded, mainly as a result of the growth of Briggs Motor Bodies, recently acquired by the Ford Motor Company, so that it was no longer limited to the manufacture of motor bodies, but now had vehicle assembly lines. The aircraft industry had also developed appreciably, mainly

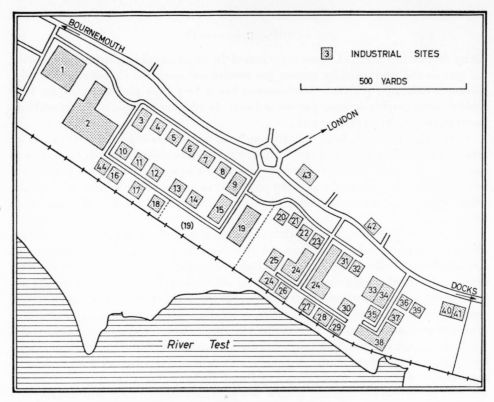

Fig. 67. The Millbrook Industrial Estate

Based on a survey by M. J. Clark and J. Lewin.

The numbers are as follows:

(1) Western Manufacturing (Reading) Ltd.—manufacturing electronic engineers; (2) Mullard (Southampton) Ltd.—semi-conductors; (3) Thomas & Evans Ltd.—soft drinks; (4) Addy Products Ltd.— chromium, cadmium and silver products; (5) Carlton Products (Southampton) Ltd.—manufacturing woodworkers; (6) Moorgreen Metal Industries Ltd.—sheet metal engineers; (7) Hobbs The Printers Ltd.; (8) Rosewalls (Southampton) Ltd.—sheet lead, lead pipes, putty; (9) B. A. Rolfe & Sons (Southampton) Ltd.—garage; (10) Tizer Ltd.—soft drinks; (11) Lea & Baxter Ltd.—cold store (meat); (12) Luff & Smith Engineering Co. Ltd.—precision engineers; (13) T. Hunt & Sons Ltd.—transport, coal and coke merchants; (14) Skinners (Southampton) Ltd.—toolmakers, jigs and fixtures; (15) Dunlop Rubber Co. Ltd.—tyres; (16) I.C.I.—'Dulux' paints depôt; (17) Yorkshire Imperial Metals Ltd.—brass, copper and plastic tubes, etc.; (18) Millblock Co. Ltd.—concrete products; (19) Calor Gas (Distributing) Co. Ltd. —calor gas and calor propane; (20) Waller Engineering Ltd.—liquid gas equipment; (21) Raleigh Industries Ltd.—cycles, etc.; (22) Southampton Waste Paper Co., Ltd.; (23) Mitchell (Millbrook) Ltd.—plastic materials; (24) Dimplex Ltd.—radiators and heating appliances; (25) Sparshatts— commercial vehicle services; (26) Coca Cola Southern Bottlers Ltd.—soft drinks; (27) Belcher (Radio Services) Ltd.—radio and T.V. maintenance; (28) F. H. Jung & Son Ltd.—sausage casings; (29) Truck Mixed Concrete (Southampton) Ltd.; (30) Light & Law Ltd.—motor engineers (also C.P.C. Ltd.); (31) Goodyear Tyre & Rubber Co. (G.B.) Ltd.—motor tyres; (32) C.P.C. Ltd.—general and structural engineers, coal hoppers; (33) S.P.D. Ltd.—warehouse keepers; (34) Rayment Tools Ltd.—tool and jig makers; (35) C. A. Ridgewell Ltd.—sheet metal engineers; (36) Stoneham Memorial Co. Ltd.—monumental masons; (37) Philip Howell (Southampton) Ltd.—hotel and bar products; (38) Davies, Turner & Co. Ltd.—transport; (39) I.B.M. World Trade Laboratories (Southampton Unit)—business machine manufacturing; (40) H.P. Bulmer & Co. Ltd.—cider depôt; (41) T. Walls & Sons Ltd.—ice-cream; (42) The Millbrook Press—printers; (43) British Oxygen Gases Ltd.—dissolved acetylene, etc.; (44) Southern Gas Board—depôt.

under the stimulus of defence purchases, but after 1957, consequent upon Government encouragement of amalgamation and reorganisation in the aircraft industry, employment declined.

The most significant industrial changes in the Southampton area since 1957 have been in the oil-refining and related industries, oil distribution, the manufacture of pharmaceutical and toilet preparations, and the electronics industries. Since the expansion of the old A.G.W.I. oil refinery by the Esso Petroleum Company, the Fawley-Hythe area has attracted large-scale industrial investment, most of which has come from American sources.

The refinery is now the largest in the United Kingdom, and merits special attention on account of its significance to the industrial development of the area. By 1963 it represented an investment of over £90 millions. It has a capacity of 11½ million tons a year and supplies 22 per cent of the country's oil requirements. The site on Southampton Water was chosen on the shores of a sheltered estuary with a deep navigable channel and unique tidal features (see pp. 60-1). Both these aspects are of vital importance to refinery location in this country, where we rely entirely on imported oil supplies. In addition, a large area of land was required, and this was available adjoining the site of a relatively small refinery which had been built and successively added to since 1920. The new refinery was completed in 1951, though since then it has been expanded very considerably.

Crude oil supplies for the refinery come mainly from the Middle Eastern and Libyan oilfields. Over 20 million tons of crude oil and finished products and over 4000 tankers are handled at the Marine Terminal (Plate XXVIII) in a year; this traffic represents nearly a third of the tonnage using the port of Southampton. The terminal has five ocean berths at which ocean-going tankers discharge crude oil or load finished products, and four berths on its landward side for the many small coastal tankers which are used to distribute products. A £2 million dredging project completed in 1962 now enables 86,000 deadweight ton tankers to be berthed with full cargoes of crude oil (see pp. 63-5).

The refinery's principal products are manufactured in thirty major processing units, varying from the relatively simple distillation process of separating crude oil into its raw fractions to vast and complex chemical plants. These shut down for planned maintenance only once every two years or so, and produce a variety of petroleum products. Such fuels as petrol, paraffin, diesel oils, gas oils, turbo-jet fuels and fuel oils are the products of largest volume, though a number of products of smaller volume, such as white spirit, lubricating oils and sulphur, are also of great importance. In more recent years the refinery has become an increasingly important supplier to the electricity-generating and gas industries. During the last five years the refinery has entered a fresh phase in production; new processes have been established to produce raw materials for the petro-chemical industry. The products manufactured include ethylene and butadiene, in the form of high purity gases supplied to chemical manufacturers for the production of polythene and synthetic rubber. The refinery, too, is a synthetic rubber manufacturer; butyl rubber, produced since 1963, is used mainly for the manufacture of inner tubes.

Products are distributed from the refinery by sea, pipeline, road and rail, though the last two account for less than 6 per cent of the total. The largest volume, about 80 per cent, moves by sea in coastal tankers to the company's ocean storage terminals situated on major estuaries, and about 10 per cent of the output is exported to Europe, mainly Denmark. Some deliveries are made direct to customers from the refinery, mostly by pipeline. Local customers include the Southern Gas Board, which receives refinery gas in Southampton via an 18-mile pipeline, the C.E.G.B. power-station at Marchwood via an 8-mile pipeline, and three chemical plants, Monsanto Chemicals, Union Carbide and the International Synthetic Rubber Company, sited adjacent to the refinery, which receive ethylene or butadiene gas by pipeline. When the new C.E.G.B. power station at Calshot is completed in 1967, deliveries of fuel oil will be made by pipeline direct from the refinery. Pipeline distribution, however, is not confined to the local area. In 1962 a 78-mile pipeline of 12-inch diameter was brought into use to supply ethylene to the new I.C.I. plant at Severnside in Gloucestershire. The year 1963 saw the completion of two further pipelines. The first was a 63-mile multi-product line linking Fawley and the Esso Storage Terminal near London Airport, and an 8-inch pipe, contained in the same trench sunk 13 feet below the floor of Southampton Water, carries liquefied petroleum gas to the North Thames Gas Board at Southall.

As oil-refining deals mainly with fluids in pipes and vessels, it is an industry which lends itself ideally to automation. The principal function is to control the physical conditions in the various refining plants, and indeed at Fawley the complexity of many of these is such that it would not be practicable to operate them without automatic control. The plants, which operate 24 hours a day and only shut down at infrequent intervals for overhaul, are operated by fewer than 250 men per shift. A further extension of automation has involved the increasing use of continuous stream analysers on the plants, which enable accurate quality control to be maintained at all times. Two electronic computers are in use at Fawley. An I.B.M. 1620 transistorised machine is used for solving technical problems of a non-routine and development nature, and an I.B.M. 1401 is employed for accounting purposes.

In such a plant it is not surprising to find that a high proportion of graduate assistance is required; over 300 professionally qualified people are employed, most of these being applied scientists. In all, the refinery employs some 3250 people and the neighbouring factories have labour forces amounting to a further several hundred persons. In fact, on account of the widespread use of automatic techniques, the employment levels are low in relation to the scale of capitalisation (in the refinery itself investment per employee amounts to £22,000). Expansion has, however, been the keynote of all the industries in this area, so that an additional sizeable labour force of several hundred people employed by contractors on extensions would seem to be a near-permanent feature of the industrial scene.

The large Shell-Mex and B.P. oil distribution centre at Hamble has also been greatly enlarged and modernised, and in 1959 a £15 million investment scheme was completed.

Light industries, of particular significance to the area on account of their size and because they employ a high proportion of women workers, include the factory of William R. Warner and Company at Eastleigh producing pharmaceutical, cosmetics and toilet preparations, and the Mullard Southampton Works, Associated Semi-Conductor Manufacturers Ltd. The former started production in 1956 and has since grown appreciably, so that it now employs some 800 persons. Construction of the Mullard factory was started in 1955 and production began in a modest way in 1956, when the floor space of the plant was 66,000 square feet; extensions in 1958 and again subsequently have more than quadrupled the working area, and the labour force is now about 2500, of whom some 60 per cent are women.

Besides the above developments, significant changes have occurred elsewhere. Vickers Armstrong Ltd., at Itchen, have developed important precision nuclear engineering activities and the design and construction of 'air-cushion' vehicles (Hovercraft) to replace aircraft engineering. In the food industry, Prices bakery (Southern Confectioners Ltd.) has so expanded that 1000 persons are employed. However, there have also been some contractions, and at Eastleigh the British Railways Wagon and Carriage Works have been reduced in size consequent on a reorganization of production in various British Railways' establishments.

With approximately one-third of the industrial population engaged in the heavier industries, whose requirements are predominantly for male labour, the proportion of women in employment tends to be low. In 1952 the proportion in the region as a whole was 26 per cent, compared with an average of 34 per cent in Great Britain; in Southampton itself the proportion was 27 per cent, in Eastleigh it was 24 per cent and in Hythe 13 per cent. As a result of the developments in electronics, pharmaceuticals and in motor vehicle manufacture, the proportion of women has since increased; in 1961 the proportion for the Southampton area was 29 per cent against a rather higher national average of 35·5 per cent, Southampton now having 31 per cent, Eastleigh 26 per cent and Hythe 17 per cent. It would seem, therefore, that there may still be a useful reserve of female labour in the Southampton area. As long as the employment position in other parts of the country continues to cause anxiety, the Government's policy concerning the distribution of industry seems likely to be that of satisfying the prior claims of these other areas for new industries rather than allowing further industrial development in Southampton. In due course this potential reserve of female labour will no doubt be allowed to contribute to the growth of the productive capacity of the British economy.

Industrial investment in the area has already taken place on a considerable scale. The region in 1962 had a working population amounting to 0·95 per cent of the total for Great Britain, yet in the period 1945 to 1961 the area of industrial building for which Industrial Development Certificates were necessary amounted to 1·32 per cent of the national total. Thus, despite Government efforts to steer industrial development to the north and west of the country, this region secured about a third more industrial building than would normally have been expected. These developments have tended to favour larger establishments, thus perpetuating the marked feature of the industrial structure already noted.

The stage of industrial development reached as a result of the changes is summarised by the classification given in Table XIV, in which manufacturing industry (including public utilities and constructional industry) has been arranged in four groups: 'growth', 'progress', 'steady' and 'declining'. This subdivision has been made by reference to the percentage change of output achieved by the constituent industries in Great Britain in 1951-61, as measured by the Index of Industrial Production. In Great Britain four groups of industries (the chemical and allied trades, vehicles, gas, electricity and water, and mechanical and electrical engineering) have all increased output by over 50 per cent. These have been designated 'growth' industries. The next class, the 'progress' industries consisting of two industrial groups (paper manufacturing and printing, and the construction industry, including building), has increased output by 45 per cent. Industries whose progress has been less spectacular (the food, drink and tobacco industries, clothing manufacture, metal trades and other manufacturing) have been designated the 'steady' industries, showing modest increases in output of between 10 and 20 per cent. Shipbuilding (with ship-repairing) and textile manufacture have been declining, with output smaller in 1961 than in 1951, the former by 3 per cent and the latter by 7 per cent.

This area has a large proportion of its employment, 56 per cent, in the 'growth' sector, compared with the national average of 36 per cent. 'Progress' industries are almost as prominent as in Great Britain as a whole. 74 per cent of the area's labour force in manufacturing and related industries is thus in the two most progressive industry groups, compared with 56 per cent nationally. A feature of these industries is that they are the largest consumers of the output of other industries in the economy and so cause growth in other sectors, particularly in the service industries. Transport and communications are affected, as also are the retail trades, by the growth and prosperity of the industrial population. The increase in production in the growth and progress sectors is of course a consequence of the increase in demand for their products, which in turn implies that these industries are well suited to the pattern of current demand. On the other hand, the Southampton area also has a larger than average proportion of its labour force employed in declining industries, but this appears to be more than counterbalanced by the high concentration of 'growth' industries in the area.

In view of this prominence of 'growth' and 'progress' groups in the Southampton area it is not surprising that during the last few years the area's employment record has been quite good, although temporarily the unemployment level has been rather high, mainly on account of the heavy seasonal and casual unemployment in ship-repairing. There is little doubt also that migration into the area because of its residential attractions has caused the unemployment rates to be higher than they would otherwise have been.

FUTURE INDUSTRIAL DEVELOPMENT

The largest recent industrial development in the Southampton area is the new oil-fired power-station at Fawley, on which work started in 1963. This enormous project will cost £70 millions, and will employ at its peak some 2000 construction workers. When commissioned in 1967 it will employ 500 men, and will produce 2,000,000 kilowatts from four turbines, an output over four times that of the Marchwood power-station, opened in 1957. The new station will take 2,000,000 tons of oil each year from the Fawley Refinery.

The only other major construction project is still in the planning stages: a dock extension likely to cost about £20 millions (see p. 293). Such a plan expresses faith in the future of the port, but it is contingent on developments between now and 1966, and may be postponed or even abandoned should expectations not be fulfilled; schemes for expanding the Docks have in fact existed since the late 1930's. But even if the scheme goes ahead as planned, the prospects for employment and the attraction of new industry to Southampton are not so bright as may appear from first impressions.

First, the dock extensions will be planned with an eye to the use of the most modern labour-saving equipment. Improvements to existing facilities, and the extension of 'containerisation', 'roll-on-roll-off' and other forms of mechanisation, would also enable more cargo to be unloaded without any increase in the labour force. If new labour agreements are arrived at, the removal of restrictive practices and greater flexibility in the use of dock labour could have such an effect that the whole expansion of cargo trade might be achieved with little or no increase in the present 1800 dockers, with 500 or so more employed seasonally in summer. If the effects of the possible decline in passenger traffic are taken into account (see p. 292), the employment prospects for dockers appear even less optimistic; the reduction of demand for dock labour on the passenger side might be greater than any gain on the cargo side. Passenger vessels require a great deal of labour for a short time, and should these sailings be reduced large numbers of men at present employed, if only from time to time on a casual basis, would be permanently redundant. Even without any decline in total passenger sailings, there is likely to be a decline in the demand for dock labour on this side, owing to the removal from service of the *Queens*, which is foreseen within a few years. One *Queen* is equivalent to ten or a dozen average-sized cargo vessels in its effect on dock employment, and any replacements for these two ships are likely to be much more economical of dock labour, as of other services.

The same considerations which lead to the conclusion that there will be little if any expansion in the demand for dock labour also apply to the ship-repairing and shipbuilding industry. At present the *Queens* require some 2000, out of a peak labour force of around 7000, for about fourteen weeks of the year, and the loss of this enormous requirement of labour will be difficult if not impossible to make good, for any replacements for the *Queens* will require far less maintenance. If more cargo vessels use the port, new contracts for repairs may well be obtained, but a great deal of new work would be needed to make up for the loss of these great vessels.

This analysis may be extended to the demand for other services provided in the town for vessels using the port. The expansion of cargo trade may lead to more office and agency work, some members of ships' crews would live in Southampton, and local merchants would be called on to supply food and fuel and other requirements. But the loss of the *Queens* would leave a huge gap to be made up in this direction also.

The Rochdale Report (see p. 291) wished to encourage the leasing of dock-estates to private industries, which would contribute to the trade of the ports, and it is natural to consider whether the threefold expansion of cargo trade might not give a big impetus to general industrial development in the area. The answer appears to be negative, for very few of the existing firms depend at all heavily on the port. The ship-repairers obviously do, Standard Telephone and Cables have to make their submarine cable near the docks, and Rank's flour-milling has to be carried on near to the discharging facilities. But other firms have no essential connection with the port. No doubt its proximity is some advantage to them for their export trade, but since they make mainly light manufactured goods, and as moreover their largest markets are within this country, this advantage is by no means decisive in their choice of location.

The conclusion appears to be that for its industrial expansion, as for its employment prospects, Southampton must depend on its general attractions for light industry, and on Government policy controlling the location of industry and population, rather than on development induced by the growth of Britain's foreign trade and of Southampton's share in it.

SEASONAL AND CASUAL UNEMPLOYMENT

One advantage will accrue from the growth in the cargo trade: employment may not be increased, but it will probably become more regular. The passenger vessels, and especially the *Queens*, have been a mixed blessing for Southampton. While contributing greatly to the growth of the port and the town, they have presented a major social and economic problem in that the employment they offer is highly irregular. The *Queens* usually arrive from New York on a Tuesday and sail on a Thursday, therefore constituting a great demand for dockers and ship-repairers in the middle of the week, who often cannot be employed on Mondays and Fridays. In addition to this casual employment, the passenger vessels also give rise to a heavy seasonal demand for ship-repairing workers. Many of these ships operate the North Atlantic route, which is unattractive in winter, and they therefore lie up for major repairs each winter, so as to maintain an almost uninterrupted service in the busy summer months. British Railways use Southampton for major repairs to their cross-Channel vessels using the ports between Dover and Weymouth, which are also in peak demand in the summer, and so their lay-up programme is organised to run from September to May. These heavy demands for shipyard workers in the winter are the basic cause of seasonal unemployment, since they give rise to a pool of men who cannot all find alternative work in the slack part of the year.

Suggestions have been made for many years for alleviating this seasonal unemployment by organised arrangements for the mobility of workers between ship-repairing and one or two other industries. But an analysis of unemployment by classes of worker tends to the conclusion that there is little chance that any substantial alleviation of the problem will be found in this direction. Some 200 shipyard labourers find work for part of the summer with the National Dock Labour Board, and others find labouring work in the building and contracting industry in and around Southampton. But the N.D.L.B. provides employment first for unemployed dockers from other ports, and only if there is still a need for more labour does it then take on shipyard workers; the need for these men is limited to the season of peak imports of fruit in mid-summer; and the capacity of the docks to take on more unskilled shipyard workers depends on the gradual expansion of this seasonal trade. The capacity of the building industry to absorb labourers during the summer is limited by the need to maintain a balance in the building labour force. The occupational analysis of ship-repairing unemployment shows that no significant numbers of skilled men whose services are required in building (plumbers, joiners, electricians and bricklayers) are available from

XLI The Nuffield Theatre and Arts Building, University of Southampton

XLII Southampton Docks, looking across the Old Docks up the Test estuary. On the day of this photograph, the gross tonnage of shipping at berth totalled over a half million, including both *Queens* and the *United States*

XLIII   R.M.S. *Queen Elizabeth* at berth in the Ocean Dock alongside the Ocean Terminal

XLIV   The New Docks, looking east along the Test water-front

XLV   The King George V Drydock, with P. & O.-Orient Line's *Canberra* (45,270 tons)

ship-repairing to balance the unskilled workers. Only if the building industry for some other reason has a relative scarcity of labourers in summer can it be expected to provide any offset to seasonal unemployment in ship-repairing.

Prospects are even poorer for finding work in summer for the ship-repairing craftsmen who are more specific to the industry: the welders, riveters, etc. Some may and do find work with construction firms at the Fawley Refinery and in other constructional and engineering work, but much of this work is not distinctly seasonal and tends to attract men away from ship-repairing at all times of year. It is just as likely to aggravate the problem of meeting the peak demands in winter as to alleviate seasonal unemployment in summer. Finally, the painters represent an intractable problem, in that no other industry can be expected to provide work appropriate to their experience in sufficient quantity to make much impression on their unemployment in the summer. In general, then, the craft structure of the seasonally unemployed shipyard workers is not conducive to their employment in the spring and summer in industries which have a seasonal fluctuation in the opposite direction to that of ship-repairing.

Another suggested solution to the problem of unemployment is that the ship-repairing firms should diversify their activities into other trades, and especially into those that can provide more employment in summer than in winter. Some have already extended into the field of general engineering: oil fuel firing equipment, electrical switchboards, work for the Atomic Energy Research Establishment, galvanising, metal spraying, cellulosing and stove enamelling. They have also obtained contracts for business related to the interior work on ships: joinery, furniture repairs, upholstery, painting and polishing, and carpet repairing and cleaning. Unfortunately, it is not easy to arrange for such work to be done at times when ship-repair work is not available. Some of the engineering work requires that men should be available continuously, for these customers may also require that work should be done within a time limit. Diversification is not likely to provide a ready solution to the problem of providing regular employment through the year.

New construction and long-term conversion work can be used to offset the seasonal fluctuation in the demand for labour arising on the side of repairs. But this offset appears to take the form primarily of the transfer of men from new work to repairs at the peak season in good years, so its effect is rather to ease the problem of meeting peak demands than to contribute directly to the relief of unemployment in slack periods, especially in the bad years. Moreover, this possibility must depend on the success of the industry in obtaining contracts for new or long-term conversion work in a difficult period for world shipbuilding as a whole and for United Kingdom shipbuilding in particular.

Any relief to seasonal unemployment by conversion work must depend on facilities being available for vessels to be laid up while the work is being done, and there is some fear in the industry that orders may be lost because of a lack of assurance that such facilities will be available. So far the firms have relied primarily on renting berths owned by the British Transport Commission, but Thornycrofts, who are mostly concerned, have now undertaken the extension of their own facilities.

The prospective removal of the *Queens* from service, and the use of the port by a larger

Ts

number of smaller cargo vessels, whose movements are not so pronouncedly seasonal, should gradually lead to a greater security of employment both in the docks and in the repair establishments. This in turn may contribute to the solution of the problems of industrial relations, which beset Southampton as so many other ports, and to the increase of efficiency.

PROBLEMS OF INDUSTRIAL RELATIONS

The Southampton area has in recent years been the scene of a most heartening example of co-operation in industry. An agreement for a significant reduction in working hours and a large wage increase in return for greater flexibility by maintenance craftsmen at the Esso Refinery, widely known as the 'Fawley Blue Book', has aroused nation-wide interest.

In the port of Southampton maintenance of passenger trade and expansion of cargo trade both require that the port should achieve the highest competitive efficiency in all aspects of its operations, and it is not exaggerating to say that its growth and prosperity depend above any other single factor upon improvement in industrial relations. One element present in the Southampton situation to a far greater extent than is the common experience in the country generally is insecurity of employment. The dock worker is 'cushioned' to some extent against the effects of irregular work by the National Dock Labour Board, which provides a minimum fall-back pay if a man reports for work twice a day and fails to obtain it. But this scheme has been increasingly criticised in recent years and is widely considered to be inadequate. Talks have been held between employers and unions in Southampton, as in London, Liverpool and elsewhere, to devise a local scheme for a measure of real decasualisation of employment. Such a step is in fact more urgent in Southampton than in other ports, since the proportion of dock workers on a regular weekly engagement is well below the national average; 10 per cent as, for example, against 35 per cent at Hull. But of course the irregularity of the arrival of ships that gives rise to this low proportion of weekly workers is also the great obstacle to any major advance.

As the National Joint Council for the industry noted, insecurity of employment produces: 'The casual attitude towards the observance of agreements and conciliation procedures, as exemplified by the industry's experience of strikes', and 'The casual attitude militating against the efficient use of manpower, as exemplified by resistance to modern methods including mechanisation and by adherence to restrictive practices.'[*] There is therefore a bargain to be struck in the form of a local agreement for a measure of decasualisation, in return for agreements on the more flexible use of manpower. The industry as a whole, both employers and workers, and therefore the port and town of Southampton, could not but gain from such an agreement.

The chief obstacle to this agreement appears likely to be the demand that 100 per cent of the existing registered dock workers should be taken on as weekly workers. If this is insisted upon, it becomes extremely difficult to make the scheme advantageous to the employers. It may be that even with greater efficiency of utilisation of labour, the expansion

[*] National Joint Council for the Port Transport Industry. Policy Directive to all Local Joint Committees. *Decasualisation*. October 1961.

of trade will be sufficient to maintain the present labour force, but the sudden transition from the existing method of working to a much more efficient organisation would probably result in the industry being over-manned for some years. If the employers had agreed generous guaranteed weekly earnings (and these would indeed have to be generous to make the scheme appear worth while to workers who at present enjoy high rates of pay when they do find work), there would inevitably be a worsening in the employers' financial situation. No solution is as yet in sight for this difficulty, though possibilities are being investigated locally, following national agreement in principle to local arrangements being made.

In the ship-repairing industry the industrial relations situation is more serious and at the same time less hopeful than in dock work. The prospects for British shipbuilding in the next few years are poor; world capacity is well in excess of the prospective demand for new ships, and British firms appear in general to be unfavourably placed in respect of costs. British output has remained virtually stationary since 1945, while that of many other countries has expanded rapidly. A vital factor in this lack of progress is the inefficient organisation of work which results from the industrial relations situation. Southampton enjoys a certain degree of security of business because of the concentration on repairs, but this probably aggravates the problem of competing for long-term conversion work and new construction. The fact that much of the labour force is only casually employed makes it difficult to retain the better workers in the industry, despite their high earnings when actually at work. The fact that industrial disputes have been relatively few in Southampton is no great comfort, for demarcation paralyses productivity at least as much in Southampton as elsewhere in Britain. With ship-owners economising on repairs, it may well be difficult for the industry to maintain its volume of employment. A larger number of men is involved, since the peak labour force of the industry is about 7000, against 2300 for dock labour. Moreover, the industry has no official scheme for guaranteed wages, so that there is no 'fall-back' pay, as for dockers from the National Dock Labour Board. It is not easy to see how any scheme of guaranteed employment could be acceptable to employers unless some lowering of the average hourly earnings while actually at work were accepted in return for guaranteed pay for a minimum number of hours each week. This would mean that employers would be paying directly for the pool of unemployment, instead of indirectly in the form of the higher earnings needed to persuade men to take the risk of frequent periods of unemployment. It would be essential to show employers that labour costs would not be increased, for they could not endure any addition to their costs under present competitive conditions.

As in the case of the dockers, it is difficult to persuade workers of the advantages of decasualisation, unless the scheme proposed involves not only no reduction in average earnings but no reduction in hourly rates. Otherwise the worker naturally tends to think of the plan as a trick to make him work longer hours for the same pay. It will also be difficult to obtain agreement on the side of the workers for any scheme that does not offer guaranteed employment to 100 per cent of the labour force. Yet a reduction of peak labour requirements as a result of greater flexibility between crafts is precisely what could make it worth while for the employers to guarantee weekly earnings. The fact that the industry suffers from seasonal as well as casual unemployment does not make the formulation of a scheme any easier.

In its present economic situation, the ship-repairing industry certainly could not afford to increase earnings in the way that Esso did at Fawley. But this does not mean that there is nothing the employers could offer in return for a revision of working rules. They could offer what the workers need most: greater security of employment. Further, the fact that the industry is operating under highly competitive conditions makes an improvement in industrial relations all the more urgent, because the present state of industrial relations in the industry is the greatest obstacle to increasing efficiency and lowering costs. It is an argument for pressing ahead at once, not for waiting for better times.

In any case, it is not true that at present the employers escape the cost of the irregularity of work, whereas with some guarantee of security of employment they would have to bear this cost. Already they are paying the cost of irregularity of work in high wages and high overtime rates needed under the present system to get workers when urgent work must be done, and they are also paying in that the work is done slowly and inefficiently. In addition, the whole quality of the labour force is probably reduced because some of the best men move to other industries which can offer better conditions. It is, of course, impossible to quantify these costs incurred by employers under the present system, which would be considerably reduced under a new labour agreement that gave some security of employment, but they are clearly considerable, and may well be as great as, or even greater than, the extra costs under a new system of guaranteed employment. Certainly, it would seem to be worth while investigating this question further.

Within the industry there is little sign of the kind of new thinking that will be needed if the joint problems of insecurity of employment on the one side, and harmful restrictive practices on the other, are to be overcome. The employers do not appear to realise that the main item they are selling is labour, because of the high proportion of labour to total costs, and that efficient use of a contented labour force would make the greatest contribution to the reduction of costs, and consequently to the ability to obtain new contracts. On both sides of the industry there is a tendency to await the outcome of national talks started in the shipbuilding industry by the Minister of Labour, before taking any local initiative. Since these discussions at the national level have gone on for a long time with no perceptible results, and since any results they might have would be very difficult to apply to the local industry owing to the great differences between it and the other centres of the shipbuilding industry, this waiting on events has all the aspects of a failure to recognise and to tackle the problem. The difficulties are great, and a solution cannot be easily arrived at; what is so depressing, however, is that there is no sign of a sufficient will even to make the attempt.

This chapter therefore concludes on a somewhat sombre note. It seemed preferable to discuss real problems facing an important section of industry in Southampton, rather than to devote the space available either entirely to a formal statistical analysis, or to a eulogy that stresses the achievements but ignores the problems that remain to be solved. As the earlier pages of this chapter have shown, Southampton is a prosperous industrial area whose structure is weighted on the side of new and rapidly growing industries. It is to be expected that it will continue to exercise a great attraction for industry and people from other parts of the country. But it also has a large sector that encounters problems similar to those of the older industrial regions, problems that will have to be solved if they are not to act as a brake on the economic and social progress of the area, and whose solution will require a new attitude of co-operation in industry.

BIBLIOGRAPHICAL NOTE

(1) Earlier surveys of industry in Southampton are: P. Ford, *Work and wealth in a modern port* (London, 1934); P. Ford and C. J. Thomas, *A survey of the industrial prospects of the Southampton Region* (Oxford, 1950).

(2) A more detailed account of the unemployment problem in ship-repairing is to be found in G. R. Denton, *Unemployment in the shipbuilding and ship-repairing industry of Southampton*, Report prepared for and published by Southampton County Borough Council (June 1962).

Note: Tables XIV to XVI are given on pp. 276-7.

Table XIV. *Employment in the Main Industries, June 1952, 1957 and 1961, Southampton Area Combined Employment Exchange Areas of Southampton, Eastleigh and Hythe*

Industries closely connected with the sea	NO. OF EMPLOYEES 1952 Male	Female	Number 1952	1957	1961	ALL EMPLOYEES Percent* 1952	1957	1961
Sea transport	7,792	563	8,355	10,310	9,553	7·6	8·2	6·9
River and port transport	2,445	36	2,481	2,540 ⎫		2·3	2·0 ⎫	
Dock and Harbour service	1,877	99	1,976	2,441 ⎬	4,820	1·8	1·9 ⎬	3·5
Shipbuilding and repairing, incl. marine engineering	10,210	334	10,544	10,617	8,903	9·6	8·4	6·4
Total	**22,324**	**1,032**	**23,356**	**25,908**	**23,276**	**21·2**	**20·5**	**16·8**
Large industries (home and export trade)								
Aircraft	4,882	1,046	5,928	7,450	3,379	5·4	5·9	2·4
Motor vehicle and aircraft accessories	1,934	217	2,151	2,484 ⎫		2·0	2·0 ⎫	
Motor vehicle manufacture	386	322	708	2,571 ⎬	4,090	0·6	2·0 ⎬	3·0
Electric cables	2,808	1,929	4,737	4,406	5,052	4·3	3·5	3·7
Tobacco	447	729	1,176	1,060	1,431	1·1	0·8	1·0
Mineral oil refining	2,252	138	2,390	3,278	3,616	2·2	2·6	2·6
Printing (excl. newspapers)	677	355	1,032	1,423	1,515	0·9	1·1	1·1
Railway and locomotive shops	3,600	177	3,777	4,197	3,893	3·4	3·3	2·8
Total	**16,986**	**4,913**	**21,899**	**26,869**	**22,976**	**20·0**	**21·2**	**16·6**
Small industries								
Electronics	42	33	75	346	3,467	0·07	0·27	2·51
Machine tools	231	16	247	407	183	0·22	0·32	0·13
Plastics	118	46	164	500	411	0·15	0·40	0·29
Pharmaceutical and toilet preparation	55	91	146	631	884	0·13	0·50	0·64
Paint, etc.	106	26	132	117	133	0·12	0·09	0·10
Carpets	88	77	165	177	221	0·15	0·14	0·16
Toys	46	117	163	34	36	0·15	0·03	0·03
Total	**686**	**406**	**1,092**	**2,212**	**5,335**	**0·99**	**1·745**	**3·85**
Service industries								
Buses	1,109	246	1,335	1,382	1,797	1·2	1·09	1·3
Public utilities—gas, electricity and water	1,849	153	2,002	2,520	2,330	1·8	1·99	1·7
Distribution	6,571	6,615	13,186	15,243	18,039	12·0	12·02	13·0
Hotel catering	705	2,866	3,571	4,283	3,297	3·2	3·38	2·4
Laundries	240	933	1,173	1,335	1,110	1·1	1·05	0·8
Motor vehicle repair	1,993	290	2,283	1,810	3,267	2·1	1·43	2·4
Local government	2,498	619	3,117	3,830	3,965	2·8	3·02	2·9
Total	**14,965**	**11,722**	**26,687**	**30,403**	**33,805**	**24·3**	**23·98**	**23·4**
Land transport								
Railway	2,858	182	3,040	2,899	3,127	2·8	2·3	2·3
Goods transport by road	1,044	125	1,169	1,175	1,534	1·1	0·9	1·1
Total	**3,902**	**307**	**4,209**	**4,074**	**4,661**	**3·8**	**3·2**	**3·4**
Other industries	22,155	10,598	32,753	37,198	48,332	29·8	29·4	35·0
Grand Total	**81,018**	**28,978**	**109,996**	**126,664**	**138,385**	**100·0**	**100·0**	**100·0**

* Columns do not always aggregate to given totals because of rounding errors.

Source: Ministry of Labour. The statistics for 1952 and 1957 have been compiled in accordance with the 1948 edition of the *Standard Industrial Classification* and those for 1961 in accordance with the 1958 edition.

Table XV. Manufacturing Industry, Public Utilities and Construction Industry Labour Forces in Four Groupings

SOUTHAMPTON AREA* AND UNITED KINGDOM, JUNE 1961

Industry Group	Southampton Area Number	Percentage	United Kingdom Percentage†
'GROWTH' INDUSTRIES:			
Total	**35,972**	**55·6**	**36·6**
Chemical and allied trades	6,232	9·6	5·0
Vehicles	11,371	17·6	8·3
Public utilities—gas, electricity and water supply	3,330	5·2	3·6
Engineering	15,039	23·2	19·8
'PROGRESS' INDUSTRIES:			
Total	**12,009**	**18·5**	**19·8**
Paper and printing	1,848	2·9	5·7
Construction	10,161	15·7	14·0
'STEADY' INDUSTRIES:			
Total	**7,467**	**11·5**	**33·4**
Food, drink and tobacco	4,180	6·5	7·5
Clothing and footwear	117	0·2	5·3
Leather and fur	37	0·1	0·6
Bricks, glass, etc.	463	0·7	3·2
Timber, furniture, etc.	1,874	2·9	2·7
Other manufacturing	138	0·2	2·9
Metal goods	489	0·8	5·2
Metal manufacture	169	0·3	5·9
DECLINING INDUSTRIES:			
Total	**9,246**	**14·3**	**10·2**
Shipbuilding	8,903	13·8	2·3
Textiles	343	0·5	7·8
Overall Total	**64,694**	**100·0**	**100·0**

* Combined Employment Exchange areas; Southampton, Eastleigh and Hythe.
† Columns do not always aggregate to given totals because of rounding errors.
Source: Ministry of Labour. Compiled according to 1958 edition of the *Standard Industrial Classification*.

Table XVI. Size Distribution of Larger Establishments Employing 100 Persons and Over

SOUTHAMPTON AREA AND UNITED KINGDOM

No. of Employees	Southampton Area, 1962 No. of Establishments	Percentage	United Kingdom, 1958 Percentage
100–499	95	71·0	81·0
500–999	18	13·4	10·9
1000 and over	21	15·7	8·0
Total	**134**	**100·0**	**100·0**

Source: *United Kingdom: Census of Production 1958* (Part 133, Table 4), Southampton: Ministry of Labour (private communication).

XVIII

THE PORT OF SOUTHAMPTON

THE natural advantages contributing to the status of the port of Southampton, described in
Chapter IV, have been appreciated by man for at least two millennia. Though many
references to the past activity of the port appear in Chapter XV, the first step in its modern
development began in 1803, when an Act of Parliament was passed establishing the Harbour
Commissioners (the predecessors of the present Harbour Board) to administer the affairs of
the port and to have jurisdiction over its waterways. The Commissioners' operations seem
now to be trivial, but at that time new ground was being explored. The powers of the
Commissioners to borrow money for developing the port were strictly limited, and as
members of a public body they could not embark on any large speculative scheme, the
success of which could not be assured. This necessitated the formation of a private company,
and in 1836 an Act was passed incorporating the Southampton Dock Company; the
building of the first dock commenced two years later. The Company later ran into financial
difficulties and in 1892 was bought by the London and South Western Railway Company,
later to become the Southern Railway Company, and the docks remained under its control
until the nationalisation of the railways in 1947. Thus the docks came into the ownership
of the British Transport Commission, under the management of the Docks and Inland
Waterways Executive, latterly the British Transport Docks Board. The port therefore is
administered by a harmonious duality of the Harbour Board and the Docks Board (Plate XLII).

THE HARBOUR BOARD

The Harbour Board is the Statutory Authority for Southampton, and its area of
jurisdiction commences from an imaginary line drawn from Stansore Point on the western
shore of Southampton Water to Hillhead on the eastern shore, and extends up the river
Hamble to Bursledon Bridge, to Woodmill on the river Itchen, to Redbridge on the river
Test and to Eling Causeway (Fig. 17). The water area comprises $18\frac{1}{4}$ square miles, 8 square
miles of which uncovers at low tide; the length of foreshore under the Board's jurisdiction
is 45 miles.

The term 'Harbour Authority' is defined in the Merchant Shipping Act of 1894 as
including any person, corporation or unincorporated body who are proprietors of or have
the duty or power of constructing, improving, managing, regulating, maintaining or lighting a harbour. The Southampton Harbour Board is such an Authority, organised as a Public

Trust operating under Private and General Acts of Parliament. It consists of sixteen appointed and ten elected members, the latter mainly being payers of dues. The Board is a non-profit making organisation, and any balance remaining after all necessary expenditure has been met is used to provide additional facilities and to keep port dues and charges at their lowest economic level.

Port Operation and Information Service

The Harbour Board is fully conscious of the fact that a ship fulfils her main function, from the owner's point of view, while at sea, and the less time occupied in operations in port the greater is her earning power. It is for this reason that emphasis is made of the port's excellent deep-water facilities, and no vessel arriving or sailing, apart from the *Queens* and the largest tankers, has to wait because of insufficient depth of water. Associated with this facility is the recognition by the Board of the need for an up-to-date Port Operation and Information Service, to assist in co-ordinating the greatly increased tanker movements at Fawley and the general shipping using Southampton Docks; after many years of careful planning the Board established such a service in 1953. In January 1958 a Harbour Surveillance Radar and V.H.F. R/T Communications System was installed at the Board's Signal Station at Calshot near the entrance to Southampton Water, with a commanding view of both the eastern and western approaches. The Signal Station is continuously manned day and night by the Board's officers, assisted by a patrol officer who maintains a continuous patrol of the port area in a Harbour launch, which is fitted with marine radar, echo-sounding and R/T equipment. As a result, the Signal Station staff is in a position to provide pilots, ships' masters, shipping companies and agents with full details of movements in the area, as well as supplying information about weather conditions, wind speeds and other essential matters especially necessary to ships during periods of poor visibility.

Buoying and Lighting

The Board is also the Local Sea Fisheries Committee and the Local Lighthouse Authority, and is responsible for the provision and maintenance of all light buoys, navigation buoys and beacon lights. The navigational lighting of the deep water channel is chiefly by means of gas buoys (burning propane gas), and is in accordance with the International System of Buoyage and Lighting of Coasts. Transit beacons have been erected at the Board's Town Quay and Royal Pier and at other selected sites to assist pilots in handling large liners and tankers. The light buoys and navigation buoys are coloured black or black and white on the starboard hand and red or red and white on the port hand. All these and other aids to navigation within the port are kept under constant review with the object of improving the port's functions.

The Town Quay and Royal Pier

The Southampton Harbour Board also owns and operates the Royal Pier and the Town Quay. The former, opened in 1833 by the Princess Victoria, is the terminal for the 'Red Funnel' passenger and car-carrying vessels operating between Southampton and the Isle of

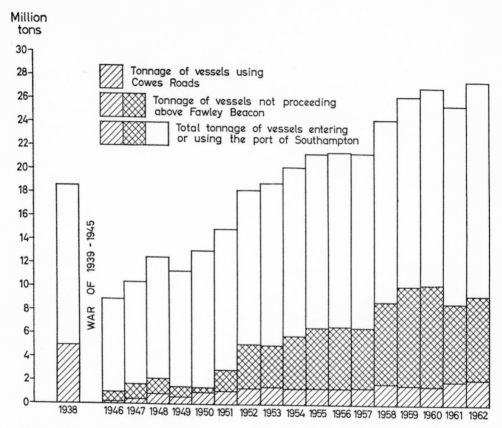

Fig. 68. Net register tonnage of shipping entering or using the port of Southampton, 1938, 1946–62
Based on the records of the Southampton Harbour Board.

Wight. During 1962 no less than 650,000 passengers were carried to and from the Isle of Wight, 150,000 were conveyed on short trips by launch, 65,000 motor vehicles were shipped or landed, and 32,000 tons of freight were moved via the Pier. In addition, 250,000 promenaders passed through the Pier's turnstiles, for it is, incidentally, a place of relaxation and entertainment.

The Town Quay provides 4500 feet of frontage, the depth of water alongside the berths having a maximum depth of 22 feet P.L.W.D. Sixteen modern electric luffing quayside cranes are provided, with capacities varying from 3 to 15 tons. Two new cranes were installed in August 1963, and early in that year tenders were invited for a further three. The open berths at the Town Quay enable vessels to dock and sail at all states of the tide without the use of tugs. Modern two-storeyed warehouses include bonded transit shed facilities, while open storage accommodation is available alongside a number of berths, used extensively in connection with imports of timber and for assembling exports. All the berths and warehouses are served by the Board's own railway system connecting with the main lines of British Railways, while good roads and lighting are provided at each berth and warehouse.

The trade at the Town Quay consists largely of traffic to and from western Europe, the Baltic countries and Canada. A considerable timber trade is undertaken at the Quay, involving direct discharge to road and railway vehicles, overside to barges, and on to the open timber store. In addition to timber and other wooden materials, substantial quantities of chemicals, fertilisers, vegetables, wallboard and motor vehicles are discharged, while the still expanding export trade includes manufactured goods, synthetic rubber, iron and steel and vehicle spares. A large tonnage of general cargo is shipped to the Isle of Wight by the Town Quay traders, who operate frequent regular daily services.

PORT TRAFFIC

Tonnage of Shipping

The total net register tonnage of shipping entering or using the port during 1962 amounted to 27,522,913, and during recent years Southampton has ranked second to London in this respect. An indication of the development of shipping using the port is given in the following Table, further illustrated by Fig. 68.

Table XVII. Net Register Tonnage and Number of Vessels entering or using the Port of Southampton

Year	No. of vessels	Net register tonnage
1928	14,846	11,446,946
1938	15,178	18,596,543
1948	11,634	12,482,975
1958	13,861	24,267,388
1961	13,950	25,397,250
1962	16,640	27,522,913

During 1962 the 27,522,913 tons of shipping entering or using the port were handled as follows:

Table XVIII. Handling of Shipping using the Port of Southampton, 1962

	No. of Ships	N.R.T.
Above Fawley Beacon		
Southampton Docks		
(British Transport Docks Board)	2,773	14,324,775
Town Quay and Royal Pier	5,220	1,068,156
River Itchen wharves	1,186	409,806
Southampton Water	577	85,640
Other wharves	618	181,214
Below Fawley Beacon		
Esso Terminal, Fawley	2,496	7,552,938
Shell-Mex Jetty, Hamble	1,170	896,888
Southampton Water	2,381	856,784
Cowes Roads	219	2,146,712
	16,640	**27,522,913**

Freight Traffic

The port of Southampton, in addition to being the principal passenger port of the United Kingdom, is also a cargo port, and the total of dry and wet cargo handled during 1962 amounted to 23,621,109 tons. The cargo can be divided into three separate sections: that handled at Southampton Docks; that handled at the Town Quay and at the various river wharves; and that handled at oil installations at the jetties of the principal oil companies established in the port.

Before the War of 1939-45, the port's total cargo trade aggregated about 2½ million tons per annum, of which 45 per cent passed through the Docks and 4 per cent comprised oil and kindred imports, the remainder being dealt with at the Town Quay and the river wharves. In 1962, of the cargo tonnage given above, no less than 21,315,512 tons consisted of oil, 964,802 tons were handled at the Town Quay and river wharves, and the balance was dealt with at Southampton Docks; the last is described in detail below. Oil is brought in large tanker shipments to the Esso Petroleum Company's refinery at Fawley (see p. 265), and to the Shell-Mex and B.P. jetties at Hamble. In addition to deliveries of refined products by road and rail tankers and by conventional tankers, smaller quantities are carried from Fawley by dracones, flexible 'sausage-like' containers. These dracones lie low in the water and are towed by small tugs; although some are in operation, they are still really in an experimental stage.

While crude oil is by far the largest single commodity handled in the port, other cargoes include:

Imports
Fruit and vegetables
Timber
Grain
Coal
Wool, hides and skins
Motor cars
Meat and dairy produce

Exports
Manufactured goods
Iron, steel and machinery
Motor vehicles
Woollens and worsteds
Scrap iron

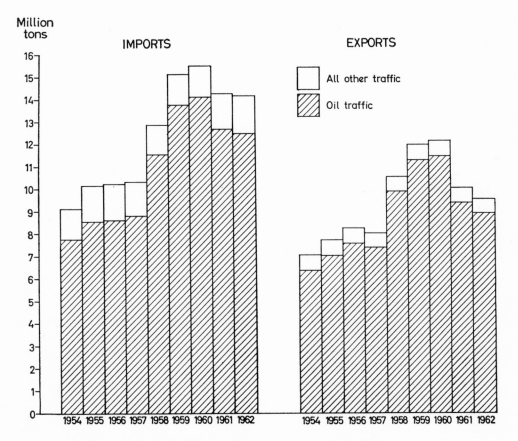

Fig. 69. Tonnage of cargo handled at the port of Southampton, 1954-62
Based on the records of the Southampton Harbour Board.

The total volume of cargo handled at the port each year since 1954 is illustrated in the following table; its breakdown into import and exports is shown on Fig. 69.

Table XIX. Tonnage of Cargo handled at the Port of Southampton

Year	Tons
1954	16,200,000
1955	17,900,000
1956	18,400,000
1957	18,400,000
1958	23,370,000
1959	27,082,284
1960	27,593,715
1961	24,269,507
1962	23,621,109

THE DOCKS

History

The Southampton Dock Company, incorporated in 1836, acquired 216 acres of land, mostly tidal mud-flats lying off the peninsula between the Test and the Itchen, for the construction of docks (Fig. 70). The Outer Dock was completed in 1842, two years after the railway between London and Southampton had been opened, and nine years later the Inner Dock was added, the only enclosed wet-dock in the port, and now unused. Later in the century river-quays were constructed along the sheltered frontage of the Itchen, and were gradually continued right round the made ground of the peninsula. From this was later excavated the Empress Dock, opened in 1890 by Queen Victoria, and now largely used for fruit-handling. By 1890 the length of quays totalled over 10,000 feet, and four dry-docks had also been completed.

In 1892 the Docks were acquired by the London and South Western Railway Company; since then the story has been one of almost continuous progress. The next major work was the Ocean Dock, completed in 1911 and originally constructed, it is said, in a successful attempt to entice the White Star Line from Liverpool. The first ship to leave this Ocean Dock was the 46,000-ton *Olympic*, in 1911. Since that date the world's largest vessels have used it (Plate XLIII), for it has a depth of 40 feet at low-water springs and of 53 feet at high-water springs. Thus the pattern of the so-called Old Docks was completed before the War of 1914-18, with fifty-one separate berths and a total quay length of over three miles; in 1913 a volume of shipping more than three times as great as in 1892 was handled.

With the grouping of the British railway companies in 1923, the Docks passed to the Southern Railway. Demands for accommodation for shipping continued to increase, and the Southern Railway Company embarked on a scheme to reclaim 400 acres of tidal mudflats along the northern fore-shore of the Test. In 1927 the enormous labour began of creating these New Docks, completed seven years later, with 1½ miles of quays, and 40 feet of water alongside even at low-water springs (Plate XLIV). The foreshore was reclaimed by dumping behind a sea-wall millions of tons of mud dredged from the Test. At its western end the King George V Drydock (Plate XLV) was completed in 1933; it is 1200 feet in length, and is designed to take a vessel of 100,000 tons.

Though the Docks suffered much damage during the War of 1939-45, this was rapidly made good, and the installations have been progressively improved to meet modern requirements, including the completion of passenger and cargo terminals, a cold store, modern handling equipment and the provision of new cranes and other mechanical appliances. These and many other schemes now in progress or projected will enhance the high reputation which Southampton enjoys for the efficient and speedy handling of ships, their passengers and cargo.

Lay-out of the Docks

The Docks are divided into two well-defined and compact areas, known as the Old Docks and New Docks

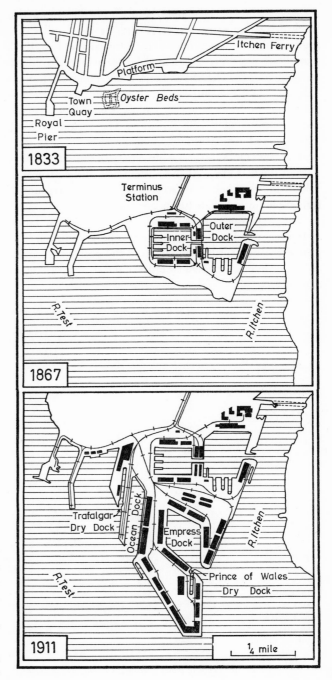

Fig. 70. Stages in growth of the Old Docks, 1833, 1867 and 1911 Based on maps in the possession of British Transport Docks Board.

respectively; reference should be made to the coloured map facing this page. The Old Docks, covering some 200 acres with nearly 4 miles of quays, form a triangle with its apex at the confluence of the rivers Itchen and Test, the Dock-head. On two sides of this triangle are river quays, indented by three large basins: the Ocean Dock, Empress Dock and Outer Dock. The Ocean Dock is the traditional home of the largest liners on the North Atlantic route; the Empress Dock is mainly concerned with the banana trade and with fruit from the Mediterranean; and the Outer Dock caters for the cross-Channel passenger and cargo ships of British Railways. The various river quays are used by miscellaneous passenger and cargo ships.

The New Docks serve a wide variety of shipping, ranging from the largest liners to small coasters (Plate XLIV). At the western end of the quay is the King George V Drydock, and behind the quayline is an area of 130 acres of reclaimed land which is developing as a thriving industrial estate (see p. 261 and Fig. 66).

The deep-water quays at both the Old and New Docks are dredged to a minimum of 40 feet, enough for the largest liners to lie alongside at low water. All quays are flanked by passenger-cargo sheds, ranging from the post-war terminals to single-storey transit sheds, and are all inter-connected by railway and road affording access at the Dock boundary to the main routes.

Table XX. Summary of Docks and Quays

Dock or quay	Year opened	Area	Nominal dredged depth below chart datum	Length of quays	Width of entrance
			ft.	ft.	ft.
New Docks	1934	—	40	8,014	—
Ocean Dock	1911	15½ acres	40	3,807	400
Test Quays and South Quay	1902	—	27–32	4,679	—
Empress Dock	1890	18½ acres	24–27	3,880	159
Itchen Quays	1895	—	20–34	4,046	—
Outer Dock	1842	16 acres	18	2,621	150

Dry-docks

	No. 7 King George V Dock		No. 6 Trafalgar Dock		No. 5 Prince of Wales Dock		No. 4		No. 3		No. 2	
Year opened	1933		1905		1895		1879		1854		1847	
	ft.	in.	ft.	in.	ft.	in.	ft.	in.	ft.	in.	ft.	in.
Length overall	1,200	0	912	3	745	0	479	9	523	0	281	0
Length at floor level	1,141	6	852	0	729	0	451	0	501	0	240	0
Width at entrance	135	0	100	0	91	0	55	0	80	0	50	0
Blocks below chart datum	35	6	20	0	18	6	9	9	8	0	1	0
Depth of sill below chart datum	37	6	22	0	22	0	10	10	11	9	1	2

To find depth of water over blocks or sill, add predicted tidal rise to above figures.

Passenger Traffic

In 1824 it is recorded that 7980 passengers used Southampton; by 1962 the annual total exceeded half a million (Fig. 71), and for the past thirty years or so there has been no serious challenge to Southampton's position as Britain's premier ocean passenger port. The latest statistics show that it deals with 62 per cent of the ocean-going passengers to and from the United Kingdom, while Southampton's share of those who travel to and from the United States and to and from South Africa amounts to 79 and 89 per cent respectively.

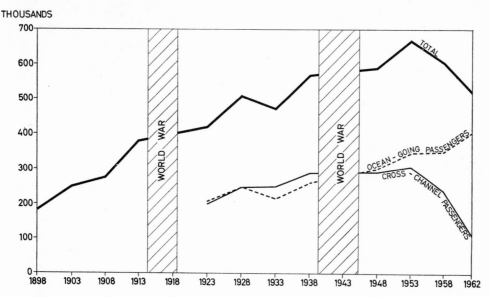

Fig. 71. Growth of number of passengers travelling via Southampton Docks, 1898-1962
Based on the records of British Transport Docks Board.

The ocean services using Southampton are provided by some thirty of the world's principal shipping companies, linking Britain with nearly a hundred world ports. On the North Atlantic the services to the United States and Canada are maintained by such famous lines as Cunard, United States Lines, French Line, Holland-America and Norddeutscher Lloyd. These services account for about 40 per cent of the traffic of the Docks (Fig. 72).

Southampton is also the principal port linking the United Kingdom with South Africa. Every Thursday at 4 p.m. the Union Castle Mail Service leaves for Capetown and other South African ports, and every Friday a sister ship berths at Southampton.

The advent of the P. & O.-Orient Line's *Oriana* and *Canberra*, both based on Southampton, together with the inauguration of services by the Europe-Australia Line and the Cogedar Line, has given an impetus to passenger trade with Australia and New Zealand, a route which is also served by the Nederland Line R.D.M., the New Zealand Shipping

Us

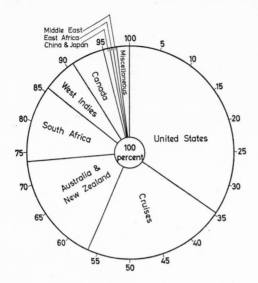

Fig. 72. Analysis of passenger traffic using Southampton Docks, according to countries of origin and destination, 1962

Based on the records of British Transport Docks Board.

Company, Royal Rotterdam Lloyd, the Shaw Savill Line and the Sitmar Line. Lines connecting Southampton with the Far East include P. & O.-Orient, Hamburg-America and Norddeutscher Lloyd, whilst the West Indies are served by Elders & Fyffes, French Line, Cia. Tras. Española, Grimaldi Line and the Royal Netherlands Steamship Company. Cross-Channel services to Havre and St. Malo are operated by British Railways. Southampton is also a main base for liner cruises, and during a current season as many as fifty are run by P. & O.-Orient, Royal Mail Lines and other companies.

Passenger Reception Facilities

It takes only four and a half days to cross the Atlantic, yet speed afloat is not by itself enough; there must also be rapid clearance of passengers and baggage at the terminal ports to enable them to reach their destinations quickly and in comfort. Nowhere is this better understood than at Southampton, where the accommodation provided for passengers has constantly been modernised and the amenities provided at the terminals have set a new standard in passenger reception.

Typical of the modern style of passenger accommodation is the Ocean Terminal (Plate XLIII), the first of the post-war terminals built at Southampton. The original sheds on this site were only single storey, but the opportunity was taken of war damage to replace them with a better type of accommodation. The problem was to provide sufficient floor space within the limitations of the site and within a reasonable distance of the quayside for dealing with a large number of passengers, up to 1700 by one of the *Queens*, bearing in mind the more complex customs and immigration procedure necessitated by post-war regulations. This was solved by the construction of a double-storey building, with the upper floor devoted exclusively to passenger reception and customs examination and the ground floor to boat-trains, cargo, stores, motor cars and quayside offices, the two floors being connected by escalators, stairways and lifts. Passenger accommodation at the Ocean Terminal consists of two reception halls, with adjoining customs examination halls. The link between ship and shore at first-floor level is by electro-hydraulic telescopic gangways connecting the ship with the entrance vestibules of the reception halls. The railway platform on the ground floor can accommodate two boat-trains simultaneously, a great boon in the rapid dispersal of passengers.

The experience gained at the Ocean Terminal has been put to good use in the design of later passenger and cargo buildings, notably at 102 berth at the New Docks. Here war-damaged sheds have been replaced by a large double-storey passenger-cargo terminal for use by the Union Castle liners on the South African service. This building provides the same amenities for passengers as at the Ocean Terminal, but greater provision has, of course, had to be made for substantial cargoes from South Africa. Other recent new building includes passenger reception halls at 105/6 berth, designed to deal with the complements of up to 2000 passengers carried in the *Oriana* and *Canberra*, and smaller halls at berths 25, 31 and 46.

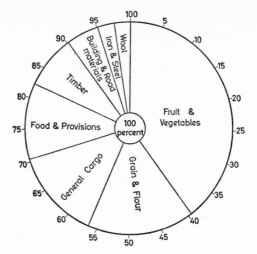

Fig. 73. Analysis of imports at Southampton Docks, 1962

Based on the records of British Transport Docks Board.

Freight Traffic

Because of its pre-eminence as a passenger port, the role of Southampton as a cargo port is apt to be overlooked, though admittedly on a national scale as yet it is not very important; in 1961 only 4 per cent of Britain's foreign trade by weight passed through the port, a proportion virtually unchanged since 1938. By value, however, Southampton stands fifth among British ports, with a total value of imports and exports of £305 million in 1962. The Docks are essentially concerned with transit rather than with storage, specialising in imports of fruit, foodstuffs, vegetables and other perishable produce which require quick handling and despatch (Figs. 73-4).

Produce from South Africa forms the biggest item of cargo; practically the whole of the deciduous and over half the citrus fruit crop from the Republic to Great Britain is landed at Southampton. The bulk of South African wines, wool, hides and skins destined for the United Kingdom is also received here, in addition to canned goods and copper. Other principal imports include vegetables from the Channel Islands, northern France and North Africa; bananas from the West Indies and West Africa; grain from Australia and Canada; meat and dairy produce from New Zealand; tobacco from the United States and India; and timber from the Baltic countries and British Columbia.

A good example of Southampton's versatility in securing and successfully coping with new traffic is shown by the decision of the French motor-manufacturing firm of Renault to use the Docks for the import of its cars into Britain. The firm has established a servicing depôt at the New Docks to which cars are brought from France in 'drive-on-drive-off' ships, resulting

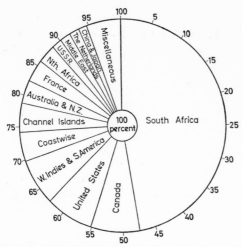

Fig. 74. Analysis of imports and exports through Southampton Docks, according to countries of origin and destination, 1962
Based on the records of British Transport Docks Board.

in a great saving of time and labour.

Exports from Southampton comprise practically a cross-section of British manufactured goods, consigned to many parts of the world. As most of the services from Southampton are by fast passenger-cargo liners on regular schedules, notably those to North America and South Africa, express freight figures largely in the export list.

The growth of holiday motoring on the Continent has prompted the introduction of two new passenger and car ferry services from Southampton Docks, both commencing in 1964. One is between Southampton and Cherbourg, for which two new 'drive-on-drive-off' ships have been built and a berth specially adapted in the Outer Dock, and the other between Southampton and Santander, the first direct car ferry service between Britain and Spain.

The proximity of Southampton to the continent of Europe makes it a convenient port for transhipment traffic to and from northern France, Belgium, the Netherlands and Germany. There is also an export trade with the Channel Islands by the cargo ships of British Railways.

Cargo Accommodation and Handling

The rapid clearance of cargo has been achieved largely by the provision of modern quayside accommodation and cargo-handling equipment, together with good rail communications, though the road-system from Southampton as yet leaves much to be desired. Typical examples of modern quayside shed design are to be found at 102 berth, completed in 1956, principally for dealing with imports from South Africa, and at berths 26/27 and 41, more recently completed for the reception of fruit and produce. The cold store situated at the western end of the New Docks alongside the deep-water quay was brought into operation in 1958, to replace the store destroyed during the War of 1939-45. It has a total refrigerated capacity of 419,000 cubic feet, which can if required be extended to take in another 220,000 cubic feet. The store is used mainly for refrigerated meat and produce from New Zealand.

Grain imports are handled at the Solent Flour Mills of Joseph Rank Ltd. at the New Docks, where four suction pipes discharge grain direct from the hold of a ship at the rate of 240 tons an hour, and transfer it to the mill's silo. The milled products are distributed over a large area of southern England by rail, road and coasting-vessel.

Bananas, another type of freight demanding specialised equipment, are dealt with at 25 berth, where the shed accommodation and discharging equipment have recently been modernised. The latter comprises four shore-based elevators and conveyors with a maximum rate of discharge of 14,400 stems an hour, compared with 9600 by the former equipment. Over 5 million stems are landed each year.

The Docks have pursued an energetic and far-sighted policy of modernisation of cargo-handling equipment. All cranes are electrically operated, varying in lifting power from a 150-ton floating crane to a 2-ton quayside crane. The quays are equipped with level-luffing rail-travelling cranes, ranging from 2 to 10 ton capacity. In addition, 15-ton diesel-electric rail-cranes are capable of travelling to any part of the Docks rail-system, and mobile diesel-electric cranes are used for quayside and shed work. A large number of fork-lift trucks, mobile cranes, ship-to-shore conveyors and other mechanical aids have been installed, so as to play their part in the more economical handling of cargo and quicker turn-round of ships.

Dry-docking and Repairing

The service available to shipowners for the maintenance, overhaul and repair of ships is one of the advantages which has helped the development of Southampton Docks (see pp. 269-72). Six dry-docks (see Table XX) owned by British Transport Docks range in length from 281 feet to 1200 feet, and provide accommodation for all types of ships up to the world's largest liner, the 83,000-ton *Queen Elizabeth*.

Ship repairs at the Docks (see p. 269) are carried out principally by the firms of Harland and Wolff and John I. Thornycroft. British Railways have a ship-repairing establishment serving the whole of their Southern Region fleet.

THE ROCHDALE COMMITTEE AND THE FUTURE

With its great natural advantages and its location in one of the most rapidly expanding regions of the country, Southampton is well placed to attract cargo trade. The Rochdale committee on the Major Ports★ recommended a high priority for the expansion of the Docks to cope with the forecast increase of imports and exports and with the trend towards larger vessels requiring deep-water berths. Whether or not the Rochdale recommendations for amalgamating ports and setting up new local port authorities are implemented, the expansion of Southampton Docks is already under active consideration by the British Transport Docks Board. However, trade will not automatically come to or be retained by Southampton; serious problems face the port in increasing the value of its commerce, and even if it does expand, for various reasons it is unlikely to provide much more employment than at the present time (see p. 272).

The first problem is that the retention of existing passenger traffic is by no means certain, and this is all the more serious since Southampton is so predominantly a passenger port.

★ *The major ports of Great Britain.* Report of the Committee of Inquiry: 1961-2. Cmnd. 1824.

The Rochdale Committee Report stresses the present relative insignificance of South-ampton as a dry-cargo port. Their figures indicated that in 1961 the total volume of imports was 12·1 million tons (excluding coastal traffic) and of exports 1·5 million tons. But no less than 11·2 million tons of imports and 1·1 million tons of exports were of petroleum, crude and refined, entering and leaving the Esso Refinery at Fawley and other private installations outside the Docks (see p. 282). Dry-cargo imports (excluding oil, but including grain, ores, timber and coal) were therefore only 0·9 million tons and dry-cargo exports 0·5 million tons, or merely 1·9 per cent and 2·6 per cent respectively of the dry-cargo imports and exports of Great Britain as a whole. The dry-cargo trade admittedly has been growing in recent years, but it is still very small, and passenger vessels are estimated to be responsible for about two-thirds of the total gross revenue of the port.

Moreover, sea-borne passenger traffic, on which Southampton depends so heavily, is under severe competition from air transport. In 1938, 96 per cent of all passengers leaving or entering Great Britain travelled by sea and only 4 per cent by air, but in 1962 air pass-engers surpassed those by sea by 6 per cent. Only the great overall expansion in foreign travel during this period has prevented the airlines from cutting into the actual number of passengers carried by sea. The total number of passengers leaving and entering the United Kingdom rose from 4,895,000 in 1938 to 14,898,000 in 1962; sea movements increased from 4,715,000 to 7,223,000, but air movements from 179,000 to 7,675,000. The big question for the future, which vitally affects Southampton, is whether air transport is going to expand so rapidly as actually to deplete the number of passengers travelling by sea. This is not the place to attempt any forecast, but competition is already intense, and the best guess is that sea-transport may by strenuous efforts be able to maintain its existing volume of traffic.

A partial solution is now being found in the diversion of passenger liners to holiday cruises in winter-time, when their services for direct transport are not in such great demand, especially on the North Atlantic route. Cruising has so far been successful and is being extended to more liners, including even the *Queen Elizabeth* and the *Queen Mary*. South-ampton is well placed geographically for this extension of cruising, situated between the greatest and most prosperous concentrations of population in the United Kingdom and the warm seas on which people may be induced to spend their holidays. But some vessels based on Southampton cruise from New York to tap the richer American market, in which case the retention of business by the shipping companies does not bring much advantage to Southampton.

However, even if sea passenger traffic for the whole country should be reduced, South-ampton may be able to obtain an increasing share of the total, which may in turn enable it to retain its present volume of passengers. In addition to attempts to build up a new market, the prospects for passenger traffic through Southampton will depend on increasing the efficiency of sea passenger transport in all its aspects, including the operation of the ships themselves, the running of the Docks, and the maintenance of the ships by local ship-repairing firms. If the struggle to maintain the demand for passenger sailing from South-ampton should not succeed, then a decline in passenger traffic would have to be offset against the anticipated expansion of cargo trade. Whether or not there was any net increase in the activity of the port would obviously depend on the balance between the contraction of the one and the expansion of the other.

The forecast increase in cargo trade is based on the Rochdale Committee's estimates of imports and exports up to 1980, which in turn are based on assumptions about the percentage annual rate of growth of the national economy, and on the further assumption that Southampton should be able to increase its share of the total overseas trade. The hopes of Southampton are pinned to the expansion of general dry-cargo trade, of which the Rochdale Committee forecast a doubling between the average for 1958-60 and 1980, on the assumption of a 3 per cent annual increase in the Gross Domestic Product.* Dry-cargo imports into Britain were forecast to increase from 18 million tons to 32 million tons, and exports from 17 million tons to 38 million tons; of this total of 35 million tons of additional dry cargo estimated for 1980, Southampton is expected to obtain 2¾ million tons. This is 8 per cent of the total increase, and would raise Southampton's dry-cargo trade from 1¼ to 4 million tons, and its share in the national total from 3 per cent to 5½ per cent. This expansion will of course be expected to proceed gradually. Half a million tons can be catered for by existing accommodation, but new berths would be needed for some 2½ million tons by 1980, and this is why the British Transport Docks Board is already considering detailed plans for a new Western Dock along the river Test between the existing New Docks and Redbridge, costing some £20 millions. If this scheme is approved, work may begin about 1966, to be completed by about 1971.

Thus further development of the port seems probable, and it will continue to play a significant part in the growth of industry and population within Southampton and its region. Despite competition from the air, the faith of the ship-owner in the future of sea-travel is evidenced by the building in recent years of such liners as *Oriana*, *Canberra*, *Transvaal Castle*, *Northern Star*, *Rotterdam* and *France*. The British Transport Docks Board, in conjunction with the Harbour Board, continues to make every endeavour to anticipate shipping developments and to satisfy the requirements of both ship-owners and shippers.

* On the more optimistic assumption of a 4 per cent rate of growth, the doubling of dry-cargo trade would be achieved by 1975.

XIX

COMMUNICATIONS

SOUTHAMPTON occupies a focal point in a chalk basin, filled with Tertiary sands and clays. The rim of exposed chalk surrounds the basin, although it has been breached by the sea on both sides of the Isle of Wight. It is widest in the north of Hampshire; the main railway to London takes 24 miles to traverse it. Except for the Avon, none of the mainland rivers crosses it and the type of gap found in the North Downs is lacking. Because of this, both rail and road have appreciable climbs over the chalk rim and, although plans were made, it has never been crossed by canal.

Changes in sea-level since Quaternary times have combined with the breaching of the Chalk to flood the lower reaches of the rivers, and tidal inlets, of which Southampton Water is predominant, are a feature of the coastline. Because of this, together with the insularity of Wight, local water transport is still of importance in this region. In general, inland communications lead from the landing places, following river valleys where possible, and then climbing to 400 feet or more to cross the chalk country. With the establishment of Southampton as the principal landing-place, it has become a focal point in a radial transport network. However, the pattern is complicated by the presence of other major traffic sources, such as Bournemouth, the combined naval base and resort of Portsmouth and Southsea, and such historic local centres as Winchester. Partly for historical reasons, the road and rail networks do not coincide. For instance, Winchester is the principal road centre, but for the railways Eastleigh is the main junction point. The communications along the coast may be treated as part of the radial system based on Southampton, but there are significant differences in the character of both road and rail to the west, to the east and to the north of the town.

ROADS

Southern Hampshire was a region of prehistoric settlement, and the trackways and ridgeways to be found on the chalk hills are mentioned in the section below on 'Rights of Way'. The first planned road system, constructed by the Romans, was based on the tribal capital of Winchester and their ports at Bitterne on the Itchen and Portchester on Portsmouth Harbour. Sections of this network are still in use. For instance, their Winchester to Silchester road now forms part of the modern A33 between Winchester and Basingstoke; the Old Sarum road is followed by an unclassified road from Winchester to Farley Mount.

With the temporary breakdown of national trade and government after the departure of the Romans, road traffic declined. Even the medieval revival was based on roads which, apart from surviving Roman sections, were not far removed from prehistoric trackways.

However, crown, church and nobility did promote some bridge building, and widened versions of medieval bridges cross the Avon at Fordingbridge and Christchurch.

But the great revival of the roads of southern Hampshire took place in the eighteenth and early nineteenth centuries, when many stretches, previously left to the scant attention of the parishes, were taken over by turnpike trusts, who met the cost of improvements by levying tolls. The toll-houses adjoined the turnpike gates and good examples survive at Romsey, Twyford and Botley. The ultimate network of turnpiked roads coincided roughly with the present A-class roads, as shown on Fig. 43, together with a few B roads. Stage wagons and stage coaches provided services which, although by modern standards were slow and expensive, were scheduled and quite reliable. Inns fulfilled the functions now divided between filling station, coach station and café, and the Star Hotel in Southampton High Street still bears an engraved stone announcing the departure of coaches for London.

The spread of railways eroded long distance road traffic, toll revenues fell, and local authorities took over the main roads. Perhaps because of the number of motoring pioneers, including Lord Montagu, who resided in the county, Hampshire was extremely progressive in tarring its main roads to meet the transition from horse-drawn vehicles to the rubber-tyred automobile. Its present road system lies mainly in the sector between the A3 Portsmouth road and the A30 to Salisbury and the West. Before the War of 1939-45, by-passes were constructed at Totton, Romsey and Winchester. At present, the capacity of the system is about adequate for the traffic for most of the time, but at peak periods congestion occurs in or near the towns. Flat junctions at Lyndhurst and Totton, and the narrow streets and complex crossings in Winchester sometimes cause delays. Since the war, considerable sections of the A31 between Winchester and Farnham have been widened into dual carriageways, and the new road to Fawley, by-passing Marchwood, is well advanced. The A33, which between Southampton and Winchester carries traffic for both London and the North, is to be relieved by a new parallel road a short distance to the west.

Outside the three county boroughs, most of the local bus services are provided by the nationalised Hants and Dorset Company. However, Southdown, Aldershot and District, and Wilts and Dorset all penetrate the area and a few independent operators survive. Of the latter, King Alfred Motor Services, operating in and around Winchester between three of the 'big company' territories, are an outstanding example. On the road haulage side, B.R.S. (Parcels) Ltd. maintains at Eastleigh the largest depôt in the south of England. An independent concern, Victory Transport Ltd., has built up an extensive delivery service based on warehouses located in the residential village of Rownhams.

BRIDGES AND FERRIES

During the great period of road improvement in the late eighteenth century, two bridges were opened to reduce the road distance from Southampton to Portsmouth by four miles. They each had spans of sufficient height and width to avoid interference with navigation; that over the Itchen at Northam is referred to below (p. 302). The bridge over the Hamble river at Bursledon was opened by a statutory company in 1798. It was linked to

the existing Southampton to Portsmouth route by a three-mile road to Bitterne to the west
and a two-mile connection to Parkgate in the east. These new roads are still distinctive, having a Roman directness about them. The Bursledon bridge was purchased by the County
Council in 1930, was subsequently freed from tolls, and was then rebuilt. Now the only
tolls which survive on Hampshire roads are payable for the use of the causeway at Lymington, and to Winchester College for a crossing by the tide-mill at Eling. Many of the bridges
of the pre-motor era have been replaced, as at Hayling Island, Portsea Island and, in 1963, at
Stockbridge. At Redbridge, replacement was associated with new approach roads, so the
old bridges over the two streams of the Test were preserved (Plate XLVII). As one of these
was built in the seventeenth century and the other in the late eighteenth, they combine with
the twentieth-century concrete bridge to illustrate well the development of bridge construction.

Intermediate between the fixed bridges and the ferries are the floating bridges, constructed mainly in the 'thirties and 'fifties of last century. These consisted of rafts with steam
engines, that hauled themselves across narrow navigable waters with strong tides by means
of chains, which normally lay on the bottom. Like ferries, their availability was restricted
but, unlike many contemporary ferries, they could carry road vehicles. Where fixed bridges
were impracticable they saved considerable road journeys—for instance, 12 miles from Cowes
to East Cowes via Newport, or less than half a mile against 15 miles round Portsmouth
Harbour from Portsmouth to Gosport. In the latter case, however, there was competition
from more rapid passenger ferries, and vehicular traffic, if its journey was an appreciable
distance from the floating bridge terminals, took the roundabout toll-free road. In 1959 there
appeared to be no chance of obtaining sufficient revenue to purchase new chains and so, in
default of an arrangement with the Portsmouth and Gosport local authorities, the bridge
was closed. The contrasting situation in Southampton is mentioned on p. 304.

The principal ferries are shown in Fig. 75, varying in size from a one-man boat at
Hamble to the modern steamers on the Isle of Wight services. The Southampton to Cowes
service is maintained by the Southampton, Isle of Wight and South of England Royal Mail
Steam Packet Company, incorporated in 1861, which has now adopted the unofficial but
time-saving title of 'Red Funnel Line'. All its paddle steamers have gone and, as suitable
facilities are available at both landing places, diesel vessels now carry both passengers and
vehicles. This is also the case on the Lymington to Yarmouth route, operated by British
Railways, although here, owing to the narrowness of the Lymington river, special double-
ended vessels, which need not turn round, are employed. Most of the Island passenger
traffic passes through Portsmouth, from which two services are operated. The passenger
boats use Ryde pier, whose length, necessitated by the gently shelving shore, is traversed by
a tramway, while the Island railway runs right out to the end of the pier. The car ferries run
to Fishbourne at the mouth of Wootton Creek, over 2 miles west of Ryde. From 1882, a
train ferry operated from Langstone to St. Helens, but this proved impractical and was
abandoned six years later.

Apart from those serving the Isle of Wight, only three ferries convey appreciable
volumes of traffic all the year round. The Eastney to Hayling boat carries a light traffic, the

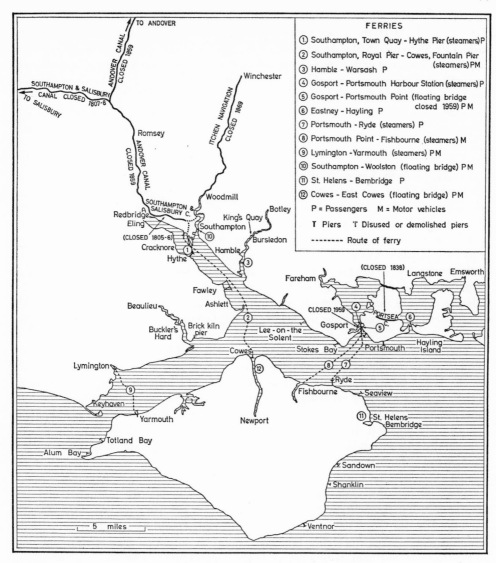

FERRIES

① Southampton, Town Quay – Hythe Pier (steamers) P
② Southampton, Royal Pier – Cowes, Fountain Pier (steamers) PM
③ Hamble – Warsash P
④ Gosport – Portsmouth Harbour Station (steamers) P
⑤ Gosport – Portsmouth Point (floating bridge closed 1959) PM
⑥ Eastney – Hayling P
⑦ Portsmouth – Ryde (steamers) P
⑧ Portsmouth Point – Fishbourne (steamers) M
⑨ Lymington – Yarmouth (steamers) PM
⑩ Southampton – Woolston (floating bridge) PM
⑪ St. Helens – Bembridge P
⑫ Cowes – East Cowes (floating bridge) PM

P = Passengers   M = Motor vehicles

⊥ Piers   ⊤ Disused or demolished piers

------- Route of ferry

Fig. 75. Ferry services in Southampton Water and the Solent

Based on miscellaneous sources, especially on information provided by Mr. J. P. M. Pannell of the Southampton Harbour Board.

Portsmouth Harbour boats a very heavy one, while the Southampton to Hythe service is also well used. At Hythe a pier about 700 yards long, traversed by an electric tramway, enables ferries to call at all states of the tide. This is the last survivor of a number of ferries linking Southampton with points on the southern side of the Test, which succumbed to the competition of buses going round by Totton. The ferry from the Town Quay to Cracknore Hard is still available, but its use necessitates special arrangements with Messrs. Husband's Shipyard.

OTHER LOCAL WATER TRANSPORT

In addition to the ferries, small trading vessels carry appreciable quantities of freight to and from the Island, the main landing places being the Medina Wharf at Cowes for coal, and Newport for general cargo. Apart from this traffic, estuarine and coastal trade has greatly declined, and inland navigation has ceased.

Improvements to the river Itchen, consisting of cuts across meanders and the provision of locks to maintain depths, took place over many years, but were virtually complete, as far as Winchester, by 1710. The Itchen Navigation finally succumbed to rail competition in 1869. Now the locks have been replaced by weirs and some of the cuts have been drained; only the towpath remains virtually intact. The best impression of the appearance of the canal is obtained by visiting the top level, which is maintained for the Winchester College boats.

There was no corresponding Test Navigation. The Andover Canal followed the valleys of the Test and the Anton as an entirely new cut; from its opening in 1796 it carried a traffic which, though steady, was insufficient to give a normal return on its capital. In 1854 the railway reached Andover via Basingstoke, and although this was a roundabout route the canal proprietors decided to meet its competition by turning themselves into a rival railway company. They closed their canal in 1859 and about 14 of its 22 miles were filled in and followed by railway tracks. Many of the abandoned meanders of the waterway were later filled in, but a number of sections, now resembling large overgrown ditches, may still be seen.

The least successful of the canals of southern Hampshire was the Salisbury and Southampton, which in fact never achieved completion. It was planned to consist of two branches from the Andover Canal, one from Kimbridge to Salisbury and the second from Redbridge to Southampton. The latter section followed roughly the line of the present railway through to the Itchen at Northam, with a branch to the Town Quay. As for much of its length it was parallel to the river Test, there was some adverse criticism, summarised by a contemporary poet as follows:

'Southampton's wise sons found their river so large,
Tho' 'twould carry a ship, 'twould not carry a barge,
But soon this defect their sage noddles supply'd
For they cut a snug ditch to run close by its side.'

Presumably, the poet was unaware that at least one canal barge had been swamped in the Test, between Redbridge and Southampton. More relevant was the fact that coasting vessels of the day could easily get up to Redbridge. However, in this pre-railway age there were hopes of a link between the Itchen Navigation and the Basingstoke Canal, and if these had materialised the Redbridge to Northam section would have formed part of a barge through-route from Andover to the Thames. Bearing in mind the convenience and cheapness of horse towage, it would seem that, although of doubtful economic value, the Southampton branch was not absurd. Unfortunately, the difficulties experienced in constructing the tunnel under the Southampton plateau did prove a major stumbling block. Engineering troubles were also encountered on the Salisbury section, funds ran out, support evaporated and so the project collapsed, leaving little behind. It was brought to mind recently when the foundations of some new flats at Redbridge penetrated its filled-up bed.

Fig. 75 also shows the Portsea Canal, part of the inland waterway route from London to Portsmouth, whose brief period of prosperity did not outlast the French threat to coastal traffic during the Napoleonic Wars. The heavy industrial traffic, which was the mainstay of the Midland and Northern canals, was lacking in southern Hampshire, and for general traffic road competition was so strong that they failed to prosper, even before the coming of the railways.

On the other hand, the barges which sailed up to the numerous landing places in the rivers and inlets of southern Hampshire enjoyed years of relative prosperity. Some, though not all, of these landing places are shown in Fig. 75; few have survived the competition of mechanised road transport. A typical run was with coal, off-loaded from a collier brig at Portsmouth or Southampton, up to the brickworks at Bailey's Hard on the Beaulieu river, with a return load of bricks. Now only a few special runs continue, such as the conveyance of coal from Portsmouth to Fareham or petroleum products from Hamble to Portsmouth.

Coastal passenger traffic has also declined, and the piers at such places as Alum Bay and Lee-on-the-Solent have been demolished. The eastern Wight resorts retain their piers, but these are used for occasional summer excursions only. Just as the motor lorry harmed the coastal freight trade, so cars and coaches have almost extinguished the coastal pleasure steamer.

RAILWAYS (Fig. 76)

The first main line in Hampshire, the London and Southampton, was completed in 1840. It entered the Itchen valley north of Winchester, crossed a meander of the river south of St. Denys by a causeway and ended at the present Terminus station on the marsh to the east of the town. Significantly, this was placed to one side, on a curve, and a branch ran past it into the Docks, then under construction by the associated Southampton Dock Company. In 1842 the Outer Dock was used for the first time by two P. & O. boats, and what were probably the first boat trains ran on to the quayside to meet them. Mainly to overcome financial difficulties, the railway company acquired the Docks in 1892 (see p. 278), and they became an integral part of the London and South Western and, from 1923, the Southern Railway system. Since 1948, as part of the nationalised transport undertaking, dock management has been separated from the railways. This reflects the increasing importance of road transport, but Southampton remains, perhaps more than any other, a railway port.

Its projects for a branch from Basingstoke to Bristol having been frustrated by the Great Western Railway, the Southampton company turned its attention to Portsmouth. Multifarious opposition kept the railway clear of the town until 1847, and the Southampton company's branch of 1841 left the main line at what was to become Eastleigh, and ran through Fareham to terminate on the western side of Portsmouth Harbour at Gosport. Even here the Service authorities were successful in preventing the penetration of moribund fortifications, and the railway ended three-quarters of a mile short of the Portsmouth ferry. However, it was Portsmouth's first railway, and in order that its people should not have to be associated with Southampton any more than they wished, the railway company changed its name to 'London and South Western'.

They provided impressive buildings, classical in style, at their three terminals at Gosport, Southampton and Nine Elms, London. All three avoided rebuilding to accommodate the growth of traffic, as each was partially replaced by another station—Gosport by Portsmouth, Southampton by the present Southampton Central, and Nine Elms when the line was extended to Waterloo in 1848. Although damaged by bombing, the magnificent colonnade of Gosport is scheduled for preservation, and this, with Southampton Terminus, which is also scheduled, provide almost unaltered examples of an early provincial station.

In 1847 the single-line extension from Southampton to Dorchester by way of Ringwood and Wareham was opened; this branched off at Northam and followed roughly the line of the derelict canal to Redbridge. Although the railway and canal tunnels under the Southampton plateau did not coincide either in level or alignment, the old tunnel does seem to have been responsible for the partial collapse of the new, just before the railway was due to open. The crisis was met by taking the trains on horse-drawn lorries through the streets, and starting them from the western side of the tunnel. The Southampton and Dorchester line was not built to the same standards as the London and Southampton, either in profile or alignment. There was no tunnel beyond Southampton, but its circuitous course, reflecting not only relief features but also the needs both to avoid standing timber in the New Forest and also to reach the towns of Ringwood, Wimborne and Wareham, earned it the nickname of 'Castleman's Corkscrew'. It did not, of course, go near Bournemouth, which was then at an embryonic stage as the 'bath chair metropolis', whose denizens seemed to have set more store by privacy and quiet than by accessibility. However, this could not last, and in 1870 the branch line from Ringwood to Christchurch was extended into Bournemouth. Eighteen years later, a cut-off line was constructed from Brockenhurst to Christchurch and, together with an 'upgraded' Christchurch to Bournemouth section, this became the new main line. What railwaymen still call the 'Old Road' declined in importance until now it has suffered the fate of inclusion in Dr. Beeching's list.

There has already been some shrinkage of the railway network, generally on the principle that the last lines to be constructed, usually carrying light traffic, have been the first to

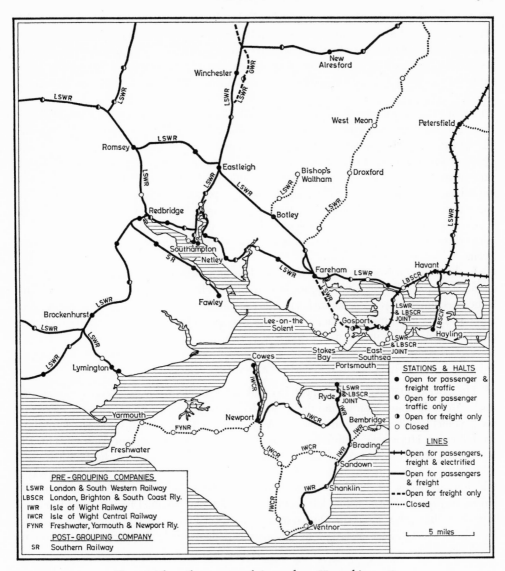

Fig. 76. The railway network in southern Hampshire, 1962
Based on information provided by British Railways.

go. It began during the War of 1914-18 with the closure of the East Southsea and Stokes Bay branches, and of the station on the Royal Pier at Southampton. (The piers at Stokes Bay and Southampton were used by the Armed Services.) Although it was not considered worth while to reopen these lines after the war, the first withdrawal for purely economic reasons came in 1930, when the passenger service to Lee-on-the-Solent was ended. This was a case of a 'dream Bournemouth' which had failed to materialise. But as shown in Fig. 77, abandonment of the weaker lines was accompanied by development of the stronger, and in 1937 the main line from London to Portsmouth was electrified for passenger traffic. To justify electrification, usually both freight and passenger trains would use electric traction, though on the Portsmouth line the increase in passenger traffic alone paid for the new equipment. Freight trains and passenger trains of steam rolling stock from other lines continued to be hauled by steam locomotives. The predominance of passenger revenue is general in Hampshire, though a striking exception is the Fawley branch, which derives much more of its revenue from freight, mainly petroleum, than from passengers. It is also exceptional in being the only Hampshire railway built since 1890—it was completed in 1925—to remain open.

In the future, it is probable that the main line to Southampton and Bournemouth will be electrified. As shown in Fig. 76, the closure of local freight depots is well advanced, and if the Beeching Plan is implemented, a number of passenger stations will follow. An increase is anticipated in commuter traffic, while losses may possibly occur in boat-train passengers, due to the increasing use of air transport.

AIR TRANSPORT

The development of air transport has had adverse effects on railways, shipping and docks. Both the trans-Atlantic and the cross-Channel routes have suffered, and the service to the Channel Islands is now transferred to Weymouth. The airports of southern Hampshire are located at Hurn near Bournemouth and at Eastleigh (Southampton Airport). Hurn is maintained by the Ministry of Civil Aviation, who have transferred the Southampton Airport to a private firm. Lack of funds has prevented the provision of hard runways, which limits the use of the airport, particularly in bad weather. Considerable development has taken place at Hurn, which has regular services to the Channel Islands and to France. However, the railways and the Docks, in which a special terminal was constructed, would have been much better placed if flying-boats had developed; they ceased operation in 1958.

TRANSPORT IN SOUTHAMPTON (Fig. 78)

The main influence on the area within the County Borough boundary has been its division by the river Itchen. In medieval times the lowest bridge was at Mansbridge, and the present narrow eighteenth-century bridge at this point forms a bottleneck on the Outer Ring Road (here part of the A27). The Northam Bridge Company completed their bridge and associated roads in 1796. The approach road from the east joined the original

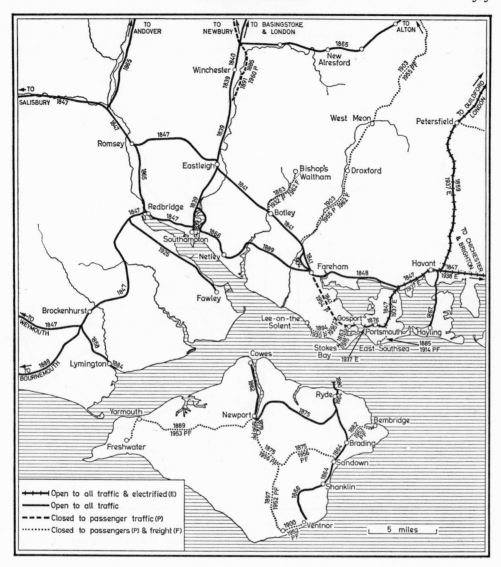

Fig. 77. The development of the railway network in southern Hampshire to 1962
Based on the successive time-tables of the independent railway companies and those provided by
British Railways.

Ws

Portsmouth road near Botley; a toll house survives on Lances Hill. The bridge was purchased by the Corporation in 1929 and freed from tolls; it was replaced in 1954. The Floating Bridge at Woolston (Plate XLVI), with its feeder roads, was opened in 1836; after the Corporation purchase of the competing Northam Bridge, its sale to the local authority became inevitable and was completed in 1934. Partly because there is no toll for passengers,

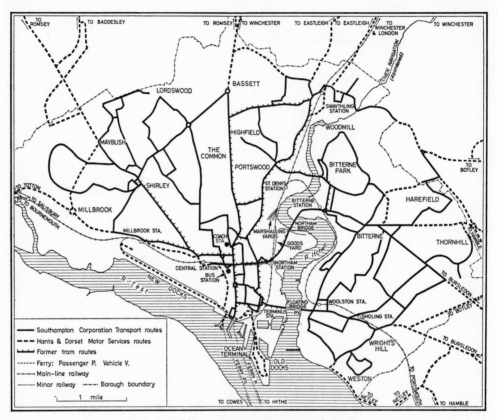

Fig. 78. Public transport services in Southampton

Based on information provided by the Southampton Corporation Transport Department, the Hants and Dorset Motor Services, and British Railways.

partly because of the good bus connections, the Floating Bridge is well used, but is scheduled to be replaced by a high level fixed bridge (see p. 342). The fourth road crossing is Cobden Bridge, originally privately owned, but subsequently purchased and rebuilt by the Corporation.

The railway crossing of the Itchen is at St. Denys, originally forming part of the 1866 branch line which served the suburbs on the eastern bank of the Itchen and terminated at the military hospital at Netley. This was the lowest possible bridge point for economic and other reasons, but it did mean that the three-quarters of a mile between the Terminus station and Woolston necessitated a rail journey of 4¼ miles. In 1889 the branch was doubled and extended to Fareham to form part of a more direct route to Portsmouth. An unusual feature of the Southampton passenger stations is that, as shown in Fig. 77, none of them has been closed, with the exception of Portswood, a temporary station opened in 1861 and replaced by St. Denys in 1866, and the boat-train station on the Royal Pier, closed in 1914. But the railway stations are used for journeys beyond the town rather than within it, and local transport has been concentrated on the roads.

Before the War of 1914-18, the radial pattern of electric tramways shown in Fig. 78 was developed. Its absence east of the river is accounted for by the limitations of the bridges and the fact that until 1920 the eastern suburbs had their own local authority—the Itchen U.D.C. Even after the 'annexation' by Southampton, only one tram route penetrated for little more than half a mile east of the river. However, the rebuilding of first Cobden and then Northam Bridge, together with the development of motor bus services, has done much to reduce the significance of the river barrier.

The present network of motor bus services is shown on Fig. 78; the general arrangement is radial, though there are some ring routes. One of the main developments of the 'thirties was the construction of new roads on either side of the medieval Bargate, which was then left on an 'island' and closed to traffic, although the trams retained their specially designed roofs which enabled them to pass under the Bargate arch until their demise in 1949. Apart from local widening schemes, the main post-war development has been of the Inner Ring Road, relieving the pressure on the High Street and Above Bar. Except for Tebourba Way, the Outer Ring Road has been formed by linking existing roads.

RIGHTS OF WAY

Few other regions in England can boast of such a wealth of prehistoric and historic remains as central south England. The downlands are covered with sites ranging from large elaborate settlements to barely perceptible burial mounds, joined by ancient trackways and ridgeways, and today they provide innumerable fascinating links with the earliest civilisations known in Britain. Though several of these tracks were subsequently used as sheep walks and some have in recent years been ploughed over, many remain which can be followed for many miles. For example, the Pilgrim's Way was probably in use thousands of years before its name was earned, though its precise route is in doubt. Much is now motor road and probably only a few sections within Wessex remain as footpaths.

Few of the Celtic routeways are traceable today, but when the Romans finally drove out the *Belgae* and the *Durotriges* from their Wessex strongholds, new ways were soon established. Two thousand years later these same Roman roads carry much of our traffic; enter or leave Winchester today and it is impossible to avoid the roads of *Venta Belgarum*.

Most of the bridleways and the footpaths have appeared during more recent history, linking farms and villages and leading to churches and inns, though the public's rights were ill-defined before the 1932 Rights of Way Act. Not until 1949, with the passing of the National Parks and Access to the Countryside Acts, was any serious effort made by local authorities to define precisely their public paths. The lengthy surveying procedure resulted in the preparation of draft maps of these rights of way, and in January 1951 Hampshire published such a map for the Rural District of Droxford, the first in the country. A little over six years later, definitive maps were completed for the whole county. The counties of Dorset, Hampshire, the Isle of Wight and Wiltshire have about 20,000 individual footpaths and bridleways, with in addition large numbers of unmetalled tracks mainly on the downland. In Hampshire alone, for instance, there are 6000 paths with a total length of about 2000 miles and a further 2000 miles of unmetalled tracks.

The 1949 Act also provided for the creation of long-distance walking routes, of which perhaps only the Pennine Way has become widely known. There is every expectation that several of these routes will shortly be designated in Wessex. A ridgeway from Sussex along the South Downs is planned, another leaving Winchester follows a modified Pilgrim's Way into Surrey, and in Dorset some of the finest cliff scenery in the south of England is included in the proposed coastal path. The last is already in good condition for much of its length, but the Army Tank Range at Lulworth makes a grievous gap, for here around Worbarrow Bay rise some of the finest cliffs. The Army at Aldershot, Bordon, Tidworth, Bovington, Lulworth and over much of Salisbury Plain are strongly entrenched, and firmly deny access to large and frequently very beautiful areas. The Navy and the Air Force too have made unpleasant marks on Wessex. Yet plenty of good long walks are to be found, and in Hampshire a number of day-long walking routes has been selected for special attention. Along these, chosen for reasons of scenery, natural history and antiquarian interest, distinctive signposts and waymarks will be erected.

Less earnest hikers will find particular pleasure in the Isle of Wight, which is more thickly strewn with footpaths than any other part of England; practically the whole coastline can be followed on foot. On the mainland Wessex includes one of the largest areas of unrestricted access in England, 65,000 acres of woodland and open heath in the New Forest, where all with countryside interests may find their pleasure.

XX

ASPECTS OF THE CIVIC SCENE

SOUTHAMPTON is not a metropolitan town and carries a provincial air in spite of its well-established position as a great passenger port. Nor is it a city; this honour might have come to it a few years ago when its population reached 200,000, but the prospect is now deferred until the area has received the attentions of the Local Government Boundary Commission.

The town has no large and independent family firms, nor is it the location of the headquarters of any of the principal shipping companies or industrial giants. Its port and its industries serve national and international concerns whose top level directorates are located elsewhere. Because of this, the civic life of the town, even in Victorian days, did not experience eminent leadership of the patronal type. Public affairs were for long in the hands of local business men, with the control of the town's major enterprise, the Docks, in the hands of a railway company. The statutory Harbour Board was a local concern, but over the years it became the centre of a balance of power contest between the Borough Council on the one hand and the port and shipping interests on the other. A parliamentary inquiry and subsequent legislation finally gave the latter a good majority representation on the Board. Thus there exists an element of formal dichotomy between the authorities for the Harbour and the Docks, and those of the town, now bridged happily by informal personal relationships and consultation. Should the Rochdale Report proposal for the formation of a single port trust be implemented, merging the statutory Harbour Board with the nationalised Docks undertaking, the Borough Council would be in no stronger relationship with the basic factors in the economy of Southampton and might well have less influence. Despite this, the Council and the Harbour Board have supported in principle the port trust proposal.

Southampton is not an industrial town in the usual sense, for its major interest in docks and shipping gives it an outlook markedly different from that of a factory town, even though there is a great deal of manufacturing industry operating both in its own right and ancillary to the port. The marked emphasis on passenger traffic gives a distinctive character to the town, although one sees in its streets only a small fraction of the people who arrive or depart by sea. The cargo trade of the port has, so far, been largely determined by its association with passenger shipping. Since the end of the War of 1939-45, however, there has been a considerable diversification of employment (see p. 259), with less dependence on docks and shipping, and this has coincided with a significant emphasis on the function of Southampton as a regional centre, which has been facilitated by its redevelopment following extensive war damage.

The Borough Council operates on a strict party basis with a post-war agreement between the parties about the proportionate allocation of aldermanic places and the alternation of the mayoralty. It is a large body, with seventy-two members, including fifteen women in 1963, and there is the usual elaborate committee system with extensive delegation of powers because of the scale of municipal business. A surprisingly wide range of decisions results from discussion and agreement without formal voting. Local elections are well fought, with the usual fluctuation of voting around 50 per cent of the electorate, and an unopposed return is a rarity. There is a tradition of decisive municipal leadership going back to pre-1939 days, though it is not now expressed in such personal terms as it used to be. Municipal ceremonial is enhanced by the fact that Southampton has the modern status of a county borough and the ancient charter status of a county, and thus appoints a sheriff as well as a mayor. Though not quite invariably, one year's sheriff is next year's mayor.

Whatever may be the views about its merits, the post-war growth of Southampton has been based on a reasonably coherent policy which has aimed at looking at least twenty years ahead. The statutory Development Plan, as explained in Chapter XXIII, endeavours to take account of all the elements involved in post-war change and growth, and to bring into effective relationship the development of docks and industry, the expansion of wholesale marketing, the planning of new elements in the major road system, the creation of a ring of post-war housing around the town periphery, some of them forming large suburbs, the location of open spaces, and the requirements of an expanded and diversified provision of education. As part of the Plan there is provision for bringing into good condition substantial sections of the old walls and other remains of the old town, especially behind the water-front, and the use, after restoration, of certain ancient buildings as museums. An overall view of the town readily shows that the large central parks, the Avenue approach to the town centre from Winchester, flanked by Southampton Common, and the division of the town by the river Itchen, have combined with other factors to give it an open character. Today the pressure of high land values and actual land shortage, together with trends in modern housing development, are increasing building density and are studding the townscape with tall blocks (Plates LI, LIII–LV). Pride in the central parks and a deep concern for the preservation of open spaces have been turned by the planning authority into a policy of open space development covering all parts of the town. This is an attempt to get the best of the two worlds, of 'openness' and high population density. The Docks, except for the western bank of the Itchen, are notable for their clean appearance. An active tree-planting policy seeks to sustain the character of Southampton as a green and pleasant place.

All this, with a parallel development of the social services, has had its implications for municipal finance. Planning and redevelopment has not, in fact, been such a heavy financial burden as was once feared, and in general commercial developers have found their contribution to rebuilding a profitable venture. The rising rateable value has partly offset the cost of reconstruction to the rates, though Southampton has a high rateable value per head of population and therefore does not benefit from the government rate deficiency grant. When the account is closed, the rate in the pound is near the national average, but with an above average expenditure per head and a good level of municipal services.

Criticism is sometimes directed at the local authority alleging a lack of cultural facilities, particularly a theatre. The history of the theatre in Southampton is not encouraging for commercial exploitation because audience support is not secure. Fortunately, the Nuffield Theatre of the University of Southampton opens in 1964. There is also a municipal project for an arts centre and theatre, as yet undated. But the cultural field is not barren. The local authority maintains an art gallery, and by 1964 it will have five specialised museums. There is a public library service, with schemes for a new central library and more branches. The Guildhall functions as a home for symphony concerts and major musical occasions. Amateurs are very active in music and drama, as they are also in painting and photography, and the Arts Festival organised by university students promises to make an important contribution to the cultural life of the area. More adventure in the cultural field really depends on the quality of public response.

A community like Southampton knows fairly well to whom it is indebted for the day-to-day conduct of the town's services and affairs after the statutory bodies and the responsible committees have made their policy decisions. The anonymity rule has nothing like the rigour of civil service practice, although wise discretion is not forgotten. So the Council's chief officers and their staffs, and in particular those who administer the family services responsible for health, welfare and the care of children, occupy a unique place in the community. The struggle with the housing shortage and with the human and technical responsibilities of slum clearance is only one of the greatly enhanced responsibilities which local authority officers have had to carry. The officers of the Harbour Board, the Docks administration, the Chamber of Commerce, the shipping agents and many others are personally known for their significant contribution to the economy of the Southampton area. With these it is right to include the trade union officers, who are deeply involved in the regulation of employment conditions in association with employers and the Ministry of Labour, and in discussions of economic developments.

The contemporary municipality is in many ways returning to an overall concern for the economic, social and personal welfare of the community such as it enjoyed before the restrictive attitude to the powers of local authorities developed in the nineteenth century. What is now happening is not so much an extension of authority as of informal influence, because of the way in which community activity now integrates itself, while becoming much more varied and complex. This is seen in Southampton as elsewhere in the extensive interlocking of personal and representative membership of the variety of bodies involved in statutory and voluntary action. Though civic responsibilities have well defined legal boundaries, they operate in fact well beyond these limits.

ARCHITECTURE

Permanent redevelopment in the town centre became possible about four years after the War of 1939-45 as a result of the easing of restrictions on capital expenditure involving building materials and labour. Above Bar, the main street of the town, then retained little of its former prosperity, but gradually the small number of temporary shops which sprang up after war devastation were swept away as permanent rebuilding occurred. An early decision had been taken that each shopping block should be designed as a unified architectural concept, with particular regard to height, scale and details of materials (Fig. 80). This was completely feasible only where the whole of a given site was available so that a grid or module could be stipulated at the outset. One of the earliest projects is sited between Pound Tree Road and Hanover Buildings, occupied almost entirely by multiple concerns. In common with other blocks of shops, it has been criticised for lack of height, but the overwhelming desire of traders for ground floor accommodation, together with the rigorous rationing of building materials, made two-storey construction only too frequent. Admittedly, much greater use of these sites would undoubtedly have been made today, and the podium of shops with tall blocks of offices or flats would have been the likely result. A particularly happy example of this kind was completed in 1963 at the Above Bar Street—Civic Centre Road—Windsor Terrace site. The work of architect Oliver Carey, it comprises an elegant and sophisticated modern building, with its huge windows and framing in black and white (Plate LII). Rising site values in the central area have produced two further multi-storey office blocks, one in Cumberland Place and the other in Brunswick Place, both in commanding positions overlooking the central parks.

A departmental store offers an architect the opportunity of producing a more completely integrated design than is possible in a block of shops with varied accommodation above them. The earliest post-war example is the Mayes building near the Bargate; the largest is that of Edwin Jones in Queensway; and perhaps the most successful architecturally is that of Tyrell and Green in Above Bar Street. The approach to the Guildhall, now in West Marlands Road, will be enhanced in a few years by a paved and landscaped pedestrian way, to be known as Guildhall Square. This will not only provide an open space, but will also relate the Civic Centre more completely with the main shopping street. Tyrell and Green's store faces the Square, and two stores are on its flanks: C. & A. Modes, completed a few years ago, and Plummers now rebuilding permanently and replacing their temporary shops on the site of the Square.

The Civic Centre, by Berry Webber (who won the competition for its design in the early 'thirties), has for long proved inadequate to cope with the expanding functions of municipal administration. A new road pattern in its vicinity, including the closing of Commercial Road to vehicular traffic, gives scope for siting a new municipal annexe, a separate central library and a new Police Headquarters. These are major projects for the near future and may well take place at the same time as the redevelopment of the last major area in the town centre, situated between the Civic Centre and Four Post Hill. It is here that a new College of Art, an Arts Centre and a theatre may be built. The central portion will be devoted to housing, whilst the western end allows for an improved railway station approach, with multi-storey car parks and commercial development.

The first part of the new Technical College has been completed (1963) in Palmerston Road, facing the parks. The main teaching block, nine storeys high, is approached by a covered way which also gives access to an Assembly Hall and Lecture Theatre. This, with four-storey teaching accommodation, forms an enclosure to a paved court and a landscaped forecourt, and located at the rear of the main block are single-storey monitor roofed workshops. A sub-surface stratum of silt here necessitated a concrete raft foundation of box shape, which forms the basement of the main building. The structural frame is of reinforced concrete and slender mullions are exposed, cast *in situ* and faced with a white Portland capstone aggregate concrete. The panels between the windows are in a blue-green ceramic tile; elsewhere facing brickwork is used. To the north of this site the construction of a Central Health Clinic is also in progress. The site levels are such that ambulances can be garaged and serviced, with other accommodation at a higher level.

The provision of an up-to-date Central Baths had for many years been the dream of townspeople. A site near the New Docks on the Western Esplanade was eventually selected; it had the advantages of being reasonably central, in the Council's ownership and with a nearby sea water supply. The fact that this land was reclaimed from the Test estuary made piling a necessity, driven to a depth of 40 feet. The indoor baths were completed just over a year ago, and future stages will provide Turkish and other special bathing facilities and an outdoor Lido.

The need for housing accommodation in the post-war period led the Council to develop great areas on the periphery of the town. The latest of these, Lordshill, virtually a town in itself, will be built near Rownhams and Nursling, between Southampton and Romsey. Lionel Brett has been appointed consultant architect and his project shows much new thought and originality. The clearance of slums has already produced some notable schemes. Messrs. Lyons and Israel's Holyrood flats (Plate LI) are sensitively handled, although with higher buildings the areas of open space would have been greater in a similar project today; economics at the time dictated a mainly four-storey development, though with some nine-storey blocks. A highly individual essay in the design of tall blocks of flats is at Lansdowne Hill, on the site of the old castle. The work of Eric Lyons, it dominates the old town, though perhaps at the expense of St. Michael's church, for so long a landmark. A decrepit area at Northam has been transformed by mixed development of maisonettes and another tall block of flats, the Council's first attempt at multi-storey housing (Plate LIII). It was followed by a further block at Redbridge (Plate LIV), and others are proposed. Private housing development, driven by land scarcity and consequent high site values, has followed suit, and the changing pattern of development is exemplified in a high block of flats in Upper Bassett.

The massive educational programme has resulted in a number of new primary and secondary schools (see p. 318), and there has been considerable experiment in construction and planning in an endeavour to equate enhanced standards of accommodation with strict cost control. The more recent schools are noteworthy for compactness of planning and the reduction of circulation areas. Interesting architectural solutions have been evolved in many cases and, although the selection of a few schools is difficult, attention is directed to Weston Park Boys' School, Moorhill Secondary School for 600 pupils, and St. George's Roman Catholic Secondary School. Hightown Secondary School at Thornhill, now under construction (1963), will accommodate 900 pupils, and is the largest of its kind in the town.

Primary schools worthy of mention are at Hightown, Wimpson (Plate LV), Mansbridge and Kanes Hill, the last two being of identical design and construction.

This brief review would not be complete without reference to the University's own rapid development, discussed in Chapter XXII, but one aspect of this work deserves comment here. The approach to the University area, both from the town centre to the south and from the north, is at present devious and undistinguished. It is a defect which may well be eliminated with the extension of the University to the boundary of the Common, which itself contains one of the main approaches to the town, that from the north.

MUSEUMS AND ART GALLERIES

Museums

The establishment and development of museum services in Southampton is a relatively new venture. The town's first museum, Tudor House in Bugle Street, was purchased by Southampton Corporation and opened to the public as an antiquarian museum in 1912. Tudor House remained the only museum until 1951, when the Guildhall over the Bargate was restored and opened as a museum of local history to commemorate the Festival of Britain year. Again, in 1960 the Corporation restored the derelict medieval fortification known as God's House Tower in Winkle Street, and converted its interior for use as a museum of local archaeology. Two other buildings, the Wool House in Bugle Street and a warehouse in French Street, are in process of restoration and conversion as museums of local maritime history and of science and industry respectively. Thus since 1950 and within little more than a decade, Southampton Corporation have founded a precinct of five specialised museums in separate buildings, four of which are scheduled ancient monuments, and all situated within the confines of the medieval walled town.

Tudor House (Plate XXXII), with its frontage facing the Norman church of St. Michael, is one of the few surviving examples of a large town house of early Tudor times. Its timber-framed structure was built by Sir John Dawtrey of Petworth, an official of the royal customs house, between 1491 and 1518, replacing a medieval building which previously occupied the site. Dawtrey represented Southampton in Parliament in 1495 and later became Sheriff of Hampshire. Towards the end of the reign of Henry VIII, Tudor House became the residence of Sir Richard Lyster, Chief Baron of the King's Exchequer, and Lord Chief Justice from 1546 to 1552. Despite much restoration, the main structure of the building remains much as it was during the sixteenth century, and provides a striking example of the domestic architecture of the period. The garden is laid out in the formal style typical of the Tudor period, and gives access to the remains of a Norman merchant's house, built about 1150-75. This Norman house was one of a group of medieval stone houses which stood on the waterfront close to the West Quay, and is one of the finest examples of Norman domestic architecture surviving in England. The house, which now has no roof or dividing floor, was in two storeys, and in the north wall can be seen a Norman fireplace. The upper windows on the west front and that on the north are original, dating from the mid-twelfth century. In the ground floor an original Norman arched doorway opens into Blue Anchor Lane, which forms the northern boundary of both the Norman house and Tudor House. Against the east wall of the Norman house a chimney dating from about the year 1200 has been erected. This was removed from 79½ High Street, Southampton, in 1953, and placed in the Norman house for preservation; it is one of only three known Norman chimneys existing in England. In about 1360, when the West Wall of the town was built, the west front of the Norman house, together with a number of others, was incorporated into the Town Walls. The original openings on the west side of the ground floor were blocked up and new ones inserted, probably intended for small cannon; if so, these are the earliest gun-ports of their kind known to exist in Britain. An area of land adjacent to Tudor House and abutting on the West Gate terraces and Town Wall has recently been acquired by the Corporation to extend the present limits of Tudor House garden. Tudor House is in itself a 'museum piece', and the policy for development of the collections has been designed to ensure that the exhibits are complementary to, and not in competition with, the interior architecture. The scope of the collections now displayed mainly covers the field of applied arts, including local topographical prints, paintings and drawings, and portraits and personalia of notable people associated with Southampton.

The Bargate Guildhall (Plate XXIX) was opened as a town museum in May 1951 by the Duke of Wellington, Lord-Lieutenant of Hampshire. This hall, built in late medieval times above the twelfth-century Norman arch of the Bargate, was used for guild meetings and town assemblies, and was the scene of many 'mayor-making' ceremonies. The Annual Court Leet was regularly held in the Guildhall from the sixteenth century until 1856, and performances by strolling players were at one time given there. The Guildhall was used as a court of justice until the opening of the Law Courts block at the Civic Centre in 1933. Since its conversion into a museum, the Bargate Guildhall has been used for temporary exhibitions, with its permanent collection illustrating civic history. An exhibit of special note is a tapestry commemorating Southampton's role as chief embarkation port for the D-Day invasion of Normandy. Provision for public access to the roof of the Bargate and for use of the ground floor for special exhibitions is planned for completion after the Wool House and Science Museums have been opened.

God's House Tower (Plate XXX), a massive defensive spur work adjoining God's House Gateway, formed the main south-eastern fortification of the town in the early fifteenth century, and is now a museum of local archaeology. Before its completed restoration and opening in 1960, only the shell of the building remained, the original floors in the main gallery and tower no longer existed and the masonry was a wreck. The work of restoration was undertaken by the Southampton Borough Architect's Department, in collaboration with the Ancient Monuments Division of the Ministry of Works. God's House Gateway, about a century earlier in date than the Tower, also forms part of the museum, the interior of the gatehouse being used as the Crawford Memorial Lecture Room. The adjoining Tower was built to protect the sluices which controlled the flow of water into the town's tidal moat and was the headquarters of the Town Gunner. The Tower and the gallery connecting it with the town's East Wall provided an extensive flank defence for God's House Gate and afforded accommodation for troops and stores. The Tower is a square three-storeyed building, with contemporary gun-ports and a wide embrasure for guns on the top. It served as a key defence post during the Hundred Years' War, when invasion by the French was a constant threat, and in 1457 when a French fleet threatened the town the guns at God's House Tower were brought into action. In the late eighteenth century the Tower became the town gaol, though ill-suited to the purpose. The gatehouse was used as a bridewell or house of correction, the felons' gaol was housed in the connecting gallery between the gatehouse and the tower, and the tower itself was used as a debtors' prison. The prison establishment was abandoned in 1855 and subsequently the buildings were used for storage purposes. God's House Tower and Gateway are named after the nearby Hospital of God's House in Winkle Street. The archaeological collections at God's House Tower illustrate the prehistoric Roman, Saxon and medieval archaeology of Southampton and district, and a series of air photographs of important archaeological sites in Wessex is also displayed. The Crawford Memorial Lecture Room commemorates the late Dr. O. G. S. Crawford, who lived at nearby Nursling, pioneer of the study of air photography as an aid to archaeology.

Opposite the Royal Pier, at the south-eastern corner of Bugle Street, stands a fine example of a medieval warehouse. This building, known as the Wool House, is now being put in order for use as the town's maritime museum. Dating from the fourteenth century, it was originally used for storing wool before shipment, a reminder of the town's commercial importance during medieval times, when wool was one of England's staple commodities and Southampton one of the chief ports for its export. During the eighteenth century the Wool House was used to confine French and Spanish prisoners of war, the names of some of whom can be seen today carved on the beams of its fine Spanish chestnut roof. The main collections at the Wool House will illustrate the maritime history of the port of Southampton, with a special section devoted to the history of yachting in Southampton Water and the Solent, and there will be a wide variety of ship models, marine paintings, navigational aids and marine engines.

Having ensured the permanent conservation of four historic buildings for use as town museums, Southampton Corporation in 1963 transferred to the care of the Museums Department an early twentieth-century tea-warehouse for conversion into a museum of science and industry. The emphasis in the collections to be acquired for the new museum will be on science as applied to industry and commerce, with educational displays built around local industry.

The Art Gallery

Southampton Art Gallery is now twenty-five years old; opened in 1939 as the final section of the Civic Centre buildings, but damaged during the War, full activity could not be renewed until 1946. The eight rooms and large Main Hall have now been redecorated, equipped with up-to-date lighting, and are being provided with suitably designed modern furniture. The gallery itself and most of the permanent collection largely owe their existence to the bequest of Robert Chipperfield of Southampton, who died in 1911, which provided a substantial part of the cost of building. An income of some £4000 a year from this bequest has enabled a wide collection to be built up. Some of the purchases made in the 1930's, before the gallery was opened, would not be possible now with the spectacular rise in prices, particularly in the field of French Impressionist painting.

For a short period before the War of 1939-45, Southampton possessed one of the wealthiest galleries in the country, for in 1932 a further bequest from another leading figure in Southampton—Frederick William Smith—augmented its income, and serious buying from both bequests began about this time, in anticipation of the building of the gallery. In making purchases Southampton has been fortunate in having, by the terms of the two bequests, the advice of the Directors of both the National Gallery and the Tate Gallery. Purchasing policy has not been rigid, but has been governed to a considerable extent by the state of the art market. Just after the War it was possible to concentrate on British painting of the eighteenth and early nineteenth centuries, while at the same time buying fairly extensively recent and contemporary British painting. This still continues, although an attempt is now being made to secure a small number of Continental Old Masters to form the nucleus of a collection before it is too late. This is particularly important, since the removal of two extensive long-term loan collections has left the gallery very weak in this field.

Sculpture is also within the gallery's purchasing policy, and a start has been made here, not only with small bronzes in the gallery but with a Rodin figure on the Art Gallery forecourt. It is hoped to add further sculpture outside as opportunity arises. Finally, a sum has been allocated from the rates to purchase a small and highly selective collection of pottery to include pieces typical of their period and style from some of the major ceramic epochs.

The strongest section of the collection at present is British painting from about 1700, with an emphasis on the eighteenth and twentieth centuries. The most outstanding painting here is Gainsborough's full-length portrait of Lord Vernon, first exhibited in London in 1767. Slightly earlier is the Reynolds of Cornet Nehemiah Winter, painted in 1759. There are two portraits by Romney and a Lawrence of Archbishop Moore of Canterbury. Landscapes include Richard Wilson, sea-pieces by Turner, Morland and de Loutherbourg, a large J. C. Ibbetson of North Wales and an interesting late landscape by Wright of Derby. In the nineteenth-century rooms are one or two pre-Raphaelites—Holman Hunt, Burne-Jones and Ford Madox Brown; amongst the earlier pictures here are a John Martin of 1812 and a large Etty. One of the two Tissots is certainly the finest painting in this room, which also contains a portrait by Sargent. British painters of this century include a strong representation of the Camden Town Group, centred on Sickert (one of whose rare self-portraits the gallery possesses); Gilman, Gore, Bevan and Ginner are all represented, in some cases by two or three examples, as well as more obscure painters like Malcolm Drummond, and associated artists such as Wyndham Lewis and Augustus John.

There are several paintings by Wilson Steer, and the next generation of painters forms another strong section of the collection, with works by Paul Nash, Matthew Smith, Stanley Spencer and Gwen John. More recent painters include Graham Sutherland, John Piper, Victor Pasmore, Ivon Hitchens, John Bratby and Roger Hilton. This section has recently been augmented by the splendid bequest of Mr. Arthur Jeffress, which includes ten Sutherlands and five Pipers. This bequest also greatly enriched the small collection of French nineteenth- and early twentieth-century paintings, of which the three most important are a large early Courbet-like Sisley of 1867, a Camille Pissaro of Louveciennes dated 1870, and a 'white period' Utrillo. Paintings by Delacroix, Corot, Tissot, Boudin, Forain, Harpignies, Bonnard, Vuillard and the Douanier Rousseau are included, as well as several by the Belgian surrealist, Delvaux.

Amongst the Flemish painters are a pair of early portraits by Van Dyck and works by Goossen van der Weyden, Jordaens and Joos de Momper, while the Dutch School includes landscapes by Philips Koninck and Isaac van Ostade, a J. D. de Heem still-life and a portrait by Nicholas Maes, as well as an interesting Cesar van Everdingen. The earliest picture in the gallery is a triptych by the fourteenth-century Florentine painter, Allegretto Nuzi, and the Italian section also has good examples of Sophonisba Anguisciola and Desiderio, and a characteristic Salvator Rosa landscape which it is interesting to compare with those by Francisque Millet and Gaspard Poussin amongst the French School. Bronzes by Maillol, Rodin, Degas and Epstein, and a few British water-colours and drawings, complete the collection as it is at present.

The Southampton Record Office

Although Southampton Corporation has a tradition of record preservation dating as far back as 1834, when a catalogue of Corporation archives was prepared, it was not until 1953 that the first archivist was appointed to organise a record office within the Town Clerk's Department. The publication of the Corporation's own records by the Southampton Record Society between 1905 and 1941, with the aid of a municipal subsidy, shows that it was not lack of interest but of qualified staff which delayed the establishment of the Office.

During its first ten years the Record Office has expanded to provide various services. The Master of the Rolls has approved it for the deposit of manorial records and the Lord Chancellor for public records. It holds not only all the older records of the Corporation, but also many private documents which have been deposited from time to time by their owners. These it tries to make available for use by the public by producing catalogues and calendars, and also by publishing a summary guide to the contents of the Office. It is also responsible for the modern title deeds and other papers of the Town Clerk's Department. Many of the older Corporation records have been published by the Southampton Record Society and its successor the Southampton Record Series, both of which the Corporation has strongly supported. The charters beginning in 1199 were printed in 1909, the *Oak Book* with its Anglo-Norman laws of the guild merchants in 1910, and the *Black Book* in 1912. More recently *The Local Port Book* of 1439-40 and the *Third Book of Remembrance*, 1514-1602, have been edited and published. The Corporation has also embarked on a policy of publication of Southampton Papers on subjects of local history, and the second edition of the *Southampton Atlas* (first published in 1907) is a new departure in record office publications in this country.

The private records include a magnificent series of solicitors' papers rescued from salvage by the Public Library at the beginning of the War of 1939-45, and since transferred to the Record Office. These contain information concerning almost all aspects of life in Southampton in the eighteenth and nineteenth centuries, as these solicitors acted as clerks to most municipal, charitable and Anglican bodies in the town. Several other large groups of solicitors' papers consist mainly of local title deeds. A number of Anglican parishes have deposited their records in the Office, and a start has been made with Nonconformist records. But perhaps pride of place among the deposited material should be given to the records of businesses. The nineteenth- and twentieth-century records of traders and industries are so rare in England and Wales that the Southampton Record Office may claim to be more favoured than most, with six large collections and several small ones.

THE CHAMBER OF COMMERCE

The Southampton Chamber of Commerce is one of the oldest voluntary associations in the town, and like many of its counterparts in other large towns and cities, it was a product of the Industrial Revolution. It has, however, two unusual characteristics. In the first place, it was originally established by a resolution of the Trade Committee of the then Town Council dated 28 January 1851, and has maintained unusually close links with the local authority ever since. In the second place, it has always contained a substantial element of retailers in its membership, and thus combines the functions of a Chamber of Commerce and a Chamber of Trade.

The Chamber became an incorporated body in 1875; among its objects were 'the promotion of the trade and commerce, the shipping and manufactures of the town and port of Southampton, and of the home, colonial and foreign trade of the United Kingdom generally; the collection and dissemination of information relating to trade, commerce, shipping and manufactures; and the promoting, supporting or opposing legislative and other measures affecting the interests of its members'. Today those objects are still a true reflection of what the Chamber sets out to do. It is managed by an elected Board of Directors of twenty-four business men, representing as far as possible the range of industry, commerce, shipping and retailing in Southampton. The Board appoints the Secretary of the Chamber, who manages and co-ordinates all its affairs. Several standing committees are responsible for special subjects, such as Distributive Trades, Transport, Shipping and Taxation, as well as *ad hoc* panels appointed from time to time to deal with particular problems.

The Chamber has some 950 member firms, varying in size from great industrial undertakings to small private retail businesses. Its revenue, used to meet the cost of maintaining a building with various facilities and the employment of a small full-time staff, is derived from members' subscriptions. Much of the staff's time is spent in dealing with inquiries on the local supply of goods and services and on all aspects of trade. The Chamber promotes various joint projects in the interests of its members or of the town as a whole, and specialises in giving advice on export documentation and procedure, tariffs and customs regulations.

The Southampton Chamber is an authorised signatory of Certificates of Origin and similar documents under the Geneva Customs Convention of 1923, issuing thousands of such items annually. It publishes a monthly journal, *Southern Gateway*, distributed to members and also sent to many destinations at home and abroad. The Chamber is represented on some thirty external organisations, and for over a hundred years it has played its full part in the civic life of the town. It is a founder member of the Association of British Chambers of Commerce, established in 1860, one of three national bodies invariably consulted by the government of the day on economic, commercial and industrial matters.

Unlike Chambers of Commerce on the Continent, which are known as 'public law bodies' and receive substantial government backing, the Southampton Chamber (as other Chambers in Britain) is purely a voluntary association of business firms. The Chamber, though often taken for granted in the outside world, is thus entirely dependent on the support and good will of its members and does not receive a penny from official sources, a rare condition today and one which the Chamber values and is determined to preserve.

EDUCATION IN SOUTHAMPTON

It is simple enough to state that Southampton has over 34,000 children in ninety-two schools, of which thirty-six (27 primary and 9 secondary) have been built since 1945, a College of Technology (including a Technical College), and a College of Art, but it is more difficult in a short space to give a picture of what goes on in these institutions. Every building used by the education services in Southampton, with a single exception, was either destroyed or more or less seriously damaged during the War of 1939-45. Now war damage has been made good, many old schools have been much improved, and 45 per cent of the children at the primary and secondary stages are working in schools built since 1950. Moreover, a new College of Technology has recently been opened. But there is still much to do on the building side, and only an adequate and steady annual capital allowance for building can ensure this, for the schools today have to cope with 70 per cent more children than in 1946.

Seventy schools cater for children of primary age. These primary schools have widened and broadened their activities since 1944 and are beginning to reconsider and expand their teaching of mathematics and even introduce the teaching of modern languages. Moreover, the growth of these schools as widely based communities, extending their activities in many directions outside school hours, has transformed them. Perhaps the most striking development that is taking place is in secondary education. The four maintained grammar schools, which between them had some 150 sixth-formers in 1946, now have considerable difficulty in finding accommodation for over 700, many of whom stay on for three years. The other secondary schools have changed so much that it is not easy to give them a common name. They are certainly not 'modern' in the connotation that this title has assumed. Almost all the children who go to them are anxious to take a course leading to an examination, either to 'O' level G.C.E. or to an appropriate examination in commercial subjects at the end of five years, or to a local examination at the end of four. In fact, some thousand children in these twenty-one secondary schools are now in their fifth year, most of them preparing for 'O' level G.C.E.—that is, many more than are taking an 'O' level course in the grammar schools. Of these, some hundred each year pass on to the sixth forms of the grammar schools,

XLVI
The river Itchen, showing
the Floating Bridge

XLVII   The bridges over the Test estuary at Redbridge

XLVIII
Above Bar, before the War
of 1939-45

XLIX
Above Bar, after wartime
destruction

L
Above Bar, after post-war
rebuilding

thus adding to their accommodation problems. In addition, local examinations in certain groups of subjects have been provided for children prepared to stay on at school to complete a four-year course. Thus a very large proportion of Southampton children leave school with some specific paper qualification that they have had to work hard to achieve. This scheme started very much as a small experiment, but even in the early days it was clear that many more children could take full advantage of the new opportunities that were being offered to them. There are two ways of accounting for this; one, which is fundamental, is that for the first time children of this level were being given an opportunity of extending themselves and their potential was therefore being more fully realised. This, however, cannot fully account for the facts, since the better children at the top of these schools were out-stripping the children at the lower end of the grammar schools. It seems clear that children at the top of one school are more stimulated than children who are at the tail end of another, and this encouragement adds impetus to their efforts. So the new scheme which had been initiated was extended because so many achieved success and satisfaction from it. The other development was unexpected, but very welcome. One of the basic ideas was that variety of opportunity should be offered, and a number of courses with rather different aims were started. As the years have gone by, this sort of specialisation has tended to fall into the background; the courses that have been most successful, and therefore have spread, are the more general ones, providing education on as wide a front as possible, without any particular aim in mind. Ten years ago the pattern included a number of courses such as seamanship, commerce, arts and crafts, farming and gardening, but now the tendency is for these courses to disappear and for children to take a wide variety of subjects in the G.C.E. or in the Southampton four-year examination.

The effect of this examination stimulus on the schools has been remarkable. The academic stimulus has affected not only the children who are actually preparing for the examination, but the rest of the school as well. There has been the growth in status of the school in the minds of parents and the townspeople as a whole. Moreover, the concentration upon examinations does not seem to have militated against the wider developments of education; in fact, the feeling that the school has something worth while to offer seems to have spread from examinations to other activities. Thus out-of-school clubs and societies, drama and music, games and athletics have all made rapid progress over the last fifteen years, and subjects not taken in examinations have been transformed.

The system of secondary education thus evolved in Southampton is essentially a flexible structure capable of still further development to provide the widest educational opportunities for children of all levels of ability. Reference has already been made to the pattern of special courses in secondary schools, and this is responding both to the increasing demand for a broad general education and to the growing readiness of parents to keep children at school beyond the statutory leaving age so that they may complete a four-, five- or seven-year course leading to an appropriate examination.

In 1963–64 nearly 45 per cent of secondary pupils are remaining at school for a fifth year and 60 per cent of the 1963 entry have embarked on five-year courses. In this and other ways the Education Authority meets the wishes of parents for their children. Experience has shown that most of the pupils concerned take full advantage of the opportunities thus afforded them. With the growth in the status of the secondary school and the accommodation provided by new buildings, it became possible in 1963 for each secondary school to function as a 'neighbourhood school' (except for one girls' school specialising in secretarial subjects), and to be linked more closely with the primary schools in its area. Each school now offers a range of four- and five-year courses related to appropriate examinations, including 'O' level G.C.E.

These developments in secondary education have blurred the division between grammar and other secondary schools. At the eleven-plus change the Southampton allocation procedure gives full weight to the child's primary school assessment and this, rather than the results of the one-day test, is the deciding factor in grammar school and grammar course entry so far as the individual pupil is concerned. The substantial movement from secondary to grammar schools at sixteen plus is proving very fruitful. It is expected that further opening up of the grammar school sixth forms will give even wider opportunities for pupils in secondary schools to pursue their full-time education beyond the age of sixteen.

Physical Education

Physical Education has developed out of all recognition during the last ten years. From the bare-foot work that had done so much to improve children's feet arose the idea of developing special climbing apparatus to strengthen and develop not only the feet but other parts of the body as well. It was felt that the earlier this apparatus could be brought into use the better. Primary schools now have their halls equipped as rather more than rudimentary gymnasia, using much apparatus that has been specially designed for Southampton schools. Similarly the gymnasia of all secondary schools built since the war have incorporated specially designed equipment. This complete rethinking of the apparatus side of physical education has been extended to other facets of the work. The importance of swimming is fully realised, and a large number of primary schools have portable teaching baths erected in playgrounds at the beginning of the summer term and fully used until the autumn. Recently more permanent baths, again built on simple principles and therefore reasonable in price, have been erected adjacent to secondary schools. Both of these supplement the opportunities offered at the Town Baths. An old mill on the river Itchen has been turned into a centre for canoeing and sailing, available not only to schools but to youth clubs, students of training colleges and universities, and to teachers. More recently instruction in rowing, judo, archery, golf, table tennis and badminton has been provided on a voluntary basis by adult clubs. Those who have been thus initiated can join these clubs when they leave school.

Handicapped Children

The provision for handicapped children has also made important advances. A unit for spastics caters for the seriously affected children from Southampton and the district around,

who cannot attend ordinary schools. A school for children who find formal learning difficult has been active for some years on the shores of Southampton Water, and a second is
about to be built for seniors in pleasant surroundings near the Southampton Sports Centre.
The introduction of light-weight hearing-aids has made it possible to assist very young
children who have less than normal hearing, and a unit under expert leadership has been
helping children from the age of two, and their mothers, to learn to use this apparatus. As
they have grown up, the children have been able to pass on to the normal infant and junior
schools to which the special unit is attached, and from which they can receive continued
support and guidance.

Further Education

Before the War of 1939-45 there was no technical college in Southampton, and technical
and commercial courses were centred on the University College. After the war a former
workhouse was converted for use as a technical college, which has grown so rapidly that
several other buildings have been taken over. Now the first instalment of the new College
of Technology is in use. At present the work in this building and in the assorted premises of
the Technical College is being organised as one college, with departments covering most
branches of science, engineering, building, commerce and the food industries, serving a
national as well as a local need. Southampton's special interest in the sea is shown by the
courses in marine engineering, naval architecture, shipbuilding, marine radio and radar,
whilst the proximity of the Fawley Refinery and its associated industries is stimulating the
development of chemical engineering. The College is one of the largest in the country,
with some 10,000 students and over 200 staff.

The College of Art is still awaiting new buildings, but meanwhile caters for some 1700
students on courses in fine and applied art. The College is the centre for advanced work in
printing in the area of the Southern College of Art, a federation of Art Colleges which
enables them to co-ordinate their courses and co-operate in wider schemes. For example,
common arrangements for diplomas for full-time study are under discussion, in line with
the system of certificates already used for certain part-time courses.

The Southampton School of Navigation situated at Warsash on the eastern shores of
Southampton Water was until recently attached to the University, but its administration is
now in the joint hands of the Hampshire and Southampton education authorities, with a
governing body on which the two authorities and the University are represented. The
school has several functions, a one-year course for Merchant Navy cadets, courses for Merchant Navy officers taking Ministry of Transport certificates of competency in navigation
up to Extra Master level, radar observer courses, and mid-apprenticeship courses of a mainly
liberal character. Other countries are represented amongst the cadet students and the school
has an international reputation.

Adult Education

The twentieth-century movement for adult education found a place in Southampton as early as October 1907, when the inaugural meeting of the Southampton Branch of the Workers' Educational Association was held in the original buildings of the Hartley University College under the chairmanship of its Principal, Dr. S. W. Richardson. The branch thus founded was based on the customary triple relationship of workers' organisations, the local education authority and the University College. This relationship is still fully expressed in the constitution of the Joint Committee for Adult Education of the University of Southampton.

The Adult Education Department of the University and the Southern District of the W.E.A. now function over an area comprising the counties of Hampshire, West Sussex, the Isle of Wight, the eastern half of Dorset and the Channel Islands. Originally the collaboration of the University and the W.E.A. related almost entirely to the promotion of three-year tutorial classes, with the University itself arranging a limited number of extension courses, in addition to those organised from both Oxford and Cambridge because of the early association of extension courses with these older universities. Tutorial classes still continue in the area in good volume, though they have been complemented by a much larger range of sessional, terminal and short courses dealing with a great variety of liberal studies.

In the period before 1938, the tutorial responsibility fell largely on the staff of the University College and on a small number of part-time tutors drawn from other educational institutions. Even then the growth of a full-time staff for adult education had begun, both in the University and the W.E.A. Today the whole district is covered by full-time tutors, seven appointed by the University and three by the W.E.A., who work closely with such organisations as Women's Institutes and Townswomen's Guilds, and with the many local groups and branches of the W.E.A.

The post-war period has seen a substantial growth of adult education, despite financial limitations, although the development of science classes has been restricted in consequence. For the session 1961-2 there were 430 classes in the University-W.E.A. area, with a student enrolment of 7675. In Southampton itself there is a large branch of the W.E.A., with 540 students and thirty-six classes in 1962-3, the majority of which are held at the University. Pressure of internal work has limited the help that can be given to adult education by the intra-mural staff, which has meant that in addition to the staff tutors a large number of part-time tutors are used, so widening the range and availability of subject teaching.

During and since the War of 1939-45 the Adult Education Department has been responsible for certain educational work in the Services. This is now mainly of a residential character, with full-time tutors conducting weekly and fortnightly tutorials for small groups at the major military centres, supplemented by a number of residential courses held in University halls of residence. A significant feature of this work is an increasing interest in various aspects of science and engineering, including lectures and demonstrations in the computer laboratory.

A more recent development of adult education is closely associated with industry and takes the form of courses for apprentices, shop stewards and other factory workers, arranged sometimes at the factory and in some cases at a university centre. This kind of adult education, while it is adapted to the special circumstances of the students, fits in well with the liberal traditions of the movement. In the Southampton area the development is mainly concerned, so far, with apprentice education at the Fawley refinery.

Notwithstanding these special provisions, the decisive factor in adult education is the demand springing from voluntary interest, since there is usually no vocational incentive as in other types of education. Most of the effective demands are met, though 'subject fashions' sometimes create difficulties. A recent report by the National Institute of Adult Education on staffing and accommodation has resulted in more thought being given to the provision of adult education centres in the larger towns. There is only one in the southern area, at Worthing, but special accommodation for adult education at the University is planned for 1964. The ten-year capital programme of the Southampton Borough Council includes a project for an Arts Centre and Theatre which would provide accommodation for the wide range of voluntary cultural organisations in the town. A final interesting aspect of adult education is the part it has played in new town development at Crawley, and also through studies by local groups of the problems of expanding towns in Hampshire.

THE PUBLIC HEALTH SERVICES OF SOUTHAMPTON

Although local records of health services, such as the supply of pure water to the Borough, can be traced as far back as the fifteenth century (see p. 98), public health services were not organised until the middle of the nineteenth century. In the year 1850 a specially appointed committee of the Southampton Local Board of Health decided to advertise for a medical officer of health, whose duties were 'to report periodically on the sanitary conditions of the town, to ascertain whether any contagious epidemic affecting the public health exists and to take charge of common lodging houses', and Dr. Francis Cooper was appointed in November 1850. In the same year the first inspector of nuisances was appointed. Dr. Cooper died from Asiatic cholera in 1865, at a time when the disease was prevalent in the town.

The history of public health in Southampton during the nineteenth century contains frequent reference to outbreaks of infectious disease, such as cholera, which spread rapidly through the poorer parts of the town. Smallpox occurred on several occasions, and diphtheria, scarlet fever and typhoid were common causes of death. Apart from dealing with such outbreaks, the health officers were also concerned with a variety of nuisances, insanitary housing conditions and lodging houses, the result of a rapidly increasing population. Many of the nineteenth-century cholera outbreaks started in seaports infected by immigrants arriving on ships from abroad. For this reason, in 1866 a doctor was appointed in Southampton to inspect every foreign immigrant ship on arrival. Subsequent reports commented on the value of this service, as there was no further introduction of cholera from immigrant ships, whereas no other port under similar circumstances escaped. In 1874 a doctor was appointed as part-time port sanitary medical officer for the Borough. National regulations which came into force early in the present century prescribed measures designed to prevent the importation of major infectious diseases and to destroy rats on ships. The Southampton Port Sanitary Authority was created in 1893, the Borough Council being made the responsible authority. The area of the Authority was extended in 1935 to include parts of Cowes Roads, the Solent and Spithead, as well as the whole of Southampton Water. In addition to dealing with communicable diseases, the port health officers are also much concerned with the supervision of accommodation for the passengers and crew of vessels and with the examination of imported foodstuffs.

The only personal health services provided by public authorities in the nineteenth century were minimum medical care for the destitute sick, and hospital care for those suffering from serious infectious disease, designed mainly to protect the community. The present century saw the development of the personal health services. In 1908 a medical officer was appointed to carry out routine medical inspections of school children, assisted part-time by a lady health visitor. Of the children examined, one-third were found to require treatment. Many of the defects found remained untreated by existing services, and local authority services came into being to treat ringworm, skin infections, and eye and other defects. An orthopaedic clinic was first held in 1930, co-operating closely with the special hospital at Alton. The school dental service was inaugurated in 1912. The first health visitor devoted some of her time to home visits, advising on the care of babies and young children, and additional visitors were soon appointed. A higher standard of midwifery had been promoted by the Central Midwives Board. Midwifery was largely domiciliary until the Maternity Unit was opened in 1936 at the Municipal Hospital. The first ante-natal clinic was held in the Borough in 1920.

One of the earliest medical institutions in the town was a dispensary, established in 1809 to provide medical attention for the poor without their having to resort to poor law relief. The Corporation contributed towards the expenses. A casualty ward of six beds was opened at the Town Quay when the docks were built, though it was closed in 1838 when the Royal South Hants Infirmary opened, to become the principal medical centre in the town. The Corporation provided a fever hospital at the West Quay, and in 1892 hired a floating port sanatorium, later to be replaced by a larger ship converted to serve as a hospital and permanently moored in the river Test. An isolation hospital was opened at Shirley in 1900. The Corporation became responsible for general hospital services in 1929, and developed the former poor law infirmary into a well equipped general hospital. Accommodation for persons suffering from tuberculosis was provided at the isolation hospital. In 1948 the operation of the National Health Service Act placed all local hospitals, voluntary and municipal, under the control of the Wessex Regional Hospital Board and of management committees appointed by the Minister of Health. The same Act made local health authorities responsible for services which are mainly domiciliary in character.

Since 1948 the public health and welfare services of Southampton have developed strikingly; only a few features can be mentioned here. They include the provision of central and branch clinics, a training centre for the subnormal opened in 1961, and a Child Guidance

Clinic; the demolition of some 1500 unfit houses since the War of 1939-45; the provision of nine homes affording residential accommodation for nearly 400 persons; the special emphasis on domiciliary health services, medico-social services and school health; and the general concern with the environmental services required by a large town and port.

The Port Health Service

Vessels arrive in Southampton from many world ports; each year a quarter of a million passengers disembark from over 2000 vessels, and over half a million tons of foodstuffs are landed at the Docks. Although quarantinable diseases such as smallpox and plague are now rarely encountered on vessels coming to this country, medical officers must be on their guard. Each year several hundred sick people are admitted to hospital from vessels arriving in the port, some of them are suffering from communicable diseases, others from diseases which are not infectious. In most cases, arrangements for admission are made through the Port Health Office, located in the Docks. Medical officers in the department also carry out duties as medical inspectors of aliens and of Commonwealth immigrants. This work is carried out in close co-operation with the immigration officers.

Sanitary inspections of vessels are made by the health inspectors, who also take routine samples of water supplies, and examine vessels for any evidence of infestation by rodents. The fact that only 1 per cent of vessels require 'deratting' before certificates of freedom from infestation are issued is a tribute to the work of the service and to the improvements in ship construction and maintenance.

Inspection and sampling of imported foodstuffs are regularly carried out. As in the town, the Borough Analyst and Public Health Laboratory Service examine samples. The great quantities of food imported, and changes in the character and types of food, require continued vigilance.

THE PRESS

Southampton is served by a single locally published newspaper, the *Southern Evening Echo*, but the oldest inhabitants can remember when the town also had four weekly papers. The last of these to survive was *The Hampshire Advertiser* (which incorporated *The Hampshire Independent* and *The Southampton Times*), ceasing publication in 1940 as a result of the war. *The Advertiser* began life as *The Southampton Herald* on 28 July 1823, with strongly Tory politics, while its Liberal rival was *The Hampshire Independent*, founded a decade later. In 1860 these were joined by *The Southampton Times*, which vigorously represented Radical opinion until the 1920's. The fourth of the local weeklies was *The Southampton Observer*, a Conservative penny paper which competed with the twopenny *Advertiser*.

Southern Newspapers Ltd., the proprietors of the *Echo*, are celebrating their centenary in 1964. The firm adopted its present title in 1927, having previously traded as the Hampshire Advertiser County Newspaper and Printing and Publishing Company, Ltd. It was originally founded for the purpose of purchasing the existing *Advertiser*, and in 1891 it bought the *Southern Echo*, which had been established in 1888 as a half-penny evening paper by Passmore Edwards, the famous philanthropist and free library pioneer. To begin with, it seems, Edwards was not keen to sell his paper; he was not in the newspaper business purely for commercial reasons. Chiefly he wanted a platform for his political and social ideals, and during its early years the *Echo* faithfully reflected the Gladstonian views of its first proprietor. Its new owners decided, wisely as events have shown, to pursue an independent, non-party policy, and the paper has maintained this line ever since.

In 1940 it appeared for the moment as though the history of the newspaper had been brought to an abrupt end. Its offices and works in Above Bar were destroyed by enemy action during the night of November 30, yet publication continued without a day's interruption, the paper being printed in Bournemouth until temporary premises could be opened on the bombed site in 1943. New headquarters on the original site were opened in 1955 by Earl Mountbatten of Burma; they incorporate one of the most up-to-date newspaper plants in the country.

The region served by the *Echo* includes most of central south England, with Southampton as its focal point; it circulates throughout Hampshire, the Isle of Wight and Wiltshire, and its sister journals, published in Bournemouth and Weymouth, serve the county of Dorset. These three evening journals and the four associated weeklies published in Bournemouth constitute an influential independent press group.

XXI

THE ORDNANCE SURVEY

CONSTRUCTION will soon start on a large group of buildings at Maybush on the road between Southampton and Romsey. These buildings, when completed, will be occupied by 3000 men and women, with their drawing and aerial survey equipment, printing machinery, map stores and all the other essentials of a national survey organisation. For the second time in its history the Ordnance Survey will make its headquarters at Southampton (Plate XXXIX).

This homecoming will be no affair of chance, as it was in 1841 when the Ordnance Survey came to Southampton for the first time. From its foundation in 1791 the Survey had been housed in the Tower of London, but in November 1841 a disastrous fire destroyed the Map Office, and a new home had to be found. By chance the choice fell on South-ampton, for the simple reason that the town provided, it was alleged, 'the only place where accommodation could be found'. That place was an empty cavalry barracks, used latterly as a Royal Military Asylum for the orphans of soldiers, at the town end of the Avenue (Plate XXXVIII). The move was made, and thus for reasons neither of policy nor suitability the administration of the national Survey was taken from its proper place in the metropolis, where it could keep in touch with the Government and science, to a then relatively small provincial town. During the years that followed, however, the disadvantages of remoteness from London diminished, and when, almost exactly a century later, the headquarters of the Survey had to return to the vicinity of London which had previously been so reluctantly left, continual efforts were made to return to its provincial home.

The first half-century of the Ordnance Survey's life before it came to Southampton had been a period of experiment and growth. The organisation was formed in a small way in 1791, when two officers of the Royal Artillery were appointed to carry out a trigonometrical survey and prepare a 1-inch map of Great Britain, mainly as a measure of defence against France. Before that time there had been no national survey, although for upwards of forty years Major-General William Roy had pointed out the imperative need for such an organisation. Though he was a convinced and ardent proponent, Roy's advocacy was for long ignored. He died the year before the Ordnance Survey was founded, yet the credit for its formation is largely his. The new Survey, having been formed for a military purpose, was placed under the Board of Ordnance and thus became known as the Ordnance Survey. The trigonometrical survey was started in 1792, the ground survey for the 1-inch map three years later, and in 1801 the first map (the 1-inch sheet of Kent) was published. Others followed at regular intervals, that of Hampshire being published in 1810 (Plate XL).

By the time that the move to Southampton took place the whole of Wales and all England south of a line from Preston to Hull had been mapped.

During the Survey's early years at Southampton the strength of the Map Office (later to be called the Ordnance Survey Office) was probably about 130, with 600 men employed on survey work in other parts of the country. In those days the staff was still mainly military, although some civilians had been recruited since 1824. While the Survey's first officers had come from the Royal Artillery, its direction was by this time in the hands of officers of the Royal Engineers, as it remains largely to this day. This combination of soldiers and civilians was to form the pattern until the War of 1939-45, and for a hundred years Southampton was to be familiar with the uniforms of the Survey's soldiers, to accept the successive Directors-General as important functionaries in the town's life and, through the skill and craftsmanship of the men which it provided, to contribute to the organisation's world-wide reputation. That first century saw the foundation of the 'Survey families', whose names occur again and again through four or five generations.

It is not easy to pick out the highlights of those early years at Southampton, but Queen Victoria herself visited the London Road offices in about 1880, as did her great-grandson, the Duke of York, later King George VI, fifty years later. It is recorded too that in 1887 the staff at Southampton prepared a beautiful Jubilee Volume illustrating the history and work of the Survey, and presented it to the Queen in person. Throughout those years the Ordnance Survey was a force to be reckoned with in local sport, excelling at cricket in particular and providing more than one player for Hampshire.

Important as those activities were in establishing the place of the Survey in the town's life, they were, of course, ancillary to the serious business of surveying and mapping the country. Work continued on the 1-inch map during the second half of the century and, perhaps even more important, 1853 saw the beginning of the 1:2500 survey. This task was to become, and remains to this day, a major feature in the Ordnance Survey's programme. The town of Southampton had, in fact, anticipated this large-scale survey by eight years, for in 1845-6 it paid the Ordnance Survey to carry out a 1:1056 scale survey for 'the Sanitary Improvement of the town'. That survey was made by Sgt. W. Campbell and his section of Royal Sappers and Miners, and the resulting thirty-three beautifully drawn manuscript plans are still the treasured possession of the Civic Record Office. The Ordnance Survey possesses an equally beautiful 6-inch scale manuscript reduction of these plans. The national 1:2500 scale survey reached Southampton in 1865, but the plans which resulted and were twice revised before the War of 1939-45 have now been replaced by modern post-war plans at the 1:1250 scale.

Apart from the survey programme, the latter decades of last century and the early years of the present saw the Southampton office experimenting with and developing new techniques in printing, photography and lithography. For example, it was here that the zincography method of printing was developed and extensive work was done on half-tone processes for lithographic printing. It is recorded too that the first year of the new century saw electricity replace steam for all the machines at the London Road office, which no doubt added to the comfort and cleanliness of the printers.

At the outbreak of the War of 1914-18 the Survey was denuded of its soldiers and many of its civilians. This did not mean the cessation of work, for Southampton became the main centre for the production of military maps. During those four years of war, Southampton sent 32 million maps to the Army, including vast quantities of large-scale trench maps which were usually wanted at very short notice.

After 1918 hard times befell the Ordnance Survey, when, in common with other Government organisations, it suffered severe cuts in its financial vote. Consequently there was a reduction in staff by some 28 per cent to a total of below a thousand, with the result that the revision programme was drastically curtailed and the mapping of the country rapidly became out of date. To Southampton, however, the London Road offices must have seemed much the same as ever—the bugle calls were still heard at the chiming of the clock on the since bombed North Range; the uniformed Royal Engineers were still there; the pattern of social life continued in its old course; and the Survey remained prominent in the local sporting world. The serious state of the national maps and plans ultimately led, however, to the appointment of a Departmental Committee under the chairmanship of the Viscount Davidson, which reported in 1938 with far-reaching recommendations. As it turned out, war intervened and these recommendations had to be laid aside for a time, but a few years later they were to become the key-stone of the Ordnance Survey's post-war programme.

As in 1914, the War of 1939-45 deprived the Survey of its military and many civilian employees. Even worse troubles were ahead, however, for on the night of 30 November, 1940, the London Road offices were badly damaged by the disastrous German air attack on Southampton and were made largely unusable. More than that, large numbers of irreplaceable manuscript records were destroyed and the phrase '. . . regret that we cannot supply this information because the documents were destroyed by enemy action' still occurs with unwelcome regularity in Ordnance Survey correspondence. Another irreplaceable loss was the great theodolite completed by Ramsden for William Roy in 1787 and used for the first trigonometrical survey of the country. Because of the damage, many of the staff had to leave the London Road offices for other parts of the town, or were moved to new buildings at the old Crabwood estate on the Romsey road, where the Ordnance Survey had begun to expand shortly before the war. Later, in 1942 and 1943, further offices were provided in Surrey at Esher and at Chessington, to which the administrative headquarters and a large section of the staff were moved. Thus Southampton ceased to be the Survey's headquarters, though it has continued to house a large proportion of the staff.

The war inevitably changed the Ordnance Survey's role, for survey work came to a virtual standstill, and all the effort was put into the production of maps for the armed forces. Maps were printed in vast numbers in those years (120 million were needed for the Normandy landings, though not all came from Southampton), and the staff were subjected to the most stringent security restrictions when maps were being prepared for operations such as the North Africa and 'D-Day' invasions.

As the war progressed and British towns were increasingly damaged by bombing, it was realised that there would be an immediate need for up-to-date mapping for the necessary post-war reconstruction programme. The Government agreed, therefore, that all major towns should be surveyed anew at the scale of 1:1250. In addition, the old 1:2500 scale County plans of the smaller towns and rural areas were to be converted to a single series on the National Grid system and revised, and the mountain and moorland areas were to be surveyed at the 6-inch scale. These, although important, were not the only mapping tasks, for the revision of maps at other scales, in particular the 1-inch and ¼-inch, had to be tackled, and in addition a completely new 1:25,000 scale map had to be provided. It was realised that the new surveys and revision, together with the necessary triangulation and levelling, would require the Survey to recruit large numbers of men and women to bring its personnel up to a total of about 5000. This recruiting and training started as soon as demobilisation got under way, all the new draughtsmen and many of the surveyors being trained at Southampton. A new feature of the post-war Ordnance Survey was that there would be no more soldier-surveyors and draughtsmen, for the Army has retained its own Military Survey units; the Ordnance Survey was to be entirely civilian (apart from its Royal Engineer officers), and Southampton was no longer to see the familiar uniform.

Soon after the war it was seen that the tasks of drawing and printing could be carried out more efficiently if the London Road and Crabwood offices were organised on a functional basis. The result was that the former became responsible for drawing and printing the large-scale plans, while the Crabwood offices took charge of the map series at scales of 6 inches to 1 mile and smaller. The London Road Division has the additional responsibility of training the Survey's draughtsmen. Southampton thus remains the centre of all the Ordnance Survey's drawing and printing activities and the place of training for its draughtsmen, surveyors, tracers and the personnel in its many printing trades. The last now also go to the School of Printing in the Southampton College of Art, and take part in printing courses organised by the Southampton Education Authority.

In order to complete the post-war programme as expeditiously as possible, the Survey has naturally had to experiment with and adopt many of the latest methods, techniques and materials. Thus the tellurometer, an electronic distance-measuring instrument, is largely used in the survey of control points; the chain has given way to aerial survey stereo-plotting equipment, and to self-reducing tacheometers which instrumentally measure distances up to 200 metres; the surveyor's paper field-sheet has been replaced by machined enamelled aluminium plates and by distortion free plastics; and in addition to drawing on enamelled plates the draughtsman now scribes on to glass or plastic. Advances in cameras and printing equipment, improved chemicals and materials, and air-conditioning have transformed the speed at which maps can be printed, not to mention the improvement in their quality. These developments have enabled the Ordnance Survey to complete by 1963 some 37,000 of the projected 47,000 new 1:1250 scale plans (the 210 plans of Southampton were published as long ago as the early 1950's), 31,000 of the 171,000 plans on 1:2500 scale, and the completely new 1-inch and ¼-inch series, as well as many other new maps. The 1-inch sheet of Southampton, published in 1960, was the first Ordnance Survey map to show Rights of Way (see p. 306), a policy which will be extended to all 1-inch and 1:25,000 Second Series sheets of England and Wales. This programme has demanded an expansion of the Southampton staff to almost 2000, mainly draughtsmen and printing tradesmen, and has led to annual printings averaging 750,000 copies of large-scale plans and 2 million copies of medium- and small-scale maps at London Road and Crabwood respectively.

The future will see further developments of the techniques that have enabled the Ordnance Survey to make so much progress with this post-war programme. For example, more extensive use will be made of aerial photography for the 1:1250 scale surveys, for the revision of the 1:2500 scale National Grid plans, the survey of the mountains and moorlands at the 6-inch scale, and for contouring the 6-inch maps; the use of plastics will be steadily developed in the drawing offices; and still better materials and equipment will further improve the standard of camera work and printing. But for the time being the grave handicap of inadequate and scattered accommodation remains, and the full benefit of improved methods and techniques cannot appear until all the headquarters administrative and technical staff are again together in one place, housed in a building properly designed for the precise and exacting work the Survey has to perform. Fortunately, that day is now not so very far ahead, and fortunately too the place is to be Southampton. When that day comes the Ordnance Survey will have truly returned home.

XXII

THE UNIVERSITY

THE University of Southampton has developed by stages out of the Hartley Institution, founded in 1862 from motives almost diametrically opposed to those which inspired the creation of the majority of English provincial universities or their embryos. Most of these were by-products of the Industrial Revolution, coming into existence in response to the need for higher education in the growing industrial towns and commercial ports, and owing their endowments to men whose wealth was derived from that Revolution. But if the Hartley Institution was a by-product of the Industrial Revolution, it was through reaction against it. Its founder, Henry Robinson Hartley, was an eccentric straggler from the eighteenth century, knowing little and liking less of the new age of docks and railways, who aimed to create, not a college for the many, but a cultural centre for the few, which might serve as a rallying-point for Southampton's intellectual *élite*. To that end he bequeathed the fortune of over £100,000 which he had inherited from two generations of successful wine-merchants in trust to the Corporation for the establishment of an 'Institution' that should promote the study of antiquities, science and literature, chiefly by means of a library, a museum and public lectures.

After Hartley's death in 1850, however, this bequest was contested by his relatives in a long lawsuit which swallowed up three-fifths of the legacy in lawyers' fees and awards to the claimants, leaving the infant Institution sadly handicapped by inadequate funds. This was the first, chronologically at least, of several reasons why the University of Southampton, despite this early endowment of its ancestor, has been later than most in reaching full and independent status. Other and more fundamental reasons were that the town, with a population of less than 50,000 at the time of the ceremonial opening of the Institution in 1862 by the Prime Minister, Lord Palmerston, was not of the same order of magnitude as the rising industrial cities of the North and Midlands, and that its chief source of revenue, the great steamship lines, was one whose magnates mostly lived and had their ties elsewhere, feeling no such obligations towards it as did the Wills family towards Bristol or Jesse Boot to Nottingham. It was, therefore, a long time before any further considerable local benefactions were forthcoming to augment the diminished endowment. An additional complication was that though Hartley's other surviving papers make his intentions clear, his will was sufficiently vaguely worded to give those who wished to see a teaching college established a chance to interpret it in their favour. The result was that the early history of the

Institution was bedevilled by bitter controversy between the partisans of the rival interpretations, who made matters worse by aligning themselves with opposed political parties in the town.

A microscopic element of class teaching was present from the outset, and was developed by the first Principal, Dr. Francis Bond, who seized the opportunity offered by the need in India after the Mutiny for engineers and telegraphists to staff the Public Works Department, and secured governmental recognition of the Institution as an approved establishment for their training. The foundation of the Royal Indian Engineering College at Cooper's Hill in 1871, however, ended this opportunity and with it the Institution's first brief era of expansion. There followed more than twenty years of slow progress under the amiable and rather whimsical guidance of T. W. Shore, a geologist and antiquary of some repute. During this period the Institution prepared its students, whose numbers dropped at first below fifty and then slowly rose again, chiefly for the examinations of the Science and Art Department at South Kensington or for entry into the older universities, the medical schools, Sandhurst, Woolwich or the Royal College of Mines. In 1885, impelled by Shore, it had the distinction of inaugurating the successful movement to obtain government grants for the university and other provincial colleges which were now coming into existence, only to experience the mortification of having its own application for a grant rejected on the grounds of its smallness and lack of both an adequate teaching staff and a properly representative governing body.

Rallying from this disappointment, the Institution, whose teaching functions were by now more and more overshadowing its original character, sought with considerable success to concentrate on development as a technical college. In this it was substantially aided by the Corporation, which took advantage of the powers recently given it by the Technical Instruction Act of 1889 to levy a rate and make therefrom a grant to the Institution for the purpose of technical education; and also by Sir Philip Magnus, an eminent authority in this field, who visited it and drew up a report for its future guidance. In pursuance of his recommendations the staff was enlarged, work for the external degrees of London University commenced, the name of 'Hartley College' was adopted, and Dr. R. W. Stewart, a man of great driving force, was appointed to succeed Shore. Under his vigorous direction and with further rate-aid from the Corporation, three stages of advance were achieved in quick succession. First, the College made a name for itself in the field of technical education; then it obtained leave from the Education Department of the Privy Council to open a day-training department for teachers in 1899, which in due course developed into a full-scale department of education; and finally it secured recognition as a university college in 1902—though Stewart himself left just before this last achievement crowned his work.

Nevertheless, its position was far from secure. The College buildings, cramped at the bottom of the High Street, had already been expanded as far as the available space allowed and were now becoming increasingly inadequate, while the finances were still precarious. The College's income, indeed, soon fell again below the minimum then required for recognition as a university college, and in 1910 it was informed that this recognition would be withdrawn in a year's time. An appeal to the Chancellor of the Exchequer secured a respite pending the result of an effort to raise further funds, but it seemed at first that this effort would fail. The Corporation came once more to the rescue in the nick of time, however, and the College entered on a new era under the inspiring leadership of its President, the scholar and philanthropist Claude G. Montefiore, and of its Principal, Dr. Alex Hill (1913-20). Land was bought at Highfield on the outskirts of the town, and new buildings were erected there which were opened by Lord Haldane in June 1914. The outbreak immediately afterwards of the War of 1914-18, during which these buildings were used as a military hospital, delayed the transfer of the College thither until 1919, however, and dislocated its development in several ways. By the time the move was possible, the steep rise in prices due to the war had considerably raised the cost of equipping the new buildings and the post-war increase in student numbers had made much more provision necessary, so that accommodation and revenue were once again inadequate and mighty efforts had to be made to enlarge them further.

During the inter-war years, and chiefly under the principalship of Kenneth H. Vickers (1922-46), the University College continued to expand, if somewhat slowly. Dr. Montefiore was a never-failing source of wise council and generous benefactions, and the Principal was a man of strong religious faith whose basic motive in his work of laying the foundations for a University of Southampton was the wish to establish a community in which men and women could learn the values of the good life and develop their qualities and characters in order to play a proper part in the service of their fellows. With this end in view he made it a cornerstone of his policy to create halls of residence (of which four were opened during this period) as soon as the finances permitted, in order that as enclaves of corporate spirit and true academic life they should serve to foster in the College as a whole the proper atmosphere of a modern university. Other additions at this time included the Turner Sims Library, the George Moore Botanical Building, and new engineering, geology and physics blocks. In view of the near neighbourhood of various marine and other engineering works, with which an increasingly close co-operation was developed, the Engineering Faculty soon became prominent, first under Professor John Eustice and then more widely under his successor Wing-Commander T. R. Cave-Browne-Cave; while among other important developments were an active extra-mural (now adult education) department and a school of navigation which provided training both for cadets aspiring to become mercantile marine officers and for serving officers studying for certificates of competence.

The effects of the second world war on the College were fundamentally different from those of the first, which had been a time of frustration and interruption of progress. It was not evacuated, and by remaining in its own buildings with their scientific and other equipment, and even obtaining leave to expand them on the engineering side, it was able to continue its work of instructing civilian students, nearly all of whom were either awaiting their call-up or were technicians in training. In addition, it provided courses for a great many service personnel. As a result the student numbers more than trebled, and although there was naturally some reduction when the service courses came to an end, the formation of a special planning committee during the war prepared it to take its full share in the post-war expansion of university education.

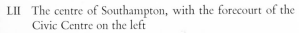

LI   Holyrood blocks of flats, with Terminus Station in the right background

LII   The centre of Southampton, with the forecourt of the Civic Centre on the left

LIII   Northam, showing the new blocks of flats

LIV   Redbridge Towers, a nineteen-storey block of flats, opened in 1962, near the western boundary of the Southampton County Borough

LV   The Millbrook area in western Southampton, with Wimpson School in the centre

LVI   The Thornhill Housing Estate, in eastern Southampton

This does not mean, however, that progress since 1945 has been all plain sailing, or the rate of expansion uniform. Three phases can be distinguished: an almost immediate post-war advance, a pause for consolidation, and then a renewed and greater advance which is still in progress. The first phase coincided with and owed much to the principalship of Sir Robert Stanford Wood (1946-52), and culminated in the College becoming by royal charter the University of Southampton in 1952, with the Duke of Wellington (who had been its President since 1949) as Chancellor and Sir Robert Wood (succeeded on his retirement later in the year by Dr. D. G. James) as Vice-Chancellor. There followed a slowing-down of this increase in student numbers and a relative lull in building operations, similar to those experienced by most British universities of comparable size in the middle 1950's. During this period the University was chiefly concerned with the organisation of new courses and other arrangements necessitated by its change of status. Subsequently, further developments of governmental policy and fresh benefactions have enabled it to plan and embark on another and larger programme of expansion in response to the needs of the present day.

THE PRESENT AND FUTURE

Since the establishment of the University in 1952 there have been no additions to the six faculties, which were named in the Royal Charter as Arts, Science, Engineering, Economics (now Social Sciences), Education and Law. While the number of departments in the faculties has only been increased slightly, the first decade of the University's existence has seen the student population rise from 933 to 1900 and the number of professorial Chairs from fifteen to thirty. By 1966-7 it is envisaged that there will be 2460 students, of whom 1060 will be in the faculties of Arts, Social Sciences, Education and Law, compared with 1400 in the faculties of Science and Engineering. It is interesting to note that the number of students in the Engineering and Science group will have increased by then to 57 per cent of the total, as against 49 per cent at the time of the establishment of the University. According to the present plans, these proportions will be maintained during the two following quinquennia, at the end of which period about 2100 students will be in Science and Engineering and 1550 students in the Arts group. By 1980 the total will be brought to 4000 by the addition of a pre-clinical medical school and by further increases in the other faculties. These increases form part of the national plan for the British Universities announced by the Chief Secretary of the Treasury in March 1962, which provides for an advance from 110,000 students in 1961-2 to 170,000 in 1973. It seems likely, however, that these national figures will be greatly increased in view of the existing pressures for the extension of University education.

To illustrate the meaning of University expansion of this extent, it is worth noting that in the proposals for the quinquennium 1962-7, submitted to the University Grants Committee, it was hoped to institute at Southampton seventeen new Chairs, and to appoint 170 additional lecturers and 200 additional laboratory technicians. Along with these staffing increases, the University foresaw a number of new academic developments. Disciplines proposed on the Arts side included American History and Literature, Archaeology, Russian Language and Literature, Italian Language and Literature and the Fine Arts. Chairs of Politics,

Ys

Sociology and Psychology were envisaged for the Faculty of Social Sciences, and a Chair of Comparative Law for the Faculty of Law. In Science and Engineering, new Chairs were proposed in Oceanography, Architecture and Building Science, Engineering Materials, Noise Technology, Control Engineering, Nuclear Engineering and Communications. It was also hoped to institute additional Chairs in several existing departments, such as Mathematics, Chemistry and Physics. A number of these new commitments has already been approved including, in particular, three lectureships in American Studies helped by initial financial support from the United States. The newly established Institute of Sound and Vibration Research is expected to be followed by an Institute of Oceanography, and it is also likely that there will be a considerable increase in the number of postgraduate courses leading to the degree of Master, of which five are already in existence. Courses of this type are likely to be of growing importance in the research activities of the University, and it is possible that eventually the total number of students taking these courses or studying for higher degrees in the normal way will amount to one-third of all the students in the faculties of Science and Engineering.

The pressure on the library facilities is constantly increasing. In the main and departmental libraries 630 seats are available at present for readers and shelving for 220,000 volumes, but by 1980 it is estimated that the Library will need to provide places for 1000 readers and shelving for 350,000 volumes. The creation of an academic library, as other new Universities have found, is a very expensive undertaking, and although the Library already has over 150,000 volumes and receives about 1300 periodicals, the rate of expenditure must be accelerated to cover the anticipated increase in the scope of scholarly interests and research. Other needs are related to Palaeography and Archives, special collections, exhibition space and photographic services.

To provide ground for all the new departmental buildings within the present restricted University site has not been considered possible, and the University proposes to acquire additional land in its immediate neighbourhood. These proposals are based on a Development Plan prepared by Sir Basil Spence, O.M., R.A., the University's consultant architect, and they make provision for the purchase of twenty-two acres, bringing the total area of the teaching site to fifty-four acres. A Public Inquiry into the proposals was held by the Ministry of Housing and Local Government in Southampton in February 1963, and if they prove acceptable to the Minister the University will be satisfied with the extended area thus made available. The density of buildings on the extended site will necessarily be high, but fortunately the entire western boundary lies along Southampton Common, which is likely to remain open land in perpetuity. The Development Plan embodies three main features: first, a central court contained by the buildings serving the general needs of the University, the Library, the Nuffield Theatre (Plate XLI), the Great Hall, the Administration Building and the Students' Union; second, the present gardens lying to the west, around which will be grouped most of the buildings of the Faculty of Science; and third, the court in the eastern part of the present precinct serving most of the early University buildings, as well as a number of more modern ones. The Engineering Buildings will be in the area lying immediately to the north of the existing Engineering departments. Although it has not proved possible to bring all the buildings for the faculties of Arts, Law, Education and Social Sciences into a single area, they will all be close to the Library, for the expansion of which there are satisfactory adjacent sites.

An important aspect of the developments is the proposed diversion of traffic (including Corporation transport) from University Road to Broadlands Road and Hartley Avenue, when they have been linked by a new road running to the east of the University. The present division of the East and West sites by University Road is dangerous as well as inconvenient, and with the growth of the University these disadvantages would be greatly increased. A new entrance to the University will be provided at the northern end of Furzedown Road, which, by affording direct access to the University from The Avenue, will greatly improve the main approach from the centre of the town.

A notable lack in the faculties in the University is Medicine. An area within the Development Plan has been earmarked for the pre-clinical buildings of a future Medical School in the hope that it will prove possible for medical teaching to be established here within the Wessex Hospital Region. At present this is the only region in the country without a teaching hospital, the value of which to the existing medical services would obviously be very great. Ideally the teaching hospital should be adjacent to the main University site, but this is unfortunately not feasible. Nevertheless, the University feels strongly that once medical teaching can begin the link between the Faculty of Medicine and the rest of the University must be strengthened by carrying out pre-clinical teaching at the main University site itself.

Some 850 students are at present living in Halls of Residence, and an important feature of the proposals for future developments relates to additional Halls. The University is well placed in this respect, since ground already in its possession in Bassett and Swaythling should meet the requirements of the development period. These sites lie no further than a mile from the main University site, and by 1980 it is hoped to provide residential accommodation for 2500 students out of the total of 4000. Most of the residential buildings will probably be in the form of traditional Halls, accommodating up to 300 students each, but it is also likely that some hundreds of students may be housed in large blocks of study-bedrooms, based on the Scandinavian pattern. No large dining-rooms or common rooms would be available for these students, who would obtain most of their meals in the Students' Union.

The Montefiore and Wellington Sports Grounds together provide thirty-five acres of playing fields at little over a mile from the main site, and in addition fifty acres of suitable land lying near the Wellington Ground have been purchased for development when the growth of the University makes this necessary. At the time of writing, the University lacks a Student Health Service, a Physical Education Department and a full-time Appointments Service. Insufficient finance has prevented the establishment of these important facilities, which are regarded as essential in a modern university, but it is hoped to make them available in the near future.

The University is confident that it will continue to make valuable contributions to the advancement of knowledge, to the national plan for increased opportunities of higher education and to the scientific and industrial needs of the Southampton region. This brief survey of future plans is written not long before the publication of the Robbins Report on Higher Education in Britain, which may lead to a considerable acceleration in the Government's plans for the expansion of university education. If this proves to be the case, 1980 may see a much larger student population in Southampton than the 4000 now proposed. Other changes arising from the Report may relate to teaching methods, to the administration of universities and to the duration and composition of courses. The University of Southampton is prepared for change and will remain ready to play its part in any new national plan and to further the cause of learning and scholarship.

XXIII

THE PLANNING OF SOUTHAMPTON

SURVEYS undertaken in connection with the Development Plan for Southampton indicate that in the past about one-fifth of its area has changed in character every twenty years; it is significant that slum clearance is now proceeding in districts built up between 80 and 100 years ago. This rate of change varies in other towns of differing size, with differing economies and with special characteristics, such, for example, as Bath or Cambridge which contain a very high proportion of buildings that for architectural or historical reasons should be retained. Southampton, however, is a dynamic place in a part of England which is under considerable pressure both from population growth and economic development, and with rising standards of living and of space requirements this rate of change is likely to increase in the future (Fig. 79).

Change and growth took place in the past by natural processes and to meet various and often conflicting pressures. Although there were draft planning schemes for Southampton before 1939, none of these reached the stage of government approval, and it is only since 1945 that a comprehensive plan has been available to guide development over the whole town.

RECONSTRUCTION

The first step in this planning process took place during the War of 1939-45, when as a result of very heavy war damage and the virtual destruction of the town's main shopping and business centre, proposals for reconstructing the central area were prepared by Professor Adshead and Mr. H. T. Cook, who was then Town Planning Officer. This was followed by action under the Town and Country Planning Act of 1944, when the Council in 1946 applied for a Declaratory Order, designating a large area in the town centre subject to compulsory acquisition for the purpose of dealing with the extensive war damage. The Order as confirmed covered 262 acres, virtually the whole of the business centre. A slightly larger area has since been made a Comprehensive Development Area as part of the approved Development Plan, under which rebuilding had been largely completed by 1963, with the exception of the area between the Civic Centre and the Central Station. Rebuilding has taken place generally in accordance with block redevelopment proposals, making provision for more regular boundaries, rear access to shops for loading and unloading, and a unified architectural treatment. The reconstruction plan for the central area itself was formally submitted to the Minister of Housing and Local Government in 1957, and was approved by him with very little modification in December 1960. It provides for an inner ring road (now completed) around the main shopping and business core, a north–south Docks Road (now

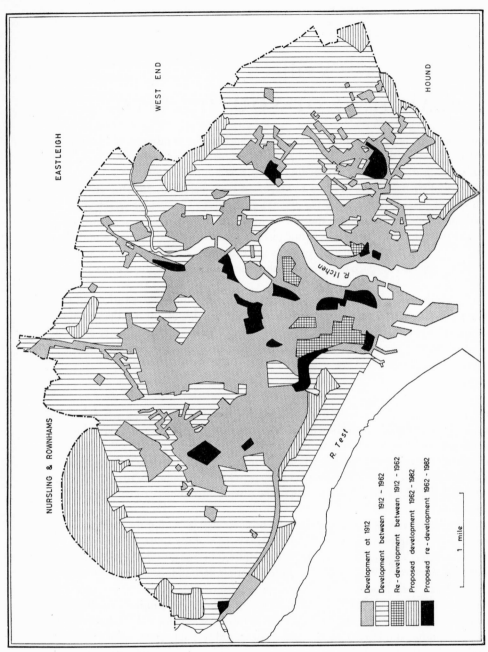

Based on the Borough Architect's Review of the Southampton Development Plan.

In the past fifty years Southampton has developed by a considerable peripheral expansion and by rebuilding in the central 'core' because of war damage or blight. Development in the next twenty years is expected to follow a similar pattern with further expansion (though on a much more limited scale than previously) and redevelopment and renewal of the older areas adjoining the town centre and in the old 'village' centres.

Fig. 79. The growth and development of Southampton, 1912–82

NURSLING & ROWNHAMS

EASTLEIGH

WEST END

HOUND

R. Itchen

R. Test

Development at 1912
Development between 1912 - 1962
Re - development between 1912 - 1962
Proposed development 1962 - 1982
Proposed re - development 1962 - 1982

1 mile

partly under construction) to link the A33 road from Winchester and London with the Old Docks without passing through the main town centre, and an inner east–west by-pass skirting the northern edge of the central parks. It defines the main use zones for shopping, offices, light industry and warehousing—in particular, a wholesale fruit and vegetable area around the lower High Street which is now virtually complete. The extent of these zones was based on a detailed survey of existing uses in 1939, the last normal period before the war. The Plan also allocated sites for public buildings, including a new health centre and a college of technology, and defined three main zones for high-density housing at Kingsland, Holyrood and in the 'old town' area west of the High Street.

THE DEVELOPMENT PLAN

The main Development Plan for the town as a whole was first undertaken under the Town and Country Planning Act of 1947. For the first time it was obligatory on planning authorities to base their plans on a comprehensive survey of their area, and also to indicate the intended or probable phasing of development as between the first five years and the following fifteen years of the twenty-year period intended to be covered by the Plan.

In Southampton the necessary surveys (which included population growth, age and condition of buildings, traffic, industry and employment, and many other aspects) and the preparation of the Development Plan itself were carried out between 1949 and 1952. The Plan was submitted to the Minister in July 1952 and approved by him with a few minor alterations in November 1956. The purpose of the Development Plan, as set out in the Written Analysis, is 'to make the best use of the available area within the borough boundaries by reserving land in suitable positions for the activities of the people who live and work in Southampton and who visit the town'. Its main objectives are:

(a) to help in maintaining Southampton as an important port;

(b) to relieve traffic congestion, particularly in the town centre, and to provide easy access to the Docks from all quarters;

(c) the reconstruction of the war-damaged shopping centre and the general improvement of shopping and business facilities in the town;

(d) the provision of sites for new industries, for the re-establishment of war-damaged industries and the re-location of existing industries at present badly sited;

(e) the clearance of obsolete housing and the use of the sites for new housing and for other purposes, as shown on the Town Map and Programme Map; the reservation of land for residential purposes to accommodate the estimated population in the next twenty years;

(f) the provision of schools for the children living in these residential areas, in positions as near as possible to their homes; and

(g) to safeguard existing public open space and woodland and provide a better balance over the town generally, and to open up where possible the river frontage to the general public.

The main features of the Development Plan can be summarised under seven major heads.

(i) *Population*. Based on the Registrar General's projection of the 1947 population, and assuming that there would be no overall balance of migration, the population of the town at the end of the twenty-year Development Plan period was expected to rise from about 180,000 to 209,000.

(ii) *Residential Development*. It was estimated at the time the Plan was prepared that sites were available for nearly 10,000 dwellings. It was intended to demolish a total of 3800 dwellings by 1971 (mainly in 'blight' areas), and, after allowing for the use of much of this cleared land for other uses, to rebuild on the remainder about 1400 new dwellings. On the basis of the proposed gross residential densities, however, land in the borough was considered to be not quite sufficient to accommodate the estimated future population.

(iii) *Industry and Employment*. The main analysis and conclusions in the Plan relating to industry and employment were based on the 1950 Interim Report, *A Survey of the Industrial Prospects of the Southampton Region*, prepared by Professor P. Ford and Mr. C. J. Thomas. The Council considered, as did this Report, that there had been an over-dependence on shipping and related activities in the past, and (with the proportion both of workers in manufacturing industry and also of female employment in particular much lower than the national average) that there was a need for the greater diversification of the industrial structure of the region and for further industrial development in the future. The Development Plan provided for the 266 acres of existing industry zoned for the same purpose to be increased to a total of 601 acres. Most of this additional area would provide for new estates on the reclaimed land behind the New Docks and on industrial estates at Northam and Millbrook.

(iv) *Shopping*. The Plan provided for the retention and reconstruction of the existing central area shopping district based on Above Bar Street (Fig. 80), with adequate facilities for loading, rear access and car parking. It also allowed for the retention of the secondary shopping centres in St. Mary Street and Bedford Place, and for the retention and improvement of the remaining shopping structure, comprising several suburban district centres, supplemented by smaller groups of shops within easy reach of all residential areas. It was also intended to redress as far as possible the over-provision on the western side of the town (Shirley) with one shop per 68 persons, as against the eastern side (Sholing) with only one shop for every 278 persons.

(v) *Communications*. The main rail, air and ferry services remained basically unaffected, though in addition a helicopter site has been reserved on Corporation-owned land between the New Docks and the Town Centre, in close proximity to the main railway and bus stations. The Plan provided for the replacement of the existing Floating Bridge, connecting Woolston and the area east of the river Itchen with the centre of Southampton, by a fixed bridge and parliamentary powers have since been obtained by the Corporation to enable this to be constructed. The road proposals for the central area have already been mentioned. For the rest of the town it was intended to retain and improve the existing road network.

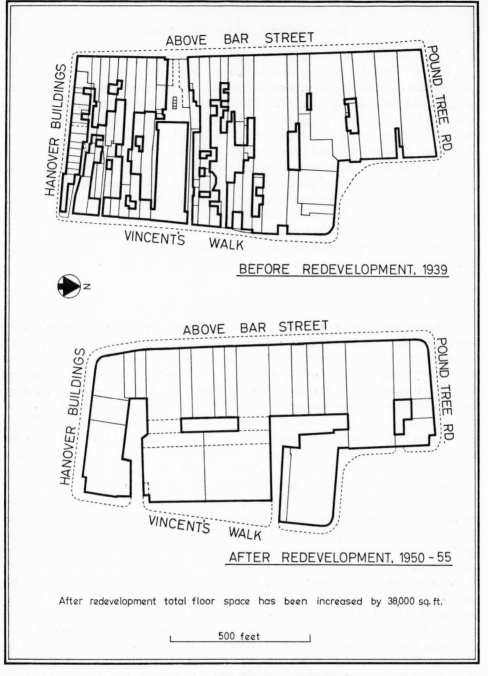

Fig. 80. Central Area block redevelopment

Based on the Southampton Development Plan, Written Analysis.
The principle adopted by the County Borough Council in controlling rebuilding of the war-damaged central area was to require new buildings to conform to an overall block scheme which provided (i) vehicular service access to *all* properties; (ii) regularised curtilages to achieve a more efficient and intensive use of land; (iii) allowed for adequate road widening and day-lighting demands; and (iv) provided opportunity for unified architectural treatment.

(vi) *Cultural and Recreational Facilities.* Southampton has a good standard of public open space, but the Plan makes further provision to improve distribution and access, to provide more space for organised games, to allow for the increased population, to open up the river frontages and to link existing open spaces. The proposals provided for an increase of public open spaces from 874 acres (4·8 acres per 1000 population) to 1379 acres (6·6 acres per 1000). Sites have been reserved for branch libraries, a new central swimming baths (of which the indoor baths are completed) and for additional allotments.

(vii) *Education.* Reservations for schools and their playing fields form one of the most significant aspects of the Development Plan. The area used for these purposes in 1950 was about 139 acres, and provision was made to increase this in twenty years to 625 acres, excluding nursery schools (for which about eighty small sites have been reserved). Longer term reservations involving standing property will have to be made to bring the sites of older schools up to Ministry of Education standards, and some of the provision for school playing fields is made in large reservations on the edge of the town.

AMENDMENTS TO THE PLAN

The 1947 Planning Act provides for amendments to the Development Plan to be submitted at any time; the first of these was the Central Area C.D.A. map. The second, the proposal to expand the University from its present student population of 1800 to 4000 by 1980 (see p. 335), which, if approved, will involve the demolition of about 120 dwellings over the next twenty years, has recently been the subject of a public inquiry. Here is an example of the necessity for planning proposals to be sufficiently flexible to take account both of long-term development and of unforeseen changes. In this case, the Council's initial Development Plan was prepared while the University was still a small University College, and well before the recent tremendous expansion of university and technical education could be envisaged.

Two major matters will have an important effect on development in Southampton. The first comprises the proposals by the Hampshire County Council (submitted in November 1958) for a 'Green Belt' closely surrounding the town (see p. 156). The second is an assessment by the County Borough Council of the town's overspill needs, which has resulted in a scheme, now approved in principle by the Minister, to develop land at Nursling and Rownhams, lying mostly outside the borough boundary on the north-western edge of the town, for residential and ancillary uses (schools, shops, open spaces, etc.) to accommodate about 20,000 people. The latter scheme is at present being worked out by a consultant architect-planner, so that building can commence as soon as possible.

Development Plans are required to be reviewed periodically, after fresh surveys have been made. This provides opportunities of taking stock of developments already effected, of examining new trends and of taking account of fresh needs. The Southampton Plan is at present (1963) being reconsidered to cover the period up to 1981, and it is clear that two major changes for which provision must be made are the increases in population growth, already greater than anticipated, and in vehicular traffic.

Population Growth

Whereas the population of the County Borough was originally estimated to grow (by natural increase alone) to 209,000 by the end of the first Development Plan period, this growth has been much faster than expected, and by mid-1962 it had already reached 206,000 (see p. 249). The revised estimate shows that the 1981 population, again taking into account natural increase alone, will be 228,000, and this figure cannot be satisfactorily accommodated within the present boundaries. In fact, the latest estimate by the Registrar General gives a population of 225,700 as early as 1972. The development proposed at Nursling and Rownhams, together with some infilling, redevelopment and urban renewal within the borough, should be adequate to cope with this increase for about ten years, but for the period beyond it will be necessary to look outside the County Borough for further sites.

Traffic and Parking

The tremendous increase in the number of motor vehicles poses two main problems: dealing with moving traffic and providing for stationary vehicles. Plans are already in hand for major improvements to the main east–west route through Southampton, particularly along Redbridge Road and sections of Bitterne Road, and for the beginnings of the north–south Docks route from the Avenue to Queen's Park.

One aspect which has been studied as part of the review of the Development Plan is the inevitable conflict between through traffic and shopping. In the town centre steps have already been taken to relieve through traffic in the main shopping street by the construction of the Inner Ring Road, and further relief will be afforded when the Docks route is completed. Rebuilding in Above Bar Street has provided for all shops to have rear access for loading and servicing, which would allow the elimination of vehicles from this street and the creation of a pedestrian precinct if in the future this is thought to be necessary; this possibility is now under discussion.

In Southampton all the main suburban 'district centres' straddle busy through-roads. Schemes have already been approved in principle by the Council for those at Bitterne (Fig. 81) and Portswood. Others are being or will be considered for Shirley and Woolston, which will eventually eliminate vehicular traffic from these shopping areas by providing by-pass routes for through traffic and service roads and car parks for the centres themselves. Future plans for dealing with moving traffic are now being formulated by the Borough Engineer, based on a recent and comprehensive traffic survey. Measures for dealing with car parking in the town centre are also under active consideration by the Borough Council. One requirement is to distinguish between short-term and long-term parking. The situation of the main shopping street, Above Bar, with the attractive parks around its northern and eastern sides, is such that any major parking provision in close proximity must be located to the west. In fact, much of this area is already reserved for parking. The substantial fall in the height of the land between the Inner Ring Road and Western Esplanade makes this area particularly suitable for multi-storey car parks, and a compulsory purchase order has recently been confirmed for part of the area to be developed for this purpose.

A number of other sites has been reserved for car parks within the town centre, but to avoid congestion it may be desirable to locate additional parks on the edge of the central area, in close proximity to the major approach roads. Substantial provision for car parking forms an essential part of the redevelopment proposals already referred to for the suburban centres.

THE FUTURE

The future of population, employment, land use and planning in the Southampton area is so likely to be influenced by a number of major factors in the near future—the current local government review, the Rochdale Report on the Docks, the possible involvement in the question of London's 'overspill', in fact, the problems of southern England generally—that it is impossible to consider these in any detail at the present time.

Within the borough itself, emphasis has already shifted first from war damage reconstruction to slum clearance, and now to the processes of gradual redevelopment, infilling and the type of improvement known as 'urban renewal'. While such processes must be initiated and encouraged if the town is to keep pace with present and future demands, it would be a mistake to assume that they can provide a complete solution to the problems created by the expansion of population. Experience shows that with all the demands on land for other purposes, redevelopment of outworn areas, even at high densities of over 100 persons to the acre, creates overspill, and this is likely to increase as the more suitable areas are dealt with and standards for new development rise. These rising standards of conditions for living, working and recreation, together with the continuing growth of population, carry with them increasing demands for more space for new and wider roads, car parks, schools and higher education establishments, open spaces, and much else that will enrich leisure in the affluent society. They also imply greater freedom of movement and choice for employers, for workers and for those wishing to retire. This expansion will obviously bring about an increased demand for all types of land use. Therefore a thriving town such as Southampton must face the very difficult problem of resolving the conflict of land use within its boundaries.

The town has a pleasant, open character which should be preserved, and yet the increase in population and these internal land use pressures will have the inevitable effect of increasing the density of certain parts of the town. It is proposed to restrict high density redevelopment to suitable areas, such as the district shopping centres and central residential suburbs. Counteracting this trend to higher densities there will be an opening up of valleys and other suitable areas for open spaces and schools; in consequence, a greater variety in form should be achieved and parts of the town will acquire a degree of urbanity which in the past has been lacking. In a well-balanced town of this size it is recognised that there is need for a wide variety of development and residential accommodation, ranging from high density neighbourhoods containing tall blocks of flats to low density suburbs of detached houses with large gardens. It is hoped that by careful control of development this variety will be perpetuated and strengthened, and trends towards overall uniformity and suburban monotony

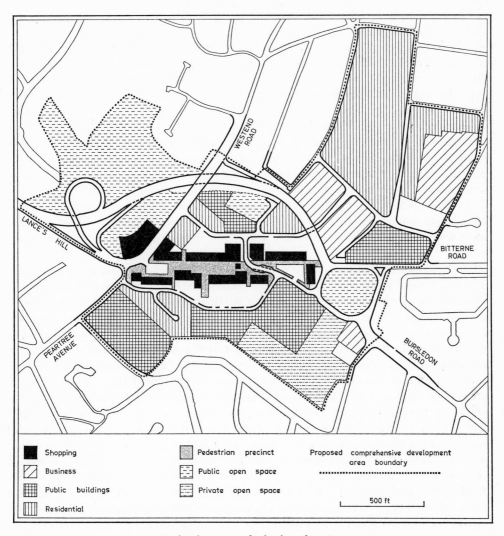

Fig. 81. Redevelopment of suburban shopping centres

Based on the County Borough Council's plan for Bitterne Shopping Centre.
This plan illustrates the principles now being followed in plans for the redevelopment of the existing suburban centres, all of which at present straddle one of the main radial roads. They are (i) segregation of through from local traffic; (ii) creation of safe and pleasant conditions for pedestrians by removing vehicles altogether from the shopping precinct; and (iii) adequate space for service access and car parking.

will be resisted; on the other hand, care must be exercised to protect the existing unity and character of certain areas.

The housing programme in Southampton, with the Council committed to building 6000 houses during the five years from 1963, is partly devoted to the replacement of a large number of unfit houses and of short-life temporary bungalows at the rate of about 600 a year. Housing achievements have already been notable; while the population of the County Borough increased by 7·8 per cent during the last decade, the number of houses increased by 24·5 per cent (see p. 249). The slum clearance programme will taper off in a few years, but it could then be replaced by a programme to deal with the large number of houses in need of improvement and with the urban renewal areas. Neither the scale nor the duration of such a programme can as yet be accurately measured. For private housing needs there will soon be little land available other than that in possession of the local authority, which can probably deal with some ten years of housing at normal rates in a new suburb adjoining the borough boundary (Lordshill, for a 20,000 population) and in an area of comprehensive development within the borough on the eastern side which may provide houses for about 3000 people.

The built-up edge of the town is approximately 3 miles radius from the town centre. This size of town affords a relatively simple structure, and travelling time between home—office—factory—school, etc., is not more than 30 minutes for any inhabitant (it also allows a high percentage of people to travel home to their mid-day meal). The land within the existing 'urban fence' (including the Lord's Hill Housing Estate) will be efficiently used and when this has been fully developed, it is considered that further growth should take place as part of existing separate communities such as Netley, Hedge End and Eastleigh, the intervening countryside being maintained as open as possible. But this must take into account the presence of the Green Belt and also the Hampshire Development Plan (Chapter XI) as it affects the Southampton area. Furthermore, the larger issues associated with London's 'overspill' may call for a radical revision of these plans. The attention now being given by the Ministry of Housing and Local Government to this problem in the metropolitan region may well bring the Southampton area into consideration for the necessary dispersal of commerce, industry and population outside the London daily commuting area. The Minister has called (May 1963) for a new attitude to the size of towns and for the rigorous re-examination of green belt patterns in connection with the expected national population increase of 7 million between 1961 and 1981. 'The worthwhile towns of the future will be big, not small; dynamic, not static', now appears to be the Ministerial view.

The possible expansion of the Docks and a greater emphasis on cargo trade (see p. 293) could have radical effects both on the transport system and also on the land requirements for industry, storage and distribution depots, and offices, which will in turn have repercussions on the land available for other uses, notably housing. The pressure for further industrialisation along the shores of Southampton Water will make it even more important to see that amenity and recreational facilities are not lost sight of. With this point in mind, the County Borough Council initiated a few years ago the formation of a conference of local authorities bordering Southampton Water to bring forward and co-ordinate positive proposals for